Time to (Re-)integrate Dissociation into Psychoanalytic Psychotherapy?

This book brings together contributions from leading authors in the field of dissociation to facilitate the pursuit of integrative clinical scholarship, connecting psychoanalytic thinking and practice with dissociation research and treatment.

Dissociation is not merely altered consciousness, it is an attack on consciousness: on memory, identity, and goal-directed action. The attempts by early psychoanalytic theorists to grapple with this clinical entity were marred by the very same frustration evinced by contemporary descriptive psychopathologists who were faced with understanding the similarities and differences between dissociative symptoms and disorders and other types of psychopathologies. The DSM-V and ICD-11 categorize at least six dissociative disorders. Some of these diagnoses have provoked controversy and skepticism. Whilst many, if not most, clinicians will have encountered various forms of dissociative psychopathology, Dissociative Identity Disorder remains an elusive and contested presentation. Perhaps in parallel to the disorder itself, it continues to be challenging for theorists and clinicians to view the field as a whole and contain the disagreements, contradictions, and paradoxes.

This book will be of use to researchers and students of clinical psychology, psychiatry, and psychotherapy. The chapters in this book were originally published as a special issue of *Psychoanalytic Psychotherapy.*

Paul Cundy is a Clinical Psychologist and Psychodynamic Psychotherapist. He is an Associate Fellow of the British Psychological Society, Leicester, UK, and Editor-in-Chief of *Psychoanalytic Psychotherapy.*

Golan Shahar is Professor of Clinical Health Psychology, Zlotowsky Chair of Neuropsychology, and Adjunct Professor of Public Health at Ben-Gurion University of the Negev where he also heads the Stress, Self & Health (STREALTH) research lab. He is also Adjunct Professor of Child Study and Adult Psychiatry at the Yale University School of Medicine and the former International Editor of *Psychoanalytic Psychotherapy.*

Time to (Re-)integrate Dissociation into Psychoanalytic Psychotherapy?

Edited by
Paul Cundy and Golan Shahar

Routledge
Taylor & Francis Group
LONDON AND NEW YORK

First published 2025
by Routledge
4 Park Square, Milton Park, Abingdon, Oxon, OX14 4RN

and by Routledge
605 Third Avenue, New York, NY 10158

Routledge is an imprint of the Taylor & Francis Group, an informa business

British Library Cataloguing-in-Publication Data
A catalogue record for this book is available from the British Library

ISBN13: 978-1-032-90914-1 (hbk)
ISBN13: 978-1-032-90918-9 (pbk)
ISBN13: 978-1-003-56061-6 (ebk)

DOI: 10.4324/9781003560616

Typeset in Times New Roman
by codeMantra

Publisher's Note
The publisher accepts responsibility for any inconsistencies that may have arisen during the conversion of this book from journal articles to book chapters, namely the inclusion of journal terminology.

Contents

Citation Information

The following chapters in this book were originally published in *Psychoanalytic Psychotherapy*, volume 37, issue 4 (2024). When citing this material, please use the original page numbering for each article, as follows:

Introduction

Time to (re-)integrate dissociation into psychoanalytic psychotherapy? An introduction to the special issue on dissociative disorders and psychoanalytic psychotherapy
Paul Cundy and Golan Shahar
Psychoanalytic Psychotherapy, volume 37, issue 4 (2023), pp. 295–299

Chapter 1

The curious reader's guide to dissociation: understanding dissociative processes, a Commentary
Richard A. Chefetz
Psychoanalytic Psychotherapy, volume 37, issue 4 (2023), pp. 300–318

Chapter 2

When daydreaming becomes maladaptive: phenomenological and psychoanalytic perspectives
Richard A. Chefetz, Nirit Soffer-Dudek and Eli Somer
Psychoanalytic Psychotherapy, volume 37, issue 4 (2023), pp. 319–338

Chapter 3

Dissociative identity disorder: a disorder of diagnostic and therapeutic paradoxes
Richard J. Loewenstein and Bethany Brand
Psychoanalytic Psychotherapy, volume 37, issue 4 (2023), pp. 339–380

Chapter 4

Dissociative depression: a psychodynamic view
Vedat Şar
Psychoanalytic Psychotherapy, volume 37, issue 4 (2023), pp . 381–428

Chapter 5

Metaphoric, metonymic and psychotic somatoform dissociation
Dana Amir
Psychoanalytic Psychotherapy, volume 37, issue 4 (2023), pp. 429–442

Chapter 6

Self-medication, traumatic reenactments, and dissociation: a psychoanalytic perspective on the relationship between childhood trauma and substance abuse
Antonino Costanzo, Gianluca Santoro and Adriano Schimmenti
Psychoanalytic Psychotherapy, volume 37, issue 4 (2023), pp. 443–466

Chapter 7

Addressing dissociation symptoms with trauma-focused mentalization-based treatment
E. Rüfenacht, L. Shaverin, J. Stubley, M. L. Smits, A. Bateman, P. Fonagy and P. Luyten
Psychoanalytic Psychotherapy, volume 37, issue 4 (2023), pp. 467–491

Chapter 8

Dissociation in suicidal depression: a Reformulated Object-Relations Theory (RORT) perspective
Golan Shahar, Morgan Robison and Thomas E. Joiner
Psychoanalytic Psychotherapy, volume 37, issue 4 (2023), pp. 492–520

Notes on Contributors

Dana Amir, University of Haifa, Israel.

A. Bateman, Psychoanalysis Unit, Department of Clinical, Educational and Health Psychology, University College London, UK.

Bethany Brand, Psychology, Towson University, USA.

Antonino Costanzo, Faculty of Human and Social Sciences, Kore University of Enna (UKE), Italy.

Richard A. Chefetz, Private Practice, Washington, DC, USA.

Paul Cundy, Psychodynamic Psychotherapy, North East London NHS Foundation Trust, London, UK.

P. Fonagy, Research Department of Clinical, Educational and Health Psychology, University College London, UK; Anna Freud Centre, London, UK.

Thomas E. Joiner, Department of Psychology, Florida State University, Tallahassee, USA.

Richard J. Loewenstein, Psychiatry, University of Maryland School of Medicine, Baltimore, USA.

P. Luyten, Research Department of Clinical, Educational and Health Psychology, University College London, UK; Faculty of Psychology and Educational Sciences, KU Leuven, Belgium.

Morgan Robison, Department of Psychology, Florida State University, Tallahassee, USA.

E. Rüfenacht, Division of Psychiatric Specialties, Department of Psychiatry, Geneva University Hospitals, Switzerland; Research Department of Clinical, Educational and Health Psychology, University College London, UK.

Gianluca Santoro, Faculty of Human and Social Sciences, Kore University of Enna (UKE), Italy.

Vedat Şar, Department of Psychiatry, Koç University School of Medicine, Istanbul, Turkey.

Adriano Schimmenti, Faculty of Human and Social Sciences, Kore University of Enna (UKE), Italy.

Golan Shahar, Department of Psychology, Ben-Gurion University of the Negev, Beer-Sheva, Israel.

L. Shaverin, Tavistock Trauma Service, Tavistock & Portman NHS Foundation Trust, London, UK; Anna Freud Centre, London, UK.

M. L. Smits, De Viersprong, Viersprong Institute for Studies on Personality Disorders, The Netherlands.

Nirit Soffer-Dudek, Department of Psychology, Ben-Gurion University of the Negev, Beersheba, Israel.

Eli Somer, School of Social Work, University of Haifa, Israel.

J. Stubley, Tavistock Trauma Service, Tavistock & Portman NHS Foundation Trust, London, UK.

Time to (re-)integrate dissociation into psychoanalytic psychotherapy? An introduction to the special issue on dissociative disorders and psychoanalytic psychotherapy

Whilst writing this introduction (14 October 2023), an entire nation – the State of Israel – is being traumatized and evidences signs of collective dissociative symptoms. An orchestrated, carefully planned attack from Gaza, by the Hamas Organization, has culminated in more than 1300 Israelis (mostly civilians) being brutally murdered and about 200 hundred Israelis kidnapped to Gaza. The consensus consolidating among Israelis these days is that the Israeli Defense Forces (IDF), arguably one of the most formidable armies worldwide, has never before been surprised and overwhelmed as it was on the Saturday of 7 October 2023, when the attack commenced. Golan Shahar, the editor of this special issue, currently providing psychological first-aid with both civilians and members of the security forces, is awed by one recurring theme reverberating in the words of virtually all the survivors with whom he works: a theme of *surrealism*. 'This is not happening', 'I barely sleep and when I wake up it is with the hope that it didn't happen' are merely some of the utterances he repeatedly hears, and they echoed his own experiences.

Psychological dissociation is The Surreal. It is an amalgamation of thoughts, emotions, and behaviors that share the common denominator of challenging the way we experience self and world. Dissociation is not merely altered consciousness, it is an attack on consciousness: on memory, identity, and goal-directed action. Freud (1919) titled it 'Unheimlich', improperly translated as 'The Uncanny' (see also Sullivan, 1953, on uncanny emotions), and for Bion (1959), it was the outcome of attacks on linking. The attempt, metaphoric as it was, by these psychoanalytic theorists to grapple with this clinical entity is marred by the very same frustration evinced by descriptive psychopathologists in the face of understanding the similarities and differences between dissociative symptoms and disorders and other types of psychopathology (Sar & Ross, 2006). Decades of theory, followed by further decades of empirical research, have advanced our understanding of experiences such as depersonalization, derealization, dissociative amnesia, self-compartmentalization, and other dissociative manifestations, but they are far from settling gnawing questions in psychopathology – with clear implications for psychotherapy – such as 'what is the difference between dissociation and psychosis?', 'is there dissociation without prior trauma?', 'can people really be dissociatively split into multiple identities?', 'what are the adaptive and maladaptive ways in which people cope with dissociative manifestations?', 'how should pathological dissociation be treated?', and more (see Chefetz, 2015; Sar & Ross, 2006).

These are the questions that serve as an impetus for developing this special issue, which brings together contributions from leading authors in the field of dissociation. The DSM-V and ICD-11 categorise a number of dissociative disorders: Depersonalisation-Derealization; Dissociative amnesia (with or without dissociative fugue); Partial Dissociative Identity disorder; Dissociative Identity disorder (DID); Dissociative neurological symptom disorder; Trance disorder; and Possession trance disorder. Some of these diagnoses have provoked controversy and skepticism. Whilst many, if not most, clinicians will have encountered various forms of dissociative psychopathology, DID remains an elusive and contested presentation. Perhaps in a parallel to the disorder itself, it continues to be challenging for theorists and clinicians to view the field as a whole and contain the disagreements, contradictions, and paradoxes. We hope and believe that this special issue will serve as an important facilitator of the pursuit of integrative clinical scholarship connecting psychoanalytic thinking and practice with dissociation research and treatment.

The special issue begins with a commentary by Richard Chefetz entitled 'The curious reader' in which he offers an overview of this complex subject and guides readers, both new and experienced, through the articles.

The next article, by Richard Chefetz, Nirit Soffer-Dudek, and Eli Somer, describes these authors' fascinating and innovative research program focusing on maladaptive daydreaming (MD). Pertaining to an excessive employment of immersive daydreaming characterized by highly absorbing fantasy, daydreaming becomes maladaptive when it is executed at the expense of living in the real world. MD appears to be incredibly prevalent and confers considerable damage to functioning and well-being and is involved in a wide array of psychiatric comorbidities. In their article, the authors locate research on MD within the psychoanalytic literature focusing on fragmentation and multiple self-states (Chefetz & Bromberg, 2004), and Winnicott's (1971) notions concerning adaptive and maladaptive imagination. Case illustrations are provided, and clinical implications are briefly discussed.

The third article, by Richard Loewenstein and Bethany Brand, provides an introduction to DID and its links to psychoanalytic theory and clinical practice. The authors propose that psychodynamically informed psychotherapy is necessary for the successful treatment of DID. They illustrate how psychoanalytic concepts such as the therapeutic alliance, the frame, conflict, defense, transference and countertransference, intersubjectivity, observing ego, projective identification, negative therapeutic reaction, regression in the service of the ego, etc. are central to successful treatment of DID. However, they also describe multiple clinical and theoretical ambiguities, paradoxes, and even apparent contradictions, which must be held in mind in order to make sense of DID. For example, in order to accurately conceptualize and work effectively with DID, psychoanalytic practitioners must incorporate domains of knowledge from other modalities, such as non-psycho-analytic views of the mind, hypnosis/hypnotherapy, developmental traumatology, as well as approaches to the therapy that may feel alien, uncomfortable, and even heterodox. The authors highlight the limited focus on this subject in mental health training programmes. This is despite the burgeoning interest in 'trauma' in the mainstream media. They present a case for increased training in the diagnosis and treatment of trauma-and-stressor-related disorders, including DID, in the context of both international prevalence data and also the proliferation of unregulated treatments lacking any theoretical basis or research evidence of efficacy.

The fourth article in this special issue, by Vedat Sar, presents a comprehensive theory of dissociative depression, a construct he himself termed. Espousing his absolute command of the psychopathology literature, Sar construes dissociative depression as a chronic and complex mood disorder characterized by both persistent depressive symptoms, intermittent major depressive episodes, and dissociative symptoms such as depersonalization, derealization, and amnesia. The importance of dissociative depression as a clinical construct lies in its ability to shed light on the complexity of depression (see Shahar, 2024), and to pave new grounds in intervention with patients manifesting treatment-resistant depression (TRD, Cuijpers, 2023). Sar locates the origins of dissociative depression in disturbances of sense of self and agency formed around developmental difficulties in separation-individuation, juxtaposed against a serious developmental traumatization. The author amasses an impressive list of continental thinkers, within and outside psychoanalysis, to substantiate his etiological theory of dissociative depression.

We continue with an article by Dana Amir, who presents an intriguing psychoanalytic and literary theory of somatoform dissociation. Drawing from her previous work integrating literary scholarship, psychoanalytic theory, and psychopathology (e.g., Amir, 2014, 2016, 2019), as well as on empirical research on somatoform dissociation (Nijenhuis et al., 1996), Amir distinguishes between three forms of somatic dissociation, each of which conforms to different literary-symbolic configurations: *The metaphorical*, in which there is a symbolic connection between the somatoform phenomenon and the traumatic content, *the metonymic*, which constitutes a revival of the traumatic experience without the ability to reflect on it, and *the psychotic*, in which the somatoform phenomenon is experienced as ego-syntonic, thus neither causes distress nor evokes thinking. Clinical vignettes illustrating each of the three forms of somatic dissociation are presented, and a fourth vignette illustrates the role of therapist's countertransference in the treatment of these conditions.

The next paper, by Antonino Costanzo, Gianluca Santoro, and Adriano Schimmenti, describes the role of self-medication in maintaining dissociative states. Using the clinical example of 'Charles', an anonymised patient with characteristics that many readers will recognise, the article explores the relationship between developmental trauma, dissociation, and substance abuse within the framework of the self-medication hypothesis. The authors describe how substance abuse can serve as a maladaptive coping strategy for attempting to regulate the overwhelming emotions that can arise from traumatic impingements on the development of attachment relationships. People who have experienced this type of developmental trauma may dissociate negative attachment memories and their accompanying emotions, with consequent compartmentalization of their internal states and impaired self-regulation abilities. In these scenarios, substance abuse can be used as an external regulator of distressing emotions, enabling the person to distance themselves from their traumatic memories and facilitating an omnipotent and self-reliant attitude. The authors assert the paramount importance for clinicians to accurately identify and address the needs of these individuals in order to develop their capacity to acknowledge, explore, and integrate their trauma memories as intrinsic elements of their identity, thereby fostering the development of a unified and cohesive self-concept.

The following article, authored by Eva Rüfenacht, Lisa Shaverin, Jo Stubley, Maaike Smits, Anthony Bateman, Peter Fonagy, and Patrick Luyten, describes their experience of adapting Mentalization-Based Treatment (MBT) for use with people with complex post-traumatic stress disorder (C-PTSD). The article introduces a novel conceptualisation and treatment approach for complex post-traumatic stress symptoms, including dissociation, derived from attachment and mentalization theories. The authors provide an overview of the different expressions of dissociation and the prevailing understanding of their links with diverse clinical manifestations and their role in trauma. They go on to reinterpret these clinical symptoms through an attachment and mentalization lens, before elaborating on their new trauma-focused mentalization-based treatment and its therapeutic objectives. The article concludes with clinical material to illustrate the application of this approach in a treatment setting.

This special issue concludes with a contribution from Golan Shahar, Morgan Robison and Thomas Joiner. Their ambitious article offers a conceptualization that integrates three bodies of literature: Joiner's Interpersonal-Psychological Theory of Suicide (IPTS), dissociation theory and research, and psychoanalytic object-relations theory, with a particular focus on social-cognitive reformulations of this theory. A case example of an adult psychotherapy patient's serious, near-lethal suicide attempt is used to illustrate this theoretical viewpoint.

The authors use the Reformulated Object Relations Theory, including a reformulation of Melanie Klein's depressive position, to propose a bridge between IPTS and dissociation theory and research. By contrasting the pathological depressive position with Ogden's concept of the historical position, and introducing a temporal axis, the authors describe how depressed individuals project their hoped-for self-with-other representations onto the future only to be met with interpersonal stress and a dearth of social support and positive events. They go on to suggest that, for the reformulated depressive position to spiral into suicidality, dissociative mechanisms must make it the only available position. A diagram is provided to illustrate the role of basic level and advanced level dissociative processes in the progression of the depressive position into suicidality.

Disclosure statement

No potential conflict of interest was reported by the author(s).

References

Amir, D. (2014). Nausea as the refusal of a mother-tongue: The psychosomatic metaphoric, metonymic and psychotic expression. In *Cleft tongue: The language of psychic structures* (pp. 111–132). Karnac Books.

Amir, D. (2016). The metaphoric, the metonymic and the psychotic aspects of obsessive-sympomatology. *International Journal of Psychoanalysis*, *97*(2), 259–280. https://doi.org/10.1111/1745-8315.12442

Amir, D. (2019). *Bearing witness to the witness: A psychoanalytic perspective on four modes of traumatic testimony.* Routledge.

Bion, W. (1959). Attacks on linking. *International Journal of Psycho-Analysis*, *40*, 5–6, 308–315.

Chefetz, R. (2015). *Intensive psychotherapy for persistent dissociative processes: The fear of feeling real.* Norton.

Chefetz, R. A., & Bromberg, P. M. (2004). Talking with "me" and "not-me": A dialogue. *Contemporary Psychoanalysis*, *40*(3), 409–464. https://doi.org/10.1080/00107530.2004.10745840

Cuijpers, P. (2023). From treatment resistance to sequential treatments of depression. *World Psychiatry*, *22*(3), 418. https://doi.org/10.1002/wps.21138

Freud, S. (1919). The uncanny. In S. Freud (Ed.), *The standard edition of the complete psychological works of Sigmund Freud: Vol. XVII. An infantile neurosis and other works* (pp. 217–256). Vintage (published 1999).

Nijenhuis, E. R. S., Spinhoven, P., Van Dyck, R., Van der Hart, O., & Vanderlinden, J. (1996). The development and psychometric characteristics of the somatoform dissociation questionnaire (SDQ-20). *Journal of Nervous & Mental Disease*, *184*(11), 688–694. https://doi.org/10.1097/00005053-199611000-00006

Sar, V., & Ross, C. (2006). Dissociative disorders as confounding factors in psychiatric research. *Psychiatric Clinics of North America*, *29*(1), 129–144. https://doi.org/10.1016/j.psc.2005.10.008

Shahar, G. (2024). *Complex depression: Role of personality and the social context.* American Psychological Association Press.

Sullivan, H. S. (1953). *The interpersonal theory of psychiatry.* Norton.

Winnicott, D. W. (1971). *Playing and reality.* Tavistock.

Paul Cundy

Golan Shahar

The curious reader's guide to dissociation: understanding dissociative processes, a commentary

Richard A. Chefetz

Associative processes that provide salience through sorting of mental content rely upon dissociative processes to remove non-salient content from awareness, like not noticing the glasses on your nose. When association fails in trauma, as capacities to assimilate and accommodate experience are outstripped by that experience being outside the usual range of human experience, then more elaborate dissociative experience like depersonalization and derealization may become active to help us tolerate our perception even if it costs the price of isolated affect or additional amnesia for experience. With repetition of traumatic experience identity confusion and identity alteration may occur, effectively generating the less common dissociative identity disorder. This guide first explores the basis of dissociative experience as a prelude to the reader's foray into the subject of this special issue of this journal. Additionally, the writer delves into aspects of the work of a world-class collection of authoritative articles to fully flesh them out or emphasize critically important perspectives. Finally, the centrality of the relationship in psychotherapy is emphasized as a requirement for effective treatment when persistent dissociative processes dominate the activities of a wounded human mind.

Curiosity can be thought of as the opposite of dissociation. Aiming to understand something is essentially associative in nature; we compare the new to the old and sort out meaning and differences. We assimilate new knowledge as it fits into our existing understanding of the world. We don't have to accommodate our frame of understanding if the new thing is not so far outside our usual experience. Trauma creates a circumstance where our ability to assimilate and accommodate may fail: what happens is just too far outside our normal range of experience to be understood. In this way, associative processes fail when there is trauma, and dissociative processes activate to fill the breach and maintain mental coherence.

Dissociation normally assists achievement of mental coherence by unconsciously discarding what lacks salience or utility. Dissociation helps us forget to notice, again, the eyeglasses on our nose, the minimal discomfort of the chair, or the old scratch on the kitchen table since none of these perceptions is of particular use after they become routine. But everyday dissociative contributions to mental coherence take on new meaning and recruit a higher level of neurobiologically patterned shifts and changes in function when a mind is threatened or overwhelmed by something traumatic. When associative processes fail and assimilation and accommodation aren't possible, there is a new impossibility in our lives, a novel reality forced down our mental throats as we swallow involuntarily. Traumatic experience potentially activates dissociative responses beyond those routinely present in post-traumatic stress disorder (PTSD), and intrusions come from outside awareness, emotional numbing is involuntary and unconscious, social withdrawal feels compelling and not well understood, startle is physiologically unbidden and involuntary; and all of these things are in the dissociative core of PTSD. The dissociative processes of depersonalization, derealization, and amnesia are most typically the replacements for failed associative processing of reality. The chronicity of trauma can create the eventual emergence of identity confusion followed, at times, by identity alteration, the creation of self-states (Siegel, 1999), or states of being (Putnam, 2016). Perhaps more simply put there are 'different ways of being you', one isolated from the other by dissociative process (Chefetz, 2015). Before talking more about self-states and their clinical significance, let's put some more flesh on the bones of some kinds of dissociative experience and what generates it.

In this writer's view, traumatic experience is not so much about the size of the bang as it is about the vulnerabilities of an individual and how their mind's responses to living their life, and relating to self and others, change indelibly after an experience (Chefetz, 2015, p. 191). It's not that there's no hope for recovery; it's that a person changes and they are never the same, again. This writer anticipates that the savvy reader will already be asking: What really constitutes a trauma if it's not the size of the bang? Are we not at risk of diluting the notion of trauma if we include things like bullying and ridicule, shaming, humiliation, and all manner of familial dysfunction resulting from chronic alcoholism, drug use, or severe mental illness like chronic psychotic illness in a parent? Martin Teicher's lab at Harvard/McLean hospital can help us here (Teicher et al., 2010) and so can attachment researchers Karlen Lyons-Ruth et al. (2006) and Giovanni Liotti (1999). While Teicher showed how emotional abuse only, not including sexual or physical, was enough to cause developmental delays in hippocampal, corpus colossal, and precuneal structural maturation, Lyons-Ruth modeled how emotional unresponsiveness was the best predictor of adult dissociation in her cohort, and Liotti opined how attachment disorganization predicted some of the development of adult dissociative disorders. Note, also, that Type A, avoidant patterns also play a role in the genesis of the dissociative disorders (Barach, 1991). You can drive a nail into the lid of a coffin using a sledgehammer and one single massive blow, or you can tap on it with a spoon, ten-thousand times, and in both cases the nail goes in (Felitti et al., 1998). We don't need big bangs to profoundly wound people. How do dissociative processes figure in this picture of chronic traumatic stress?

Depersonalization is the experience of feeling somehow, often inarticulately, not real. The classic out-of-body experience is not typical, though it certainly is reported. More typically there's an odd feeling of somehow not being fully connected to one's body. This is often associated with a sense of emotional deadness or being numb, and this lack of feeling can become exquisitely painful, sometimes prompting self-harming behaviors in a desperate attempt to prove a body is alive. Derealization is the sense of the world being not real, phony, fake; colors are muted, edges of objects are indistinct, the world is seen as if through a veil (Simeon & Abugel, 2006). Most people with this level of activated dissociative process have much more depersonalization experience than derealization. In fact, if somebody is new to any kind of psychotherapy treatment, and an assessment for depersonalization reveals none, then the chance of their having a complex dissociative disorder is low.

It may be useful to think of depersonalization as a kind of nifty, adjustable, emotional circuit breaker; it activates with intolerable emotional pain, but, once established, it activates with even just a flicker of an increase in pain. Mediated by the insula (located at the temporal-parietal junction), interoception, our ability to know gut feelings, is impaired by depersonalization (Sierra et al., 2002). When we don't know feeling, then we lose the major contextualizing quality of interpersonal human experience. If depersonalization goes on 'over-drive', then a full out-of-body experience might occur. Yes, I am saying that dissociative disorders and their underlying processes are significantly about emergency states of affective down-regulation that persist after a trauma. The persistence of activated dissociative processes cause the most trouble, it seems, as returning home from the battlefield with depersonalization in a protective always-on mode is not conducive to a loving relationship with spouse or children. The same goes if leaving an abusive home setting, finally; when does the protective dissociative process deactivate? Let's go back to basic dissociative processes for another moment and then jump into self-state territory.

'How's your memory?' That's not a typical question asked of a thirty-year-old, or younger, person. If you take the risk of asking, it's very important to be able to respond to: 'Funny you should ask, my memory is terrible, but not always, and the inconsistency drives me and my family crazy'. Most memory disturbance related to dissociative processes is of the 'Swiss cheese' variety, small pieces of memory go missing (Loewenstein, 1991). Yes, large, more global chunks can be missing, too. But it's the small stuff that's most telling, and distinct from the memory issues of older ages. In a clinical interview, when it seems as if my patient has forgotten what we've just talked about or is suddenly looking around the room as if trying to get oriented, even though we've been talking for fifteen minutes, I may stop the action and ask if they can tell me what indeed we have been talking about. If they're hesitant and then respond with a kind of memory that's more of the gist of things than an actual clear memory, I've learned to specifically ask them: "Do you have a clear memory or is it more like you somehow know, sort-of, what we've talked about, but the feeling is more like you read about it in the newspaper than you were truly in the experience? This kind of experience, if confirmed, hints at a change in their state of consciousness between the time of the actual experience and their effort at recollection. It's as if the mental space they were just in is now next door and they get the vibe about what happened, but not the veridical experience, not the clearly felt sense of knowing.

This kind of discontinuity of experience is ubiquitous in people with activated dissociative processes, and it's also true they've learned to not only try to hide this from others but also to not notice the discontinuity themselves. After all, it's kind of normal, and so while it's not normal to the observant clinician the normal discontinuity does not have salience and is easily deflected. Some deflections are more intentional: 'I'm not going to talk or think about that because it will just get me upset'. The psychological process we think of as isolation generally refers to isolation of affect, but, in fact, this dissociative process can also refer to the compartmentalization of a mind and isolated subjectivity. In addition to psychodynamics of isolation and deflection there are those of exclusion, a process descriptive of how a mind keeps intrusive flashback quality mental content out of awareness on a routine basis.

A multiple self-state psychology of mind is a naturalistic perspective of the mental structure of a mind supported by infant research and an enormity of literature in relational psychoanalysis and the dissociative disorders (Beebe et al., 2012; Bromberg, 1998; Chefetz, 2015; Davies & Frawley, 1992; Howell, 2005; Lyons-Ruth, 2003; Main & Hesse, 1990; Mitchell, 1991; Ogawa et al., 1997; Putnam, 1997, 2016; Slade, 2014; Stern, 1997; Tronick et al., 1978; Wolff, 1987). A 'state of mind' has been proposed to be " … a pattern of activation of recruited systems within the brain responsible for (1) perceptual bias, (2) emotional tone and regulation, (3) memory processes, (4) mental models, and (5) behavioral response patterns (Siegel, 1999). This kind of organization may be further biased by profound experiences of depersonalization that as one of several life experiences predicts that being up on the ceiling and watching the poor little girl below being raped creates a perceptually and psychodynamically powerful conviction of self-other, e.g., the not-me experience and the pseudo-delusion of separateness in the identity alteration of dissociative identity disorder (DID) (Chefetz, 2015; Chefetz & Bromberg, 2004; Kluft, 1985) amongst several proposed mechanisms for the generation of the experience of alternate identities, not all of which have had traumatic experience, as per their relatively separate belief systems and biases (Putnam, 2016; Siegel, 1999). Frankly, the most important reason any clinician could have as to why knowing about and being able to speak with a person about self-state experience is because people with self-state experience will feel understood. This felt sense of being understood creates the beginnings of a sense of emotional safety, as if a patient is saying: 'Oh, they get it about me! I didn't understand it myself until they started talking this way, but now it makes so much sense that I just feel relieved, and, honestly, I'm also a little bit scared of what I might learn next'. A felt sense of safety initiates feelings toward secure attachment and goes a distance toward creating a therapeutic alliance.

While the genesis of a dissociative disorder may depend in large part upon initiatory experiences of one kind of trauma or another that leads to depersonalization, the place where many clinicians' sense of credulity falters about things dissociative is in appreciating the nuances or reality of identity alteration. Such was my personal experience in talking with the editor of this special edition of this Journal, Golan Shahar (personal communications, July, 2022). Familiar with each other from interactions on a listserv, Golan challenged me to show him switches between self-states, and then convinced they existed after watching a video via zoom screen-sharing, he asked for a video of switching with amnesia for the switch. He was genuinely moved by what he saw in a different patient (both patients had given me permission to use their video files for teaching purposes). Still, as I'll discuss later, appreciating that a person with DID is listening from more than one center of initiative/identity is a weirdness that one senior colleague admonished me years ago to never forget is a factor in a clinician's difficulty in understanding dissociative experiences. That is part of the reason why my focus is more generally on dissociative processes rather than dissociative disorders. If you look for a person to walk into your office with a dissociative disorder, then you'll rarely meet one. If you become educated about how to discern the presence of depersonalization, the nuances of dissociative amnesia, and how to listen for patient stories related to discontinuities in a person's subjective experience of consciousness, then you will find more people with dissociative disorders than you ever imagined existed.

Commentary

Dissociative identity disorder: a disorder of diagnostic and therapeutic paradoxes

The most detailed and on-point article in this journal dedicated to understanding dissociation is Brand and Loewenstein on the paradoxes inherent in the diagnosis and treatment of DID. Picking out the most salient aspects of this paper is like asking somebody to find the high point on a mile high plateau: there is an enormity of richness. Nevertheless, there's a couple of things I think a curious reader ought to be sure to notice. I've chosen to start with this article because it contains the underlying theory and clinical examples for much of the rest of the articles here.

The expertise that informed the writing of this paper is extraordinary. As such, it is not quite for the uninitiated. If you're not at all familiar with dissociation or the dissociative disorders, then you will come to appreciate the value of this article over time. Perhaps you'll take the advice of this writer and try and read it through on the surface the first time you go through it. Get the lay of the land, so to speak. Read the other articles in this issue, and then come back and read this one in more depth. Still, it will be a while before you can appreciate all it has to offer. For now, I'm going to emphasize and elaborate upon some of the aspects of this article that you may do well to take with you on your first reading. Let's start with a little more psychoanalytic history and perspective.

Pierre Janet got a lot right when he wrote about disaggregation and mental states early on (Janet, 1901), but his work was eclipsed by that of Freud and the concept of repression, a much easier thing to imagine than dissociation and hypnoid states. Melanie Klein's work on the developmental achievement of a depressive position after the initial paranoid-schizoid position and her discussion of splitting (Segal, 1979) figures centrally as descriptive of dissociative dynamics if that lens is used for focus (see, also: Shahar, in this journal). Fast forward to Ronald Fairbairn who wrote about internal object relations (Fairbairn, 1944) that just happen to have a hand-in-glove fit with the psychodynamics of dissociative experience in dissociative identity disorder. Harry Guntrip's work with schizoid phenomena and the in and out program (Guntrip, 1969) is another important milepost describing dissociative psychodynamics. Donald Winnicott, who analyzed Guntrip after an inadequate analysis with Fairbairn, wrote unknowingly about depersonalization in a dream at the end of his paper on hate in the countertransference (Winnicott, 1949). However, he also frequently wrote about dissociative experience at some length, but without much fanfare; consider the implications of his work on true and false self (Winnicott, 1960). If you have PEP-WEB, then search for Winnicott's work and the term dissociation. There were 26 'hits' when I just checked. Bowlby wrote about detachment and segregated subsystems in addition to his notion of internal working models, a kind of schematic of the world-view of a self-state (Bretherton, 1987). Finally, just for fun, look up Herbert Rosenfeld's analysis of a schizophrenic state with depersonalization (Rosenfeld, 1947). And, if I may be permitted, check out this writer's discussion of Nina Farhi's case of a psychotic woman. Farhi's discussion, after mine, holds a key to understanding where things dissociative were in the Winnicottian literature (Chefetz, 2008). More recently see the work of Bromberg, Stern, Davies, Howell & Itzkowitz, as well as Chefetz, as noted earlier. Dissociative processes and experiences were very much part of psychoanalysis; they were just hidden in plain sight.

Thinking about splitting in the context of its misuse in describing dissociative experience ought to include Klein's notion of the child keeping apart the good and bad objects and therefore splitting their internal experience of a parental figure. It is much more parsimonious to consider that unintegrated aspects of the child's experience held in different self-states with contradictory internal working models typical of Type D attachment, preclude integration of the good and bad. There would not be enough emotional safety to know that the mother who hurt you was the mother who was also good to you and that you were living with both mothers. The two notions have to be kept separate to tolerate the distress and disruption of being around a mother with contradictory multiple self-states.

Winnicott gave us another useful perspective that also deserves addition to the author's review of psychoanalytic perspectives and DID, the transitional object (Winnicott, 1953). There is a paradox related to dissociative processes in the title of his article: the first not-me possession. To possess something is to own it, and yet, since it is not-me it is not owned. This points to the distinction between me and not-me. Of course, Calvin and Hobbs ought be consulted on these matters (Spitz & Handler, 1993). From their perspective they are engaged in active fantasy that has the felt impact of relatedness, attributions of personality, and a particular external space in which activity occurs, but which clearly must be imagined in order to take place. A discussion of Winnicott's ideas regarding imagination and fantasy is too complex for this task, but the point is that in dissociative identity disorder there is the same kind of possession and not-me experience, even when the existence of another self-state is denied, and it all happens intrapsychically. We know that there is a kind of implicit knowing about one state and another (Huntjens et al., 2006). In addition, the internal worlds of people with DID often are represented by a kind of landscape (O'Neil, 1997) that may be thought of as an interim place for living, a kind of transitional internal space (Chefetz, 2015).

I would commend to your attention the section of this paper on shame and humiliation experience. Because shame is always relational (DeYoung, 2015), the paradox will occur that the more intense the relationship between patient and therapist the more the patient, at some level, will expect to be humiliated or shamed by the therapist. This is consistent with negative therapeutic reactions, and the reality of how, as the authors note, sadistic abuse consists, in part, of spoiling the good. An in-depth review of the negative therapeutic reaction is available (Wurmser & Jarass, 2013), though some psychoanalytic writers have opined that the negative therapeutic reaction is more related to countertransference misattribution than anything, in particular, happening in the patient (Philip Bromberg, personal communication, 2016).

Maladaptive daydreaming

Eli Somer coined the term maladaptive daydreaming (MD) (Somer, 2002) and has led research efforts and cultivated a wide range of investigation into this prevalent but previously unknown experience. There is a conceptual continuum from normal daydreaming, through the intense absorption of maladaptive daydreaming, on into the internal worlds and experiences of people with dissociative identity disorder. Central to understanding the psychodynamics of maladaptive daydreaming are two forms of mental regulation: narrative regulation and affect regulation. The former is about the stories we tell ourselves about the life we have: 'I had a normal childhood, no different, really, than anybody else in my neighborhood. Yeah, there was a lot of drinking and drugging going on, but that was true of all the families I got to know. Yeah, just normal, like everybody else'. When asking questions like those on the Adult Attachment Interview people tend to be surprisingly revealing, often with some internal distress, as they respond to queries like: 'So, can you tell me what kind of parent your father was, and use specific examples, please?' Painful reality ensues, and the contrast with the regulatory narrative is stark. Such histories came pouring out of Somer's patients as he skillfully explored reality. People sought out treatment with him after searching the internet for something that matched their internal experience and they found maladaptive daydreaming.

This writer reported on the unusual experience of having a former consultee of his contact Dr. Somer about maladaptive daydreaming and talk about her dissociative identity disorder and interactions with this writer. It gave us an opportunity to look at her experience of both maladaptive daydreaming patterns and those of DID. As noted in the article, affect regulation is a primary outcome of maladaptive daydreaming and dissociative processes, in DID. A clinician's capacity to work in an emotion-focused paradigm may be important for progress in these treatments. I look forward to seeing treatment outcome studies in the literature as consciousness for maladaptive daydreaming increases in clinical settings.

Dissociative depression

Those readers who have encountered what is often referred to as 'treatment resistant depression' may find some advantages in considering what Vedat Şar has offered in this extensive review of depression in the context of dissociative adaptations to living. For example, this writer was covering for another physician who was on vacation when consultation was sought by one of their patients because of despair over continued depression without response to medication or psychotherapy. 'Tell me about your depression, please? What is your depression like, what is your experience?'

> What do you mean? I'm depressed. Isn't that enough to say? I mean, like, you're a psychiatrist, you know what depression is!
>
> Yes, of course I do. You are exactly correct. Still, each person has their own private experience of depression, and I'd like to understand yours. Can you give me an example of when you feel depressed, please?
>
> Oh, that's easy. I regularly go to work, sit down at my computer, and the next time I realize I'm at my desk three hours have gone by and I have no idea what happened to the time. It's just lost, and I feel miserable again. I have no idea what is going on in my life or how to deal with it. If that's not depressing, then nothing is!

This man had dissociative amnesia, profound depersonalization and derealization, and evidence for self-state activity. He felt enormously relieved that somebody could help him make sense of his 'depression'. In his descriptions of dissociative depression, Şar casts a wide net and reviews much of the etiology of depression, in general. For our purposes let's focus on three aspects of dissociative experience that influence the trajectory of depression when dissociative processes are highly active: depersonalization, discontinuity of experience and skills, and identity alteration.

Depersonalization experience is often hidden behind complaints of not being able to feel feelings, feeling disconnected from life and others, and feeling unreal, as if floating in a great void completely underwater with life going on at the surface that is inaccessible. This loss of feeling and feeling painfully unreal (Simeon & Abugel, 2006) is part and parcel of dissociative depression as well as depersonalization. Alexithymia and cognitive failures associated with difficulty identifying feelings leave people feeling isolated and unable to relate to others (Simeon et al., 2009). Imagine the pain of being respectfully and tenderly touched on the cheek by somebody who is very caring and you feeling nothing, a giant absence of anything, hollowed out. Consider what it's like to go to the office on Monday and spend the whole day fully engaged in a task only to arrive on Tuesday morning and have so little recognition of what was done on Monday that it takes you all day to even figure out what happened or that you were actually the person who did that work? This kind of discontinuity of experience extends to knowing how to operate machines and other office equipment and is part of a reasonable mental status examination (Loewenstein, 1991) if there's a hint of depersonalization in your initial screening review of systems. Discontinuity is often related to gross shifts in self-state activity where, for example, being frightened by somebody's bullying in an office setting might provoke a frightened child-like response in a person, a sense of lost adult capacities associated with a feeling of just wanting to go home and hide under the bed covers. Not only is this demoralizing, but it's confusing, and, of course, depressing. Lastly, consider how in DID the full power of the not-me position of alternate self-states leads to alienation from self and others. Losing capacities and abilities is demoralizing. Meeting with a spouse who bullies and provokes a switch into either a passive-submissive child-like state vs. a raging, in your face and destructive self-state might be enough to make any partner, spouse, friend or family members step back and tell you that you're crazy, a conclusion a person with a hidden dissociative disorder often comes to without help from others. This, also, is depressing.

Şar offers us a number of handles with which we can pursue the workup of treatment resistant depression. His broad perspectives add depth to the existing literature. A reader who becomes familiar with the subjective experiences of living with a dissociative disorder will be armed to explore identity confusion, emotional dysphoria, body dysmorphia, poor memory in a younger person, and the distress associated with feeling emotionally isolated from self and other. These perspectives have much to contribute to the practice of psychotherapy.

Metaphoric, metonymic, and psychotic somatoform dissociation

Dana Amir's theoretical perspective melds some of the ideas of Bion, Lacan, and McDougal in a thoughtful and interesting discussion of three aspects of somatoform dissociation. She describes the metaphoric somatic pathway as one that carries a capacity for symbolization forward while the metonymic is one without symbolization that is relegated to the use of action, traumatic enactive repetition (knowing) to tell the story of that which cannot be symbolized (Bardy & Mottet, 2006). Each of these ways of conceptualizing somatoform adaptations to trauma are useful in the context of thinking about people who present in consultation and seem to have no medical explanation for their symptoms. It may evoke, in a thoughtful clinician, a need to conceptualize a conversation mechanism. Symbolization and enactive repetition are the first two mechanisms Amir denotes. The third, psychotic, was more interesting and unusual for this reader. It always catches my attention when casework involving trauma or dissociation has an aspect that is called psychotic.

Amir's patient is reminiscent of those encountered in the negative therapeutic reaction where nothing good or meaningful is allowed to stand (Wurmser & Jarass, 2013) as well as the presence of trance logic, an essence of hypnosis (Orne, 1959) and a centerpiece of the internal worlds of DID. In fact, in the patient labeled psychotic, trance logic was visible in mother's relative indifference to father's incest of the daughter/patient, and, also, father's apparent lack of interest in his daughter's well-being. Trance logic is the juxtaposition of logically incompatible thoughts, feelings, ideas, or actions without anxiety, hysterical indifference. My sense is that this person was enacting the trance logical attitudes of both parents, and the degree of that betrayal was unbearable and left her ensconced in a somatic refuge. 'It troubles my mother' is a statement about the extent to which this now adult woman is emotionally insistent upon occupying the space assigned to her by both her parents (not caring about her well-being) and uses blinding levels of denial (dissociation) of her own pain, humiliation, and rage at her mistreatment.

In the patient with vocalization Amir emphatically states that the patient under consideration did not have dissociative identity disorder. However, she goes on to describe the patient productive of three different kinds of sustained vocalizations: a male voice, a mechanical voice, and then a beautiful and heartfelt singing voice. I recognized the origin of the lyrics as belonging to a popular song, There is a Ship. Here is the full set of lyrics, and what is absent in the text of the article may be telling:

https://www.youtube.com/watch?v=8DAlv3suXkQ
Lyrics

There is a ship and she sails the sea
She's loaded deep, as deep can be
But not as deep as the love I'm in
I know not if I sink or swim

I leaned my back against an oak
Thinking it was a trusty tree
But first it bent and then it broke
Just as my love proved false to me

Oh, love is gentle, and love is kind
The sweetest flower when first it's new
But love grows old and waxes cold
And fades away like the mornin' dew

The water is wide, I cannot get o'er
Neither have I the wings to fly
Give me a boat that can carry two
And both shall row my love and I
Source: Musixmatch

Songwriters: Noel Paul Stookey/Milton T. Okun/Peter Yarrow/Mary Allin Travers

'I leaned my back against an oak ... but first it bent and then it broke, just as my love proved false to me'. The song that moved both Amir and the patient to tears was metaphoric, and metonymic, there was symbolization and a kind of enactment. The tears shed told the story of profound loss of a love that could not be, an incestuous relationship of the patient with her brother. However, the stanza quoted above was left out of the words in Amir's article, and I am imagining also left out of what the patient sang. Yes, there was vocal association, and also, I'm especially curious about those three different voices potentially representing a very carefully hidden in plain sight DID, the vocal dissociation. There are times, in my experience, where the only crack in the patient's capacity to not know about their dissociation is in vocalizations that might be missed if a clinician did not fully pursue that territory. Amir is not a novice. Still, while also not a novice, I've been fooled by a patient or two who are faster at spackling over the cracks in their discontinuities than I have been at noticing the presence of the crack.

For now, I'm just grateful for the pleasure of reading a different kind of take on how to think about somatization as metaphoric and metonymic. It has been useful to add this to my reference points about conversion and somatization.

Childhood trauma and substance abuse

Costanzo, Santoro, and Schimmenti present a complex case of DID with clinical detail for both dissociative process and use of substances in typically failed efforts to regulate affect. This exposition clashes with the medical model of addiction as a lifetime biological illness from which relief is achieved with regular management but without real hope for definitive resolution of the addictive tendency or vulnerability. The authors propose that relief of the patient's substance use rests not in medication management or group supportive psychotherapy but in working through childhood psychodynamic burdens. My personal experience in over forty years of trauma treatment is in synchrony with their perspective. There are also some areas of investigation and concern that may deserve additional elaboration.

First, the burden of carrying shame often falls upon the shoulders of internal self-states capable of counter-affective compensation: shame states and fears of annihilation may occur through the use of grandiosity, as we can understand through the lens of self psychology (Wolf, 1988). In the context of DID, contempt is often used where one self-state asserts another is lacking potency, efficacy, or being a coward, having a fearful response to adversity. In other words, normal vulnerability is shamed by a contemptuous and dismissive internal ridicule. Yes, this is an echo of what in other psychotherapeutic contexts is called a harsh super-ego (Wurmser, 2000). In DID this dynamic occurs when an aspect of self hides shame and humiliation feelings in the self-state persona of a tough, take-no-prisoners sadistic perpetrator imago, and internally enacts abuse by inflicting shame and humiliation on other internal self-states. This is a paradoxical protector/perpetrator self-state, holding an enormity of emotional pain in a soft and vulnerable core surrounded by a hard outer shell of grandiose, sadistic, and contemptuous bravado (When appropriate, I have joked with patients about this as a version of M&M chocolate candy, and the point gets communicated quickly). Relief of this dynamic often occurs through an empathic stance with the perpetrator self-state that aims to make conscious the hidden shame and humiliation stored in the memory of this perpetrator self-state and under the blanket of omnipotent and sometimes magical scenes of abuse (Chefetz, 2017; Howell, 2002). What seems magical to the observing clinician, however, is not reflected in the lived experience of the patient that makes use of trance logic so that internal threats are uncritically accepted as reality.

Second, reliance upon substances for the relief of toxic and deeply painful affect cannot be accomplished without providing an affect modifying substitute that does not involve the use of substances (Brand et al., 2022; Napier, 1994; Vermilyea, 2000). In my observation, these kinds of grounding exercises are essential to the conduct of a trauma-focused psychotherapy. Significantly, there is wide acceptance of the use of mindfulness meditation and yoga practice in the treatment of trauma (Boyd et al., 2018; Taylor et al., 2020). Additionally, teaching self-hypnosis for affect regulation can be a powerful and self-esteem building option as dissociative capacities that phenotypically resemble hypnotic states are turned into resources that allow for reduction of intense affect that otherwise generate both emotional storms and self-destructive behavior: this represents a perverse affect regulation by punishing or enacting trauma dynamics on an often depersonalized body (Bradley et al., 2019; Farber, 2008; Ford & Gómez, 2015).

Lastly, since the dissociative disorders represent disorders of hiddenness (dissociative symptoms are often not noticed by either patient or clinician and need to be suspected in clinical settings where people are labeled treatment resistant or simply untreatable), it behooves the thoughtful clinician to develop a model of the kind of presentation these people will make in an intake or evaluation. Unresolvable depression, difficult or impossible to resolve anxiety, history of developmental (attachment) trauma, blunt trauma, victim of bullying, high ACE score (Felitti et al., 1998), eating disorder, substance use disorder, multiple failed therapies and/or failed personal relationships all can point toward a hidden dissociative disorder. The key screening feature beyond getting a good history is to become fluent in the nuances of depersonalization to be able to inquire about these experiences at a level beyond the simplistic and unusual out-of-body experience. Familiarity with an interview about dissociative experience is valuable (Loewenstein, 1991) as is use of the Cambridge Depersonalization Scale (Sierra & Berrios, 2000). Familiarity with the basic principles of the presentation of dissociative processes, as described earlier, is essential.

Trauma focused mentalization based therapy

Mentalization based treatment (MBT) has earned its place in the world of trauma treatment through painstaking and systematic theory building and clinical research. Rüfenacht, et.al. engaged with this writer as a reviewer of their contribution with a fruitful and respectful exchange about both the value of a trauma-informed approach to dissociative experience with MBT and a broadening of their lens and focus on dissociative processes hidden in work with complex trauma and post-traumatic disorders. Their product is excellent, and I recommend it to you as both well-written and authoritative. I would like to add only one comment regarding a more general perspective about chronic, complex post-traumatic stress disorders (cPTSD) as it relates to dissociative processes and disorders. (The introduction to Brand and Loewenstein, in this journal, provides additional data about the perspective I spell out, below.)

The centerpiece at issue is that in a population of people with cPTSD there is going to be a significant subgroup of unrecognized dissociative disorder presentations. In fact, a recent study concludes:

> The largest mean dissociation scores were found in dissociative disorders (mean scores > 35), followed by posttraumatic stress disorder, borderline personality disorder, and conversion disorder (mean scores > 25). Somatic symptom disorder, substance-related and addictive disorders, feeding and eating disorders, schizophrenia, anxiety disorder, OCD, and most affective disorders also showed mean dissociation scores > 15. Bipolar disorders yielded the lowest dissociation scores (mean score, 14.8) … The findings underline the importance of careful psychopathological assessment of dissociative symptoms in the entire range of mental disorders. (Lyssenko et al., 2018)

In another study, a metanalysis of research involving measurement of dissociation in the context of PTSD, the authors concluded:

> (1) Dissociation is moderately related to trauma exposure and severity; (2) dissociation symptoms rise sharply immediately after trauma exposure, then gradually decline for most, but stay high for some; (3) dissociation is clearly, consistently, and very strongly related to the presence and severity of *DSM–IV* PTSD symptoms; (4) the presence of high dissociation raises the probability of the presence and high levels of PTSD symptoms; and (5) dissociative symptoms relate as strongly to the three PTSD symptom clusters as they do to one another. These conclusions can provide the basis for consideration of various models of the causal relationships among traumatic stress, dissociation, and PTSD and recommendations about diagnostic criteria for PTSD. (Carlson et al., 2012)

It would seem conceivable that while the authors are focused on a view that the population of people they see with cPTSD are treatable with trauma focused MBT, it would be this writer's opinion that there is a likely cohort of their patient population with not only high dissociation but with undiagnosed dissociative disorders. Part of the problem with doing research is that the more things you consider the less control you have over your data. This is important in research and it also may constrain results. While trauma focused MBT is clearly valuable and useful, it behooves the thoughtful clinician to do extensive screening for the dissociative disorders if treating a population with cPTSD. I look forward to additional work from these authors that takes a second look at their patient population and ferrets out the extent to which dissociative disorders are present. Of course, then the problem arises: If I show there is a dissociative disorder, then under the rules of an investigational review board, won't I be required to responsibly provide treatment for somebody with a new diagnosis evoked by my research? For clinicians who are not used to treating a person with a dissociative disorder this expectancy might create a reluctance to do more pointed research. Of course, if it's not studied, then that doesn't mean it doesn't exist.

Dissociation & suicidal depression: a reformulated object relations theory perspective

Shahar, Robison and Joiner have written a complex paper that combines a theory of suicide, a view of dissociation related to Melanie Klein's work, and an exploration of a reformulated object relations theory. Thoughts of suicide are a sad routine feature in the psychotherapy of people who have activated dissociative processes in the context of a complex dissociative disorder, and the authors' review of that literature is informative. A dissociative disorder adds the dimension of multiple self-state psychology, and that is at the core of the case of Nirit, who brought with her The Terminator and Niriti. This constellation of the overwhelmingly powerful internal object and the innocent little child is emblematic of an internal object world centered around the abuse of a child. Nirit was distressed that Terminator and Niriti were so detached, not by their presence. Why was that?

The authors enlarge Klein's notion of anxiety as motivator and expand it to include the potential for negative emotion. I would spell that as shame, humiliation, mortification, helplessness, hopelessness, terror, horror, abjection, self-loathing, and self-disgust, amongst others of their ilk. Regarding repression, I would spell that as dissociation representing a model of mind where the comings and goings of self-states predict the presence or absence of consciousness for elements of experience, view of the world, cognitive capacity, and the core affective orientation of self-states in relation to others, both inside and outside a dissociative mind. I value inclusion of projective identification in the author's theorizing, though I have stated elsewhere that nothing is projected into the other, it is already there, though perhaps in a different context; but the affective core of the projection is activated in the other through processes of unconscious communication generated by regular interaction over time (Chefetz, 2015). It is the clinician's denial of their own affectivity that is often at the core of difficult enactments and requires delicate handling to bring into awareness (Bromberg, 2003; Chefetz, 2003). I heartily endorse the author's idea of a multiple-position psychology as related to a multiple self-state psychology, and recommend considering that's what Fairbairn did, but in a different language (Fairbairn, 1944). I believe that a central affect dimension that remains to be added to the author's theory is the notion of affective arousal, and levels associated with terror, not simply fear or anxiety, if consideration of dissociation is going to be used.

Dissociation in suicidality doesn't require actual annihilation of a position, just a simple switch from one self-state to another accomplishes the deed. Countering this kind of switch often takes the shape of engaging with the suicidal self-state, exploring their world-view, core affect, and motivations, and then following up by asking about the others Inside and how they feel, what they think, and 'What would they vote for?'

In my comments related to Costanzo, Santoro, and Schimmenti, I described problems attendant to persecutor/protector states. This is how Terminator could be understood. I would offer that Terminator secretly held unbearable levels of shame, humiliation, etc, related to childhood abuse and adult failures to make her world the way Nirit thought it should be by using her intelligence and wit, amongst other talents. I believe that the super-capable physician, Nirit, survived her suicide attempts because they were not efforts to die, but rather efforts to see if anybody cared enough to save her (something archaic younger states likely would not believe in their time-warped constellation). Efforts to call attention to the pain in Terminator were hidden behind their bravado. I believe that going forward, direct communication with Terminator as a 'real' object is required, and the empathic attunement to Terminator's pain will create a moment of transformation as 'the worst' is accepted by another who listens and cares.

Conclusion

After all, it's in the relationship that healing occurs. After trauma, people are noted to be both the problem and part of the solution. It's the challenge of being a good enough clinician in combination with recognizing that as clinicians, we're not so different from our patients. Eventually we help turn the tide and people heal. I hope the words I've written in this commentary contributes to such healing.

Disclosure statement

No potential conflict of interest was reported by the author(s).

References

Barach, P. (1991). Multiple personality as an attachment disorder. *Dissociation*, *4*(3), 117–123.

Bardy, B., & Mottet, D. (2006). Enactive/06: Enaction & complexity. In *Third International Conference on Enactive Interfaces*.

Beebe, B., Lachmann, F., Markese, S., & Bahrick, L. (2012). On the origins of disorganized attachment and internal working models: Paper I. A dyadic systems approach. *Psychoanalytic Dialogues*, *22*(2), 253–272. https://doi.org/10.1080/10481885.2012.666147

Boyd, J. E., Lanius, R. A., & McKinnon, M. C. (2018). Mindfulness-based treatments for posttraumatic stress disorder: A review of the treatment literature and neurobiological evidence. *Journal of Psychiatry and Neuroscience*, *43*(1), 7–25. https://doi.org/10.1503/jpn.170021

Bradley, A., Karatzias, T., & Coyle, E. (2019). Derealization and self-harm strategies are used to regulate disgust, fear, and sadness in adult survivors of childhood sexual abuse. *Clinical Psychology & Psychotherapy*, *26*(1), 94–104. https://doi.org/10.1002/cpp.2333

Brand, B. L., Schielke, H., Schiavone, F., & Lanius, R. A. (2022). *Finding solid ground: Overcoming obstacles in trauma treatment*. Oxford University Press.

Bretherton, I. (1987). New perspectives on attachment relations: Security, communication, and internal working models.

Bromberg, P. M. (1998). *Standing in the spaces*. The Analytic Press.

Bromberg, P. M. (2003). One need not be a house to be haunted: On enactment, dissociation, and the dread of "Not-me". *Psychoanalytic Dialogues*, *13*(5), 689–710. https://doi.org/10.1080/10481881309348764

Carlson, E. B., Dalenberg, C., & McDade Montez, E. (2012). Dissociation in posttraumatic stress disorder part I: Definitions and review of research. *Psychological Trauma: Theory, Research, Practice, & Policy*, *4*(5), 479. https://doi.org/10.1037/a0027748

Chefetz, R. A. (2003). Healing haunted hearts–toward a model for integrating subjectivity: Commentary on papers by Philip Bromberg and Gerald Stechler. *Psychoanalytic Dialogues*, *13*(5), 727–742. https://doi.org/10.1080/10481881309348766

Chefetz, R. A. (2008). *Nolens volens* out of darkness—From the depersonal to the "really" personal. *Contemporary Psychoanalysis*, *44*(1), 18–40. https://doi.org/10.1080/00107530.2008.10745946

Chefetz, R. A. (2015). *Intensive psychotherapy for persistent dissociative processes: The fear of feeling real*. W.W. Norton.

Chefetz, R. A. (2017). Issues in consultation for treatments with distressed activated abuser/protector self-states in dissociative identity disorder. *Journal of Trauma & Dissociation*, *18*(3), 465–475. https://doi.org/10.1080/15299732.2017.1295428

Chefetz, R. A., & Bromberg, P. M. (2004). Talking with "me" and "not-me": A dialogue. *Contemporary Psychoanalysis*, *40*(3), 409–464. https://doi.org/10.1080/00107530.2004.10745840

Davies, J. M., & Frawley, M. G. (1992). Dissociative processes and transference-countertransference paradigms in the psychoanalytically oriented treatment of adult survivors of childhood sexual abuse. *Psychoanalytic Dialogues*, *2*(1), 5–36. https://doi.org/10.1080/10481889209538920

DeYoung, P. A. (2015). *Understanding and treating chronic shame: A relational/Neurobiological approach*. Routledge.

Fairbairn, W. R. D. (1944). Endopsychic structure considered in terms of object-relationships. *International Journal of Psychoanalysis*, *25*, 70–92.

Farber, S. K. (2008). Dissociation, traumatic attachments, and self-harm: Eating disorders and self-mutilation. *Clinical Social Work Journal*, *36*(1), 63–72. https://doi.org/10.1007/s10615-007-0104-6

Felitti, V. J., Anda, R. F., Nordenberg, D., Williamson, D. F., Spitz, A. M., Edwards, V., Koss, M. P., & Marks, J. S. (1998). Relationship of childhood abuse and household dysfunction to many of the leading causes of death in adults. The Adverse Childhood Experiences (ACE) study. *American Journal of Preventive Medicine*, *14*(4), 245–258. https://doi.org/10.1016/S0749-3797(98)00017-8

Ford, J. D., & Gómez, J. M. (2015). Self-injury and suicidality: The impact of trauma and dissociation. *Journal of Trauma & Dissociation*, *16*(3), 225–231. Taylor & Francis. https://doi.org/10.1080/15299732.2015.989648

Guntrip, H. (1969). *Schizoid phenomena, object relations and the self.* International Universities Press, Inc.

Howell, E. F. (2002). Back to the "states" victim and abuser state in borderline personality disorder. *Psychoanalytic Dialogues*, *12*(6), 921–957. https://doi.org/10.1080/10481881209348713

Howell, E. F. (2005). *The dissociative mind*. Analytic Press.

Huntjens, R. L. J. C., Peters, M. L., Woertman, L., Bovenschen, L. M., Martin, R. C., & Postma, A. (2006). Inter-identity amnesia in dissociative identity disorder: A simulated memory impairment? *Psychological Medicine*, *36*(6), 857–864. https://doi.org/10.1017/S0033291706007100

Janet, P. (1901). *The mental state of hystericals: A study of mental stigmata and mental accidents*. GP Putnam's Sons.

Kluft, R. P. (Ed.). (1985). *Childhood antecedants of multiple personality.* American Psychiatric Press, Inc.

Liotti, G. (1999). Disorganization of attachment as a model for understanding dissociative psychopathology. In J. Solomon & C. George (Eds.), *Attachment disorganization* (pp. 291–317). Guilford Press.

Loewenstein, R. J. (1991). An office mental status examination for complex chronic dissociative symptoms and multiple personality disorder. In R. J. Loewenstein (Ed.), *Psychiatric clinics of North America* (Vol. 14, pp. 567–604). W.B. Saunders Company.

Lyons-Ruth, K. (2003). Dissociation and the parent-infant dialogue: A longitudinal perspective from attachment research. *Journal of the American Psychoanalytic Association*, *51*(3), 883–911. https://doi.org/10.1177/00030651030510031501

Lyons-Ruth, K., Dutra, L., Schuder, M. R., & Bianchi, I. (2006). From infant attachment disorganization to adult dissociation: Relational adaptations or traumatic experiences? In R. A. Chefetz (Ed.), *Dissociative disorders: An expanding window into the psychobiology of mind* (Vol. 29, pp. 63–86). Saunders.

Lyssenko, L., Schmahl, C., Bockhacker, L., Vonderlin, R., Bohus, M., & Kleindienst, N. (2018). Dissociation in psychiatric disorders: A meta-analysis of studies using the dissociative experiences scale. *American Journal of Psychiatry, 175*(1), 37–46. https://doi.org/10.1176/appi.ajp.2017.17010025

Main, M., & Hesse, E. (1990). Parents' unresolved traumatic experiences are related to infant disorganized attachment status: Is frightened and/or frightening parental behavior the linking mechanism? In M. T. Greenberg, D. Ciccheti, & E. M. Cummings (Eds.), *Attachment in the preschool years: Theory, research, and intervention* (pp. 161–182). The University of Chicago.

Mitchell, S. A. (1991). Contemporary perspectives on self: Toward an integration. *Psychoanalytic Dialogues, 1*(2), 121–147. https://doi.org/10.1080/10481889109538889

Napier, N. J. (1994). *Getting through the day: Strategies for adults hurt as children*. W.W. Norton.

Ogawa, J. R., Sroufe, L. A., Weinfield, N. S., Carlson, E. A., & Egelend, B. (1997). Development and the fragmented self: Longitudinal study of dissociative symptomatology in a nonclinical sample. *Development and Psychopathology, 9*(4), 855–879. https://doi.org/10.1017/S0954579497001478

O'Neil, J. A. (1997). Expanding the psychoanalytic view of the intrapsychic: Psychic conflict in the inscape. *Dissociation: Progress in the Dissociative Disorders, 10*(4), 192–202.

Orne, M. T. (1959). The nature of hypnosis: Artifact and essence. *The Journal of Abnormal and Social Psychology, 58*(3), 277–299. https://doi.org/10.1037/h0046128

Putnam, F. W. (1997). *Dissociation in children and adolescents*. The Guilford Press.

Putnam, F. W. (2016). *The way we are: How states of mind influence our identities, personality, and potential for change*. IPBooks.Net.

Rosenfeld, H. (1947). Analysis of a schizophrenic state with depersonalization. *The International Journal of Psycho-Analysis, 28*, 130.

Segal, H. (1979). *Klein*. Karnac.

Siegel, D. J. (1999). *The developing mind: Toward a neurobiology of interpersonal experience*. Guilford Press.

Sierra, M., & Berrios, G. E. (2000). The Cambridge depersonalisation scale: A new instrument for the measurement of depersonalisation. *Psychiatry Research, 93*(2), 153–164. https://doi.org/10.1016/S0165-1781(00)00100-1

Sierra, M., Senior, C., Dalton, J., McDonough, M., Bond, A., Phillips, M. L., O'Dwyer, A. M., & David, A. S. (2002). Autonomic response in depersonalization disorder. *Archives of General Psychiatry, 59*(9), 833–838. https://doi.org/10.1001/archpsyc.59.9.833

Simeon, D., & Abugel, J. (2006). *Feeling unreal: Depersonalization disorder and the loss of the self*. Oxford University Press.

Simeon, D., Giesbrecht, T., Knutelska, M., Smith, R. J., & Smith, L. M. (2009). Alexithymia, absorption, and cognitive failures in depersonalization disorder: A comparison to posttraumatic stress disorder and healthy volunteers. *Journal of Nervous and Mental Disease, 197*(7), 492–498. https://doi.org/10.1097/NMD.0b013e3181aaef6b

Slade, A. (2014). Imagining fear: Attachment, threat, and psychic experience. *Psychoanalytic Dialogues, 24*(3), 253–266. https://doi.org/10.1080/10481885.2014.911608

Somer, E. (2002). Maladaptive daydreaming: A qualitative inquiry. *Journal of Contemporary Psychotherapy, 32*(2/3), 197–212. https://doi.org/10.1023/A:1020597026919

Spitz, E., & Handler. (1993). Calvin and hobbes postmodern and psychoanalytic perspectives. *Psychoanalytic Review, 80*(1), 55–82.

Stern, D. B. (1997). *Unformulated experience: From dissociation to imagination in psychoanalysis*. The Analytic Press.
Taylor, J., McLean, L., Korner, A., Stratton, E., & Glozier, N. (2020). Mindfulness and yoga for psychological trauma: Systematic review and meta-analysis. *Journal of Trauma & Dissociation*, *21*(5), 536–573. https://doi.org/10.1080/15299732.2020.1760167
Teicher, M. H., Samson, J. A., Sheu, Y.-S., Polcari, A., & McGreenery, C. E. (2010). Hurtful words: Association of exposure of peer verbal abuse with elevated psychiatric symptom scores and corpus callosum abnormalities. *American Journal of Psychiatry*, *167*(12), 1464–1471. https://doi.org/10.1176/appi.ajp.2010.10010030
Tronick, E., Als, H., Adamson, L., Wise, S., & Brazelton, T. B. (1978). The infant's response to entrapment between contradictory messages in face-to-face interaction. *Journal of the American Academy of Child Psychiatry*, *17*(1), 1–13. https://doi.org/10.1016/S0002-7138(09)62273-1
Vermilyea, E. G. (2000). *Growing beyond survival: A self-help tool-kit for managing traumatic stress*. Sidran Press.
Winnicott, D. W. (1949). Hate in the countertransference. *International Journal of Psychoanalysis*, *30*, 69–75.
Winnicott, D. W. (1953). Transitional objects and transitional phenomena: A study of the first not-me possession. *International Journal of Psychoanalysis*, *34*(part 2), 89–97.
Winnicott, D. W. (1960). Ego distortion in terms of true and false self. In R. Khan and M. Masud (Eds.), *The maturational processes and the facilitating environment (1965)* (pp. 140–152). Hogarth Press and the Institute of Psycho-Analysis.
Wolf, E. S. (1988). *Treating the self: Elements of clinical self psychology*. Guilford Press.
Wolff, P. (1987). *The development of behavioral states and the expression of emotions in early infancy: New proposals for investigation*. University of Chicago Press.
Wurmser, L. (2000). *The power of the inner judge: Psychodynamic treatment of the severe neuroses*. Jason Aronson.
Wurmser, L., & Jarass, H. (Eds.). (2013). *Nothing good is allowed to stand: An integrative view of the negative therapeutic reaction*. Routledge.

When daydreaming becomes maladaptive: phenomenological and psychoanalytic perspectives

Richard A. Chefetz, Nirit Soffer-Dudek and Eli Somer

Maladaptive daydreaming (MD) is the excessive employment of immersive daydreaming characterized by highly absorbing fantasy experiences that become a preferred focus of consciousness at the expense of living in the real world. Active dissociative processes like depersonalization and derealization, including those also characteristic of dissociative identity disorder (DID): amnesia, identity confusion, and identity alteration, may be present and, like in DID, seem to be psychodynamically driven. Comorbidity with attention deficit disorder, obsessive-compulsive disorder, post-traumatic stress disorder, and others is typical. Often associated with profound shame experience, it is, like DID, a condition that tends to be concealed and requires a clinician to be knowledgeable about its nature before a diagnosis can occur and effective treatment be initiated. We introduce the concept, explore its clinical associations and manifestations, and provide several case vignettes to illustrate the breadth and depth of this potentially debilitating variation on daydreaming.

Life could be unbearably mundane without the pleasure of a daydream, a narrative fiction thematically playing out the work of the mind's storyteller. Daydreams often happen in a state of deep absorption of attention. Total immersion or absorption may be directed towards adaptive goals (immersion into a task at work or playing a game with enthusiasm, e.g., Zadik et al., 2022) or might sometimes reflect a tendency to drift off into vivid, engaging personal reverie. These absorbing, subjectively alive experiences may compete with external reality when there is intense immersion. There are probably many readers who have remarked with amazement that they have been so absorbed in their thoughts they have lost track of attending to their needs at hand; in common parlance, some people talk about off-task immersion as being 'zoned-out' (whereas on-task immersion may be referred to as being 'in the zone'). A person who appears to be 'zoned out' may actually be highly focused on an internal event. While this kind of state is often associated with normal intense absorption, have you ever wondered what it would be like to find a particular mental state more interesting than real life?

Preliminary findings in a population study estimate that about 2.5% of people have a clinical-level impairment from such consuming immersive daydreams (Soffer-Dudek & Theodor-Katz, 2022). This epidemiological finding suggests that MD may be three times as prevalent as schizophrenia (van Os & Kapur, 2009). It is consistent with the literature on certain dissociative disorders (Sar et al., 2007). So, it's not rare, and it's also not routine, requiring clinicians to know about this kind of maladaptive daydreaming (MD) and similar problems in order to ask about them.

Shame often exists for those people afflicted by behavior that feels outside their control, e.g., alcoholism, binge-eating disorder, or obsessive-compulsive disorder (OCD). People tend to hide the shame-laden content of their experiences (Carvalho et al., 2022). A now classic example of this is dissociative identity disorder (DID), previously too often diagnosed as schizophrenia because some people with DID have the experience of hearing voices of the non-bizarre variety (Kluft, 1987). Unfortunately, many clinicians are not aware enough of the importance of such a differential diagnosis (Longden, 2010). Revealing such heard voices might be an unwanted entrée to hospital admission and anti-psychotic medication. Revealing an inner world of immersive daydreaming in which four hours or more of each day (Soffer-Dudek & Somer, 2018 are spent actively fantasizing at the expense of working, studying, or nurturing social ties might cause some anxiety. A person reporting this might believe they are crazy, especially if they reveal they prefer it to ordinary reality. Daydreaming is a routine pastime. However, when daydreaming becomes compelling, unbidden, and unavoidable, and the everyday function of a person's life lays fallow in their calendar, then there's a problem of real dysfunction.

Shame appears to play a significant role in the psychodynamics of relational trauma, which is thought to have links to both MD and DID. In the case of DID, dissociative processes seem to create conditions that nurture a pseudo-delusion of separateness, eventually giving rise to characteristic alter personalities or not-me self-states of DID (Chefetz & Bromberg, 2004). Similarly, in MD, a shame-generated counter-phobic immersive fantasy of a beloved and/or capable me seems to be a possible equivalent process. The concept beloved-me stems from the idea that experiencing shame leads to feeling unworthy of love and devalued. Thus, the opposite of shame might not be pride, but rather the feeling of being beloved (Chefetz, 2021). The vignettes following this theoretical discussion shed some light on the presence of beloved/capable me in MD scenarios. In MD, it appears that positive qualities are added to a re-constructed self-esteem, whereas in DID, negative qualities are misattributed to an Other (alter personality) through a self-shunning process.

Daydreaming is part of clinical history, particularly that of psychoanalysis (e.g., Raphling, 1996; Freud, 1908), and has its rightful place alongside the study of dreams and parasomnias. Although Winnicott (1971) distinguished between adaptive and maladaptive fantasizing, Somer originally identified MD as a suggested syndrome (Somer, 2002). Comorbid clinical constructs may include obsessive-compulsive spectrum disorders (Salomon-Small et al., 2021), addictive disorders (Pietkiewicz et al., 2018), and attention deficit hyperactivity disorder (ADHD), yet, they are distinct (Theodor-Katz et al., 2022. Autism spectrum disorder is also comorbid with MD (West et al., 2023). While they share similarities, such as preoccupation with the internal world and in stereotypical repetitive movements, they differ in that MD does not involve an impairment in social understanding.

MD is characterized by intense immersion or absorption, which aligns with one of the characteristics of hypnosis (Orne, 1962) and is a prominent factor in dissociative experience (Soffer-Dudek & Somer, 2022; Soffer-Dudek et al., 2015). Individuals with a strong tendency for spontaneous absorption may become engrossed in internal events at the expense of being responsive to their surroundings, resulting in a reduced sense of agency and increased automatisms (Bregman-Hai et al., 2020; Soffer-Dudek & Somer, 2022). This loss of continuity in subjective experience is essential in defining dissociative experiences (Schimmenti & Şar, 2019) and may possibly lead to a sense of experiential disconnectedness and self-incoherence in MD. Significantly, there are mixed presentations of MD and dissociative disorders (Soffer-Dudek & Somer, 2022). In people with MD, the symptoms mentioned above create a clinical picture where daydreams are compulsive and subsume reality. An adaptive, rather than dysfunctional, engagement with daydreaming might involve valuing immersive daydreaming as an activity while still dedicating more time, effort, libido, and interest to one's actual life. The diagnosis of dissociative trance disorder can be made only if the patient shows disruption of identity and altered consciousness to the surroundings that may be perceived as an experience of being controlled by an external supernatural power. Trance disorder only applies to those who experience an unusual involuntary event, and neither a regular activity nor a part of a broadly accepted religious practice, and any organic causes such as traumatic brain injury, epilepsy, and the effects of any psychoactive substances have to be ruled out (APA, 2013).

Daydreaming

Daydreaming and mind-wandering from one's present reality involve focusing on internal images and thoughts. These psychological processes can facilitate future planning or creative thinking (Klinger, 1971; Singer, 1974). This human experience has long been described as a 'stream' of thought or consciousness (James, 1890). Mental activity unrelated to the task at hand is loosely called 'mind-wandering' (Baird et al., 2014; Smallwood, 2013; Smallwood & Schooler, 2015). Killingsworth and Gilbert (2010) demonstrated that people's minds wander over 50% of waking time; while significant, focusing on external perceptions is not necessarily the dominant share of our daily experience.

In contrast to mind-wandering, daydreaming denotes active fantasizing characterized by continuous, vivid, and emotionally engaging internal storytelling with a coherent narrative (Theodor-Katz et al., 2022. This differs from unguided thoughts that race from topic to topic without a particular course or aim, characterizing ADHD (Irving & Thompson, 2018; Theodor-Katz et al., 2022. Fantasizing is a free and spontaneous mental activity, more controlled than nocturnal dreaming but with fewer constraints and control than goal-directed thought (Christoff et al., 2016).

Nocturnal dreaming and the loosely labeled 'mind wandering' are both associated with the default mode network and have been suggested to use the same simulation processes (Domhoff, 2011). However, due to the hypoactivation of some prefrontal regions when creating oneiric scenes (Dang-Vu et al., 2007), daydreaming may engender a much more organized, coherent, continuous, and guided narrative than dreaming. In addition to this structural difference between mental states associated with dream-like activity, there seem to be individual differences, probably along a continuum of mental ability for fanciful, vivid, immersive daydreaming, which may or may not become maladaptive (West & Somer, 2019). Under what conditions do immersive fantasies impinge upon one's waking life, culminating in MD?

MD has been suggested as a nosological classification for a new psychiatric disorder: excessive, compulsive/addictive absorption in fantasies causing significant clinical distress or dysfunction in academic, vocational, or social contexts (Bigelsen & Schupak, 2011; Somer, 2002; Somer et al., 2017). Listening to evocative music and engaging in stereotypical movements such as pacing or spinning are highly hypnotic and may facilitate absorbed daydreaming states. Daydreamers may engage in facial expressions and mouthing as they become increasingly engrossed. They may laugh, weep, or move in tandem with imagined characters. Adult immersive daydreamers seem aware enough of their environments to avoid accidents or public embarrassment. People with MD distinguish fantasy from reality but yearn for their addictive fantasy (Bigelsen et al., 2016; Soffer-Dudek & Somer, 2018). Solitude allows undisturbed immersion in daydreaming without the need for concealment. Shame is typical for this consuming behavior that alters relatedness and impedes life's goals.

MD is associated with difficulties in emotion regulation and insecure attachment (Chirico et al., 2022; Greene et al., 2020; Mariani et al., 2022; Sándor et al., 2021). Maladaptive daydreamers may develop this behavior in response to adversity like trauma or social anxiety (Soffer-Dudek & Somer, 2022). In one daily diary study, 65.9% of daydreaming episodes functioned as a distraction from an unpleasant reality, 48.9% as a means to regulate painful feelings, and 27.6% served as a distraction from painful memories (Wen et al., 2022). This suggests a compensatory role for MD with themes such as an ideal self, emotional support, social competency, or gaining recognition (Somer, 2002; Somer et al., 2016a, 2016b). Trauma-related compensatory themes may also be present with a repetitive portrayal of the daydreamer as a rescuer, a victim, or a perpetrator (Somer et al., 2021). Unlike 'fixed' post-traumatic flashbacks, MD scenes are creative, flexible, and ever-changing, like different episodes in a TV series (Soffer-Dudek & Somer, 2022).

From a multiple self-state perspective (Bromberg, 2009), daydreaming may allow experimentation with different self-states within a relatively safe inner space. As a character in a vivid fantasy, the daydreamer can reify a complex version of self with its own set of motivations, emotional responses, wishes, memories, and goals. The daydreamer temporarily allows herself to adopt that identity in a self-generated alternate reality. In most people, daydreaming of a version of themselves is probably normal and even adaptive. It can facilitate rehearsing desired future scenarios to promote their later attainment in real life. Indeed, daydreams that functioned as 'planning and rehearsing' were associated with more positive post-daydream moods (Wen et al., 2022). In its adaptive form, this process could generate an integrated set of self-states that make up a coherent self-narrative (e.g., 'a part of me can be assertive at work when needed'). In MD, however, the experimentation and expression of these covert selves are so highly gratifying that individuals prefer daydreaming to actual living.

Moreover, MD may entrench the disconnection and dissociation between the individual's self-states, leaving the person with a sense of fragmentation and a not-me experience (Chefetz & Bromberg, 2004). Returning to outer reality, people with MD face the harsh realization of the ever-widening gap between their fantasies and actual lives, creating further despair and self-criticism. Derealization occurs as the fantasy experience feels much more real than reality (Soffer-Dudek & Somer, 2022). Life is experienced as empty, disappointing, or dismal (Somer et al., 2019). More than 30 years before the term MD was coined, Winnicott (1971) contrasted adaptive with maladaptive daydreaming by differentiating between 'imagination' and 'fantasy'. An imagining person is projecting their current self onto the future, permitting the coexistence of the present and the future in one's mind. Conversely, fantasy means that the fantasizing self cannot envision the daydreamed character as 'me', which prohibits the continuity of the self (Bromberg, 2013; Winnicott, 1971). Maladaptive daydreamers have described their experience as living in multiple worlds or layers with varying degrees of active dissociative processes, e.g., depersonalization (Soffer-Dudek & Somer, 2022; Somer et al., 2019). The failure of the daydreamed experience to be integrated with the living self leads to post-daydreaming distress (Soffer-Dudek & Somer, 2018; Wen et al., 2022): shame, loneliness, decreased self-esteem, and social dysfunction (Ferrante et al., 2020; Soffer-Dudek & Somer, 2018; Theodor-Katz et al., 2022; Wen et al., 2022). MD, as actual coping, is inefficient, creating a vicious cycle that contributes to avoiding one's problems and alienation from potential social support sources. Many do not feel comfortable sharing their problem with mental health care professionals for fear of being misunderstood. Those who disclose their problems often experience unempathetic or unhelpful responses from family and friends.

Naïve practitioners dismissed their concerns and provided unsuitable or insufficient diagnoses (Bigelsen & Schupak, 2011; Somer et al., 2016a), leading them to seek help online and support the medicalizing of MD (Bershtling & Somer, 2018).

The following three case vignettes are illustrative of the breadth of clinical presentations of MD.

Gail

Gail is a 41-year-old female computer engineer living in Israel, married, and a mother of two girls. She first contacted me (Somer) via an email describing her shock at learning that her years-long secretive mental activity had a name. Concerned and embarrassed by her disruptive mental compulsion, she had Googled her symptoms only to discover that her experience was shared by countless people worldwide. Their detailed descriptions of addiction to vivid daydreaming sounded strikingly familiar.

> I was dumbfounded to discover that many people suffer from this. I always thought I was the only weirdo in the world with this problem ... much to my surprise, your name came up in MD online communities, so I decided to seek you out and ask you before I change my mind if you would agree to treat me.

Gail sought therapy to control her time-consuming daydreaming, about which she felt humiliated. She was relieved that she finally revealed her secret but often prefaced her disclosures with self-disparaging comments like: '*I am so stupid*', '*This is SO embarrassing ...* ' and, '*I hope you won't laugh at me for sharing this with you*'. She used to spend most of her off-task time in her fantasy worlds, usually pretending to listen to others while interacting with invisible internal protagonists. Her daydreaming seeped into her work time, leaving her zoned-out for long periods in front of her computer, seemingly absorbed in figuring out an elusive bug in the code. She was concerned about her insufficient sleep due to her preference to daydream. She felt awful for daydreaming while caring for her children and guilty about her fantasies' contents.

Like her, her father was a computer engineer at a thriving global hi-tech company. Gail described him as emotionally absent. He seldom expressed pride in her achievements, often was critical of her eating habits and choice of clothing, and regularly commented on her unshaven body hair. Gail described her mother, a commercial lawyer, as an attractive woman who valued her career much more than homemaking. Although the parents earned substantial salaries, they led a spartan lifestyle. They provided Gail with all the essentials but often refused requests for what they regarded as unnecessary extras, for example, a camera she wanted for her birthday and a pair of quality branded tennis shoes. Gail's maternal grandmother, who lived nearby and provided comfort and emotional support, was a significant figure in her life. Since childhood, she has always enjoyed the company of her imaginary companions. They showed up as she was pacing back and forth on the worn-out path of her bedroom carpet, listening to her favorite music. Notably, many individuals with MD report physical movements that accompany fantasy immersion; perhaps they represent self-soothing or hypnotizing behaviors aimed at discharging psychophysiological stress.

Gail was an excellent student. She was very insecure about her physical appearance. She displayed an emotionally avoidant social style. She was constantly worried about embarrassing herself, hesitant about meeting strangers, and feared criticism with the regular ensuing reflexive blushing and shame.

With tears in her eyes, she admitted that she spent most of her day having imaginary interactions with Michael, her first teenage boyfriend. He had left her heartbroken when he unexpectedly broke up with her. He was the first boy who showed interest in her as a young woman, and it was with him that she had her first sexual encounter. His sudden abandonment left her feeling taken advantage of and humiliated. Unfortunately, this event mimicked her parents' emotional distancing and may have solidified her shame-based social withdrawal. These experiences were consistent with her later daydreaming themes and her yearning to recover self-esteem. Her main daydreaming themes revolved around impressing Michael and making him realize what a regretful mistake he committed by giving up on such a successful woman. Here is how she presented her problem:

> First, I need to apologize in advance for the shallow and childish content of my daydreaming. How can an accomplished woman like me waste her time on such stupid fantasies? ... at any rate, in all my daydreams, without exception, I look fabulous: I have a stunning figure and stylish clothes, and I am gorgeous. Michael is featured in most of my daydreams. I imagine him being present when I am successful, witty, popular, or cool. I insert him into scenarios where I am praised for professional achievement or solving a difficult computer programming problem. He is there as I move sensually on the dance floor or happily embrace my husband. I see Michael looking longingly at me from the corner of my eye. I also have daydreams that do not feature Michael. Still, in all these cases, I am either very attractive or highly successful: I am a lead dancer in a Broadway blockbuster, a top Silicone Valley Hi-Tech CEO calls to offer me a senior management position, or I invest wisely in the stock exchange and make millions of dollars ... I hesitate to say ... This is sooo embarrassing ... OK, let it out, Gail. So, lately, I have been daydreaming that I have been blissfully married to Michael. I can't figure it out because I love Tom (her husband) so much. Michael is no match for him. So annoying, I am an awful person...

Gail always recognized the irrationality of her fantasy life. She maintained that her adolescent crush would not have been a suitable match for her and that she was fortunate to be married to her successful and attractive husband. Still, the urge to taunt Michael in her fantasies 17 years after the boy broke up with her was unrelenting. This constellation was a psychodynamic treasure trove of unconscious motivations, but was it necessary to explore this in-depth to effect change and give her relief? Or rather, would a cognitive-behavioral approach focused on the obsessive-compulsive/addictive aspects of her experience be effective?

Our therapy initially focused on exploring Gail's motivation to control her rush-producing imaginary retaliations and self-aggrandizing fantasies. She understood the compensatory function of her narcissistic imaginings. She also knew that her insatiable thirst to be recognized as attractive and successful was rooted in her childhood pain and adolescent suffering. Yet, rather than working on the level of dynamic insight, she enthusiastically adopted one of my formulations of her problem as an addictive OCD-like craving that was impossible to satisfy. The opportunity to regard her unceasing self-aggrandizing imaginings as irritating but meaningless symptoms may have diminished their emotional weight and the ensuing shame. Reducing the problem to a futile compulsion helped Gail to separate herself from the behavior by objectifying it as a pointless annoyance that could be eradicated. At my suggestion, she added the following affirmations as part of a daily self-motivating routine:

> I want to share my current life's joys and achievements with the hurt child within me.
>
> I have a behavioral addiction. I refuse to be an addict.

These self-affirmations were both succinct and complex. They conveyed a compassionate insight into the childhood origins of her pain, a cognizance of her self-worth, an awareness of the need to anchor herself mindfully in the present, and a confident resolution to control her condition.

What followed was a series of meetings in which I provided self-esteem-building skills to return control of her emotional life to her and reduce her dependence upon MD for self-soothing. She became increasingly present in her external world through mindfulness meditation and monitoring her daydreaming patterns, interventions that help reduce MD symptoms (Herscu et al., 2023). I encouraged her to practice these tasks daily. In session, we discussed things that mattered to Gail: her family and work. Excel charts she meticulously kept showed a steady decline in the time spent in fantasy. After about 20 weekly sessions over six months, the MD time curve had leveled off and remained stable at about 90 minutes daily, down from up to 5 hours of incessant daily daydreaming. Gail was proud to report that Michael was no longer featured in her fantasy scripts. 'But *you still daydream'*, I remarked. '*Can you share what is happening in your inner world these days?*' I asked. '*Sure,*' she replied smilingly.

> We meet in your office, and we talk. I complain about hardships at work, and you offer your perspective. I will tell you about my daily life with Tom. I reminisce about my childhood and youth, and you listen empathically. I also like to brag about my achievements and how well I am feeling these days, and I can tell you are pleased and quite proud of me. You don't say it, but I can hear your thoughts, and sometimes I respond to them … I know that your thoughts represent what

> I think about myself, but I still believe these might be opinions and thoughts you may have of me.

To ask for her final authorization for this text, I wrote Gail many months after we ended the treatment to inquire about her well-being and ask for final approval of her case description. Here is her reply:

> Wow, I agree with this description and consent to use it. Thank you for asking my permission; it means a lot to me. I read the first emails to you, and I had a bit of trouble believing it was me. I could always convey what I had been through, but it's still amazing how deep I was in this MD, that these were my words, and how much it is a thing of the past now…Good luck with the publication of the paper.
> Gail

This case represents a classic transference cure from one perspective. From another perspective, Gail has simply replaced a dysfunctional and preoccupying pain-reducing MD scene with a script that honors her emotions, asserts her dignity, allows her to feel cared about, and gives her some benevolent internal objects upon which she can rely for emotional sustenance. It is an efficient and effective remedy.

Rachel

Rachel emailed me (Somer) for a consultation about her emotional suffering. Different mental health professionals had given her several diagnoses, but she never felt they understood her condition correctly. She was an ultra-orthodox Jewish woman from a radical breakaway Hasidic dynasty. She was 32 years old and the mother of six children. Her husband worked part-time as a salesperson in a technical shop and was a student at an institute of advanced rabbinical literature for married men. As is the custom among fundamentalist Hasidic women, she covered her clean-shaven head with a tight headscarf.

Rachel's mother was the seventh of nine children. Mother was orphaned at age 10. Rachel's father was the youngest of 10 children, born in quick succession. Before his birth, his father got sick with cancer. His paternal grandmother couldn't care for him as a newborn, so he was sent to an 'orphanage' for a few months. Rachel's parents were divorced. Her father remarried before Rachel's Bat Mitzvah, and the family moved from America to Jerusalem, Israel when Rachel was 14. Besides being provided a home and food, she felt no one cared for her physically or emotionally.

I asked Rachel to describe her recollections of her childhood and current condition. Here is what she wrote:

> My parents started home and family on the heels of their unresolved childhood traumas, with very little support. So here are my reflections on my growing-up years:

I'm the 10th out of 11 children. What I remember as the most stressful growing up was the heavy weight of financial distress. The kids in my family weren't sheltered from anything. Lack of money was always the front and center issue, permeating every aspect of life, from the weekly grocery order through the new school year to family events like Bar-Mitzvahs and weddings. More than my sisters, I have always taken it to heart and rarely asked for something new. I would babysit at other people's houses, which I loved as a change from my boring home, and for the opportunity to put a few dollars into my mom's purse. There were many other stresses, and everything was out in the open. My father was a daydreamer who often paced around for long hours, talking to himself. I think he has a bit of autism, and he maintained a very superficial relationship with my mother and us kids.

My mother is very introverted. She tolerated no nonsense. Nonsense to her is anything emotions-related or anything out of the straight and narrow. I felt very choked and stifled at home. In her defense, I would say that she did the best she could with what she had and gave us a lot of good childhood memories too. My unmet needs for unconditional acceptance and intense closeness caused me to shut down and start functioning like a robot.

At age 7, I contracted a severe infection, which kept me home for a few weeks during the school year and left me physically weak and suffering from muscle aches and other unpleasant physical issues for many years. So physically and emotionally, I was the family drama queen, probably making my sisters very jealous.

Whereas I tuned out with daydreams, my sister, a year my senior, got her satisfaction from bullying, and I was the ideal target; high-strung, highly sensitive, and over-responsive. I learned to always be on guard and avoid any show of vulnerability.

I always needed to portray myself as 'perfect', hoping to be liked. Therefore, my pride kept me from ever confiding in anyone or reaching out for help. Although I don't think there even was someone safe to whom I could've turned.

My family was part of a seceding rabbinical court. As such, we weren't part of the neighborhood social circle. I was shy, quiet, and nerdy in elementary school, but I was untamed, boisterous, and daring with a friend. In middle school, I became less avoidant, was disruptive in class, restless and inattentive. I was frequently punished for that. Academically I was effortlessly a straight-A student. But my social life was terrible. I failed to maintain lasting friendships due to my insecurities and lack of emotional expression.

Before high school, I decided to become a beloved 'perfect', and my acting out changed to acting in. I was portrayed as a model student and tried to absorb clues for socially appropriate behavior by observing others. I was like a chameleon attempting to be like whomever I was with. I was then able to maintain neutral relationships.

To this day, I have difficulty focusing on a conversation and being part of a social circle. I can be my best self if I feel accepted, respected, and in the company of people, I appreciate ... These factors severely limit my enjoyment of social situations ... Therefore, I lose interest in participating...I generally do better one-on-one than in groups, as I tend to lose focus and drift away. But even one-on-one exhausts me. Being playful and fun is an ability I've never mastered.

Maladaptive Daydreaming

> I'm not sure when it started, but I remember the content of my daydreams since age 11. They always centered around someone, usually a female teacher or a camp counselor, whom I loved and wanted a deeper relationship with – someone who embodied my untapped potential. I would fantasize about her all day, creating elaborate scenes where I gained her admiration, and I'd replay it often, tweaking the details until it was perfect. In my daydreams, I'm the ideal version of myself: fluid, expressive, grounded, connected, confident, assertive, validated, and surrounded by a cohort of admirers. The qualifier would change periodically as crushes came and went. When one ended, like after a school year, I would experience withdrawal and cry a lot, faced with the reality that my fantasies now have no chance of ever coming true. I remember one in particular when I was 17 and aware of what I was doing. I broke off our relationship, telling her that I was too obsessed with her and that it was setting me back in my self-growth. Afterward, I felt like I'm going crazy.
>
> Currently, I don't indulge in such elaborate themes anymore. Around my kids, I'm forced to be present, and then I feel a lot of tension in my body, and I'm restless, irritable, and discontent. Today I often find myself in a daydream as a means of trying to figure things out. Like I'll fantasize about a conversation to hashing out details, plans, or benefits/drawbacks of something. Or as a way of clarifying my emotions.
>
> In reality, I have a hard time identifying what I'm feeling ... When something excites me, I'll find out about that after I daydream of sharing this excitement with someone...There's another function to my daydreams of which I recently became aware. I often experience disproportionately intense feelings; though I know they are invalid, I can't escape them. e.g., my husband comments, and I get really, really angry for no good reason. Despite my efforts to manage my emotions, nothing helps. I calm down only when I daydream about a scenario where I'm in a safe environment and free to release my anger.

Rachel provides us with insights into the different ways MD helps her regulate emotions. She, like Gail, was a child with unmet emotional needs who relied on MD for soothing or comfort in the face of traumatic stress that impinged upon the development of a positive and cohesive identity. In what follows, we turn to the association of MD with trauma and dissociation, and present one final case vignette.

Maladaptive daydreaming and dissociative identity disorder (DID)

At the center of traumatic experiences are unbearable levels of affective arousal: anxiety, fear, terror, horror, etc., and the collapse of the capacity to generate personal narrative: failures of assimilation and accommodation (Horowitz, 1982). Additionally, DID relies on several alterations of perception (Steinberg, 2000) which require considerable creativity of the mind: (1) the use of circuit-breaker-like depersonalization and derealization to down-regulate affective intensity: altering embodiment, perception, and memory to remove intolerable experiences from consciousness; (2) identity confusion that makes knowing self as through a fog; and (3) identity alteration that takes these operations to their logical conclusion through the construction of the experience of an alternate sense of self in a not-me position that allows a person to say: 'That didn't happen to me!' Add to this the frequent reports of people with DID living in an inner landscape (O'Neil, 1997), and there is a fertile garden to grow speculation about the potential for MD mechanisms to overlap with the lived experience of DID (Ross et al., 2020; Soffer-Dudek & Somer, 2022). Engaging in MD provides an alternative mode of affect and narrative regulation accomplished not by the piecemeal changing of the perception of reality, as in DID, but in adding, en bloc, an entire alternate internal reality in which a person can live a totally different experience through the dissociative capacity inherent in the hypnotic absorption of immersive daydreaming. Whereas individuals with DID both: (1) alter their perception of ongoing experience and (2) create an incomplete alternate inner reality, MD focuses on perfecting the second 'solution'. It's not that a person with DID can't tell the difference between internal and external. It's just that the significance can be successfully ignored. In MD, the significance is understood, and the internal absorption is often a source of shame or ongoing self-criticism prompted by the loss of healthy functioning in the world. Table 1 summarizes key similarities and differences between MD and DID.

The mixing of MD and DID self-regulatory function is visible in the following report of a 35-year-old woman with DID, for whom Chefetz consulted over three years ago (second opinion about DID) and who recently independently wrote Somer after reading about MD on the web. Her language holds both her recognition and her ongoing doubt about her experiences.

Leila

> I was first diagnosed with DD-NOS [Dissociative Disorder, Not Otherwise Specified] and then DID over a decade ago [2009]; re-diagnosed with DID a few years back, and yet I am constantly in a state of argument/denial about it. When I first learned about MD, I didn't think I related to it because I do experience some amnesia and a definite loss of executive function in the parts of my system who fully experience their personhood. However, a spark lit once I began reading about the overlap and intersection of dissociative disorders and MD. THIS is my experience! MD that I consciously recall. . .alongside dissociative fugues that I do not recall – both different and yet intertwined.
>
> As a child, I LIVED in my inner world. It was far more real than my outer world, and I got all my emotional needs met there . . . Around the age of twenty-five, something shifted. I felt I 'stepped forward' and began living in the outer world, and my inner one became practically inaccessible. . .I still have an inner world, but it is not nearly as elaborate or accessible, and I can't escape to it in the same way.

With its corresponding responsibilities, Leila's transition into adulthood demanded more careful attention to her external reality and was, therefore, incompatible with extensive fantasizing. However, the mounting need to cope with the stressors of daily life seemed to have activated her dissociative disorder.

Table 1.

	Capacity for Internal Immersion	Regard for Internal Immersion	Depersonalization	Derealization	Amnesia	Identity Confusion	Identity Alteration	Trance Logic	Transitional Space
MD	Intense	Enjoys and also regrets, knows it is fantasy, but still may prefer to living in the world	May occur, but not as robust as DID	Unusual, but may occur	No	No	No	No	Yes, and knows they are fantasy; tend to assure that regular responsibilities are fulfilled.States with positive attributes added and enjoyed in fantasy. States with positive attributes added and enjoyed in fantasy.
DID	Intense	Often disrupted by intrusions from Internal self-states; may prefer living inwardly to being in the world; May not regard the real world as having more significance than the inner world.	Robust	Robust, but usually not as robust as for Depersonalization	May be global, but more typically micro-amnesias; amnesia for amnesia typical	Routine	Robust	Yes	Yes, and may prefer them and avoid real world with major consequences.States with negative attributes isolated from awareness. States with negative attributes isolated from awareness.

> Enter dissociative disorder treatment. I was diagnosed with a dissociative disorder in my early 20s before I ever "stepped forward" and lost access to the fantasy world that got me through life. I ran from the diagnosis for a long time, but it became impossible to ignore once I reached a point in my therapy … A couple of people in my inner world nowadays are the same ones who existed when I was a child. They do not have shared lived experience, nor do they ever take over the executive function. They serve as a support system for other parts who have shared lived experience with me and take over the executive function.

Leila differentiates between her DID identities, who respond to external stressors and alter their perception of ongoing experience, and her old MD protagonists, who provide a supportive alternate inner reality. She describes the two sets of inner protagonists as having distinct and complementary functions.

> For a long time, I've felt invalid – like I must be making something up without meaning to – because it made no sense why these different "types" of parts existed…I am intrigued by this 2020 study (Ross, 2020) that suggests that there may be two mechanisms at play in some dissociative disorders: one that results in the structural dissociation of "alters" and another more like MD. I can only say that my own experience suggests that, for me, yes, both are at play – even still as an adult. Moreover, I believe it may be possible to leverage the MD "mechanism" in therapy and on one's own time to improve functioning and stability overall (e.g., to create changes in the internal world to provide certain supports and processes that improve functioning in the external world). Or, at least, I have done this without knowing what I was doing …

Since MD results from a creative mechanism, Leila suggests that the MD world could be employed to support the functioning of the DID alter system. Leila strongly believes that MD and DID can be coexisting complementing processes:

> There's no question in my mind that I experienced MD. I fit the classic definition: hours, days, etc., absorbed into a fantasy world, living out fictional storylines that matched what many others seem to report (themes of war, abuse, physical and sexual violence, protection, and caretaking). This helped meet our emotional/caretaking needs that my parents did not meet in real life. Mark and Nicholas, and Nate were literally "characters" in those early stories. I suppose maybe they are some evidence that the MD mechanism - whatever it is - still exists in this brain. At the same time, we experienced continuous trauma and neglect from birth and were clearly losing time even very early in childhood. So, I believe structural dissociation must've been at play as well … I think that the MD mechanism is still there and that maybe this is what I engage in to change the inner landscape.

Discussion

The pain and suffering of persons with either MD or DID are not to be denied. Naturalistic unconscious management of intolerable experience, profound neglect, emotional violence, and physical or sexual abuse can be psychologically drastic. An affectively overwhelmed mind may unconsciously reorganize the perception of experience, guided by existing psychodynamics, to maintain the essential elements of identity. These are suggested to be the experience of agency in taking action (being a 'doer'), the experience of self in relation to others, and a sense of existence through the occupation of space or location (Shafer, 1980). In DID, people who experience depersonalization lose much of their self-identity. For example, the out-of-body experience means giving up agency. You can't be a 'doer' if you don't have a body. Similarly, I could not subjectively experience a trauma as happening to me, my body, if I am depersonalized and viewing the action from up on the ceiling, rather than looking at someone punching me in the face, prior to being raped. Dissociative processes injure selfhood by partially annihilating the context of experience. The payoff is to end fear. The price is to live rigidly and alone.

Similarly, living in an MD alternate internal reality can regulate shame, humiliation, panic, or profound anxiety. The advantage is to escape painful feelings. The cost is to disengage from people around you and be bereft of the satisfaction of honest intimacy, tenderness, and love. Fantasy experiences with lost boyfriends may appease a wounded mind, but the hunger remains once the fantasy turns off because the wound is not addressed, nor is the loss grieved. The need to repeat occurs to reapply the temporary balm, an obsessional/addictive pattern. The self-regulatory nature of MD and DID create alienation from self and other (Soffer-Dudek & Somer, 2022) and isolation from painful affect at a steep price.

At the developmental center of the lives of Gail, Rachel, and Leila are histories of profound emotional pain or neglect. Lest the reader believe that emotional injury doesn't compare with physical or sexual abuse, we believe it worth noting the neurodevelopmental delays found in emotionally abused children (Teicher & Samson, 2016) and that attachment research has suggested the best predictor of adult dissociation is emotionally unresponsive parenting (Lyons-Ruth et al., 2006). One problem associated with the Lyons-Ruth study, and all the other longitudinal attachment studies that discuss dissociation, is that no formal dissociative disorder diagnostic testing has ever been conducted. Investigational review boards require provisions be made for treating individuals who may be activated by studying their difficulties. Thus, attachment researchers cannot definitely assert or deny the severity of dissociative experiences in their cohorts. Ample research links MD with attachment insecurity (Mariani et al., 2022), OCD (Salomon-Small et al., 2021), and ADHD (Theodor-Katz et al., 2022). From an affect theory perspective, these are all failed efforts at emotion regulation (Sándor et al., 2021). Parents who are incapable of supporting their child in regulating their emotions leave a vacancy in their mind for such a soothing function. As a result, the abused or neglected child may find solace in imagined soothing daydream characters, replacing unresponsive real objects with internal ones. This can disrupt the normal process of healthy internalizing of a soothing or regulating function, which is essential for developing the ability to regulate emotions without the need for daydreamed aids. Improvement in emotion regulation seems critical, also, in DID (Nester et al., 2022). Thus, though the literature on the treatment of MD has only begun (e.g., Herscu et al., 2023), it is likely that an integrative approach, combining OCD/addiction interventions with a psychodynamic, emotion-focused perspective, may be in order. The treatment of DID is generally one of psychodynamic orientation (Chefetz & Bromberg, 2004), yet, as the treatment of Gail reminds us, careful assessment of a particular person's capacities and needs might lead to the amelioration of dysfunction and attainment of a productive life without insight-oriented therapy. Indeed, MD symptoms were significantly decreased in a randomized controlled trial that implemented monitoring and mindfulness training without specifically addressing daydream contents. However, only partial reductions were achieved, suggesting that targeting the associated underlying psychodynamic conflicts manifested in the fantasy content may prove to be invaluable in treating this condition. Research on a psychodynamic approach to treating MD is needed.

Conclusion

MD is a well-thought-out construct describing in detail the painful advent of immersive daydreaming that only partially solves the problems of emotionally painful experiences, often of childhood. It has properties that may occur in tandem with DID, and there is a partial overlap between the two diagnoses (Soffer-Dudek & Somer, 2022). If DID is present, it may better explain MD symptoms, however, both diagnoses may coexist. Immersive daydreaming itself is a naturalistic occurrence and is not necessarily pathological. Psychopathology ensues with the accompanying mounting distress or the loss of function in a person's life. Future studies are needed to address the paucity of treatment data. As a preliminary to that, the writers believe the education of clinicians about MD, including its relationship to DID, must become a routine part of clinical education.

Disclosure statement

No potential conflict of interest was reported by the author(s).

References

Baird, B., Smallwood, J., Lutz, A., & Schooler, J. W. (2014). The decoupled mind: Mind-wandering disrupts cortical phase-locking to perceptual events. *Journal of Cognitive Neuroscience*, *26*(11), 2596–2607. https://doi.org/10.1162/jocn_a_00656

Bershtling, O. D. & Somer, E. (2018). The micro-politics of a new mental condition: Legitimization in maladaptive daydreamers' discourse. *The Qualitative Report*, *23*(8), 1983–2002. https://doi.org/10.46743/2160-3715/2018.3466

Bigelsen, J., Lehrfeld, J. M., Jopp, D. S., & Somer, E. (2016). Maladaptive daydreaming: Evidence for an under-researched mental health disorder. *Consciousness and Cognition*, *42*, 254–266. https://doi.org/10.1016/j.concog.2016.03.017

Bigelsen, J. & Schupak, C. (2011). Compulsive fantasy: Proposed evidence of an under-reported syndrome through a systematic study of 90 self-identified non-normative fantasizers. *Consciousness and Cognition*, *20*(4), 1634–1648. https://doi.org/10.1016/j.concog.2011.08.013

Bregman-Hai, N., Kessler, Y., & Soffer-Dudek, N. (2020). Who wrote that? Automaticity and reduced sense of agency in individuals prone to dissociative absorption. *Consciousness & Cognition*, *78*, 102861. https://doi.org/10.1016/j.concog.2019.102861

Bromberg, P. M. (2009). Multiple self-states, the relational mind, and dissociation: A psychoanalytic perspective. In P. F. Dell & J. A. O'Neil (Eds.), *Dissociation and the dissociative disorders: DSM-V and beyond* (pp. 637–652). Routledge/Taylor & Francis Group.

Bromberg, P. M. (2013). Hidden in plain sight: Thoughts on imagination and the lived unconscious. *Psychoanalytic Dialogues: The International Journal of Relational Perspectives*, *23*(1), 1–14. https://doi.org/10.1080/10481885.2013.754275

Carvalho, S. A., Carvalho, F., Fonseca, L., Santos, G., & Castilho, P. (2022). Beyond the centrality of shame: How self-concealment and fear of receiving compassion from others impact psychological suffering in transgender adults. *Journal of Homosexuality*. Advance online publication. https://doi.org/10.1080/00918369.2022.2114398

Chefetz, R. A. (2021). Attackments: Subjugation, shame, and the attachment to painful affects and objects. In O. B. Epstein (Ed.), *Shame matters: Attachment and relational perspectives for psychotherapists* (pp. 60–76). Routledge.

Chefetz, R. A., & Bromberg, P. M. (2004). Talking with "me" and "not-me": A dialogue. *Contemporary Psychoanalysis*, *40*(3), 409–464. https://doi.org/10.1080/00107530.2004.10745840

Chirico, I., Volpato, E., Landi, G., Bassi, G., Mancinelli, E., Gagliardini, G., Gemignani, M., Gizzi, G., Manari, T., Moretta, T., Rellini, E., Saltarelli, B., Mariani, R., & Musetti, A. (2022). Maladaptive daydreaming and its relationship with psychopathological symptoms, emotion regulation, and problematic social networking sites use: A network analysis approach. *International Journal of Mental Health Addiction*. Advance view. https://doi.org/10.1007/s11469-022-00938-3

Christoff, K., Irving, Z. C., Fox, K. C. R., Spreng, R. N., & Andrews-Hanna, J. R. (2016). Mind-wandering as spontaneous thought: A dynamic framework. *Nature Reviews Neuroscience*, *17*(11), 718–731. https://doi.org/10.1038/nrn.2016.113

Dang-Vu, T. T., Desseilles, M., Petit, D., Mazza, S., Montplaisir, J., & Maquet, P. (2007). Neuroimaging in sleep medicine. *Sleep Medicine*, *8*(4), 349–372. https://doi.org/10.1016/j.sleep.2007.03.006

Domhoff, G. W. (2011). The neural substrate for dreaming: Is it a subsystem of the default network? *Consciousness and Cognition*, *20*(4), 1163–1174. https://doi.org/10.1016/j.concog.2011.03.001

Ferrante, E., Marino, A., Guglielmucci, F., & Schimmenti, A. (2020). The mediating role of dissociation and shame in the relationship between emotional trauma and Maladaptive daydreaming. *Psychology of Consciousness: Theory, Research, & Practice*, *9*(1), 27–39. https://doi.org/10.1037/cns0000253

Freud, S. (1908). Creative writers and day-dreaming. In J. Strachey (Ed.), *The Standard Edition of the Complete Psychological Works of Sigmund Freud, Volume IX (1906–1908)* (pp. 141–153). Jensen's 'Gradiva' and Other Works. London: Hogarth Press.

Greene, T., West, M., & Somer, E. (2020). Maladaptive daydreaming and emotional regulation difficulties: A network analysis. *Psychiatry Research*, *285*, 112799. https://doi.org/10.1016/j.psychres.2020.112799

Herscu, O., Somer, E., Federman, A., & Soffer-Dudek, N. (2023). Mindfulness meditation and self-monitoring reduced maladaptive daydreaming symptoms: A randomized controlled trial of a brief self-guided web-based program. *Journal of Consulting and Clinical Psychology*. Advance online publication. https://doi.org/10.1037/ccp0000790

Horowitz, M. J. (1982). Psychological processes induced by illness, injury, and loss. In T. Millon, C. Green, & R. Meagher (Eds.), *Handbook of clinical health psychology* (pp. 53–67). Plenum. https://doi.org/10.1007/978-1-4613-3412-5_3

Irving, Z. C. & Thompson, E. (2018). The philosophy of mind wandering. In K. C. Fox & K. Christoff (Eds.), *The oxford handbook of spontaneous thought*. Oxford University Press. https://doi.org/10.1093/oxfordhb/9780190464745.013.19

James, W. (1890). *The principles of psychology*. Macmillan & Co. https://doi.org/10.1037/10538-000

Killingsworth, M. A. & Gilbert, D. T. (2010). A wandering mind is an unhappy mind. *Science*, *330*(6006), 932. https://doi.org/10.1126/science.1192439

Klinger, E. (1971). *Structure and functions of fantasy*. Wiley-Interscience.

Kluft, R. P. (1987). First-rank symptoms as a diagnostic clue to multiple personality disorder. *International Journal of Offshore and Polar Engineering*, *144*(3), 293–298. https://doi.org/10.1176/ajp.144.3.293

Longden, E. (2010). Making sense of voices: A personal story of recovery. *Psychosis*, *2* (3), 255–259. https://doi.org/10.1080/17522439.2010.512667

Lyons-Ruth, K., Dutra, L., Schuder, M. R., & Bianchi, I.(2006). From infant attachment disorganization to adult dissociation: Relational adaptations or traumatic experiences? In R. A. Chefetz (Eds.), *Dissociative disorders: An expanding window into the psychobiology of mind Psychiatric Clinics* (Vol. 29, pp. 63–86. Oxford: Elsevier. https://doi.org/10.1016/j.psc.2005.10.011

Mariani, R., Musetti, A., DiMonte, C., Danskin, K., Franceschini, C., & Christian, C. (2022). Maladaptive daydreaming in relation to linguistic features and attachment style. *International Journal of Environmental Research and Public Health*, *19*(1), 386. https://doi.org/10.3390/ijerph19010386

Nester, M. S., Brand, B. L., Schielke, H. J., & Kumar, S. (2022). An examination of the relations between emotion dysregulation, dissociation, and self-injury among dissociative disorder patients. *European Journal of Psychotraumatology*, *13*(1), 2031592. https://doi.org/10.1080/20008198.2022.2031592

O'Neil, J. A. (1997). Expanding the psychoanalytic view of the intrapsychic: Psychic conflict in the inscape. *Dissociation: Progress in the Dissociative Disorders*, *10*(4), 192–202.

Pietkiewicz, I. J., Nęcki, S., Bańbura, A., & Tomalski, R. (2018). Maladaptive daydreaming as a new form of behavioral addiction. *Journal of Behavioural Addictions*, *7*(3), 838–843. https://doi.org/10.1556/2006.7.2018.95

Raphling, D. (1996). The interpretation of daydreams, I. *Journal of the American Psychoanalytic Association*, *44*(2), 533–547.

Ross, C. A., Ridgway, J., & George, N. (2020). Maladaptive daydreaming, dissociation, and the dissociative disorders. *Psychiatric Research and Clinical Practice*, *2*(2), 53–61. https://doi.org/10.1176/appi.prcp.20190050

Salomon-Small, G., Somer, E., Harel, M., & Soffer-Dudek, N. (2021). Maladaptive daydreaming and obsessive-compulsive symptoms: A confirmatory and exploratory investigation of shared mechanisms. *Journal of Psychiatric Research*, *136*, 343–350. https://doi.org/10.1016/j.jpsychires.2021.02.017

Sándor, A., Bugán, A., Nagy, A., Bogdán, L. S., & Molnár, L. (2021). Attachment characteristics and emotion regulation difficulties among maladaptive and normal daydreamers. *Current Psychology*, *42*(2), 1617–1634. advance view. https://doi.org/10.1007/s12144-021-01546-5

Sar, V., Akyüz, G., & Doğan, O. (2007). Prevalence of dissociative disorders among women in the general population. *Psychiatry Research*, *149*(1–3), 169–176. https://doi.org/10.1016/j.psychres.2006.01.005

Schimmenti, A. & Şar, V. (2019). A correlation network analysis of dissociative experiences. *Journal of Trauma & Dissociation*, *20*(4), 402–419. https://doi.org/10.1080/15299732.2019.1572045

Shafer, R. (1980). Narration in the psychoanalytic dialogue. *Critical Inquiry*, *7*(1), 29–53. https://doi.org/10.1086/448087

Singer, J. L. (1974). Daydreaming and the stream of thought. *American Scientist*, *62*(4), 417–425. https://doi.org/10.2307/27844990

Smallwood, J. (2013). Distinguishing how from why the mind wanders: A process–occurrence framework for self-generated mental activity. *Psychological Bulletin*, *139*(3), 519–535. https://doi.org/10.1037/a0030010

Smallwood, J. & Schooler, J. W. (2015). The science of mind wandering: Empirically navigating the stream of consciousness. *Annual Review of Psychology*, *66*(1), 487–518. https://doi.org/10.1146/annurev-psych-010814-015331

Soffer-Dudek, N. & Somer, E. (2018). Trapped in a daydream: Daily elevations in maladaptive daydreaming are associated with daily psychopathological symptoms. *Frontiers in Psychiatry*, *9*, 1–14. https://doi.org/10.3389/fpsyt.2018.00194

Soffer-Dudek, N., Lassri, D., Soffer-Dudek, N., & Shahar, G. (2015). Dissociative absorption: An empirically unique, clinically relevant, dissociative factor. *Consciousness and Cognition*, *36*, 338–351. https://doi.org/10.1016/j.concog.2015.07.013

Soffer-Dudek, N. & Somer, E. (2022).Maladaptive daydreaming is a dissociative disorder: Supporting evidence and theory. In M. J. Dorahy, S. N. Gold, & J. A. O'Neil (Eds.), *Dissociation and the dissociative disorders: Past, present, future* (2nd ed., pp. 547–559). Taylor & Francis. https://doi.org/10.4324/9781003057314-41

Soffer-Dudek, N. & Theodor-Katz, N. (2022). Maladaptive daydreaming: Epidemiological data on a newly identified syndrome. *Frontiers in Psychiatry*, *13*, 871041. https://doi.org/10.3389/fpsyt.2022.871041

Somer, E. (2002). Maladaptive daydreaming: A qualitative inquiry. *Journal of Contemporary Psychotherapy*, *32*(2/3), 197–212. https://doi.org/10.1023/A152

Somer, E., Abu-Rayya, H. M., & Brenner, R. (2021). Childhood trauma and maladaptive daydreaming: Fantasy functions and themes in a multi-country sample. *Journal of Trauma & Dissociation*, *22*(3), 288–303. https://doi.org/10.1080/15299732.2020.1809599

Somer, E., Soffer Dudek, N., Ross, C. A., & Halpern, N. (2017). Maladaptive daydreaming: Proposed diagnostic criteria and their assessment with a structured clinical interview. *Psychology of Consciousness: Theory, Research, & Practice*, *4*(2), 176–189. https://doi.org/10.1037/cns0000114

Somer, E., Somer, L., & Halpern, N. (2019). Representations of maladaptive daydreaming and the self: A qualitative analysis of drawings. *The Arts in Psychotherapy*, *63*, 102–110. https://doi.org/10.1016/j.aip.2018.12.004

Somer, E., Somer, L., & Jopp, D. S. (2016a). Childhood antecedents and maintaining factors in maladaptive daydreaming. *Journal of Nervous and Mental Disease*, *204*(6), 471–478. https://doi.org/10.1097/NMD.0000000000000507

Somer, E., Somer, L., & Jopp, D. S. (2016b). Parallel lives: A phenomenological study of the lived experience of maladaptive daydreaming. *Journal of Trauma and Dissociation*, *17*(5), 561–576. https://doi.org/10.1080/15299732.2016.1160463

Steinberg, M. (2000). Advances in the clinical assessment of dissociation: The SCID-D-R. *Bulletin of the Menninger Clinic*, *64*(2), 146–163.

Teicher, M. H. & Samson, J. A. (2016). Annual research review: Enduring neurobiological effects of childhood abuse and neglect. *Journal of Child Psychology and Psychiatry, and Allied Disciplines*, *57*(3), 241–266. https://doi.org/10.1111/jcpp.12507

Theodor-Katz, N., Somer, E., Hesseg, R. M., & Soffer-Dudek, N. (2022). Could immersive daydreaming underlie a deficit in attention? The prevalence and characteristics of maladaptive daydreaming in individuals with attention-deficit/hyperactivity disorder. *Journal of Clinical Psychology*, *78*(11), 2309–2328. https://doi.org/10.1002/jclp.23355

van Os, J. & Kapur, S. (2009). Schizophrenia. *The Lancet*, *374*(9690), 635–645. https://doi.org/10.1016/S0140-6736(09)60995-8

Wen, H., Soffer-Dudek, N., & Somer, E. (2022). Daily feelings and the affective valence of daydreams in maladaptive daydreaming: A longitudinal analysis. *Psychology of Consciousness: Theory, Research, & Practice*, Advanced view. https://doi.org/10.1037/cns0000293

West, M. J. & Somer, E. (2019). Empathy, emotion regulation, and creativity in immersive and maladaptive daydreaming. *Imagination, Cognition and Personality*, *39*(4), 358–373. https://doi.org/10.1177/0276236619864277

West, M. J., Somer, E., & Eigsti, I. M. (2023). Shared challenges and cooccurrence of maladaptive daydreaming and autism spectrum disorder. *Advances in Neurodevelopmental Disorders*, *7*(1), 77–87. https://doi.org/10.1007/s41252-022-00279-1

Winnicott, D. W. (1971). *Playing and reality*. Tavistock.

Zadik, M., Bregman-Hai, N., & Soffer-Dudek, N. (2022). Are you "in the zone" or "disconnected"? flow, dissociative absorption and their adaptive and maladaptive correlates. *Journal of Anomalous Experience and Cognition*, *2*(2), 316–361. https://doi.org/10.31156/jaex.23915

Dissociative identity disorder: a disorder of diagnostic and therapeutic paradoxes

Richard J. Loewenstein and Bethany Brand

Dissociative identity disorder (DID) is life-long, childhood-onset, posttraumatic developmental disorder where chronic early-life maltreatment and attachment disturbances prevents the child's development of a continuous sense of self across emotional states, relationships, and social contexts. As development proceeds, these self-states acquire a sense of themselves, a capacity for information processing, memory, emotion, and behavior. Conceptualizing DID involves paradoxes and apparent contradictions. DID has been categorized as a severe mental illness with major psychiatric comorbidities. Studies show that DID individuals have a unique personality organization with repeated, often covert posttraumatic reactivity, especially in relationships (e.g., therapy). Paradoxically, research shows that, during development, DID individuals preserve psychological resiliencies consistent with responsivity to long-term, psychodynamically informed treatment. These include, when not stressed, capacities for therapeutic alliance, reality testing, and observing ego.

Introduction

Dissociative identity disorder (DID) is a potentially life-long, childhood-onset, posttraumatic developmental disorder where chronic early life maltreatment, trauma, and attachment disturbances prevent the child's consolidation of a continuous sense of self across emotional states, relationships, and social contexts. As development proceeds, these dissociative self-states acquire a sense of themselves, a capacity for information processing, memory, emotion, and behavior. This paper is an introduction to dissociative identity disorder (DID) and its conceptual and clinical links to psychoanalytic[1] thinking. We argue that successful treatment of DID requires a psychodynamically informed psychotherapy and DID should be of major interest to psychoanalysts.

The relationship between dissociation, dissociative disorders (DD), dissociative identity disorder (DID), and psychoanalysis is long, fraught, and mostly conspicuous by its absence. DID is a condition of multiple clinical and theoretical ambiguities, paradoxes, and even apparent contradictions, and these must be held in one's mind to make sense of the disorder, or to at least to accept a level of ongoing cognitive dissonance. Among these is that, despite its classification as a severe mental illness with significant co-morbidities and disability (Johnson et al., 2006; Loewenstein, 2018; Loewenstein et al., 2017; Mueller-Pfeiffer et al., 2012), psychoanalytic concepts (therapeutic alliance, therapeutic frame, conflict, defense, transference, countertransference, observing ego, intersubjectivity, projective identification, negative therapeutic reaction, regression in the service of the ego, etc.) are foundational in informing successful DID treatment. However, at the same time, in order to accurately conceptualize and work effectively with DID, psychoanalysts must incorporate domains of knowledge from several literatures outside virtually all schools of psychoanalysis, such as non-psychoanalytic views of the mind, hypnosis/hypnotherapy, developmental traumatology, as well as approaches to the therapy that may feel alien, uncomfortable, and even heterodox.

Very few graduate mental health programs provide any training in dissociation/DD. In the authors' experience, there is usually *minimal training in PTSD in these programs*, despite the ubiquity of celebrity 'tell all' accounts, plays, novels, TV series, and movies where trauma (child maltreatment, rape, trafficking, combat trauma, etc.) is central to the story. Also, there is a burgeoning money-making industry of 'trauma experts' giving in-person and online trainings – and even offering 'certification' typically in their own copyrighted, non-academically studied methods – for diagnosis and treatment trauma-and-stressor-related disorders, including DID.

This is unfortunate as the US lifetime prevalence of PTSD is about 6–7% (3.6% in men, 9.7% in women), with rape, sexual assault, and physically violent attacks the most likely to produce PTSD (Kessler et al., 2005). International, general population epidemiological studies show that the 1-year prevalence of DID is 1.5%, with a lifetime prevalence possibly as high as 3.5% (Loewenstein, 2018). The US National Comorbidity Study Replication (NCS-R) found that the one-month prevalence of pathological dissociation (PD), severe dissociative symptoms consistent with diagnoses of DID, dissociative amnesia (DA), and severe forms of depersonalization/derealization disorder (DDD), was about 4.8%; this is consistent with a large, prospective Finnish general population study that found about 3.5% prevalence for PD both at baseline and 3 year follow-up (Simeon & Putnam, 2022). In the NCS-R study of PD, multiple forms of childhood maltreatment (physical, sexual, and emotional abuse, neglect), suicidality, and psychiatric hospitalizations strongly correlated with PD, but not with other diagnoses in the NCS-R. Also, it is unfortunate that, with the ascendance of behavioral and psychopharmacological models in psychology and psychiatry, few mental health training programs give more than cursory attention to psychoanalytic concepts, typically as part of a 'survey' of different treatment models (CBT, psychodynamic, etc.).

Brief introduction to other domains of knowledge important to understand dissociation and DID

Discrete Behavioral States Theory (DBST), development, and dissociation

DBST is a transtheoretical, translational *theory of human consciousness*. DBST elucidates human experience across myriad normal and pathological domains. DBST helps align many apparently different conceptual domains (e.g., understanding human development, mind/brain/body relationships, and psychopathology, and is particularly helpful in understanding DID). For extensive discussions, the reader is referred to Putnam (1997, 2016), and Loewenstein and Putnam (2022). DBST can unify understanding of many aspects of normal and pathological human functioning [e.g., emotional states; daydreaming; eating; toileting; artistic states; work states; private states; group states (e.g., at a concert; peak experiences, etc.)]. Psychoanalyst Mardi Horowitz (1979) has written about the process of psychotherapy using a behavioral states model. Transdiagnostically, most psychiatric disorders can be conceptualized as 'state-change' disorders (e.g., mood disorders, anxiety disorders, substance use disorders) as well as self-destructive, suicidal, and high-risk behaviors that attempt to modulate negative states. In particular, DBST synthesizes theoretical and clinical conceptualization of psychological trauma, dissociation, and trauma-and-stressor related (TSRD) and dissociative disorders (DD) as paradigmatic state-change disorders.

The study of infant states, the child's development of more complex states, and the co-regulation of caregiver and infant/child states is a transtheoretical model to account for normal and pathological development. DBST underlies a developmentally informed model of DID as a posttraumatic developmental disorder where extreme, malevolent, unpredictable early life traumatic states and attachment pathology interfere with the development of a unified sense of self across states, relationships, and contexts.

Hypnotic capacity and hypnotizability

'Hypnosis' is a 19th century misnomer for a partially genetically determined capacity for inner focused attention, reduced peripheral awareness, and responsivity to hypnotic suggestion (Elkins et al., 2015). Hypnotic states are a subset of DBS. Kluft (2018a, 2018b, 2018c, 2019) has written the definitive psychoanalytic and intellectual history of Freud's views of hypnosis and recommends a rapprochement between psychoanalysis and the hypnosis field. There is a non-normal distribution of hypnotizability in the general population, with a small group of high hypnotizables in the 'tail' of the distribution. DID individuals naturalistically manifest the highest hypnotic capacity of any clinical group. They shift in and out of auto-hypnotic states in their daily lives (Loewenstein, 1991). The expert consensus guidelines for treating DID indicate that, because of this, *no* treatment of DID occurs without hypnosis (Chu et al., 2011). Training in hypnosis can be immensely helpful for clinicians to track auto-hypnotic phenomena during therapy, and to provide psychoeducation about what DID patients may experience as distressing dyscontrol.[2] Therapeutic hypnosis is not a treatment, but a set of techniques that facilitate treatment. Hypnotic interventions for DID can be used throughout treatment to facilitate symptom reduction, both in therapy and by the patient using self-hypnosis to manage symptoms outside of therapy; improved internal cooperation, communication, collaboration, and empathy among self-states; to facilitate safe, paced processing of trauma memories, and for assistance with unification of self-states (Kluft, 1989, 1992, 2018a, 2018b, 2018c, 2019).

Trance logic

'Trance logic' is characteristic of highly hypnotizable people in deep trance. The person limits cognitive dissonance by acknowledging both outer reality as well as their hypnotic reality. In DID, the trance logic concept can clarify how the DID individual tolerates logical contradictions between profoundly divergent beliefs, as well as imaginative, secondary structuring of self-state systems, that logically could not coexist in a single human being. It is best illustrated by example; a DID patient presented in therapy as a self-state insisting it was 20 years earlier. When told the correct date, she said, 'Oh Wow! We're in the future!'

Betrayal trauma theory

Betrayal Trauma Theory (BTT) and attachment theory, particularly of Type D attachment patterns, are related ideas and inform the work with DID patients. Type D attachment patterns (disoriented- disorganized) in infants are associated with maternal dissociation and abusiveness, and result in adolescent and adult dissociation, as well as other behavioral problems (Putnam, 1997, 2016). To briefly summarize type D attachment theory, infants may experience a type of 'fight-flight' responses to an unpredictably 'frightening' and/or 'frightened' ('hostile-helpless') caregiver. In the Strange Situation paradigm, type D babies exhibit contradictory attachment responses/relational states or dazed trance states in response to reunion with the mother. This has been called 'fright' or 'fear without solution'; the child desperately needs the parent yet pulls away in fear or goes into a trance state to tolerate connection with the mother. Primate survival requires attachment; infants will produce attachment behavior most likely to be successful with disturbed caregivers (Putnam, 2016). Attachment requires dissociation of the attachment schema from those with awareness of the dangerous parent.

A DID patient captured these conflicted attachment demands, 'It was really hard to attach to people who were trying to kill me'.

Originally, BTT was developed to assess whether delayed recall of childhood maltreatment was not only related to the extremity of the trauma, but to other factors. BTT is a cognitive developmental analogue to Type D attachment. Here, due to frightened/frightening abusive caregivers, the developing child must separate schemas for attachment from schemas for betrayal (maltreatment). BTT is associated with higher dissociation, higher rates of dissociative amnesia, and more physical symptoms in trauma survivors (Loewenstein et al., 2017).

Shame and the psychotherapy of DID

Therapists should develop competence in recognizing, understanding, and working with shame as it is universal in all patients, but is particularly endemic and pervasive in posttraumatic disorders, and is a dominant, profound presence in all aspects of DID treatment (Kluft, 2007, 2016; Nathanson, 1992). Shame is typically universally conveyed with eyes averted, head and body bowed, body slumped, and/or hands over the eyes, hair over the eyes; there may be halting speech, nervous laughter, and almost all forms of negative self-talk are shame based (e.g., stupid, weird, freaky, a mutant, a coward, horrible, needy – often the most shame-filled term; Herman, 2011; Loewenstein, 2022). Nathanson follows the model of Tomkins (see Nathanson, 1992) that there are 9 universal, biologically and genetically based affects that can be cross-culturally observed. These include interest-excitement; enjoyment-joy (related to pride); a 'neutral' state, surprise-startle that ablates the current affect and orients the person towards a stimulus that may require a different response; fear-terror; distress-anguish; anger-rage; disgust; dissmell[3]; and shame-humiliation. To briefly summarize a complex discussion, by the time we are adults, these basic physiological affects have become organized around myriad past experiences with each of these organized into 'emotions'. For example, a patient described shame as a 'magnet'. When he experienced it, it brought up an excruciating multi-sensory library of past shame experiences. Nathanson proposed the existence of defensive 'scripts' that attempt to moderate adverse emotions, in particular, shame. Nathanson describes a 'compass of shame' scripts including self-attack (self-shaming); avoidance (including cognitive avoidance, but particularly drug and alcohol use, nonsuicidal self-injury, high-risk behaviors, etc.); withdrawal (related to avoidance, but a literal or psychological 'leaving' from the shaming situation), and attack the other (bullying, intimate partner violence, sexual violence, etc., where humiliation/mortification is the delivery system for power, dominance, and control).

Dissociative identity disorder (DID)

DID is the most severe, chronic DD, and, in addition to self-state formation manifests symptoms of all other DDs (e.g., dissociative amnesia, depersonalization/derealization, as well as spontaneous trance and auto-hypnotic symptoms, among others).

DID and trauma

Multiple studies show that individuals with DID have the highest rates of childhood maltreatment of any clinical group in psychiatry, typically exceeding 90% for all types of abuse (Loewenstein et al., 2017). In general, maltreatment includes multiple episodes of physical, sexual, emotional abuse; often accompanied by emotional, physical, and medical neglect. Substantiation of trauma reports in DID includes a study of DID children that documented over 90% substantiation of maltreatment by social and medical services (Hornstein & Putnam, 1992); Also, detailed documentation of trauma was found in a forensic case series including documentation in school, medical, and social service records of extreme, often nearly homicidal maltreatment, by caregivers; adult scars that correlated with specific childhood maltreatment events; and evidence of severe childhood dissociative symptoms that had been misdiagnosed or ignored throughout life (D. O. Lewis et al., 1997). Case series have documented relatives' later-life admissions of being aware of and/or witnessing previously denied maltreatment in their DID-diagnosed family members (Kluft, 1998).

What DID is NOT

DID is not a splitting or shattering of some stable aspect of a person's psyche, which breaks down into other 'parts' as a protection against the impact of trauma. Our language about the mind is *metaphorical*, and these metaphors can implicitly determine our theories of mind, and, in turn, our understanding of patients (e.g., terms like 'sequestration' or 'compartmentalization' of trauma in DID does not refer to little structures with doors in the DID brain where trauma memories are stored). Talking about the mind and DID inevitably requires physical *metaphors* that some of which concretize and reify the mind, e.g., 'splitting', 'compartmentalization', 'structure', etc. Kluft conceptualizes DID self-states as 'structured defensive processes'.

In psychoanalysis, the conflation of 'splitting' mental 'structures' in dissociation may have been pre-figured in Freud's paper on 'the Ego and the Id' referencing 'splitting of the ego' (Freud, 1923). There is a similar use of the splitting metaphor for dissociation/DID in writings in the hypnosis and other psychological literatures as well as the popular media ('split personality'). This metaphor contributes to a persistent, concretized, reified, and fundamentally misleading way of conceptualizing DID. Because we think or feel that DID individuals are 'split', or they say the 'feel fragmented, split up', we have reified the mind as if these metaphors are conceptually correct.

A tenacious hold on the splitting metaphor makes it harder to shift paradigms. Clinicians should open their minds to a different view, rather than trying to stuff dissociation/DID into the splitting concept, where it does not fit (block that metaphor!). Process metaphors better approximate DID phenomenology (e.g., division, disconnection, discontinuity, detachment, distancing, duplication/reduplication, polarization, systemization, etc.). Some structure metaphors are inevitable (e.g., compartmentalization, sequestration, layering) but notice these metaphors are not those of 'horizontal or vertical splitting' or that the DID mind is made up of 'parts', another physical, reified, mechanistic metaphor. This term has been widely promulgated by the neo-Janetian *structural* dissociation theorists (Van der Hart et al., 2006; italics added) with DID self-states defined as 'dissociative parts of the personality'.

Reification of DID as 'separate people in one body'

For more than 40 years experts in the field (e.g., the authors of this paper, Richard P. Kluft, M.D., Ph.D, Frank Putnam, M.D., David Spiegel, M.D., all editions of the International Society for the Study of Trauma and Dissociation (ISSTD) Treatment Guidelines for Adults with DID, the DSM-5-TR, et al.) have explicitly written that DID is *not* a condition of separate 'people', but a disorder of subjective self-division that may be more, *or typically less*, secondarily personified and elaborated with different names, descriptors, etc. (Brand et al., 2016; Chu et al., 2011; Kluft, 1992; Loewenstein, 2020; Loewenstein et al., 2017; Loewenstein & Ross, 1992; Putnam, 1992; Spiegel et al., 2011). For example, Kluft (1992) states that 'It often is difficult to keep in mind that although the alters are not separate people, *they do embody different personified adaptive strategies and are guided by and express very different attitudes toward one another, significant objects, the treatment, and the therapist*' (p.149, italics added).

Further, all of the above, as well as the DSM-5-TR definitively state that these elaborations and personifications are *not essential to the diagnosis of DID, and are related to myriad complex socio-cultural, psychodynamic, defensive, and other processes*. These secondary elaborations can be conceptualized as the 'identity' aspects of DID (e.g., age, gender identity, sex, religion, ethnicity, profession, etc.). The expert consensus is that the DID human being/person is held responsible for all behavior, even when disavowed by amnesia, lack of control, or the agency of another self-state. Also, the consensus is that holding the DID person responsible for behavior is crucial for therapeutic progress, and to do otherwise invites regression and therapeutic impasse (Beahrs, 1994; Kluft, 1993; Loewenstein, 2020).

It is the critics of the trauma/dissociation concept that have focused on these media-based stereotypes, often to caricature the DID concept, as well as that of delayed recall of trauma memories (P. McHugh, 1995). Some have been outspoken, hostile critics of psychoanalysis throughout their careers and have specifically blamed 'Freudian' theories of 'repression' for 'the epidemic' of supposed therapeutically confabulated trauma memories and 'iatrogenic' DID (Crews, 1995; P. R. McHugh, 2008).

OK, so what is DID, already?

Lose the picture of the shattered, split mirror.

Instead, picture a never-put-together jigsaw puzzle with all those clearly formed and boundaried pieces – often shaped and colored subtly differently from one another – lying on top of each other in the box, with the box completely full of pieces. That is a more realistic image to get the diagnostic, clinical, and psychodynamic 'feel' of DID.

When Dr Loewenstein lectures on DID, he uses (with permission) artwork by DID patients. We wish the reader could see these, as they illustrate the psychological organization of DID in ways that transcend words. Whether the artist has formal training or not, the pictures are highly complex, often filling the entire paper with myriad forms. Frequently, the art depicts subtly overlapping, but carefully *boundaried* human faces, mouths, eyes, sometimes partly hidden bodies, hands, feet, words, shapes, as if all these human entities were flowing across, overlapping around, behind, below, and above one another.

Sometimes, the art is not representational but depicts multi-colored shapes, often with similar complex relationships, again, drawn with careful boundaries around each shape. Other art works may depict multiple personified representations, also organized beside, above, below, around one another, talking with one another, with larger beings looming in the corner, etc. The clarity of the boundaries, even with all the apparent overlap of the images is striking.

These images evoke striking aspects of the paradoxical nature of DID. DID patients produce these highly complex, often obsessionally detailed, strikingly boundaried artistic creations, even when overwhelmed, decompensated and hospitalized with severe PTSD symptoms (e.g., flashbacks in multiple sensory modalities, nightmares disrupting sleep; confusion of past/present, disorientation to the present); dissociative symptoms (e.g., rapid, dysfunctional shifting/shifting of self-states, ongoing dissociative amnesia, confusion, dissociative hallucinosis of self-state voices); and in acute safety crises (e.g., struggling with nonsuicidal self-injury; suicidal impulses, urges, and plans; eating disorders). Data from studies using structured diagnostic instruments show that when DID patients meet BPD diagnostic criteria, they are typically decompensated, and most no longer meet BPD criteria when stabilized (Ross et al., 2014; Sar et al., 2017).

Conversely, there is a literature on a subgroup of BPD with high dissociation scores on self-report screening measures (Schmahl et al., 2013). They differ from non-dissociative BPD patients in a number of ways, including poorer response to standard BPD treatment models (Kleindienst et al., 2016). Studying BPD patients with diagnostic measures for DD finds a substantial subgroup (50% or more) that meet diagnostic criteria for DID or DA (Korzekwa et al., 2009; Sar et al., 2014). Rather than DID being a variant of BPD, DID is a categorically different disorder with (discussed below) a significantly different personality organization. Indeed, the data suggest that BPD patients, especially those with dissociative features, should be screened with diagnostic inventories for DD/DID.

DID and developmental trauma: an etiological discussion

DID is most accurately described as a childhood-onset posttraumatic developmental disorder where the traumatized child – with a genetic predisposition to dissociate (Becker-Blease et al, 2004; Yaylaci, 2017) – cannot complete the normal developmental processes that establish a unitary subjective sense of self that typically occur before the age of 5–6 (Putnam, 1997, 2016). Traumatic experiences – particularly repeated, malevolent, unpredictable maltreatment perpetrated by caregivers produce extreme, overwhelming states. Also, abusive parents usually provide little or highly inconsistent soothing and restorative experiences. Thus, the child is left to attempt to recover from these states, typically by a global dissociative shut-down.

Repetitive extreme traumas and dissociative shutdown states are compounded by targeted betrayal, blame, double binds, and attacks on the child's sense of self, if not the child's entire reality. Typically, these parents (and/or other perpetrators) blame, mock, and humiliate the child for being distressed, hurt, helpless. Almost universally, they blame the child for causing the maltreatment, often for contradictory reasons: punishment for being 'bad', or a reward for being 'good'; the child is 'seduced' by the adult; the act was done to clean the dirty child; the child wanted it, needed it, asked for it, etc. Abusers may insist that the child's distress should be suppressed, and/or the child cannot be distressed since 'nothing happened', and/or the child needs 'to forget' what happened – sometimes actually (with and without awareness) using hypnotic commands for amnesia.

Mostly, DID children are not 'abused'. They are tortured, often with extreme, systematic, sadistic calculation.

Some DID individuals report an early childhood history of multiple painful medical/surgical procedures that they endured with little or no comfort (e.g., repeated genital surgeries). These patients typically report being left for long periods of time in the hospital without their parents. Others describe maltreatment by staff in addition to the medical/surgical issues, including sexual, physical, and emotional cruelty (e.g., a nurse saying, 'if you don't stop crying, you'll never see your parents again!'). Others have been described as experiencing extreme wartime/terrorism-related trauma, including kidnapping by armed groups, and being forced to act as child 'soldiers' or sex-slaves, etc. (Draijer & Van Zon, 2013; Kelly et al., 2016).

These myriad assaults, and the attachment disturbances these produce (typically consistent with type D attachment pathology), interfere with development of normal metacognitive processes (typically during ages 1–6) that assist with the consolidation of a unified sense of self across different relational (e.g., with parents, siblings, others); social (e.g., at school, at home, with peers); and emotional states (e.g., excited, humiliated, enraged). The DID child often experiences further discontinuities between the reality of a chronically dangerous, unpredictably violent, sadistic home life and the insistence that the family appear to be 'perfect' in the outside world (e.g., at church, school, public events). There may be additional disconnected realities: with friends and friends' families, where sometimes the DID child is amazed to experience a 'normal', non-violent, actually caring family environment. As the child gets older, there may be more disconnected 'realities' at camp, athletics, etc.

Type D Attachment and Betrayal Trauma

Data on type D attachment and BTT help with additional understanding of self-state formation. Faced with the problem of attaching to caregivers who are at times profoundly abusive (typically *both* frightening and frightened), DID patients develop self-states that can experience attachment by dissociating betrayal, as well as self-states that experience and recall trauma by caregivers, and eschew attachment (Freyd, 1996). Maltreatment in DID often begins before the development of object constancy. The DID child may experience the nighttime abusive daddy as literally a different daddy from the daddy during the daytime – with self-states developing congruent with the 'different' parents (Putnam, 1997). DID patients report, as do most male and female childhood sexual abuse survivors, that males, particularly father figures were their most common 'primary' abuser. However, a substantial minority will report that maternal figures or other older females were the 'primary' perpetrator.

As described later, many different people, both male and female, may be perpetrators within the DID family, and/or outside it. In modal DID families with a male 'primary' abuser, the maternal figure is ultimately understood to be complicit in some way – from complete emotional or physical absence to active, ongoing involvement. Different self-states may already have developed to adapt to disturbed early attachment patterns with the maternal caregiver. Developmentally, additional self-states may arise in response to the ongoing experience of different 'mommies'. Sometimes one or both parents may also suffer with DID leading the child to develop self-states to attempt to congruently mirror the parents' self-states.

These patterns often continue into adulthood and can help understand how deeply attached some DID patients are to perpetrator caregivers, with some even continuing to experience incestuous abuse well into adulthood (Middleton, 2013). From a developmental point of view, the deeply attached self-states are life-saving. Normal human development cannot occur without some attachment experiences (Putnam, 2016). However, recovery requires that the DID patient live safely in the present. This means safety from dangerous relationships, including from members of the family or origin. This may involve a complex, grueling therapy process, with many attachment-based twists and turns.

Affect theory, shame, and DID

In DID, and in other survivors of childhood maltreatment, attachment and humiliation can be experienced as literally simultaneous as attempts by the child to seek warmth, nurturance and comfort is responded to with emotional, physical, and/or sexual violence; in its simplest form, 'I'll give you something to cry about'. Herman (2011) describes another aspect of the unwinnable predicament for the abused child in seeking attachment and comfort from cruel caregivers. Here there is a primal humiliation that fuses with attachment needs. Due to this bind of necessarily needing a caregiver for survival who is also endangering one's physical or mental survival, self-states may offer a solution. That is, self-states that dissociate betrayal are a tolerable method for being with the caregiver, typically in a humiliated, passive manner. Some perpetrators humiliate the child for being helpless. These states may become utterly convinced that they are all bad, so evil that they deserve nothing other than defilement, abuse, and punishment.

Self-states and self-state systems

The basic developmental disturbance in DID is located in the self-systems, in varying discrete behavioral states of being where our 'selves' are organized. Thus, we posit that dissociative 'self-state' is conceptually, developmentally, and clinically far more accurate for the subjective self-divisions in DID than 'identity',[4] 'personality', 'alter', 'part', etc. Also, this counters the notion that there is a core mental structure in DID that is shattered, split into 'parts' or 'pieces'. DID patients will present with a central self/identity state usually with the legal name of the person. Even so, the above developmental model avoids the notion of the 'real person' and their 'parts'. Clinicians who hold the notion of 'the real person and their parts' miss that self-states are a complex, dynamic adaptation, not just symptoms. This may lead to a treatment focused on suppression or ablation of the parts (symptoms), with psychic hegemony by the 'real person' (Yalom, 1989). Usually, this results in a compliant outcome, patient flight, treatment stalemate, or a massive decompensation, as self-states fight against being ignored or 'killed off' by creating crises, engaging in unsafe behavior, etc., which in turn leads to more suppressive 'treatment'. DID patients commonly say things like, 'She *thinks* she's the "real one". Ha! We created her when we started high school, cuz we needed someone to function there'.

More accurately, our imagination can envision infinite possible 'selves' – a far more helpful notion for conceptualization, diagnosis, and treatment of DID. Sometimes, self-states' qualities, descriptors, and psychodynamic shaping have a childlike imaginative playfulness, yet simultaneously have grimly serious psychodynamic content based in surviving childhood torture.

In addition to malevolent people in the DID child's life, there may be positive people with whom the DID child can identify, if only briefly. This can include other caring, loving, supportive relatives, nannies, teachers, other children's parents, caregivers, neighbors, etc., as well as positive experiences with the parents (e.g., a DID parent with both abusive and fun-loving, seemingly compassionate self-states). These may be introjected and secondarily personified as benevolent, supportive self-states. The development of self-states/systems are adaptations to these many issues, not only 'trauma', but the relational and emotionally tortuous ways the abuse is represented to the child. As Sullivan (1953) posited, self-state systems start to develop that reflect the myriad relational patterns of the DID individual's caregivers. Concisely, self-states develop that are congruent to the different 'multiple realities' with which the child interacts.

Later development

Over time, the child's developing internal senses of self may come to reflect the dangerousness, disorganization, and conflict evident across the various relationships and environments with which they are involved. Some self-states may become subjectively personified and organize along independent developmental trajectories. In adolescence, the issues of separation and individuation, identity formation, sexuality, and autonomy from family are major developmental tasks. Dissociative adolescents have major difficulties with these, as well as attempts to move on from traumatic experiences (Kluft, 2000). These tasks may be complicated by ongoing intrafamilial violence, exploitation outside the home, as well as more positive and nurturing experiences (finding a safe friend with whose family the teen can stay). They may develop more complex and elaborated self-states and self-states systems to attempt to manage these challenges. Many of these may begin to manifest marked internal conflict, for example, self-states that deny that anything 'bad' happens in the family, and those who 'know'. This process can involve creation of self-states with different roles that may become more complex as these expand (e.g., 'school', 'home', 'church', 'friends'/different 'friend groups', et al.); intrapsychic and emotional functions (e.g., 'detached observer', 'angry one'); relationships to trauma (e.g., ones who 'know', ones who have no memory), relationship to ongoing abuse ('the sexy little boy', 'the whore'), and secondary elaborations (e.g., names, accents, wardrobe, hair style, behaviors).

DID may also be shaped by later traumatic experiences. DID patients report high rates of severe, multi-year, peer bullying, sometimes involving physical or sexual assaults. Bullying increases the DID child's trauma burden and often leads to more disconnection from others. Also, child abuse victims are more vulnerable to extrafamilial perpetrators who will preferentially seek out vulnerable children for sexual abuse. Thus, the typical adult DID patient reports additional extrafamilial sexual abuse with perpetrators including male and female teachers, coaches, guidance counselors, physicians, therapists, priests, nuns, ministers, rabbis, imams, deacons, et al. Some DID patients describe being trafficked in their families, and/or by organized criminal pedophile groups among extrafamilial perpetrators. Criminological research indicates three types of often overlapping organized abuse groups: in the community, in institutions (schools, religious institutions, etc.), and within families (Salter, 2013). DID individuals continue to be vulnerable to abuse and exploitation in adult life, including high rates of multiple sexual assaults, intimate partner violence, trafficking, etc. (see Loewenstein et al., 2017).

Self-state development and dynamics

In the clinical examples that follow, we illustrate the complex nature the development of self-states/systems. There is no 'one' way to understand their psychodynamic organization. For example, one view is that DID is solely based in attachment disturbances; that self-states *only* represent aspects of highly changeable attachment patterns (Brown & Elliott, 2016).

Self-state formation represents myriad attempts to adapt, to survive, to live in 'multiple realities' at home and in the world, to manage relationships, and to try to manage to hold on to attachments to dangerous people. Some self-states are described as having limited, but important progressive developmental qualities; even so, these are tinged with themes of abuse and neglect. A DID patient reported that, starting when she was very little, she experienced self-states that 'came' to assist with developmental tasks that were interfered with by parental malevolence and neglect. One came to help her stop wetting the bed (she was beaten, made to stand outside for hours in her wet night clothes for enuresis). Similarly, she was tormented for sucking her thumb; another 'older one' came and helped her stop that. Another 'one' was described as coming to school to teach her how to tie her shoes (her parents ignored needs like this, and she already felt 'different' at school).

Trauma is not 'optional' for the DID individual

The developmental life experience of the DID child is that it is not optional to experience humiliating danger, malevolence, cruelty, neglect, and betrayal from those on whom the child depends. *It is not whether the child is harmed, only when and how badly.* A major aspect of the life-long adaptation of the DID individual is the impossibility of avoiding being hurt, but 'making the least worst' of degrading, mortifying maltreatment, accompanied by betrayal at the deepest personal, social, institutional, and cultural levels. The core trauma/dissociation psychodynamics of the DID individual is to organize self-states and self-state systems around this postulate. Clinicians working with DID are more successful when they can decode this paradoxical 'logic' that explains symptoms, and most effectively leads to their resolution, by shifting 'survival' adaptations to 'recovery' adaptations. Seemingly intractable, dangerous, self-destructive behavior may be based on mitigating the effects of murderous childhood violence. One patient said, 'Hurting myself when I was a kid made my mother hurt me less, cuz I had "taken care of it" for her.' Clinicians who can think in terms of family-systems theory, general systems theory, etc. may find this a more comfortable way of thinking about DID. One DID patient's creative resilience is shown in the following. As long as she could remember, her icy, narcissistic mother repeatedly told her that 'nobody loves you' and 'nowhere is safe'. The patient created two self-states: 'nobody' who loved her; and 'nowhere' who was safe.

Observers have characterized the senior author's work with DID as, 'eclectic, psychodynamically oriented group and family therapy for one person'.

Similarly, Kluft (2000, 2007), following Kris (1982), describes that DID patients' dissociative amnesia is not based in memories being 'unconscious'. Rather, as in Janetian theory, the mind is made up of self-systems with distributed, conscious, state-dependent memory. Thus, as Kluft suggests, there is conscious withholding, 'reluctance' to share what is known, often due to shame, to 'protect' other self-states, and/or to perpetrator threats to maintain silence, etc. Accordingly, a clinician can struggle futilely to help an amnestic self-state recall what is missing (e.g., who went to Atlantic City last week and won $1000.00). Instead, one asks for those in the mind who know what occurred, even agreeing to the continuation of the protective amnesia (hypnotic trance-logical amnesia suggestion) for self-states who cannot tolerate knowing yet.

State transitions in DID: state switching; state shifting

In the model of DID as highly elaborated 'separate people' in a split mind, another stereotype is dramatic switching with strikingly different presentations, like a parade of single people emerging from a revolving door. Marked switching to highly different self-state presentations does occur. However, it is often associated with poorer life adaptation, life problems, disability, and/or is a symptom of decompensation. In general, DID is characterized by subtle state shifting, where minimal overt changes occur in the person's demeanor, and to the extent this is recognized by others, it is primarily with the designation that the person is 'changeable', 'moody', 'bipolar', etc. The person's dissociative amnesia is often dismissed as being 'forgetful', 'getting dementia', 'being absent minded', etc. Actually, in many DID patients, most of the DID self-states *manifest intrapsychically*, and not in direct behavioral role enactments.

The neurobiological, developmental, phenomenological, clinical, and treatment outcome data all support a model of DID as the 'state of multiple, simultaneous states', organized as an overall self-state system, made up of multiple self-state (sub) systems. Phenomenologically, these are characterized by overlap, interference, influence, intrusion, as well as cooperation and coordination among self-states/systems; the latter to better manage life functioning. Dissociative amnesia during therapy is often related to subtle state shifting (sometimes called 'microdissociations'), and/or impingement on the surface self-states from the self-states 'behind them'. Much of the clinical presentation can be metaphorically described as the moment-to-moment summation of self-state 'vectors' that at a point in time in therapy result in a particular configuration of self-states/systems that are manifested intrapsychically.

One can conceptualize interventions at the level of self-states that present directly in 'person-like' ways: most often as interventions by 'talking over', that is, by asking for input from self-states/systems not on the dissociative surface (Kluft, 2005, 2006), as well as by directing comments to 'the whole mind', 'the whole human being'. Observers have characterized the senior author's work with DID as, "eclectic, psychodynamically oriented group and family therapy for one person".The entire mind of the DID individual is not sub-divided. There are many functions, capacities and behavior that occur in a unified way. Kluft has metaphorically termed this a psychological 'double-entry bookkeeping system' (as cited in (Loewenstein, 2022, p. 774)). For example, in therapy, a DID patient was experiencing defensively motivated, continual anterograde dissociative amnesia, forgetting everything discussed in therapy as it occurred. This process was unresponsive to any clarification, confrontation, interpretation, etc. When, in frustration, her therapist asked, 'if you are unable to remember anything, how are you going to find your car in the parking lot when you leave?' She answered breezily and trance-logically, 'Oh, that's different'.

Also, there are issues that are unconscious in the classic sense, 'across the whole mind', often about global transference issues, that require interpretation of a number of different dissociated transference elements that lead to understanding of a broader transference pattern and its origins. Medications are not effective in DID patients if they do not treat psychopharmacological target symptoms experienced across the whole human being's mind.

Clinicians often ask, 'Why would you work with self-states?' Based on the foregoing, the question really is: 'Why wouldn't you work with self-states?'.

More DID paradoxes, complexity, and ambiguity: the psychological organization of DID as viewed through psychological assessment

Our understanding of the psychological organization of DID originated in our collaboration with Judith Armstrong, Ph.D., and her pioneering methodology for psychological assessment of this population. She decided to study DID as a self-system, rather than following previous testing studies. She began by inviting, using the patient's own terminology, all 'divergent self-aspects' to participate in the testing (Armstrong, 1991, p. 536). Also, she asked to debrief the person afterwards to explore their responses to testing. This approach demonstrates why it is so important (and commonsensical) to work with all aspects of the DID person's mind in therapy. As with any other person, accurate assessment (or psychotherapy) is unlikely to be successful without the full psychological participation of the patient.

Traumatic content on the Rorschach

Armstrong found that DID patients gave responses on the Rorschach that were filled with malevolent associations – imagery of aggression, blood, sex, and anatomy as well as morbid, damaged objects and people. Classically, this response pattern would have been interpreted as indicative of psychotic thought disorder. Armstrong realized that, to survive, the DID child had always to be alert for possible predictors of threat. These fear-based responses represented *accurate, survival-based reality testing.* She developed the Trauma Content score (sum of percepts of aggression, blood, sex, anatomy, and morbid divided by the number of response; Armstrong & Loewenstein, 1990). Across studies, DID patients show an *average* of 50% of their Rorschach percepts contain Trauma Content (Brand et al., 2006). Trauma responses can also occur with other assessments. A bright patient performed well on the WAIS except for the block design. In the debriefing, she recalled being locked repeatedly by her mother in a toy box containing blocks.

Paradoxical resilience

The trauma content on the testing was not the only new finding. Paradoxically, the psychological assessment research showed that DID is simultaneously a resilient adaptation that preserves and allows more normal development of important psychological capacities. We hypothesized that extreme forms of state-dependent learning might be at least a partial explanation linked to 'sequestration' of traumatic experiences that permits more normal development of adaptive, mind/brain capacities.

The psychological organization of DID is *highly complex and multi-faceted.* DID patients show higher cognitive complexity scores on the Rorschach than clinical and non-clinical subjects, including psychotic and borderline patients (B. Brand et al., 2009). This can become problematic when DID patients' defenses against continual profound trauma include elaboration of and overinvolvement in their inner worlds, a psychological withdrawal based on the belief that to 'be' in the world is too dangerous and toxic. Other differences include that DID patients have preservation of a capacity for good reality testing, when not posttraumatically activated/stressed; the ability to take distance on posttraumatic cognitive distortions; a capability to see relationships as possibly supportive, despite being exposed to extreme levels of betrayal and violence; a survival instinct and stubborn hopefulness; preserved creativity; and a highly developed capability to observe their psychological processes – observing ego capacity. In our data, the latter was significantly better in DID even compared to normal, non-clinical controls (Armstrong, 1991; Armstrong & Loewenstein, 1990; Brand et al., 2009; Brand et al., 2006). Some authors postulate that DID individuals lack the capacity for mentalization (Steele, 2009). However, this capacity can be observed in therapy, when the DID patient is not overwhelmed by posttraumatic responding. These adaptive and resilient capacities make it feasible for DID patients to develop a therapeutic alliance, and engage in insight-oriented, psychodynamically informed psychotherapy. Also, these capacities indicate DID patients' ability to successfully use metaphors and similes in therapy.

Additional findings include that DID individuals have *avoidant and obsessional personality features*, rather than the often-assumed histrionic personality structure. DID individuals rely on intellectualization with a tendency to try to back away from emotions. Intellectualization and the attempts at 'compartmentalization' of psychological experience fits with obsessional personality features. A subgroup of DID patients has trauma-based obsessive-compulsive symptoms (e.g., 'If I always arrange things in my room a certain way, I will be safe'). Some meet diagnostic criteria for obsessive-compulsive disorder. Survivors of childhood trauma often attempt to exert rigid, obsessional control over themselves, their minds, and other people (e.g., the clinician). DID patients frequently show this pattern, especially in their often-stubborn reluctance to explore their inner experience, and in attempts to control the therapist and the therapy (Kluft, 1994). Like other obsessionals, DID patients feel better when they make sense of things. They respond positively (overall) with psychoeducation about their disorders and treatment. They experience marked relief when they make sense of behavior that otherwise feels shamefully out of control.

A patient described that she never could go to bed before 2 A.M. Over the years, she tried all kinds of 'strategies' for good 'sleep hygiene'; she tried 'will power', alcohol, street drugs, psychiatric medications, etc. The pattern never changed. Even if she went to bed before 2 A.M., she could not fall asleep until 2 A.M. Finally, when asked to reflect on this in therapy (note the observing ego and ability to think clearly here) she realized that 'When I was growing up, I figured out that, if, by 2 A.M. my father hadn't come into my room to attack me, he wasn't coming. So, I could feel safe to go to sleep. I found out that there were [self-states] that I didn't know about who were still trying to protect me by staying up. We did some internal communication together and they found they could stop living in "trauma time". They realize he's dead, we live in a safe place now and have a safe relationship, we don't have to keep the secrets. We can talk about things in therapy. And they can help us by helping decide when we want to go to sleep'. She said, 'I didn't like remembering that, but I am so relieved that I'm not crazy. This finally makes sense!'.

Multi-level responding

Another paradoxical finding in the DID assessment research is multi-level responding, illustrating the 'state of multiple simultaneous states' phenomenology. For example, when asked for the definition of 'perimeter' on the WAIS, the patient said, 'I don't know'. At the same time, seemingly without awareness, her hand traced a circle in the air (Armstrong, 1994; Armstrong & Loewenstein, 1990). In another example, when a disorganized adolescent inpatient was asked how far it was from New York to San Francisco, she said, 'I don't know, but the lady in white says it's 3000 miles'. The 'lady in white' was a visual hallucination described as persecuting the patient from the corner of the room. In the first example, the sensorimotor responding was more sophisticated than the verbal responding. In the second, it was the hallucination that held the conflict-free information. These paradoxical phenomena are common in DID treatment and the patient's daily lives.

Posttraumatic responding, psychological resilience, and dissociative defenses

During psychotherapy, DID individuals typically experience continual multi-level, subtle, posttraumatic reactivity that can coincide with, and at times overwhelm the capacities for logical thinking and self-observation. Psychotherapy is an important attachment relationship; accordingly, traumatic reactivity will infuse the transference (and countertransference). This is consistent with the DID child's developmental experience of continual anticipation of unpredictable danger and threat from those on whom they relied, if not loved. Thus, overtly, or covertly, the basic, dominant transference themes are based in anticipated betrayal by the therapist, who will inevitably turn to the patient to get their narcissistic needs met, often in sexual ways, defined (see below) as *traumatic transference*.

For DID patients, attachments have only two possible outcomes. If the therapist does not betray and exploit the patient, the only other possible outcome is that the 'nice' therapist will abandon the 'bad' patient, typically precipitously. DID patients have been inculcated with the belief that their badness causes maltreatment and abandonment. In the abandonment scenario, the patient's badness overwhelms and drives away the therapist. Common distorted beliefs include that the therapist will blame the patient for abuse and shun the patient because of their badness. Also, there are fears of needing 'too much' from the therapist (and also that this could lead the therapist to abuse the patient); being 'too complicated' for the therapist to 'deal with'; having had 'too many bad things happen' that the therapist cannot tolerate hearing about, and so on. Often, DID patients will report that therapists *literally* have said these things to them, increasing their immense shame burden. Problematic and frankly exploitative psychiatric and psychotherapeutic encounters are common in the history of DID patients. This will compound the traumatic transference as the setting of therapy itself is now experienced as potentially dangerous.

Defenses against trauma intrusions

During Rorschach testing, some DID patients become frightened of the cards because the nature of the task pulls for traumatic material, thereby overwhelming their normal tendency to avoid and disconnect from trauma via dissociation. They may briefly lose their grounding in current reality, sometimes even have flashbacks during testing. Some individuals show biphasic PTSD-like responding. Here, neutral, or even pleasant images may be followed by traumatic intrusions – a process that may parallel the DID patient's developmental experience of something neutral or good, suddenly contaminated by danger, with dissociation as the only possible response. On testing, when the attempts at dissociative distancing fail, the individual may go into flashback, lose psychological distance and reality orientation, and even view the card itself as a literal danger.

The assessment research provides a structured way to observe these processes and illuminate what occurs in therapy. As trauma intrudes during psychological assessment, DID patients may attempt to avoid it by changing topics (maybe a result of a self-state shift), emotional numbing and detachment, dissociative distancing, sudden depersonalization/derealization, and autohypnotic strategies, or mixtures of these. Autohypnotic defenses can include hyperfocus[5] on tiny areas of the Rorschach card rarely noticed by other patients. Typically, this leads to highly detailed fantasy-based responses that serve to protect the individual from PTSD intrusions stimulated by the card ('that's the tiny, hidden entrance to a cave that is guarded by these two gargoyles who are making sure that no one can get inside the cave'). At another level, there are both a sexual-trauma, defensive image (small cave, no one can get inside), and multiplicity-based – and possibly scary- responses (two gargoyles). Multiplicity responses are also common in DID Rorschach protocols.

In another example, a man reported seeing a common image on the Rorschach, with good reality testing ('that's a bat flying'). This was followed by a personalized trauma content intrusion with perceptual distortions ('that's my dead cat that my dad ran over on purpose with his car'. The patient then appeared frightened to touch the card, as if it were a dangerous stimulus. He then said, 'a man's, uh, thing, going into someone's butt'), followed by an intellectualized and dissociative response in which the percept was seen from a distance, then a derealization response seeing the world at a distance, as if watching a movie ('now I see a spirit rising up into the sky, way above the clouds'). In follow-up questioning after completion of the Rorschach, the man showed some embarrassment about the 'weird, scary stuff I saw'. He shared that a traumatized child state reported the middle two percepts while non-traumatized, older self-states saw the two more benign images.

This response pattern may also occur during therapy. The patient may show good reality testing, followed by increasing flashback responding with decreasing reality orientation, then dissociative distancing (e.g., depersonalization), finally followed by an embarrassed detached disavowal. This shows some of the differences between DID and psychotic responding described in the literature and supported by data. Specifically, DID patients have distance from and are fearful of apparent psychotic or bizarre experiences (e.g., they are aware that hearing the voices of self-states is 'crazy' and they may feel shame reporting hearing voices). Similarly, the DID patient may respond with apologetic shame and distress over experiencing extreme trauma content. This contrasts with psychotic individuals who have delusional explanations for perceptual alterations and no ego distance on thought-disordered content (Laddis & Dell, 2012).

When more severely disrupted by traumatic material on testing, DID individuals lose distance and may go into full flashback. This is analogous to DID patients becoming increasingly activated by interpersonal trauma cues. They may engage the in kinds of defensive strategies as described during testing but may become increasingly unable to hold back posttraumatic intrusions. They may enter a full flashback and lose reality awareness, and/or switch to self-states that embody trauma experiences and project these onto therapy and the therapist. Along with this, the patients lose access to their resilient capacities, including temporary lack of self-observation, poor reality testing, interpersonal reactivity, and severe trauma-based cognitive distortions.

The distortions, often about the therapist, may be so illogical that they appear delusional. Even during such times, they are 'quasi-delusional' in that there are often other self-states that can be accessed who retain intact reality testing and insight (Loewenstein, 2022). For example, when a woman with a Ph.D. was in a severely traumatized child state, she insisted that her dead perpetrator could still harm her because he threatened he would always be able to know, and 'if you tell anyone, I'll kill you'. Adult self-states retained awareness that this was manipulation intended to silence her and protect the abuser from being discovered. Nonetheless, it took repeated working through over months for the entire system of self-states to recognize she was safe from this man. This example illustrates that both the thought-disordered and reality-based thinking coexisted, but only attending to both allowed the reality oriented, insightful understanding to be integrated across self-state systems. This also exemplifies why it is crucial to work with self-states, as they are *resources* and not 'just symptoms'. Also, therapists need to learn how to help DID patients get grounded, and contain flashback material by active involvement in stabilizing the patient. A good introduction is the evidence-based, *Finding Solid Ground program* (Brand et al., 2022; Schielke et al., 2022).

Assessment research and differences between DID and BPD

Based on the DID assessment research Armstrong (1991, 1994) reframed responses on the Rorschach that classically would have been conceptualized as 'borderline splitting'. Looking at the totality of the paradoxical data, she concluded that in DID, the concepts of trauma-based 'fractionation' and 'polarization' are more accurate than splitting. The DID child grew up in dramatically different realities: sometimes caregivers were nurturing and safe, yet these same caregivers unpredictably but inevitably turn vicious. This required the child to survive these incomprehensibly polarized experiences by developing self-states that could attempt to manage radically different parental behavior. Also, our neurobiological responses to danger and threat activate before the cortex – the 'thinking brain' – to provide automatic, instinctive responses without shades of grey (e.g., run immediately that way from the sabretooth tiger, don't sit and reflect on the size of the teeth). It would have been dangerous during experiences of life-threat, to perceive and think in 'shades of grey' such as 'My Mommy loves me but also chases me with a knife'.

In the Rorschach case above, the man could perceive others as collaborative and cooperative ('two women carrying a basket') yet also as malevolent and dangerous, followed by being able to step back, literally getting distance on the trauma-based perceptions by seeing a kinder image of a spiritual figure that could 'rise above' the awful intrusions. On testing, Armstrong described how DID patients could step away from trauma-based responding, displaying some awareness of their contradictory responses. This is not typically possible for individuals with BPD.

Armstrong brilliantly captured fundamental differences between DID and BPD: 'Although the two groups share certain superficial similarities, a BPD patient can be conceptualized as one who has split outer reality into extreme polarities to protect his or her own psychic integrity. A DID patient can be understood as someone who has divided and compartmentalized his or her inner reality to maintain object-relatedness' (Personal Communication, October 1989, Baltimore, MD).

DID and observing ego

The observing ego is essential for change-oriented, psychodynamic treatment. Almost all DID patients indicate they 'know' information 'intellectually', such as children are not responsible for abuse, but they will articulate, 'that doesn't change what I feel about myself' (i.e., shame and self-blame for trauma). Intellectualization can be defensive in DID treatment but worked with as a *beginning framework* from which to gradually erode entrenched trauma-based beliefs. Also, the obsessional personality features in DID make these patients responsive to using organizing concepts like this in goal setting for clinical work.

The multi-level responding patterns in DID mean that clinicians can, at times of decompensation, traumatic transference, and/or flashbacks, find self-states with observing ego and better reality testing, that may assist in making sense of what is going on and finding interventions. On the other hand, a controlling self-state may be consciously creating disruptions, e.g., 'causing the flashbacks' to 'keep her from telling secrets' which can be understood as avoidance of discussion of difficult memories and emotions. It may serve (in the traumatic transference) to prevent the patient from getting too close and being hurt by the clinician. Only by working with such self-states and identifying their paradoxical protective function, can these situations be fully resolved. For example, virtually all DID individuals report extremely dire threats to them or those they love if they 'tell'. First, one needs to make sure there are no *current, active threats* from perpetrators. If current threats are not present, then the therapist needs to carefully work through the fears before other self-states start to talk in therapy in detail about trauma experiences. In a classic psychoanalytic sense, one is working with the defenses before the genetic material. Overriding this type of protest and identifying too rapidly with 'talking about trauma is good', paves the way to more decompensation and disaster, without any useful working through of trauma.

Phasic trauma treatment for DID

Consistent with treatment of complex trauma (Herman, 1992), treatment of DID follows a three-stage treatment model (Brand, McNary et al., 2013; Brand et al., 2019; Chu et al., 2011). The first stage emphasizes safety and stabilization and often requires years of treatment. The second stage involves the processing and grieving of trauma, although earlier in treatment, trauma is openly acknowledged and referred to, yet without detailed exploration or attempts to get to the full range of emotion and betrayal experienced. This stage often takes years due to the multitude of traumas experienced by DID patients, safety issues that arise during trauma processing, and the need to continue supporting daily functioning and managing internal cooperation among states. The third stage emphasizes greater integration within the patient as well as into the community, with less focus on trauma as issues related to relationships, career, and existential meaning take priority. In DID, some patients desire and achieve 'unification', that is, fusion of all self-states into a culturally congruent, non-dissociative self-system. 'Fusion' is a process where two or more self-states subjectively combine all their attributes, losing subjective seperateness. 'Integration', the process of undoing all forms of dissociative defenses, starts with any dissociative separateness, and continues after the last 'final fusion' (Kluft, 1988). Most patients achieve a 'resolution', that is, substantial decrease in dissociation, often with some fusions, and better functioning with more adaptive, coordinating self-systems with markedly less overt internal conflict.

Initial interventions and pacing of treatment (stage 1)

DID treatment must be carefully paced so that the patient is not flooded with overwhelming emotions and dysregulated PTSD intrusions. Premature focus on detailed, affectively charged material will decompensate DID patients (Kluft, 2013). An overarching goal is working towards more cooperative functioning of self-states and more flexible control over dissociative and autohypnotic defenses. DID experts advise that attending to safety, emotion regulation, and management of dissociation and PTSD symptoms are crucial treatment targets in the first stage as well as throughout the treatment (Brand, McNary et al., 2013; Chu et al., 2011). Individuals with DDs indicate that they engage in self-injury in response to trauma-related intrusions, overwhelming emotions (most commonly shame states, as well as anger, sadness, and self-loathing), stressors, and severe symptoms including dissociation although, at treatment onset, few understand the reasons they engage in self-injury (Nester et al., 2022).

Research aligns with the expert consensus guidelines and expert surveys about the treatment of DID: treatment must address safety and guide patients in developing recovery-oriented methods for managing emotion, unsafe urges, and PTSD and dysregulated dissociative symptoms (Brand, McNary et al., 2013; Brand et al., 2019; Chu et al., 2011). Specialized inpatient or residential DID treatment that is consistent with the expert guidelines can benefit patients, especially for major safety crises and decompensations (Brand, Classen, McNary et al., 2009; Ellason & Ross, 1997; Jepsen et al., 2014). Patients respond with significant improvement in safety and in many symptom domains to an outpatient psychotherapy combined with a dissociation-focused adjunctive psychoeducational program (Brand, Classen, Lanius et al., 2009; Brand et al., 2013; Brand et al., 2019). Patients and their therapists, who also participated in the study learn skills for managing unsafe urges, emotion regulation, and symptom management. It guides patients to learn the purposes of their self-harming and risky behavior, and to gradually identify and practice recovery-oriented self-regulation. In DID and other traumatized patients, self-destructive, high-risk, substance-abusing, and other dangerous behaviors *are used as regulators of overwhelming emotions, memories, severe symptoms, and relationship issues*. Interventions based on suppression of 'bad behavior', such as the unfortunately all-too common response from clinicians, 'I am so disappointed that you hurt yourself again', actually increases shame (and often covert anger) and will increase these behaviors.

The evidence-based program, *Finding Solid Ground*, encouraged the identification and working through trauma-based distortions about getting safer and using non-trauma-based self-regulation (e.g., shame scripts: 'I don't deserve to feel better', 'Letting down my guard is a trick and I will get hurt if I relax'; 'better to do it to myself first before I get hurt by someone else' etc.; Brand et al., 2022; Schielke et al., 2022). Books detailing this program are available (Brand et al., 2022; Schielke et al., 2022) as well as training in this model (topddstudy.com).

Among many initial interventions, clinicians can help patients develop distance from trauma. For example, when discussing trauma, clinicians can ask for trauma to be shared at the 'headline level', rather than the 'full story' with details that can cause cascading intrusive symptoms and flashbacks (Loewenstein, 2006). DID patients frequently experience 'emotional' flashbacks (Loewenstein, 1993, 2006), responding in extreme ways to a current situation, without recognizing it's posttraumatic 'supercharging'. The *Finding Solid Ground* program refers to this as a '90–10 reaction', borrowing the term from Jon Allen and colleagues: the current situation is important and giving rise to some of the emotion (often roughly 10%), yet most ("90%, give or take) of the emotionality is triggered due to similarities with a traumatic experience or relational pattern (L. Lewis et al., 2004). Both sources of emotion are important and must be validated, including if the therapist has said something inartful, blundered, etc. Due to recognizing the trauma-based source of their upsurge of emotions, patients feel 'less crazy' and more in control.

The overarching concept involves separation of past and present. Helping the DID patient use their observing ego is essential in understanding and resolving many seemingly intractable issues. For example, refractory self-injury often stems from complex layers of meaning/

dissociated experience. These may involve ablation of current emotional agony; a show of power over one's body no matter what the adults (including therapists) want; means of self-punishment (a self-attack shame and/or anger script); and reenactments of past trauma, and combinations. For example, a woman with DID vaginally and anally inserted caustic substances and sharp objects to feel power over past traumas that she could not control, to show shame/disgust/rage towards self-states and her body that 'betrayed me' by having an age-inappropriate genital 'response' to sexual assault, and to attempt to get rid of these self-states. In terms of shame/affect theory, she was enacting a mixture of avoidance, self-attack, and attack-the-other disguised as self-attack. Stabilization of these behaviors and lasting change among states can only occur after the trauma-based roots of these conflicts/behaviors are recognized and after states are empathized with for their attempts to find ways of having power, managing shame, and covertly 'telling their stories' of trauma.

The initial interventions may involve psychoeducation about the functions of self-harm, emotions and their (lack of) regulation; alexithymia; shame scripts; as well as insisting on therapeutic agreements for cessation of all forms of dangerousness to self/dangerousness to others. It is imperative for the clinician to stand up for the importance of safety of the patient and to focus on the trauma-based rationalizations that drive unsafe behaviors (Loewenstein, 1993). Simultaneously and paradoxically the clinician attempts to help the patient/whole mind to look at these behaviors as logically related to survival when maltreatment was unavoidable.[6] Even entrenched suicidal states are trying to help, although it can take considerable work to discover how they are trying to support survival. For example, one paradoxical protector state was asked about the first time 'he' attempted suicide; the first attempt involved jumping out of a second story window in an attempt to stop, via suicide, being forced to participate in being filmed while being raped by traffickers.[7] This state stopped decades-long rumination about, and ceased attempting suicide, only after being validated for suffering as well as the defiant stance he took against the pedophiles who were ruthlessly using him. Other self-states' terror of this self-state eased and their appreciation grew once they recognized this self-state 'held' memories of horrific abuse (i.e., 'protecting the others from remembering'), and was attempting to thwart what he perceived to be current day efforts to undermine his declaration of autonomy, control, and freedom from harm. The therapist guided the patient to shift the paradoxical, life-affirming survival strategies rooted in childhood to present day, life-affirming, recovery supportive strategies. The *Finding Solid Ground* program explains this method, as well as others, for 'separating past from present'.

A large subgroup of DID patients refuse to open up beyond the minimum about their self-state systems and trauma history. Theirs is a long-term stage 1 psychotherapy, where the goal is to help the patient maintain safety, reduce treatment at more restrictive levels of care, and help them manage as well as possible in everyday life. Some may function at the level of the seriously and persistently mentally ill. There may be myriad dynamics for this, extreme intolerance of shame is often a major one. Others may not be able to tolerate seeing clearly the need to exit, from relationships with reported perpetrators. Some have retreated from reality and prefer to live as much as possible in complex, fantasized inner worlds that are more gratifying than their often-grim outside reality (e.g., subsisting on disability; estranged from their own children and family of origin; limited social supports; chronic medical problems, some related to self-destructive behavior; substance abuse, and the patients' trauma-related phobia of seeking medical care, etc.)

Psychodynamics of phasic trauma treatment: putting it together

A complete psychoanalytic formulation of phasic treatment for DID likely would involve at minimum a long monograph. Putting together the foregoing discussions, working with DID can be conceptualized as learning a new language. DID individuals often respond positively to the metaphor that they feel they grew up in an entirely different culture, even though they look, talk, and dress like 'regular people', know the cultural touchstones, etc. However, deep down they resonate with the metaphor of growing up in a different world, with different rules, different customs. One DID patient who grew up to be a successful mental health practitioner and agency director, described how as a child and an adolescent, she and her brother would sit and 'watch the normal people, trying to figure out how to be like that'. Even with her life successes and having her own children, she still felt fundamentally that she might as well have grown up in New Guinea, for all that the 'regular world' made sense.

This is a language of the person's world, inner life, defensive structures, attachments, identifications, superego functions, etc., that is their entire life adaptation is organized around – not just trauma – but the inescapable and unpredictable inevitability of being savagely harmed and betrayed potentially by any seemingly positive attachment figure. And then blamed for it.

Do you believe me?

Research shows that delayed recall of trauma memory is no less accurate than 'continuous memory'.[8] When studied with documentation of the events (e.g., delayed patient recall; trauma-based injuries; perpetrator confession), either can be essentially accurate, partially accurate, or confabulated (Dalenberg, 2006). In order to provide ongoing informed consent about this in therapy, the clinician should develop solid familiarity with the complex literatures on autobiographical memory, trauma memory; delayed recall of trauma memory; memory fallibility about trauma as well as non-trauma memory (e.g., Brown et al., 1998; Dalenberg, 2006; Dalenberg et al., 2012; Dalenberg et al., 2014, 2020; Loewenstein et al., 2017; Lynn et al., 2014). Informed consent is necessarily an ongoing process, particularly because, early in therapy, the DID patient generally thinks in trauma-based terms: 'all lies' versus 'all true'.

The clinical pragmatics are more straightforward, especially if one recalls the discussion of the development of 'multiple reality disorder' as the DID individual grows up. If the DID person, as it often happens early in therapy, with a pleading, desperate quality asks, 'do you believe me?' The clinician can answer, 'That sounds like you all feel very desperate about this. But I wasn't there. The real question is, do *you believe you?*'

In the DID patient, there is a deep conflict over belief versus disbelief about the person's own history, and, indeed, whether they actually 'have' DID. Trance-logically, different self-state groups will take opposing positions about this. The core BPD theme is often conceptualized as the defensive use of splitting into an all good versus an all-bad perception of self and other, and its impact on transference, countertransference, and projective identification. In DID treatment, there is a deep *belief/disbelief division*, that is reflected in transference, countertransference, projective identification, and, indeed in academics and the culture at large. Child abuse histories reported in psychotherapy are mostly unverifiable. Therapy is not a forensic enterprise; and therapists make poor detectives – and vice versa. Even if the person's abuser is jailed for abusing them, there may not be specific documentation for a panoply of criminal atrocities described by the patient during therapy. Sometimes relatives describe witnessing assaults on the patient that they deny recalling. The therapy-long task becomes helping the DID person make sense of their autobiography, which may include reconstruction, and may change over time. Thus, therapists should avoid closure and 'validation' or 'invalidation' of any specific memory material. Sometimes improbable material has a trauma-based reality to it. As one thoughtful DID patient said, 'It's not that I want you to believe me. I want you *to believe in me to figure it out*'.

For example, DID patients, often those who report organized sadistic abuse, sometimes doggedly insist that prominent political figures (even deceased ones) abused them. Decoding these reports typically involves perpetrator deception: wearing masks and saying they are the prominent person; making strong commands to an acutely traumatized, often drugged, sleep-deprived, highly hypnotizable dissociative child to 'see' Satan, or Lucifer, or a prominent political or media figure. The child will 'see' what is commanded, and it becomes part of autobiographical material. One patient described this as perpetrators using illusion to make what she called 'created realities'; adding another frequently bizarre dimension to the multiple realities. This, and related strategies may also be perpetrators' attempt to contaminate the child's memory so that, if they were accused of child abuse crimes, the victim's account will seem hopelessly improbable. Soon this will involve virtual reality glasses and AI, if not already.

For example, a patient who later achieved full fusion/integration of self-states had described and abreacted a memory of her baby sister being 'murdered' in an elaborate occultist ritual carried out by her family, their minister and members of their rural, fundamentalist religious sect. After substantial fusion of self-states, she said she saw this event differently. She said, 'You know when I grew up, Satan was supposed to be everywhere. If a cow died in the field, Satan did it. I deeply resented my baby sister since she was so preferred over me. Again and again, I wished that she would die. When she actually died of an infection, they held a big service in our church. I couldn't tolerate the idea that I must have "murdered" her. So, I constructed her death as being murdered by Satan in a Satanic service'. However, whether one, or even either version, represents historical reality remains unknowable. On the other hand, many DID patients do not revise trauma reports during therapy, but they make more sense in terms of the overall history, and resolution of the conflict over multiple realities. For example, the patient in the prior example had to face another horror of her growing up: antibiotics and 'Satanic' medical care were anathema to her parents and church. Her sister was prayed over until she died. In a prosaic sense, they *did* murder her sister.

Multiplicity in therapy

Kluft (1992, 2000, 2022) describes that few DID patients can tolerate a relatively unmodified psychoanalytic or intensive psychodynamic psychotherapy. DID individuals present with a broad range of functioning. Some are high functioning professionals, entrepreneurs, etc. Others function at the level of the chronically and persistently mentally ill. Most are somewhere in the middle. The vast majority struggle with major issues with safety, PTSD and mood disorder symptoms. The latter usually, at best, are mildly responsive to psychopharmacological treatments (see Loewenstein et al., 2017). Thus, the first stage of DID treatment usually requires a great deal of activity by the clinician around managing, and markedly reducing patients' reliance on self-regulation via unsafety. The Treatment of Patients with Dissociative Disorders (TOP DD) Network study showed that the stabilization model, including specifically working with self-states, led to a massive reduction in nonsuicidal self-injury in patients where this had been virtually a daily or weekly behavior (Brand et al., 2019). TOP DD data also show that working in the 3-phase treatment model *reduced* the level of dissociative symptoms, not increased them (Brand & Loewenstein, 2014; Brand et al., 2022; Schielke et al., 2022).

How does the therapist relate to the DID human being in therapy? Based on the notion that complex self-divisions are adaptive and represent major aspects of material, the therapist needs to find a way to envision the patient *as if* they are made up of a multitude of 'people'. This may require trance logic, or, as an alternative, regression in the service of the ego (Loewenstein & Ross, 1992), or similar strategy to maintain the idea of a single human mind who can show a mixture of unity and dissociatively divided processes. Kluft (1993) posits that the holding environment by the DID clinician should be a warm, engaged demeanor, as silence may feel angrily critical, and reinforces shame. The therapist must bear in mind that all self-states are equally subjectively real, and understanding their history and psychodynamic meaning is the basic task. Typically, everyday self-states will say, 'they are all a part of me', and therapists use that phraseology. It is rare that DID self-states will agree that they are 'part' of other self-states. The narcissism of the everyday states may be affected (and the therapist needs to address that as well), but it is more helpful (and accurate) to say, 'You are all part of a single human being, with a single human mind. If some of you agree that you are "part" of someone else, then we will address you accordingly'.

In terms of dissociative amnesia, from the perspective of 'everyday self-states' who are adapted to managing the person's everyday life, there may be 'out of awareness behavior'. From the perspective of the self-states who enact the behavior, there is no amnesia, they have a first-person perspective on what occurred (e.g., nonsuicidal self-injury). Thus, without making efforts to 'find' and work with these self-destructive self-states, the chances of reducing dangerousness to self are markedly reduced. The therapist needs to ask to speak with those states by a method called talking through. Hence, the idea of group and family therapy for one person. Also, 'talking through' by self-states is much less disruptive than frank switching, and implicitly invites more collectively unified functioning. It is best to address a collectivity: 'I am asking everyone to listen' is an implicitly unifying phrase, especially when commenting on issues across different self-states/systems, as well as saying 'you all' as second person plural when addressing the patient.

As noted above, experienced therapists usually are working with self-states at the level of their dynamics, not their personified qualities (e.g., 'There are some of you [therapist may name the group] deny that anything problematic affected your childhood, others [named group] of you say the opposite. I'd like to ask everyone; how can we begin a civil discussion between these groups to address these differing perspectives?') Paradoxically, the therapist's phobia of 'reinforcing' separateness by refusing to talk like this, avoiding words like 'People' to describe self-states, actually drives separateness. If the word 'people' fits the person's subjective reality, or if a patient insists 'we are not part of her:', refusing to use the preferred vocabulary typically drives the patient to dig in their heels: 'I'll show you that I'm NOT part of her!' One DID patient divided her self-systems into 'the parts and the people', requiring exploration of the meaning of the distinction, not a struggle over vocabulary.

Traumatic transference and countertransference: a therapeutic road map

Spiegel, 1986 defined traumatic transference in DID treatment as follows: *'The patient unconsciously expects that the therapist, despite overt helpfulness and concern, will exploit the patient for his or her own narcissistic gratification'* (p. 72). Similarly, the data on transference in other traumatized populations supports this view. In psychoanalytic studies of treatment of

Vietnam veterans and survivors of incest and childhood sexual abuse, the basic transference patterns were negative and posttraumatic (Lindy, 1989; Davies & Frawley, 1994). Typically, much of the traumatic transference is concealed and avoided, mimicking what the child learned to do with perpetrators: appease and be submissive and outwardly agreeable, while inwardly hiding mistrust, fear, anger, and disagreement. At other times, it is concealed in dangerousness to self/dangerousness to others, high-risk behaviors, acting in, and acting out.

Classic traumatic transference/countertransference scenarios include the following. The therapist is seen as a potential abuser. The therapist may literally be seen as a perpetrator (or someone else) from the past (flashback transference). The therapist may be perceived as the unprotective bystander who looked away while the child was being harmed, or the 'stupid', self-important 'good' person to whom the patient may have directly or indirectly disclosed the abuse but who then failed to do anything to protect the child. The therapist may be viewed as the co-abusing parent. This ranges from supposedly 'unaware' to actively involved in maltreatment. The therapist may be perceived as a good person, but who will ultimately abandon the patient, often after repeatedly promising to 'always be there'. The therapist may work hard to prove how caring they are; this can lead to taking on the role of 'rescuer' role, another transference/countertransference dynamic. The therapist may symbolically become the helpless child, unable to stop the patient's aggression, either in subtle, direct (verbal attack), and/or indirect forms (e.g., endless safety crises with the implicit message: someone can violently harm someone as much as they want, and you can't do anything about it).

These themes may shift seemingly kaleidoscopically. The therapist may need to ask 'all to listen' and enumerate the specific traumatic transference dynamics: 'Various ones of you are viewing me this way; others this other way; others this additional way. It all seems related to being in relationships with dangerous people'. The therapist might add at another process level of traumatic transference, 'I think you all are showing me that your experience growing up was so chaotic, confusing, and violent, that you never could predict how anyone was going to behave; and you never could predict whom you had to be to survive'. One patient wrote of her mother as follows, ' ... [S]o I think having multiple people inside to comprehend the multiple realities of the environment makes sense. Kind of like, 'who do you need now? The person who knows you hate them? The person who you tell you love? Someone else? Who should I be now? The person that knows you rape us? Someone who doesn't know?'.

Mind control transference

DID patients who report continual, concerted psychological invasion by perpetrators may perceive therapists as involved in mind control dynamics

(Loewenstein, 1993, 2022; Salter, 1995). Here, the therapist's concern and helpfulness are experienced by the patient as only serving to gain access to the patient's mind to control and enslave the patient; a 'mind-control transference'. Often this occurs when the patient has been exploited in organized sadistic abuse involving trafficking where there is an attempt to enslave the child, in order to provide a better 'product'. Thus, these patients paradoxically experience 'being known', 'being seen' in therapy as profoundly dangerous, not a relief and a validation. Sometimes, this type of sadistic psychological invasion can uncannily parallel psychotherapy. Perpetrators may use phrases similar to those used by therapists (e.g., 'I want you to share everything that comes to mind without omitting anything'). Some DID patients report having been abused by physicians or mental health professionals; this type of abuse necessarily complicates and lengthens the course of DID treatment.

To some extent, all DID treatment has something of mind-control transference. However, when mind control has been a major part of the childhood violence, its dynamics will dominate treatment, as the therapeutic task of understanding the patient is contaminated by perpetrator behavior that wanted 'information' about the patient and their mind. Also, it requires the therapist to go far outside typical psychotherapy training and learn about attempts at enslavement of human beings. This includes indoctrination techniques in totalitarian groups; coercive control tactics in intimate partner violence and by pimps and traffickers to enslave their victims; interrogation techniques; mind control in destructive cults; techniques used by authoritarian dictators; use of drugging, sleep deprivation, and destructive hypnosis on children; concentration camp experiences, etc.

Another aspect of learning the language of DID has to do with the presence of evil in the quotidian world. Seemingly 'normal', sometimes even prominent people, create for their DID children a psychological prison or concentration camp, except without barbed wire, guards, dogs. We do not have a model for this; seemingly 'good' people commit atrocities against children.[9] The patients themselves struggle with this. 'Everyone always told me how great my mom was, she was so kind and understanding. How lucky I was. Yeah, and she tormented me every day of my life. Why was she so good to other people and not me? You tell me it wasn't my fault. But I'm the common denominator for all of it [being sexually assaulted by both parents]. I must have made them that way'.

Common clinical issues have a traumatic transference dimension, without which the problem usually cannot be solved. For example, DID patients often have self-state conflicts over taking medication. Some self-states desperately seek medication as an anodyne, and other self-states eschew medication. In the former state, the patient tends to overuse medications (e.g., benzodiazepines) creating a need for the prescriber to set limits on, or discontinue the drug. Some DID patients desperately overuse almost any drug, sometimes creating problems with side effects and drug interactions. Another DID patient may fail to reliably take prescribed medication that benefits them, even alternating with overuse.

Several traumatic transference issues may be in play, especially if the patient reports being drugged during abuse. The overuse may reflect being given drugs that made the abuse more tolerable (e.g., opiates, benzodiazepines). The desperate overuse/demands for dose increases may reflect a subtle partial flashback to being assaulted, begging the perpetrators for the medications that 'knocked me out'. On the other hand, the refusal of drugs may stem from a fear of being controlled by the perpetrators' drugging; because at other times the patient would beg for medications, and the perpetrators would mockingly refuse to give them to her. This led to self-states who embodied a dogged refusal to be sedated, no matter how much the 'other' self-states took. In the hospital for surgery, one DID patient resisted 'going under' with general anesthesia to the point that surgery needed to be cancelled. Surgery went forward with the patient tolerating anesthesia after the clinician asked to speak to the drug-resisting self-states, acknowledged that drugs had been used adversely on her, and supported the self-states fundamentally positive attempts to resist being put in that position again.

Even without a history of drugging, another common trauma-based fear in DID is that, once the patient 'feels better' on the meds, then the psychiatrist will control the patient, have something over him/her; will 'want something from the patient' in order to keep prescribing. The patient will 'need' the therapist for the drugs. These patterns typically underlie illogical statements of concern about becoming 'addicted' to psychiatric medications, and/or accompanying continual misuse of street drugs.

Trauma-based, dissociation-based countertransference also occurs and can be crucial to decoding the therapeutic situation. One of the classic countertransference dynamics in DID is that clinicians may feel frustrated, irritated, exhausted, deskilled or even helpless to effect change, since many DID patients are desperate to hide their self-states, avoid and/or disavow trauma history, with the therapist feeling like they are doing all the work and carrying the treatment (Kluft, 1994). At other times, the therapist may feel overwhelmed at the extremity of the patient's trauma history, the sense that the nightmare of the patients' life will never end.

However, these can be decoded as projective identifications of the patient's experience of growing up, and often their later life: they were overwhelmed, exhausted, desperate, and helpless to change their situation, and perpetrators denied their distress and insisted that the patient tolerate 'more'. The clinician may say, 'I'd like all self-states to listen. I think you are giving me a graduate education in what your experience has been for much of your life. How helpless and overwhelmed you felt, and yet abusers kept insisting you do more'. Sometimes, this situation is associated with intractable suicidality. Often, this can reflect that there is an 'emotional' flashback, memories of what the patient *felt and thought* during past experience.

Here, the patient experiences, without conscious connection, their own childhood suicidality. This combines with the current suicidality, often with previously amnestic self-states consciously feeling suicidal around increasing awareness of trauma memories and their attachment implications. As discussed previously, the therapeutic intervention is to work on each level separately: with the self-states that hold previously dissociated recollection of childhood suicidality, and also work with the 'everyday' self-states whose suicidality is related to decreased dissociation of trauma memories. Also, suicidality may have a paradoxical 'life-affirming' aspect. As in a previous example, DID patients report that childhood suicidality was a protest against uncontrollable adversity; it represented a 'No. I'm not doing this anymore. I die and it stops. I have the power and I am more powerful than the bad people'. Alternatively, there may be self-states that believe in an afterlife where 'God doesn't let little children get hurt and starved'; or simply being 'at peace' in the ground. Paradoxically, in childhood, contemplating death was an affirmation against maltreatment. In the present, the patient can use the same positive affirmation to shift this 'survival' strategy to the 'recovery' strategy of self-states pulling together for recovery and affirmation of life in the present.

Understanding self-states' functions

How can children survive such deprivation and aloneness? DID children often use their imaginations, auto-hypnotic, and dissociative processes to survive. One patient imagined she was out in the rose garden smelling the beautiful roses during her drunken father's rapes (avoidance, withdrawal shame scripts as noted above). Others create a self-state that speaks to them with kindness or who coaches them through tasks; some create animal states that they experience as comforting and safer than humans (again shame avoidance, withdrawal). Other shame-scripts may include the development of sexualized self-states in childhood, who initiate 'sex' (rape) with perpetrators, to mitigate the accompanying violence (attack other; avoidance shame scripts; Kluft, 2017).

This type of self-state is experienced as mortifying by most other self-states and may be treated with a type of internal apartheid. For other self-states, they embody the certainty that 'I made it happen', which of course was reinforced by perpetrators. Also, these states may approach/invite all men sexually. This is often a test of the male therapist (and female therapists where there was female perpetration). The response, understanding the language of DID should be to talk to all self-states, focus on the specific protective function of these self-states (also, getting it over with, since 'waiting is the worst'), educate the patient and discuss this in compass-of-shame terms, and reframe the protective nature of these self-states. They came into existence to make the inevitable 'less worst' (there is no single worst in the development of DID; there are many 'worsts'). This will be tested repeatedly. These self-states may embody the words, gestures, and dress of women and men in prostitution, pornography, etc. It can be discomfiting for therapists to experience our societally conditioned responses to this type of overt seductiveness, and to make the appropriate trauma-dissociation-shame script interpretations.

Another intolerable emotion for many DID patients is pride in themselves ('don't say the P word!' says the patient). If they do something worthy of praise (or receive praise, including from therapists), they rapidly attempt to denigrate it. Some feel a compulsion to punish themselves if they are praised. If the patient says anything negative about an abusive or neglectful parent, they often experience internal castigation, and may feel urges to self-harm. These are typically reenactments of attachment-betrayal-humiliation scenarios. That is, normal needs and feelings of attachment, or other types of positive experiences (e.g., pride in one's accomplishment) were met with verbal humiliation or reprisal ('So you think you are better than me, your mother?') or overt punishment. Patients may report that any friendship or object, including pets, they were attached to were taken away, destroyed, or killed. And they were blamed for these losses. Often, self-states embody the abusive parent, and others embody themselves as children, frequently internally reenacting situations with the parent.

The internalized perpetrator has many paradoxically protective functions, and these can be analyzed in terms of trauma-dissociation as well as shame dynamics. This represents an internalized attack other script. Mortifying experiences are inevitable. These self-states serve as eidetic warnings to attempt to avoid being blind-sided (one more time) by attack. They take control over the inevitable, 'If I throw myself on the floor, you can kick me. But you can't throw me any lower', said one patient. Often, they are attempts to warn about betrayal/humiliation in attachment, any attachment. Especially to the therapist.

Negative therapeutic reaction in DID

Another common dynamic in DID treatment is the negative therapeutic reaction (NTR; Chefetz, 2015). Freud (1923) originally defined it as a patient's unexpected symptomatic worsening, often after brief improvement, when the therapist predicts that an intervention should logically lead to symptom amelioration. A classical explanation for NTR in DID is the patient's malignant, punishing superego, their entrenched belief in their core badness interferes with anything positive to be internalized. Thus, when such a DID patient experiences improvement (e.g., by use of a helpful hypnotic technique in therapy for posttraumatic distress), there is a redoubling of symptoms and the technique no longer works, and further attempts to use it bring about escalating distress. Often paradoxical protector perpetrator 'introjects' claim responsibility for these punishments.

However, there is a more fundamental cause of NTR in DID, based on the discussion of attachment/betrayal/humiliation. Many DID perpetrators, particularly sadistic ones, appear to wait for the child to be absorbed in something positive, like reading a book or playing, to pounce on them and attack. They may promise to 'not do that again', wait for the child to relax their guard, then attack again. Anything nice, like the child getting a toy as a gift, will result in this being taken from him/her with sadistic assaults to 'prove' to the child that they will be 'gotten' any time anything positive occurs. One patient's mother thought her little son was so 'generous' that he always gave his toys away to other children. He was attempting to avoid sadistically savage sexual and physical assaults from his older brothers and their psychopathic neighborhood friends. Whenever he felt good about something, they destroyed it, or made him destroy it. This had included torturing his new puppy almost to death, then insisting that the boy kill the puppy to put it out of its misery. Then, they continually taunted him that he had 'killed' his dog and must be a 'crazy, mad dog killer'.

In treatment as an adult, this DID man said, 'I learned to never trust anything good. Anything that was good, turned really bad'. This is an excruciatingly painful dilemma, that one's positive feelings, joy, excitement, pride becomes an immediate, extreme danger signal and must be obliterated. In this DID patient, introjects of his brothers and their confederates made sure to 'make something bad happen' to preempt 'outsiders' from doing it first. His tormentors also made him believe that they would make him kill his parents, like the dog, if he did not do what they wanted. Not surprisingly, he had introjects of his clueless, dissociated mother, and his alcoholic father who had savagely beaten his brothers, but sobered up when the patient was a small child, and, unlike his brothers, was treated kindly by his father. He had an 'insane mad dog killer' who had to be imprisoned in an imaginal dungeon. He found a secret ghost of his dog in his mind who told him that it was not his fault that it had been killed, but he should never let anyone know that the dog was there to support him. He was utterly terrified to reveal this in therapy and had a safety crisis after doing so.

This is a vital dynamic to understand in DID treatment. We have yet to treat a DID patient who does not recognize the phrase that 'the other shoe will drop' when anything feels or seems OK or calm. Generally, they experience this as a basic law of the universe. To avoid the profound mortification of, one more time, being so 'stupid' as to be blindsided by the 'other shoe', the DID patient must find to a way to expeditiously get rid of the good, the calm feeling, the enjoyment of something, etc.; 'waiting' for the unpredictably humiliating other shoe is 'the worst'.

Working on these dynamics requires education about shame and affect theory, and specifically about the compass of shame, within whose framework DID patients universally see themselves. In addition, it is helpful for the therapist to observe that all of us have our own compass of shame, and that human beings in general utterly despise experiencing shame/humiliation and make major efforts to defend against them. Nathanson (1992) observes that recognition of our own shame experiences is essential in empathically assisting patients with theirs. DID therapists, especially early on, may feel their own shame at the difficulties in conducting these therapies. In interventions around shame, it is helpful to recognize when there is projective identification of the patient's shame, and what is our own shame contribution. Decoding this may also help frame one's responses to the patient's shame by recognizing the connections with our own. For example, 'it is particularly hard when we are feeling ashamed, and someone we care about not only doesn't offer us empathy, but actually reinforces the shame. I wonder if some of you felt that I was doing that when I said … '

Further, one educates the patient about the NTR and the form that it takes in DID. How fundamentally cruel it is to rob someone of their ability to tolerate anything good, safe, calm. The patient can then be invited to risk tolerating and testing feeling OK, even a few seconds, with the invitation to paradoxical protectors, and others who may have thoughts about this to talk with the clinician about what they observe. Typically, this is experienced as becoming tense, then agitated, then frantic. So, it is important to not go beyond the stage of tension, to pull back and gently empathize with this predicament. As this is slowly, repeatedly worked on, at many levels, other emotions come up. For example, attack self/internal attack other scripts get activated, often combined with anger. Under the anger, there is usually sadness and grieving. These are often experienced as more intolerable than the shame or the anger. The NTR may be a defense against the sadness and the grief, as never-ending trauma memories may conceal this. It comes with the recognition that the DID patient's loved ones treated them as a hated, objectified thing, not a human. Not only was the hatred repeatedly and aggressively directed into the DID individual. There was fundamentally a hate-filled, targeted neglect of the most basic human needs.

One patient said, weeping, 'I was an orphan! Everyone hated me! I was utterly alone and under attack. And our family looked perfectly wonderful. And I could not have known that and survived as a kid. I barely can think about it now'.

In conclusion, DID is a developmental adaptation to profoundly chaotic and abusive childhood experiences. DID individuals have a unique personality organization based on dissociative self-states that include psychological resiliencies such as observing ego and an ability to develop a therapeutic alliance, alongside trauma-based reactivity, beliefs, and traumatic transference reactions. Research illustrates that long-term, psychodynamically informed treatment that focuses on improving safety and stabilization, understanding and working through traumatic transference and traumatic experiences, and acknowledging and working with self-states results in considerable benefits for patients.

Notes

1. For simplicity, we will use the terms "psychoanalytic' interchangeably with 'psychodynamic' in this paper, albeit not all psychodynamically oriented clinicians are psychoanalysts; and there are theoretical schisms among psychoanalytic/psychodynamic schools. Also, unless specifically noted, for simplicity and space considerations, we will use the term 'clinician', 'therapist', or 'practioner' to include clinicians, researchers, academicians, theorists, et al of any background or theoretical perspective.
2. Therapists trained in hypnosis require additional training to work with trauma and dissociation in psychotherapy. Training in hypnosis for complex trauma and DDs is offered by the American Society for Clinical Hypnosis (https://www.asch.net/aws/ASCH/pt/sp/home_page).
3. Disgust is summarized by drinking spoiled milk (yuk!); dissmell is smelling the spoiled mild before drinking it (pew).
4. Self and identity are linked but distinct concepts. Self is our subjective 'I' and 'me', our moment-to-moment sense of our 'selves'. It is tied to our memory of our history, and that we can see ourselves in the future (autonoetic consciousness). Identity is

more about our longer-term descriptors, some more internalized than others: sex, gender, age, ethnicity, religion, social class, profession, and many others. Identity can be negatively used against people in racist, sexist, and similar denigration of the 'other'. In DID, the secondary elaborations of the self-states are understood as identity enactments.

5. Hypnotic inductions may begin by having the patient 'hyperfocus' on something (e.g., the place where 2 walls connect at the corner of the room). Often, this is followed by eye-closure as the patient enters hypnotic trance.
6. The clinician must ascertain if the patient is currently in an abusive contemporary relationship (e.g., violent relationships; ongoing involvement with perpetrators, etc.), as the patient will see self-destructive behavior as a life-long necessity for survival. Helping trauma survivors exit abusive relationships is usually a long, grueling process that can be painful for the therapist to endure, as the patient repeatedly returns to be hurt, and new ways of coping are overwhelmed by more humiliating, controlling perpetration.
7. It is recommended that terms like 'child pornography', 'child prostitution' be replaced by more descriptive terms as the former may imply some active involvement by exploited, trafficked child.
8. The notion of 'continuous memory' is itself problematic since we do not continually remember our autobiography. This is among the many terminological issues in this area that are outside the scope of this paper (e.g., 'recovered memory'; one can say all memories are 'recovered'). The intrapsychic process of dissociation is different from that of 'repression'; large blocks of experience are unavailable in dissociation, not relatively singular memories. The subjective experience of delayed recall is different, and is often accompanied by intense emotions at minimum, and more often frank PTSD intrusive symptoms.
9. A real-world example of this mixture of good and evil is that of Daniel Gadjusek who won the Nobel Prize for medicine for his work on what are now called prion diseases. However, he used his research site in New Guinea to bring back and adopt over 50 young boys, many of whom he sexually abused and trafficked among his friends. Goudsmit (2009). Daniel Carleton Gajdusek (1923–2008). *Nature, 457* (7228), 394–394. https://doi.org/10.1038/457394a

Disclosure statement

No potential conflict of interest was reported by the author(s).

References

Armstrong, J. G. (1991). The psychological organization of multiple personality disordered patients as revealed in psychological testing. *Psychiatric Clinics of North America*, *14*(3), 533–546. https://doi.org/10.1016/S0193-953X(18)30288-0

Armstrong, J. G. (1994). Reflections on multiple personality disorder as a developmentally complex adaptation. *Psychoanalytic Study of the Child*, *50*(1), 349–364. https://doi.org/10.1080/00797308.1994.11823068

Armstrong, J. G., & Loewenstein, R. J. (1990). Characteristics of patients with multiple personality and dissociative disorders on psychological testing. *Journal of Nervous and Mental Disease*, *178*(7), 448–454. https://doi.org/10.1097/00005053-199007000-00006

Beahrs, J. O. (1994). Dissociative identity disorder: Adaptive deception of self and others. *Bulletin of the American Academy of Psychiatry and the Law*, *22*(2), 223–237.

Becker-Blease, K. A., Deater-Deckard, K., Eley, T., Freyd, J. J., Stevenson, J., & Plomin, R. (2004). A genetic analysis of individual differences in dissociative behaviors in childhood and adolescence. *Journal of Child Psychology and Psychiatry*, *45*(3), 522–532. https://doi.org/10.1111/j.1469-7610.2004.00242.x

Brand, B., & Loewenstein, R. J. (2014). Does phasic trauma treatment make patients with dissociative identity disorder treatment more dissociative? *Journal of Trauma & Dissociation*, *15*(1), 52–65. https://doi.org/10.1080/15299732.2013.828150

Brand, B., Armstrong, J. A., Loewenstein, R. J., & McNary, S. W. (2009). Personality differences on the Rorschach of dissociative identity disorder, borderline personality disorder, and psychotic inpatients. *Psychological Trauma: Theory, Research, Practice, and Policy*, *1*(3), 188–205. https://doi.org/10.1037/a0016561

Brand, B. L., Armstrong, J. G., & Loewenstein, R. J. (2006). Psychological assessment of patients with dissociative identity disorder. *Psychiatric Clinics of North America*, *29* (1), 145–168, x. https://doi.org/10.1016/j.psc.2005.10.014

Brand, B. L., Classen, C. C., Lanius, R. A., Loewenstein, R. J., McNary, S., Pain, C., & Putnam, F. (2009). A naturalistic study of dissociative identity disorder and dissociative disorder not otherwise specified patients treated by community clinicians. *Psychological Trauma: Theory, Research, Practice, and Policy*, *1*(2), 153–171. https://doi.org/10.1037/a0016210

Brand, B. L., Classen, C. C., McNary, S. W., & Zaveri, P. (2009). A review of dissociative disorders treatment studies. *Journal of Nervous and Mental Disease*, *197*(9), 646–654. https://doi.org/10.1097/NMD.0b013e3181b3afaa

Brand, B. L., McNary, S. W., Myrick, A. C., Classen, C. C., Lanius, R., Loewenstein, R. J., Pain, C., & Putnam, F. W. (2012). A longitudinal naturalistic study of patients with dissociative disorders treated by community clinicians. *Psychological Trauma: Theory, Research, Practice, and Policy*, *5*(4), 301–308.

Brand, B. L., McNary, S. W., Myrick, A. C., Classen, C. C., Lanius, R., Loewenstein, R. J., Pain, C., & Putnam, F. W. (2013). A longitudinal naturalistic study of patients with dissociative disorders treated by community clinicians. *Psychological Trauma: Theory, Research, Practice, and Policy*, *5*(4), 301–308. https://doi.org/10.1037/a0027654

Brand, B. L., Sar, V., Stavropoulos, P., Kruger, C., Korzekwa, M., Martinez-Taboas, A., & Middleton, W. (2016). Separating fact from fiction: An empirical examination of six myths about dissociative identity disorder. *Harvard Review of Psychiatry*, *24*(4), 257–270. https://doi.org/10.1097/HRP.0000000000000100

Brand, B. L., Schielke, H. J., Putnam, K. T., Putnam, F. W., Loewenstein, R. J., Myrick, A., Jepsen, E. K. K., Langeland, W., Steele, K., Classen, C. C., & Lanius, R. A. (2019). An online educational program for individuals with dissociative disorders and their clinicians: 1-year and 2-year follow-up. *Journal of Traumatic Stress*, *32*(1), 156–166. https://doi.org/10.1002/jts.22370

Brand, B. L., Schielke, H. J., Schiavone, F., & Lanius, R. A. (2022). *Finding Solid Ground: Overcoming Obstacles in Trauma Treatment*. Oxford University Press.

Brown, D. P., & Elliott, D. S. (2016). *Attachment disturbances in adults: Treatment for comprehensive repair*. W.W. Norton and Co.

Brown, D., Scheflin, A. W., & Hammond, D. C. (1998). *Memory, trauma, treatment, and the law*. Norton.

Chefetz, R. A. (2015). *Intensive psychotherapy for persistent dissociative processes: The fear of feeling real*. W.W. Norton & Company.

Chu, J. A., Dell, P. F., Somer, E., Van der Hart, O., Cardeña, E., Barach, P. M., Loewenstein, R. J., Brand, B., Golston, J. C., Courtois, C. A., Bowman, E. S., Classen, C., Dorahy, M., Sar, V., Gelinas, D. J., Fine, C. G., Paulson, S., Kluft, R. P., & Twombly, J.; International Society for the Study of Dissociation. (2011).

Guidelines for treating dissociative identity disorder in adults, third revision. *Journal of Trauma and Dissociation*, *12*(2), 115–187.
Crews, F. C. (1995). *The memory wars; Freud's legacy in dispute*.
Dalenberg, C. (2006). Recovered memory and the Daubert criteria: Recovered memory as professionally tested, peer reviewed, and accepted in the relevant scientific community. *Trauma, Violence & Abuse*, *7*(4), 274–310.
Dalenberg, C. J., Brand, B. L., Gleaves, D. H., Dorahy, M. J., Loewenstein, R. J., Cardena, E., Frewen, P. A., Carlson, E. B., & Spiegel, D. (2012). Evaluation of the evidence for the trauma and fantasy models of dissociation. *Psychological Bulletin*, *138*(3), 550–588. https://doi.org/10.1037/a0027447
Dalenberg, C. J., Brand, B. L., Loewenstein, R. J., Frewen, P. A., & Spiegel, D. (2020). Inviting scientific discourse on traumatic dissociation: Progress made and obstacles to further resolution. *Psychological Injury and Law*, *13*(2), 135–154. https://doi.org/10.1007/s12207-020-09376-9
Dalenberg, C. J., Brand, B. L., Loewenstein, R. J., Gleaves, D. H., Dorahy, M. J., Cardena, E., Frewen, P. A., Carlson, E. B., & Spiegel, D. (2014). Reality versus fantasy: Reply to Lynn et al. (2014). *Psychological Bulletin*, *140*(3), 911–920. https://doi.org/10.1037/a0036685
Davies, J. M., & Frawley, M. G. (1994). *Treating the adult survivor of childhood sexual abuse: A psychoanalytic perspective*. Basic Books.
Draijer, N., & Van Zon, P. (2013). Transference-focused psychotherapy with former child soldiers: Meeting the murderous self. *Journal of Trauma and Dissociation*, *14*(2), 170–183. https://doi.org/10.1080/15299732.2013.724339
Elkins, G. R., Barabasz, A. F., Council, J. R., & Spiegel, D. (2015). Advancing research and practice: The revised APA division 30 definition of hypnosis. *American Journal of Clinical Hypnosis*, *57*(4), 378–385. https://doi.org/10.1080/00029157.2015.1011465
Ellason, J. W., & Ross, C. A. (1997). Two-year follow-up of inpatients with dissociative identity disorder. *American Journal of Psychiatry*, *154*(6), 832–839. http://ajp.psychiatryonline.org/cgi/content/abstract/154/6/832
Freud, S. (1923). The ego and the id. In J. Strachey (Ed.), *Volume XX of The complete psychological works of Sigmund Freud* (Vol. II, pp. 69–99). Hogarth Press.
Freyd, J. J. (1996). *betrayal trauma: the logic of forgetting childhood abuse*. Harvard.
Goudsmit, J. (2009). Daniel Carleton Gajdusek (1923–2008). *Nature*, *457*(7228), 394. https://doi.org/10.1038/457394a
Herman, J. L. (1992). *Trauma and recovery*. Basic Books.
Herman, J. L. (2011). Posttraumatic stress disorder as a shame disorder. In J. P. Tangney & R. L. Dearing (Eds.), *Shame in the therapy hour* (pp. 261–275). American Psychological Association.
Hornstein, N., & Putnam, F. W. (1992). Clinical phenomenology of child and adolescent dissociative disorders. *The Journal of the American Academy of Child & Adolescent Psychiatry*, *31*, 1077–1085. https://doi.org/10.1097/00004583-199211000-00013
Horowitz, M. J. (1979). *States of mind: Analysis of change in psychotherapy*. Plenum.
Jepsen, E. K. K., Langeland, W., Sexton, H., & Heir, T. (2014). Inpatient treatment for early sexually abused adults: A naturalistic 12-month follow-up study. *Psychological Trauma: Theory, Research, Practice and Policy*, *6*(2), 142–151. https://doi.org/10.1037/a0031646
Johnson, J. G., Cohena, P., Kasena, K., & Brook, J. S. (2006). Dissociative disorders among adults in the community, impaired functioning, and axis I and II comorbidity. *Journal of Psychiatric Research*, *40*(2), 131–140. https://doi.org/10.1016/j.jpsychires.2005.03.003
Kelly, J. T., Branham, L., & Decker, M. R. (2016). Abducted children and youth in lord's resistance army in Northeastern Democratic Republic of the Congo (DRC):

Mechanisms of indoctrination and control. *Conflict and Health*, *10*(1), 11. https://doi.org/10.1186/s13031-016-0078

Kessler, R. C., Berglund, P. A., Demler, O., Jin, R., Merikangas, K. R., & Walters, E. E. (2005). Lifetime prevalence and age-of-onset distributions of DSM-IV disorders in the National Comorbidity Replication. *Archives of General Psychiatry*, *62*(6), 593–602. https://doi.org/10.1001/archpsyc.62.6.593

Kleindienst, N., Priebe, K., Görg, N., Dyer, A., Steil, R., Lyssenko, L., Winter, D., Schmahl, C., & Bohus, M. (2016). State dissociation moderates response to dialectical behavior therapy for posttraumatic stress disorder in women with and without borderline personality disorder. *European Journal of Psychotraumatology*, *7*(1), 30375. https://doi.org/10.3402/ejpt.v7.30375

Kluft, R. P. (1988). The postunification treatment of multiple personality disorder: First findings. *American Journal of Psychotherapy*, *42*(2), 212–228. https://doi.org/10.1176/appi.psychotherapy.1988.42.2.212

Kluft, R. P. (1989). Playing for time: Temporizing techniques in the treatment of multiple personality disorder. *American Journal of Clinical Hypnosis*, *32*(2), 90–97. https://doi.org/10.1080/00029157.1989.10402806

Kluft, R. P. (1992). Discussion: A specialist's perspective on multiple personality disorder. *Psychoanalytic Inquiry*, *14*(1), 139–171. https://doi.org/10.1080/07351699209533887

Kluft, R. P. (1993). Basic principles in conducing the psychotherapy of multiple personality disorder. In R. P. Kluft & C. G. Fine (Eds.), *Clinical perspectives on multiple personality disorder* (pp. 19–50). American Psychiatric Press.

Kluft, R. P. (1994). Countertransference in the treatment of multiple personality disorder. In J. P. Wilson & J. D. Lindy (Eds.), *Countertransference in the treatment of PTSD* (pp. 122–150). Guilford.

Kluft, R. P. (1998). Reflections on the traumatic memories of dissociative identity disorder patients. In S. J. Lynn & K. M. McConkey (Eds.), *Truth in memory* (pp. 304–322). Guilford.

Kluft, R. P. (2000). The psychoanalytic psychotherapy of dissociative identity disorder in the context of trauma therapy. *Psychoanalytic Inquiry*, *20*(2), 259–286. https://doi.org/10.1080/07351692009348887

Kluft, R. P. (2005). Diagnosing dissociative identity disorder. *Psychiatric Annals*, *35*(8), 633–643. https://doi.org/10.3928/00485713-20050801-05

Kluft, R. P. (2006). Dealing with alters: A pragmatic clinical perspective. *Psychiatric Clinics of North America*, *29*(1), 281–304. https://doi.org/10.1016/j.psc.2005.10.010

Kluft, R. P. (2007). Applications of innate affect theory to the understanding and treatment of dissociative identity disorder. In E. Vermetten, M. Dorahy, & D. Spiegel (Eds.), *Traumatic dissociation* (pp. 301–316). American Psychiatric Press.

Kluft, R. P. (2016). The wounded self in trauma treatment. *American Journal of Clinical Hypnosis*, *59*(1), 69–87. https://doi.org/10.1080/00029157.2016.1163659

Kluft, R. P. (2017). Weaponized sex: Defensive pseudo-erotic aggression in the service of safety. *Journal of Trauma & Dissociation*, *18*(3), 259–283. https://doi.org/10.1080/15299732.2017.1295376

Kluft, R. P. (2018a). Freud's rejection of hypnosis, Part I: The genesis of a rift. *American Journal of Clinical Hypnosis*, *60*(4), 307–323.

Kluft, R. P. (2018b). Freud's rejection of hypnosis, Part II: The perpetuation of a rift. *American Journal of Clinical Hypnosis*, *60*(4), 324–347. https://doi.org/10.1080/00029157.2018.1426326

Kluft, R. P. (2018c). Reconsidering hypnosis and psychoanalysis: Toward creating a context for understanding. *American Journal of Clinical Hypnosis*, *60*(3), 201–215. https://doi.org/10.1080/00029157.2018.1400810

Kluft, R. P. (2019). Freud's rejection of hypnosis: Perspectives old and new: Part III of III - Toward healing the rift: Enriching both hypnosis and psychoanalysis. *American Journal of Clinical Hypnosis*, *61*(3), 208–226.

Korzekwa, M. I., Dell, P. F., Links, P. S., Thabane, L., & Fougere, P. (2009). Dissociation in borderline personality disorder: A detailed look. *Journal of Trauma and Dissociation*, *10*(3), 346–367. https://doi.org/10.1080/15299730902956838

Kris, A. O. (1982). *Free association: Method and process*. Yale University Press.

Laddis, A., & Dell, P. F. (2012). Dissociation and psychosis in dissociative identity disorder and schizophrenia. *Journal of Trauma and Dissociation*, *13*(4), 397–413. https://doi.org/10.1080/15299732.2012.664967

Lewis, D. O., Yeager, C. A., Swica, Y., Pincus, J. H., & Lewis, M. (1997). Objective documentation of child abuse and dissociation in 12 murderers with dissociative identity disorder. *American Journal of Psychiatry*, *154*(12), 1703–1710. https://doi.org/10.1176/ajp.154.12.1703

Lewis, L., Kelly, K., & Allen, J. G. (2004). *Restoring hope and trust: An illustrated guide to mastering trauma*. Sidran Press.

Lindy, J. D. (1989). Transference and post-traumatic stress disorder. *The Journal of the American Academy of Psychoanalysis*, *17*, 397–413. https://doi.org/10.1521/jaap.1.1989.17.3.397

Loewenstein, R. J. (1991). An office mental status examination for chronic complex dissociative symptoms and multiple personality disorder. *Psychiatric Clinics of North America*, *14*(3), 567–604. https://doi.org/10.1016/S0193-953X(18)30290-9

Loewenstein, R. J. (1993). Posttraumatic and dissociative aspects of transference and countertransference in the treatment of multiple personality disorder. In R. P. Kluft & C. G. Fine (Eds.), *Clinical perspectives on multiple personality disorder* (pp. 51–85). American Psychiatric Press.

Loewenstein, R. J. (2006). DID 101: A hands-on clinical guide to the stabilization phase of dissociative identity disorder treatment. *Psychiatric Clinics of North America*, *29* (1), 305–332. https://doi.org/10.1016/j.psc.2005.10.005

Loewenstein, R. J. (2018). Dissociation debates: Everything you know is wrong. *Dialogues in Clinical Neuroscience*, *20*(3), 229–242. https://doi.org/10.31887/DCNS.2018.20.3/rloewenstein

Loewenstein, R. J. (2020). Firebug! Dissociative identity disorder? Malingering? Or …? An intensive case study of an arsonist. *Psychological Injury and Law*, *13*(2), 187–224.

Loewenstein, R. J. (2022). Conceptual foundations for long-term psychotherapy of dissociative identity. In M. Dorahy, S. Gold, & J. O'Neill (Eds.), *Dissociation and the dissociative disorders: Past, present, future* (2nd ed., pp. 770–789). Routledge.

Loewenstein, R. J., Frewen, P. A., & Lewis-Fernández, R. (2017). Dissociative disorders. In B. J. Sadock, V. A. Sadock, & P. Ruiz (Eds.), *Kaplan & Sadock's Comprehensive Textbook of Psychiatry* (10th ed., Vol. 1, pp. 1866–1952). Wolters Kluwer/ Lippincott Williams & Wilkens.

Loewenstein, R. J., & Putnam, F. W. (2022). Discrete behavioral state theory. In M. Dorahy, S. Gold, & J. O'Neill (Eds.), *Dissociation and the dissociative disorders: past, present, future* (2nd ed., Vol. 2, pp. 281–296). Routledge.

Loewenstein, R. J., & Ross, D. (1992). Multiple personality and psychoanalysis: An introduction. *Psychoanalytic Inquiry*, *12*, 3–48. https://doi.org/10.1080/07351699209533881

Lynn, S. J., Lilienfeld, S. O., Merckelbach, H., Giesbrecht, T., McNally, R. J., Loftus, E. F., Bruck, M., Garry, M., & Malaktaris, A. (2014). The trauma model of dissociation: Inconvenient truths and stubborn fictions. Comment on Dalenberg etal. (2012). *Psychological Bulletin*, *140*(3), 896–910. https://doi.org/10.1037/a0035570

McHugh, P. (1995). Witches, multiple personalities, and other psychiatric artifacts. *Nature Medicine*, *1*(2), 110–114. https://doi.org/10.1038/nm0295-110

McHugh, P. R. (2008). *Try to remember: Psychiatry's clash over meaning, memory, and mind*. Dana Press.

Middleton, W. (2013). Ongoing incestuous abuse during adulthood. *Journal of Trauma and Dissociation*, *14*(3), 251–272. https://doi.org/10.1080/15299732.2012.736932

Mueller-Pfeiffer, C., Rufibach, K., Perron, N., Wyss, D., Kuenzler, C., Prezewowsky, C., Pitman, R. K., & Rufer, M. (2012). Global functioning and disability in dissociative disorders. *Psychiatry Research*, *200*(2–3), 475–481. https://doi.org/10.1016/j.psychres.2012.04.028

Nathanson, D. L. (1992). *Shame and pride: Affect, sex, and the birth of the self*. Norton.

Nester, M. S., Boi, C., Brand, B. L., & Schielke, H. J. (2022). The reasons dissociative disorder patients self-injure. *European Journal of Psychotraumatology*, *13*(1), 2026738. https://doi.org/10.1080/20008198.2022.2026738

Putnam, F. W. (1992). Discussion: Are alter personalities fragments or figments? *Psychoanalytic Inquiry*, *12*(1), 95–111. https://doi.org/10.1080/07351699209533884

Putnam, F. W. (1997). *Dissociation in children and adolescents: A developmental model*. Guilford.

Putnam, F. W. (2016). *The way we are: How states of mind influence our identities, personality, and potential for change*. IUP.

Ross, C. A., Ferrell, L., & Schroeder, E. (2014). Co-occurrence of dissociative identity disorder and borderline personality disorder. *Journal of Trauma and Dissociation*, *15* (1), 79–90. https://doi.org/10.1080/15299732.2013.834861

Salter, A. (1995). *Transforming trauma: A guide to understanding and treating adult survivors of child sexual abuse*. Sage.

Salter, M. (2013). *Organized sadistic abuse*. Routledge.

Sar, V., Alioglu, F., Akyuz, G., & Karabulut, S. (2014). Dissociative amnesia in dissociative disorders and borderline personality disorder: Self-rating assessment in a college population. *Journal of Trauma and Dissociation*, *15*(4), 477–493. https://doi.org/10.1080/15299732.2014.902415

Sar, V., Alioglu, F., Akyuz, G., Tayakisi, E., Ogulmus, E. F., & Sonmez, D. (2017). Awareness of identity alteration and diagnostic preference between borderline personality disorder and dissociative disorders. *Journal of Trauma and Dissociation*, *18* (5), 693–709. https://doi.org/10.1080/15299732.2016.1267684

Schielke, H. J., Brand, B. L., & Lanius, R. A. (2022). *The finding solid ground program workbook: Overcoming obstacles in trauma recovery*. Oxford University Press.

Schmahl, C., Arvastson, L., Tamm, J. A., Bohus, M., Abdourahman, A., & Antonijevic, I. (2013). Gene expression profiles in relation to tension and dissociation in borderline personality disorder. *PloS One*, *8*(8), e70787.

Simeon, D., & Putnam, F. (2022). Pathological dissociation in the National Comorbidity Survey Replication (NCS-R): Prevalence, morbidity, comorbidity, and childhood maltreatment. *Journal of Trauma and Dissociation*, 1–14. https://doi.org/10.1080/15299732.2022.2064580

Spiegel, D. (1986). Dissociation, double binds, and posttraumatic stress. In B. G. Braun (Ed.), *The treatment of multiple personality disorder* (pp. 61–77). American Psychiatric Association.

Spiegel, D., Loewenstein, R. J., Lewis-Fernandez, R., Sar, V., Simeon, D., Vermetten, E., Cardena, E., & Dell, P. F. (2011). Dissociative disorders in DSM-5. *Depression and Anxiety*, *28*(9), 824–852. https://doi.org/10.1002/da.20874

Steele, K. (2009). Reflections on integration, mentalization, and institutional realization. *Journal of Trauma and Dissociation*, *10*(1), 1–8. https://doi.org/10.1080/15299730802488668

Sullivan, H. S. (1953). *The interpersonal theory of psychiatry*. Norton.

van der Hart, O., Nijenhuis, E. R. S., & Steele, K. (2006). *The haunted self.* W.W. Norton & Co.

Yalom, I. D. (1989). Therapeutic monogamy. In *Love's Executioner and Other Tales of Psychotherapy* (pp. 215–233). Basic Books.

Yaylaci, F. T., Cicchetti, D., Rogosch, F. A., Bulut, O., & Hetzel, S. R. (2017). The interactive effects of child maltreatment and the FK506 binding protein 5 gene (FKBP5) on dissociative symptoms in adolescence. *Development & Psychopathology*, *29*(3), 1105–1117.

Dissociative depression: a psychodynamic view

Vedat Şar

Dissociative depression is a complex and chronic mood disorder characterized by a combination of persistent depressive symptoms and intermittent major depressive episodes. A key feature of dissociative depression is the existence of dissociative symptoms that are linked to prolonged stress experienced during childhood and infancy. Disturbances of sense of self and agency are core indicators of the disorder. Common symptoms include thoughts of guilt and worthlessness, difficulties with concentration and decision-making, changes in appetite and sleep, and suicidal ideation. Additionally, individuals may exhibit various expressive patterns such as borderline phenomena, psychoticism, trauma-related enactments, and attempts at control through somatization, compensatory narcissism, and obsessions. One challenge is that dissociative depression often does not respond well to biological treatments alone. Psychotherapeutic interventions that do not specifically address the dissociative aspect may also be ineffective. The required comprehensive approach involves working through layers of therapeutic reality to reverse the process that led to the status quo. An intensive psychodynamic practice with a renewed theoretical understanding (Dialectical Dynamic Therapy-DDT) is necessary to identify the leverage points that can bring about radical inner change. The aim is to alleviate the barriers that prevent individuals from realizing their full potential assigned in the beginning of life.

Introduction

Depression may occur as a 'common final pathway' of various psychiatric disorders as well as mental processes. Some individuals experience depressive episodes as part of a 'primary' mood disorder previously referred to as 'endogenous' or 'unipolar/bipolar' depression. Such episodes may have a genetic component to its causation where life events are seen as precipitating factors. On the other hand, a significant number of people develop chronic mild depression known as 'dysthymia', or full-blown episodes called 'major' depression in response to ongoing or past stressful life experiences. This type of depression is often termed 'reactive' or 'neurotic' depression, which can also be influenced by temperament, character, personality traits, and/or developmental processes. The latter factors may have contributed to a long-standing maladaptive state, occasionally punctuated by crisis episodes. Although there can be some overlap between these different forms of depression, many individuals experience a 'double' depression, characterized by major depression episodes occurring alongside dysthymic depression.

While standard biological treatments, as proposed by the medical model of psychiatry, often yield positive outcomes for 'primary' depression, there is a subset of depressed patients who show poor response to well-established treatment algorithms. These individuals are considered treatment resistant. *Dissociative depression*, as outlined in one of my previous works (Şar, 2011), comprises a significant proportion of such resistant or persistent cases. It is important to understand the unique characteristics and challenges associated with dissociative depression in order to provide appropriate and effective interventions for these individuals. From an empirical standpoint, dissociative depression is characterized by the presence of significant dissociative symptoms alongside depressive features. Descriptively, it is typically a chronic or dysthymic form of depression. It can manifest as a 'double' depression where major depressive episodes coexist with dysthymic symptoms. Research conducted among women in the general population revealed that the prevalence of current major depression was 10.0% (Şar & Ozturk, 2013). When examining individuals with a comorbidity of lifetime dissociative disorders, the prevalence was found to be 4.1%. This indicates that almost half of the currently depressive patients in the study suffered from dissociative depression.

A closer examination of the individuals with dissociative depression reveals that they have often experienced chronic environmental stress throughout their lives, typically beginning in early childhood (Şar et al., 2013). This stress is frequently associated with various forms of abuse (sexual, emotional, or physical) and neglect (physical or emotional). Other factors such as early parental loss (Şar, 1989), growing up in extreme poverty, or educational deprivation (Şar & Ozturk, 2013) can also have profound mental influences on individuals, potentially contributing to the development of dissociative depression. Additionally, subtle traumatization within seemingly functional families is not uncommon. Last but not least, despite their essential role in healing and treating illnesses, medical services can also inadvertently become sources of trauma for children. For example, extended stays in incubators without sufficient interpersonal contact and repeated painful surgical procedures during childhood may have lifelong psychological effects (Diseth, 2006).

As a general guideline, the consequences of such developmental adversities tend to respond better to psychotherapeutic interventions than solely relying on biological treatments (Nemeroff et al., 2003). However, it is crucial to accurately diagnose dissociative depression and provide specifically tailored psychotherapeutic approaches to effectively address this challenge. For instance, a small controlled longitudinal study focusing on cognitive-behavioral therapy conducted on a group setting with female depressive migrants actually showed a worsening in outcome measures (Renner, 2011), underscoring the need for careful consideration of treatment modalities and their suitability for a particular subtype of a known psychopathology.

While there are various theories exploring the causes of depression along a biopsychosocial spectrum, it is important to establish an operational definition to delve into the psychodynamics of the proposed concept. Here is an initial step towards such a definition: Depression can be understood as a psycho-biological condition that arises during the process of *transitioning between two states of being*. This transition involves adapting to (accommodation) and integrating (assimilation) changes in both one's internal world and external reality. Absolutely, the process of transitioning and the resolution of a traumatic experience can share similarities in some aspects, even if the challenges themselves differ in scope and intensity. These dynamics are closely linked to an 'update' in *self-identity*regardless of age (Şar, 2017a). Dissociative depression, however, can be understood as a state of prolonged and *incomplete* transition. This condition of being 'stuck in transition' is believed to be caused by a traumatic background that interferes with the creative synthesis of one's past and future (Bühler & Heim, 2001). This creates a dynamic vicious cycle, wherein progress toward resolution is possible if supportive interventions from the external world are available. Rituals, whether experienced individually, provided by the community, or facilitated through professional psychotherapy (Van der Hart, 1983), are considered essential in facilitating these transitions.

It is important to acknowledge that embarking on a journey of inner change often entails pain and struggle as one navigates the new and unfamiliar territory. In their theory of positive disintegration, Polish psychiatrist Dabrowski (1964) hypothesized that the common initial integration of a developing individual, primarily based on socialization, does not truly reflect their potential. To break down this initial integration, crises and disintegrations are necessary, typically provided by life experiences. These disintegrations can be seen as the person can achieve developmental solutions in response to the challenges they face. Arising from a developmental potential within individuals, such crises are characterized by intense anxieties and depressions. This perspective suggests that there are expectations regarding one's development, progress, and growth, with both negative and positive possibilities, while safeguarding one's unique 'core' existence (Şar, 2019).

This understanding of dissociative depression highlights the concept of *dividedness*, where different states of mind encompass a range of psychological capacities including cognition, behavior, sensorimotor function, memory, perception, and identity. These 'ego states' (Watkins & Watkins, 1997) are believed by some authors to form the foundation of an individual's development over time (Putnam, 2016). They can lead to both suffering due to a lack of integration and provide opportunities for therapeutic intervention by serving as inner resources. *The pathogenesis and mechanism of dividedness thus play a significant role in making dissociative depression a distinct phenomenon.*

In the following sections of this paper, before delving into the differences between dissociative and non-dissociative depression, it will be important to explore the concept of dividedness from different angles, including its traumatic origins. This exploration will provide a foundation for understanding a proposed model of the mind that is suitable for treating trauma-related conditions, including dissociative depression. Additionally, this paper will address the defense and coping mechanisms employed by individuals seeking *security and safety.* Following the section on dividedness and the model of the mind, the paper will present various aspects of dissociative depression in context of strategies of temperance of a fragmented inner world including a proposal of *dissociative mood disorder.* Finally, the paper will outline a general strategy for healing. This strategy will encompass various therapeutic approaches and interventions aimed at addressing the dividedness and its underlying traumatic antecedents. The conclusion of the paper will tie together the different sections, highlighting their interconnectedness and their contribution to our understanding of dissociative depression. Overall, the extended exploration of dividedness, the proposed model of the mind, the specific sections on aspects of dissociative depression, healing, and conclusion are all integral parts of the comprehensive description and explanation of what dissociative depression entails.

Dividedness

The concept of dividedness extends beyond the explicit term of dissociation and holds significance in psychology, psychiatry, and psychoanalysis. One example is the theory of mind by Hughlings Jackson, a British neurologist from the 19th century. Jackson's theory conceptualized the 'self' as being divided into two aspects: subject and object, or subject consciousness ('I') and object consciousness. According to Jackson, each of them was only half themselves, and in fact, the self was associated with the emergence of 'introspection of consciousness'. In Jackson's framework, the self is considered a manifestation of the highest level of consciousness, characterized by 'doubling' or 'parallel concomitance' (Meares, 1999). This doubling is established through the reflective capacity that allows individuals to become aware of their individual experience, providing them with a sense of inner life.The phenomenon of dissociation paradoxically involves the uncoupling of consciousness, or undoubling of the self.

Jackson claimed that dissociation arises from a disruption of cerebral functions that develop late and appear last in evolutionary terms (Meares, 1999). His contemporary, French physician and psychologist Pierre Janet proposed several mechanisms operating under this umbrella, such as mental automatisms and autonomous complexes, which are organized around a hierarchy of the central nervous system as described by Jackson (Meares, 1999). Interestingly, Jackson understood that automatisms were activated during a dreamy state as a consequence of neuronal *exhaustion*, an assumption Janet also agreed upon (Van der Hart & Horst, 1989). Namely, Janet's energetic view of mental illness assumes that because of an inappropriate reaction pattern, the individual is unable to master a difficult situation and has to make great efforts in the attempt to surmount it. This continual effort produces fatigue or even exhaustion (Bühler & Heim, 2001). Indeed, exhaustion is one of the ways cumulative (complex) psychological traumatization settles and aggravates dissociative depression.

General psychiatric perspective

Pierre Janet is credited with using the word 'desaggregation', which has been translated as 'dissociation' in English (Van der Hart & Horst, 1989). This concept was derived from his understanding of mental health which he associated with one's personal capacity to integrate diverse psychological functions. Janet's approach has been taken as the basis for the definition of dissociation in DSM-5 as a disruption or discontinuity of the usually integrated psychological functions (American Psychiatric Association, 2013).

Interestingly, psychological dividedness was a subject of interest to artists and poets even before it gained attention from clinicians. Examples of this in characters such as Raskolnikov, literally meaning 'divided man', in Dostoevsky's novel, and Dr.Jekyll and Mr.Hyde in Stevenson's work. The love interest among clinician and researchers, however, came across a long-lasting challenge after the end of the 19th century. In fact, the year 1913 was a turning point in psychiatry and academic psychology: it seems to be the time when 'inner world' started to be replaced by 'behaviorism' (Meares, 1999). The focus on alleged 'objective' quality of behavior ('surface') was seen as more suitable for observing and gathering 'evidence' about mental states. Just around this turning point, Swiss psychiatrist Eugen Bleuler (1911/1950) made another major step when he utilized the concept of dividedness to replace Kraepelin's dementia praecox with 'schizo-phrenia' (split-mind). This shift led to the redundancy of a separate dissociative disorder category, and dissociation entered into silence within mainstream psychiatry for more than half a century.

Nevertheless, broader perspectives on the multiplicity of the psyche were still maintained as seen in an other Swiss psychiatrist Carl Gustav Jung's theory of archetypes. Unlike among clinicians and researchers, interest in and expressions about dissociation has subtly but successfully continued through the artistic world as well (e.g., movies, literature, popular music). The latter track was not without complications that dissociation was assumed to be merely a subject of art rather than science by sceptikers. They misinterpreted artwork or used uninformed portrayals of dissociative disorders instead of recognizing the clinical experience. Among psychoanalysts, the British school of object relationship was the movement that addressed 'part-object' representations and relationships; i.e., mental fragmentation related to developmental stress. Austrian-American psychoanalyst Heinz Kohut's (1971) subsequent 'self-psychology' was focused on 'self-objects' rather than part-objects; i.e., damaged or poorly shaped boundaries between the internal and external world, with a weak self prone to fragmentation (experienced as depersonalization/derealization) as a consequence of deficient emotional support early in life. Unfortunately, such movements never referred to dissociation as a concept explicitly, an attitude that has continued among many streams of psychotherapy until the present time.

While Bleuler's movement broadened the concept of a chronic, devastating mental illness for decades toward a more optimistic perspective including psychogenesis, the initiation of 'lithium carbonate' by the Australian psychiatrist John Cade (1949) as a treatment for mania forced a *narrower* definition of schizophrenia for pragmatic reasons: prior to the availability of effective mood stabilizers like lithium, many individuals with mood disorders were misdiagnosed as having schizophrenia due to overlapping symptoms. The subsequent advancements in biological psychiatry, supported by technological developments, and increased access to psychotherapy in mainstream psychiatry for patients with relatively severe conditions through the utilization of 'parameters' rather than staying in the 'therapeutic absence'. These developments ushered in a neo-Kraepelinian era regarding the so called 'schizo-phrenic' disorder.

It was exactly the period when dissociative disorders started to return to the scene to fill the gap that was tried to be covered by reawakening older concepts such as French physician Pierre Briquet's syndrome ('hysteria'). The latter became the somatization disorder in the subsequent DSM-III (American Psychiatric Association, 1980) which hardly represented the whole spectrum of dissociative phenomena or even the older concept of 'hysteria'. In fact, this strictly medical model of psychiatric disorders was a harsh response to the psychodynamic tradition, which led to vague boundaries between entities. The aim was to introduce precise diagnostic criteria to the field and to conduct descriptive and statistical research as valid for other branches of medicine (Purtell et al., 1951).

Nosological fragmentation

The medical model of psychiatry is based on diagnoses of phenomenologically defined syndromes referred to as disorders. Treatment algorithms designed to target psychiatric disorders try to rely on evidence derived from empirical research as much as possible. However, studies conducted on pure diagnostic populations hardly reflect the real clinical situation in mental health, because *co-morbidity* is almost the rule rather than the exception in psychiatry (Sar & Ross, 2006). The principle of Occam's razor paradoxically contributes to such nosological fragmentation; i.e., excessive comorbidity. For example, dissociative (formerly hysterical) psychosis, an officially neglected but clinically living entity, turns into an oxymoron because psychosis and dissociation belong to separate domains of psychopathology. In this sense, psychiatric research has lagged behind clinical practice and experience for decades (Şar, 2022c).

In fact, high levels of co-morbidity for many psychiatric disorders cannot be simply an artifact of imprecise diagnostic criteria; rather, they must reflect a multifactorial etiology of psychiatric disorders and a need for multimodal treatment strategies (Ross, 2000). Namely, co-morbidity in psychiatry is not something that all patients have in common. It is linked to certain risk factors. Accumulating research demonstrates that a history of traumatic childhood is associated with several mental health conditions in adulthood that are partly independent of the predominant diagnosis. One of them is a high degree of lifetime and current general psychiatric co-morbidity. Thus, unlike for biologically based psychiatric disorders, in traumatized populations, the medical model usually leads to nosological fragmentation, which interferes with the standards of treatment planning within the scope of mainstream psychiatry.

Dissociation has been found to accompany various psychiatric conditions, as demonstrated in a meta-analysis (Lyssenko et al., 2018). This has led to conceptualization of dissociation, depersonalization and derealization in particular, as a transdiagnostic symptom that may be relevant across various forms of psychopathology (e.g., Ellickson-Larew et al., 2020; Lanius et al., 2018; Lynn et al., 2022; Sommer et al., 2021). Not only childhood trauma, but dissociation also predicts a higher frequency of psychiatric comorbidity and vice versa. This overlap raises questions about the role of dissociation in relationships between concurrent psychiatric entities.

Interaction of entities

Indeed, considering dissociative depression as a unitary process rather than a construct based solely on comorbidity raises the question of the mechanisms underlying such interaction.The 'duality (interaction) model' (Sar et al., 2010) proposed for such conditions suggests that concurrent or subsequent psychopathologies may interact with (trigger or emerge as a complication of) each other, even if they are qualitatively distinct. Lynn et al. (2022) propose that dissociation and dissociative disorders can be understood as failures of normally adaptive systems and functions. They suggest several potentially interactive variables including sleep disturbances, impaired self-regulation and inhibition of negative cognitions and affects, hyperassociation and set shifts, and deficits in reality testing, source attributions, and metacognition.

Childhood trauma is generally associated with higher levels of dissociation in adult PTSD (Evren et al., 2011). A study on an adolescent population highlights the relationship between age of trauma onset, dissociation, and depression (Kyte et al., 2023). It found that there was a significant interaction between the age of trauma onset and the severity of dissociation in predicting depression. Specifically, the study found that the association between dissociation and depression was stronger for participants who experienced trauma at an older age, suggesting a more negative impact for those exposed to trauma later in adolescence. Additionally, a general interaction between dissociation and age at intake was observed, predicting internalizing problems. The association between dissociation and internalizing problems was stronger for older participants compared to younger participants. This suggests that the relationship between dissociation and internalizing problems may be more pronounced in older adolescents, potentially indicating a greater vulnerability to maladaptation following later experiences of trauma (Kyte et al., 2023).

In another study, depersonalization/derealization symptoms were found to have strong predictive power for internalizing psychopathology, even when controlling for neuroticism (Ellickson-Larew et al., 2020). The authors proposed that depersonalization and derealization symptoms are particularly relevant to depression due to their association with sleep alterations and to panic due to a combination of physiological and cognitive factors (Soffer-Dudek, 2014). Additionally, absorption was identified as a dissociative factor specifically relevant to obsessive-compulsive disorder (OCD) due to its association with poor confidence in reality monitoring. Dissociative amnesia was also hypothesized to interact with OCD and depressive symptoms in different ways (Ellickson-Larew et al., 2020).

Sommer et al. (2021) indicated that dissociation was associated with self-harm and suicide attempts, especially among individuals with BPD. However, this association was suggested to be driven in part by a third variable, such as other symptoms of PTSD or BPD Foote et al. (2008) found significant associations between several diagnoses (dissociative disorder; BPD; PTSD; alcohol abuse/dependence) and multiple suicide attempter status. However, when these diagnoses were entered in a logistic regression, a highly significant association remained only for dissociative disorder diagnosis.

The review conducted by Lanius et al. (2018) supports the notion of emotional overmodulation as a model underlying dissociative experiences across various disorders. This model of dissociation served as the foundation for the inclusion of the dissociative subtype of PTSD in DSM-5. The overmodulation model suggests that dissociation involves excessive regulation of emotions. However, it is important to note that dissociation is a bimodal mechanism that can also manifest in 'positive' symptoms related to undermodulation (Van der Hart et al., 2006). In two studies conducted by Şar et al. (2001, 2007) on patients with chronic dissociative disorders, hypoperfusion (or hypoactivity) was observed in the orbitofrontal region during resting state. This finding indicates the possibility of disinhibition rather than overmodulation as a contributing factor to dissociative symptoms.

In fact, different aspects of dissociation, such as depersonalization-derealization, amnesia, absorption, obsessions, and internalizing psychopathology, seem to represent various 'off' modes where certain mental processes are suppressed or inhibited. These 'off' modes can lead to a sense of detachment, disconnection, and a blurring of reality. On the other hand, features like disinhibition, enactments, and borderline phenomena may represent 'on' modes, where certain mental processes are heightened or activated. The interaction between these 'on' and 'off' modes can contribute to the complex presentation of dissociative depression.

Developmental aspects of dividedness

In the stream of psychoanalysis in the 20th century, the concept of dividedness was adopted by the so-called object-relation theorists. They also emphasized that the structure of the psyche is shaped by actual human experience rather than solely by internal conflicts with instinctual drives. Fairbairn's (1952) concept of 'schizoid' individual highlighted the presence of mental 'dividedness' resulting from groups of traumatic memories that become separated or 'split-off' from the conscious 'central ego'. This fragmentation led to a withdrawal from interpersonal interactions and a preoccupation with inner reality. These individuals displayed characteristics such as isolation, detachment, and a sense of omnipotence. Fairbairn's ideas on the development of splitting as a defense mechanism can be seen as relevant in understanding the concept of dissociation today.

The 'splitting defense' allows the child to hate the rejecting object and to love the exciting object. Consequently, the individual cannot develop 'object constancy' which is the ability to see a person's goodness, even when they are being rejected or frustrated by that person. According to Fairbairn, the child has also to dissociate memories of themselves during the interpersonally rejecting interactions into the 'antilibidinal ego'. These memories of the child's self which are loaded with fear, defeat, shame and humiliation, cannot be tolerated consciously too. Thus, not only the object but the subject is also divided. Fairbairn described this shift as one ego state represses another ego state that the person experiences the world through a 'multiplicity of egos'. This description fits today's dissociative disorders of identity very well.

Indeed, North American psychoanalyst Sullivan (1953) described three basic ways we see ourselves, which he called the 'bad-me', the 'good-me', and the 'not-me'. The 'bad-me' consists of the aspects of the self that one considers negative and therefore hides from others, and possibly even the self. Anxiety can result from recognizing the bad part of ourselves, for example, when remembering an embarrassing moment or experiencing guilt from a past action. The 'good-me' is all that seems positive and all that we like about ourselves. This is the part we share with the world because it produces no anxiety. The 'not-me' part represents the aspects of ourselves that are so anxiety-provoking that we reject them as a part of us. The 'not-me' is hidden from awareness.

Underlining earliest origins of dividedness (Şar, 2020), British psychoanalyst Melanie Klein (1987) suggested that pre-verbal anxiety in infancy catalyzed the formation of the splitting. She proposed paranoid-schizoid and depressive *positions*, which should become the predominant modes of mind in the first year of life. This theory assumes that these positions may become active from time to time throughout one's entire life. In the context of dissociative depression, it can be argued that it aligns more with the paranoid-schizoid position. Namely, depressive position requires a shift toward generalization of the experiences to the entire 'psyche'; i.e., ownership of them by all aspects of the individual rather than a 'split' or 'mosaic' field. Such generalizations, however, require a new balance within oneself between the internal and external worlds.

Splitting as a defense was adopted as the main mechanism of borderline personality disorder (BPD) by the Chilean-North American psychoanalyst Otto Kernberg (1967), later. Indeed, devaluation and idealization experiences are among main diagnostic criteria of BPD in DSM-5 (American Psychiatric Association, 2013). Although splitting and dissociation are kept traditionally and theoretically separate as horizontal and vertical divisions, in fact, there is no clinical evidence showing that they are different mechanisms. Thus, Australian psychiatrist Meares (2012) proposes that BPD is itself a dissociative disorder. Indeed, there is large descriptive overlap between BPD (Sar et al., 2003, 2006, 2014a; Şar, 2017a, 2017b) and dissociative disorders whereas the role of childhood abuse and neglect is also obvious in BPD (Herman et al., 1989).

Attachment, loss, and detachment

Arieti and Bemporad (1980) emphasized the role of a *dominant other* in the lives of individuals experiencing depression. This dominant other can be a person, institution, idea, or any significant aspect of one's life that holds great importance and meaning. When a concrete or imagined loss occurs, such as the death of a loved one, the end of a significant relationship, or the failure of an important goal, it can lead to profound feelings of grief, sadness, and despair. In some cases, the loss of this dominant other leaves a void that cannot be easily replaced or fulfilled by any substitute, resulting in a lack of a backup plan (a viable B-plan). Nevertheless, this pattern corresponds to a problematic attachment style among other factors.

With its background in childhood trauma, predisposition to dissociative depression is particularly related to early life events which are experienced as a loss.Different than the classical theory of mourning, Bowlby (1980) termed a young child's response to the loss of his mother-figure as the phase of 'detachment'. This phase is regularly seen whenever a child between the ages of about six months and three years has spent a week or more without his mother's or a specially assigned substitute's care. Attachment behavior is almost completely absent when he first meets his mother again. When the loved figure is believed to be temporarily absent the response is one of anxiety, when he or she appears to be permanently absent it is one of pain and mourning.Because of the persistent and insatiable nature of the yearning for the lost figure, pain is inevitable. A sense of guilt and a fear of retaliation prevail alongside *anger and hatred*. Even in healthy mourning, a person's anger is often directed towards the person lost, though it may equally often be directed towards other persons, including the self.

Bowlby's (1980) hypothesis suggests that the main mechanism of defense after loss is *not* identification with the lossed object. He mentioned the emergence of two *principal systems* or the 'two selves' in the aftermath of a significant loss. The first system, which governs everyday life, operates under the assumption that the lost attachment figure is no longer accessible, leading the individual to become self-sufficient. This system is conscious and readily accessible (Bowlby, 1962). The other system is, however, segregated and unconscious. It represents the attachment desires, thoughts, feelings, and memories associated with the lost figure. This system carries some missing elements such as personal and autobiographical memories. The deactivated system with marginal access to consciousness is organized on the assumption that the mother is still accessible and that, somehow, she can either be recovered in this world or the next. Evidence of this system's existence is fragmentary and may only emerge intermittently. This process of defensive exclusion remains active either because the caregiver disconfirms the perception of the child or because the child wants to protect the internal image of the caregiver. Freud (1927) applied the term 'split in the ego' for this condition.Following this line of thought, Duschinsky and White (2019) consider loss as a traumatic situation that evokes a type of defense what Fairbairn and Melanie Klein understand as splitting (dividing).

More specifically, Liotti (1999) considers dissociation as spontaneous activation of the attachment and defense systems. Indeed, the link between insecure attachment and dissociative disorders (Barach, 1991; Liotti, 1992; Lyons-Ruth et al., 2006), as well as BPD is well established. Bowlby (1988) stated that infants seek proximity to an identified attachment figure in situations of perceived distress or alarm for the purpose of survival. Indeed, dissociative self states are related to disorganized attachment (Blizard, 2003). Attachment disorganization involves the disaggregated representations of the self and the caregiver in infants mind (Main, 1991). Disorganized-disoriented (D) attachment (Main & Solomon, 1986) is composed of sequential or simultaneous displays of contradictory attachment patterns. Attachment perspective of dissociation explains the development of multiple and conflictual representations of the self-with-others (Schimmenti, 2022).

Dividedness and interpersonal space

Sullivan (1953) emphasized that personality cannot be isolated from the interpersonal relationships in which a person lives. Even the field of personality disorders is currently moving toward 'interpersonal relationship disorders' (Wright et al., 2022). Among object-relations theorists, Guntrip (1969) worked extensively with patients who were detached and socially withdrawn. These individuals who were called 'schizoid' at this period, were unable to form meaningful human relations. They were characterized by introversion, self-sufficiency, a sense of superiority, and loneliness. Guntrip considered the self as the fundamental psychological capacity which is to be grown through psychotherapy. In this way, the alienated, withdrawn self was given an opportunity for development in a relationship to be finally put in touch with other persons and objects.

However, for a long time, those patients were considered as having 'weak ego' (pre-psychotic or 'borderline' in a general sense; i.e., between psychosis and neurosis) that in-depth psychotherapy including psychoanalytic approaches was considered contra-indicated for these individuals due to concerns about psychotic decompensation because of interpersonal anxiety ('need-fear dilemma', Burnham et al., 1969) and fragile boundaries. In fact, schizotypal and dissociative mechanisms are qualitatively different (Bowlby, 1980) including their neurobiology and response to drug treatment, and in contrast to the former beliefs, the latter group benefits from and even needs intensive psychotherapy. Thus, *it is one of the significant mis-assumptions of psychiatry and psychoanalysis to assign 'dividedness' to 'schizo'-phrenia instead of (dissociative) depression.*

Being interested in psychotherapy of schizophrenic disorder, loneliness was a key feature of Sullivan's (1953) theory. He made the first mention of the 'significant other' in the literatüre. Sullivan believed that anxiety existed primarily in the context of social interactions.He introduced concepts such as 'selective inattention' and 'personifications' as mechanisms through which individuals alleviate social anxiety. Selective inattention refers to the tendency to selectively focus on certain aspects of the social environment while ignoring others. This selective attention helps individuals manage their anxiety by avoiding certain social cues or situations that may be anxiety-provoking. Personifications, on the other hand, are mental images or representations of oneself and others that are shaped by social interactions and selective attention. They serve as a way for individuals to understand themselves and the world around them. Defense mechanisms reduce anxiety, but they can also cause a misperception of reality.

Parental responses lead to patterns of attachment as internal working models (IWM's) which guide the individual's feelings, thoughts, and expectations in later relationships. The developmental segregated mental states in childhood, epitomizing the presence of conflicting and incompatible sets within the IWM, represents a royal road to dissociation (Schimmenti, 2022). Liotti (2006) suggested that the shifts among the multiple IWMs of developmentally traumatized individuals correspond to the drama triangle elaborated by Karpman (1968); i.e., the interactions between the main characters oscillate between the roles of the *benevolent rescuer, the malevolent persecutor, and the helpless victim*. Interpersonal psychoanalysis (Blizard & Bluhm, 1994; Howell, 2003) underlines the role of dissociation even in BPD criteria in the context of Karpman's triangle. For example, idealization and devaluation represent the perspectives of the victim and abuser, respectively. Therapeutic interventions aimed at disavowal of the 'attachment to the perpetrator', both inside the internal world and in external reality, are necessary to eliminate such destructive bonds. Disavowal of the attachment to the perpetrator, however, may require some type of trauma resolution too (Brown & Elliott, 2016).

The link between attachment theory and the drama triangle is further represented in the model of *attachment to the perpetrator and shift of locus of control* (Ross, 1997, 2000) which allows the victim to achieve a subjective sense of control in the abusive condition. Namely, even in an abusive and/or neglectful environment, the child must develop attachment to the caretaker, whereas the modules of the mind that maintain attachment behavior are disconnected from those taking in the traumatic information from the outside world. Paradoxically, the child only feels safe when the abusive 'caretaker' (the perpetrator) is nearby. The helpless child continues to identify with the aggressor and shifts locus of control inside his or her personality. The victim's rationalizations of the abuser's behavior as his or her own fault reinforce the shift in locus of control. This problem of attachment to the perpetrator can be acted out throughout life. However, while the illusion of control created in the child's mind is developmentally protective, it must be broken in adulthood in the face of outside reality.

Liotti's (2006) theory of dissociation has four implications which are closely related to this situation: (1) pathological dissociation should be viewed as a primarily intersubjective reality hindering the integrative processes of consciousness, rather than as an intrapsychic defense against mental pain; (2) early defenses against attachment-related dissociation are based on interpersonal controlling strategies that inhibit the attachment system; (3) dissociative symptoms emerge as a consequence of the collapse of these defensive strategies in the face of events that powerfully activate the attachment system; (4) psychotherapy of pathological dissociation should be a phase-oriented process focused primarily on achieving attachment security, and only secondarily on trauma work.

The context

Winnicott (1973) claimed the need for a 'holding environment' for the healthy development of the child, which he extended to schools and the community. With its trauma-related origin, family psychopathology is an essential part of the psychopathogenesis of dissociative depression. Dysfunctional communication styles of families (e.g., pseudomutuality, marital schism, schizophrenogenic mother, double bind, rubber fence) which were once proposed to be a factor in the psychogenesis of schizophrenia, are in fact descriptive of dissociative patients' families (Spiegel, 1986). Such dysfunctionalities threaten the unity of mind from early on in life and settle negative cognitive-schemas of guilt and shame (Ross, 1997).

Boundaries: omissions and intrusions

Major forms of childhood trauma may be divided into omission (neglect) and intrusion (abuse) types. Another division may be between bodily (sexual and/or physical abuse and neglect) and cognitive-emotional (emotional abuse and neglect) types of adversities which may initiate different coping mechanisms. While omission and intrusion both refer to a threat to personal and interpersonal boundaries in different ways, both bodily and cognitive-emotional maltreatment constitutes a threat to self-control (i.e., self-regulation) of one's internal (i.e., mind and emotions) and external (i.e., body and behavior) worlds. Disturbances of boundary and self-control are central consequences of cumulative traumatization that must be monitored and dealt with throughout every treatment until recovery.

In a college population study (Şar et al., 2017), intrusion types of childhood trauma led to a diagnosis of BPD rather than a dissociative disorder. The latter was predicted by childhood emotional neglect and minimization of trauma. In this college study (Şar et al., 2017), as an internally experienced identity disturbance, *mental intrusions from within* were predicted by denial or minimization of trauma history (i.e., idealization of the perpetrator-caretaker). The latter phenomenon seems to represent the *diminished awareness of trauma* (betrayal by others adopted by oneself defensively) as the origin of a *disturbed sense of self and agency.*

In fact, BPD/DID phenomena and Other Specified Dissociative Disorders (OSDD) represent two core syndromes with either an undermodulated (on mode) or overmodulated (off mode) quality. As such, OSDD is a 'partial' syndrome that does not show the entire symptom set of the dissociation spectrum.Apparently, rather than DID, OSDD seems to have played the predominant role in prediction of dissociative disorders by emotional neglect (omission type of trauma) because the severity of dissociation is already correlated with number of concurrent BPD features.

In the same college population study (Şar et al., 2017), omission types of childhood trauma tended to result in *bodily self-detachment* (depersonalization) and detachment from *external reality* (derealization), both of which have been shown to be significant predictors of self-mutilation (Şar, Alioğlu, & Akyüz, 2017; Şar, Alioğlu, Akyüz, Tayakısı, et al., 2017). Bodily self-detachment was predicted by physical and emotional neglect but not by any type of abuse, albeit the latter may have been underreported due to *denial (minimization) or amnesia.* Indeed, this pattern of disowning the body (Ataria, 2016) was associated with dissociative amnesia. In fact, omission does not exclude co-presence of intrusion type of trauma but the difference seems to be in the ways of coping styles. Namely, the difference is observed in multivariate statistical analysis as an advantage of artificial separation of the main effects. Although the prevalence of abuse might be lower in a college population compared to a clinical one as a limitation, it is unlikely that this possibility skewed the findings about these associations as reported in a previous paper derived from the same study population (Şar et al., 2006).

In a study conducted on patients with schizophrenic disorder, while emotional neglect was equally common among patients with and without elevated dissociation scores, intrusion type of childhood trauma and BPD features seemed to be associated with further *nosological fragmentation; i.e., higher general psychiatric comorbidity* including mood disorders (Sar et al., 2010). In an other study on a college population, however, the combination of emotional neglect and OP/OC (Şar & Türk-Kurtça, 2021) was a predictor of *dissociative depression*. The latter was related to ambivalence in interpersonal relationships, as represented by preoccupied and fearful types of attachment as further predictors.A recent study on a college population suggested that being male, being a single child, having depression, having psychotic-like experiences, lower family functioning, and lower psychological resilience were independently associated with childhood OP/OC experiences (Zhang et al., 2023). Interestingly, OP/OC experiences were associated with depression in only females, and associated with anxiety in only males.

The combination of overprotection-overcontrol (OP/OC) (intrusion presented as love and care or normative caretaking) with emotional neglect represents a double-bind in the relationship with a caretaker. This is a type of 'betrayal' (Freyd, 1994), a phenomenon that turns an experience into trauma by disrupting the subject's perception of reality (Şar et al., 2021). Typically, these parents are oppressive-restrictive and prone to boundary violations. Different than verbal emotional abuse, the relatively invisible quality of this type of maltreatment creates both anger and guilt which can not be validated through expressing outside. Such interpersonal interference may have started 'very early' (Şar, 2020) in life, affecting the developmental period of mirroring by the primary caretaker (Fonagy et al., 2002).

Aggressive-rejecting-conflictual and narcissistic-identificatory-fusionary types of object relationships seem to have different consequences in terms of the experience of belonging to a larger context or greater whole, whether this is family, community, or any conception of what that wider context might look like or comprise (Battegay, 1977). Coping with abuse and neglect seems to lead to different types of 'identification with the aggressor'. While abuse would more readily lead to *projective identification* (close to BPD), emotional neglect boosts *introjective identification* (close to DID). When considering artificially as a separate pathway, introjective identification is indeed more close to DID than BPD, because it has a focus'inside' of the patient. Representing two faces of the same coin, dissociative people divide themselves in order to maintain object-relatedness (off-mode), individuals with BPD, however, divide the external world to maintain their unity (on-mode) (Richard Loewenstein, workshop, paraphrased from J.G. Armstrong, 1989, Chicago, 2019).

Nevertheless, one should not forget that BPD and dissociative disorders overlap to a large extent (Şar et al., 2006). Thus, these separate pathways on inner dynamics as well as omission and intrusion type of traumatization may occur in the same person with both diagnoses concurrently. Introjective and projective identifications play a crucial role in this overlap and co-occurrence. These mechanisms, being the opposite of each other, oscillate, co-occur, and even manifest bilaterally within the same individuals including in the therapeutic relationship.

Oppression, submission, and uprising

A common aspect of dysfunctional families is damaged boundaries, which constitute initial examples of similar experiences in the life of the affected individuals. These 'apparently normal' or quasi-ordinary (in fact, dissociative) families are characterized by affect dysregulation, leading to angry outbursts in abusive members with resulting chronic traumatization of others, in particular, their offspring. Members of this type of family report childhood traumata more frequently than control group, suggesting trans-generational transmission of trauma-related psychopathology (Öztürk & Şar, 2005).

Subtle or overt oppression (both individual and societal) is a powerful factor in the genesis of dissociation (Şar & Ozturk, 2013).A type of family nurturing 'complaisant overadjustment' (Öztürk, 1976; Öztürk & Gögüs, 1973; Öztürk & Öztürk, 1981) in their younger members is of particular importance for dissociative depression as it represents a type of 'enslaving'. Complaisant overadjustment is defined as an enduring attitude aimed at pleasing others despite being overburdened by duties (e.g., being in the service of family members; self-sacrifice for others' interests). This attitude usually serves to maintain a given role in the family supposed to be for the subject's own good. The potential patient tries to please the family members by being 'perfect' in this role. This submissive attitude is usually a consequence of the pattern of attachment to the perpetrator.

Possibly related to the given family role as well, research on children and adults with somatic dissociation (conversion) symptoms suggests the importance of early birth order as a risk factor (Öztürk, 1976; Sar & Sar, 1991). Namely, German family therapist Helm Stierlin (1982) underlined the concept of delegating members in a family context which has implications for intergenerational transmission of trauma and promotion of an expanded sociological self (e.g., older child as a replacement of the father or mother).For example, ambitious expectations such as 'perfect child' as a narcissistic proximity are common in middle class families which is not only overwhelming to the offspring but also interfere with the development of a 'true self'.

Women are still in a disadvantageous position in many cultures or subcultures in terms of restrictions on self-expression. Arranged marriages at a young age, limited access to education, and quasi-religious gender-related oppression are examples of such restrictions. Age-related hierarchy within extended families can create unhealthy dynamics, such as enmeshment and violations of boundaries. Such intrusions may happen in the form of chronic and repetitive *interference ('müdahele')* from family members (Karaaslan et al., 2004) particularly in daily activities can have a detrimental effect on a woman's mental health. This form of control and intrusion can be emotionally abusive, with criticism and belittling being used as means of exerting power and dominance over the woman.

Rising prevalence of dissociative experiences (having a mean DES score equal to 30 or above) from 8.9% to 31.8% among young adults over a 25-year interval (Şar & Türk-Kurtça, 2021; Yargic et al., 1995) highlight the impact of psychosocial influences on the emergence of psychopathology which is a unique finding not observed in other psychiatric disorders. Dividedness of societal scope is widespread in this era of post-globalism (e.g., abrupt migration of large masses, rising economic inequalities, uprising of disadvantaged societal layers alongside the increasing tendency, ability, and willingness to express oneself co-present with oppressive practices) which is a fertile ground for individual dissociation.Oppression at a societal level can shape collective cognitions leading individuals either to submit to or, alternatively, to an anarchic response who should, in fact, vote for their own emancipation (Şar & Ozturk, 2013). These observations underline the importance of social factors on emergence of dissociative depression possibly influencing its prevalence in the community. The possibility of heightened self-awareness, readiness to express internal experiences, and reduced stigma around mental health should also be taken into account while examining and interpreting the rising prevalence data on self-reported dissociation.

The temperance

The capacity of abrupt changes in the psychological condition of dissociative patients led the author to hypothesize a structure of mind which can be crucial in further empirical research too. This model assumes that the self-system and internal moderation of adaptive functions constitute distinct domains although they may interact. Quick changes in psychiatric conditions are hypothesized to represent on and off switchings of the internal moderation system.

The tripartite self-system

The theory of 'functional dissociation of the self' (Sar & Öztürk, 2007) proposes that as individuals develop, there is a natural separation between the *sociological self* and the *psychological self* as they adapt and adjust to the external world. Being an oxymoron itself like Kohut's concept of self-object, the sociological self is not a societal but rather an individual entity. Basically, and unique to this theory, the sociological self takes on the role of protecting the psychological self from traumatic stressors and acts as an interface between the internal world and external reality. The psychological self, however, remains hidden and acts as an adviser while 'the self in the relation with others' (Kierkegaard, 1849/1983) is represented by the sociological self to defensively prevent destruction due to potential challenges of the external world. The psychological self, by definition, is hypothesized to be a unitary entity, while the sociological self serves as an interface with the external world and carries IWMs with interpersonal components.

This understanding assumes developmentally a *two-stage development of mental fragmentation*. The detachment of the sociological and psychological selves from each other is the primary dissociation rather than the emergence of alternate personality formations. Similarly, Farina et al. (2019) propose that the 'disintegrative' process should be considered the disruption mechanism whereas the dissociative process consists of the functional reorganization of mind into enduring parallel-distinct structures (Şar et al., 2017). Apparently, dysintegration starts very early in context of disorganized attachment while emergence of alternate personality states is the consequence of segregation as a defense against dysintegration (Schimmenti, 2022).

The sociological and psychological selves, which are inherent to normal psychological development, are not explicitly discernible at a clinical level. Instead, it is the traumatic self, emerging as a result of traumatic experiences, that presents itself through various clinical phenomena and seeks therapeutic help. In fact, the traumatic self separates from the psychological self in order to maintain its unity and protect it from the impact of trauma.Being closely connected to the fragmented sociological self, alternate personality states can have various relationships with the traumatic self and the internal moderator, but they are not permanent parts of them.The enduring symptomatology, including dissociative depression, seems to be a derivative (i.e., resistance) of the traumatic self. The sociological and psychological selves, however, play a role in the overall process, operating as the context in which this dynamics unfold.

When there is suboptimal psychological development, the balance between the sociological self and the psychological self can be disrupted. The sociological self, lacking internal nurturance, becomes detached from the psychological self, leading to its enlargement and fragmentation. Meanwhile, the psychological self remains intact, releasing the traumatic self as a separate entity. This traumatic self carries the burden of traumatic experiences and seeks assistance through symptomatic manifestations in a clinical context. It also serves to prevent the sociological self from inadvertently causing harm to the psychological self.However, there can be a subsequent adoption of the traumatic self by the sociological self, which hinders the processing of its resistances and inhibits the integration of the self. To address these challenges, it is essential to facilitate the processing of traumatic material within the context of the psychological self that can confront and navigate reality with inner strength.

To facilitate healing and integration, it is necessary for the traumatic self to return to its original place within the psychological self. However, this process requires effectively managing the resistances associated with the traumatic self. These resistances can manifest as traumatic obsessions, disruptions in interpersonal mutuality (such as diminished cooperation in psychotherapy), and depressive symptoms (Öztürk & Şar, 2016). Thus, depression can be viewed as one of the resistances of the traumatic self. The most malignant and non-adaptive behavioral outcome may be an unusually enlarged traumatic self that 'possesses' the sociological self rather than being controlled by the latter.

An expanded sociological self, disconnected from the unitary, authentic, and compassionate psychological self of an individual (Sar & Öztürk, 2007) can lead to what is referred to as a 'false self disorder' (Winnicott, 1973) or an 'as if personality' (Deutsch, 1934). In such circumstances, the person may present a facade or adaptive persona to conform to external demands, but it does not genuinely represent their inner identity. Instead, the individual becomes like a chameleon, altering their personality to please others or gain social and professional advantages. This transformation occurswhen an 'outside-directed' (Battegay, 1977; Riesman, 1950) individual becomes an 'apparatchik'with an overadapted, *reversible personality* (Sar & Öztürk, 2007; Şar & Ozturk, 2013). This state can be seen as a 'self-imposed' form of an identity disturbance, where the individual willingly engages in a prolonged and intense effort to mold themselves according to external expectations or perceived benefits. This phenomenon aligns with the concept of the 'identity disturbance due to prolonged and intense coercive persuation' as described in DSM-5 (American Psychiatric Association, 2013).

The internal moderator

The concept of internal moderation is a fundamental aspect of understanding the regulation of mental processes and psychological functioning within an individual. It proposes that there exists a central control mechanism, the internal moderator, that plays a crucial role in governing the expression and perception of various mental content, including emotions, behaviors, memories, and sensori-motor functions. The internal moderator acts as an 'on and off switch', allowing or restricting the functioning of these mental processes based on the current context and needs of the individual. Indeed, each of these two modes do not exist as binary, all-or-nothing options. Instead, they operate along a spectrum of severity, allowing for various degrees of engagement or restriction. A wider discrepancy between the two modes ('dissonance') refers to relatively increased tension in the internal moderation system.

The internal moderator is also responsible for associating time, space, and person (interpersonal bond) with different psychological functions alongside allocating energy to these functions. This governance likely refers to the process of evaluating and regulating the alignment or congruence ('match-mismatch') between various psychological factors both internally and in context of interacting with others. This process of evaluation and regulation also contributes to the establishment of interpersonal mutuality ('resonance'), where the individual's experiences and responses are aligned with those of others and other situational needs. When functioning optimally, the internal moderator fosters a harmonious relationship between different elements of the self and the external world, leading to a more stable and integrated sense of self and improved psychological functioning. It allows for effective emotional regulation, cognitive flexibility, and adaptive behaviors in various situations.

A trans-diagnostic concept encompassing both 'normal' functioning and pathological conditions, internal moderator is the center of the personal *temperance and fine-tuning*.It is seen as a neutral function, comparable to a system of artificial intelligence as it impartially regulates mental processes based on the individual's needs and the context. Additionally, the internal moderator is not a static entity but may continue to mature and develop through 'deep learning', meaning that it can adapt and refine its functioning based on experiences and feedback. From a biological perspective, the internal moderator may have underlying neurological and physiological mechanisms that govern its functioning. While the self-system, which includes a person's sense of identity and self-concept, may have more psychological and cognitive aspects, the internal moderator's biological underpinnings may be of interest to the medical model of psychiatry and potential biological treatment approaches.

The unique aspect of this theory is its proposition that the internal moderation function is *distinct* from the self-system. However, despite their separation, imbalances within the self-system may affect the accuracy and effectiveness of internal moderation, and vice versa. The presence of internal and external security measures between hiddenness and expression such as defenses and coping mechanisms further stretches the functional capacity of the internal moderator, leading to difficulties in managing the tension between 'on' and 'off' states (Şar, 2023b).The internal moderator's functional elasticity refers to its ability to adapt and manage changing loads and demands through managing the tension between on and off states.

In dissociative depression and other dissociative conditions, the internal moderator is often 'overwhelmed' due to the imbalance within the tripartite self-system. Restoring the overwhelmed internal moderator to a state of balance is essential for individuals to return to daily functioning and improve their psychological well-being. Thus, the internal moderator has the potential for recovery and its loss of function is reversible in dissociative depression and other post-traumatic conditions. Importantly, the impairment of the internal moderator in conditions like schizophrenia and bipolar disorder is more profound and may require additional and different treatment approaches. While psychotherapeutic interventions can still be beneficial, the level of impairment may necessitate medical and pharmacological interventions as well.

The theory of functional dissociation of self (Sar & Öztürk, 2007) acknowledges that emotions are not solely experienced by an overarching and integrated self but can be distributed across the different entities of the individual's mind. This view is especially relevant for individuals with dissociative disorders, where the sense of self may be fragmented.The internal moderator is depicted as a carrier of emotions, delivering them to different entities within the self-system without claiming ownership, similar to a 'forklift'. When the internal moderator is functionally impaired, affect dysregulation can occur, which is best addressed through psychotherapy utilizing the tripartite self-system rather than relying solely on pharmacological interventions like mood stabilizers.

Internal moderation is not a meta-psychological concept but a psychobiological capacity that can be measured in a standard fashion (Ayas et al., 2023): the Internal Moderation Questionnaire (IMQ). As such, the concept of internal moderation holds relevance beyond dissociative depression and applies to general psychiatry as well including psychodynamic psychotherapy research, psychopharmacological industry, and neuroscience. Last but not least, this new paradigm is capable to inspire studies on artificial intelligence and behavioral economics such as consumer behavior and financial decision-making (Kahneman, 2011).

Layers of reality

The exploration of multiple perspectives of reality has been a recurring theme in literature and cinema, with writers and filmmakers often delving into the complexities of perception and self-identity. Works such as British expatriate writer Lawrence Durrell's 'Alexandria Quartet' (written throughout 1957–1960) and Japanese movie director Akira Kurosawa's award-winning masterpiece Riesman (1950) examine how different individuals may perceive the same events and how it influences their sense of self and identity through different "way (s) of 'seeing' (Berger, 1972) and 'being seen' (Mungan, 1982/1990).In a comprehensive review on trauma and identity formation in the context of re-synchronization between internal world and external realities, Şar et al. (2017) introduces the concept of 'parallel-distinct structures' of the mind. This concept is further developed in the framework of Dialectical Dynamic Therapy (DDT) (Şar, 2022b), which incorporates the idea of 'layers' representing different pathways of reality in addressing one's mind. The concept of separate layers becomes particularly relevant in the treatment of dissociative disorders of identity (Şar, 2023b).

Dissociation and reality perception

Dissociation can be understood as a *desynchronization between different aspects of oneself and between one's internal world and external reality.* On the other hand, this desynchronization allows for the coexistence of multiple subjective versions of reality within an individual's internal world. Kluft (1993) mentioned 'multiple reality disorder', Chefetz (2003) referred to 'isolated subjectivities',

Bromberg (1998) described the experience of 'standing in the spaces' between different realities, Sar and Öztürk (2007) discussed the presence of 'sociological and psychological realities'.

Schimmenti and Şar (2019) highlight that dissociation encompasses not only compartmentalization but also alterations of consciousness which result in a temporarily narrowed perception of reality. In this context, dissociation allows for a simulation of reality by 'reducing' its complexity, a mechanism which is underlined as a neurobiological common ground of creativity in art and science (Kandel, 2016). Perspectives about reality are organized in horizontal and vertical layers., and while an 'integrated mode of consciousness' (Winkelman, 2011) is possible temporarily, the 'parallel-distinct' structures of internal world and external reality are necessary for maintaining a sense of 'actuality'. The latter refers to the version of reality that aligns with the minimum requirements of consensus among larger groups of people.

When analysed in the framework of the tripartite self-system, the sociological self takes on the role of the executive organ in negotiating reality, while the psychological self and the internal moderator work to nurture an 'integrated mode of consciousness' (Winkelman, 2011) as much as possible. In certain situations, such as hypnosis, the sociological self is more prone to task-focused fragmentation. In these instances, the therapist takes on the role of the internal moderator for the patient, essentially acting as a temporary guide and navigator of the individual's consciousness. This process is akin to taking over the task from the 'automatic pilot', meaning that the therapist helps the patient step away from habitual responses to stimuli, emotions, and thoughts. This is the domain of the interpersonally shared cognitions which can be misused by one of the partners of an allegedly symbiotic but in fact parasitarian relationship.

Mot-a-mot thinking and cognitive flexibility

Patients with a chronic dissociative disorder usually have cognitive insight overall and into their illness except during an episode of dissociative psychosis (Şar et al., 2012). Cognitive insight is empirically defined as the difference between *self-reflection* and *self-certainty* (Beck et al., 2004). If combined with diminished self-reflection, elevated self-certainty would lead to delusional thinking. Interestingly, individuals with a chronic dissociative disorder have elevated self-certainty to a scope unusual for non-psychotic disorders. Indeed, self-reflection is not disturbed in dissociative disorders, such that the increased self-certainty does not undermine the cognitive insight in the final analysis.This is described as the 'dissociation paradox' (Şar et al., 2012). In fact, this condition reflects the preponderance of the sociological self in a 'fight' mode against perceived threat. It implies that the heightened self-certainty is a protective mechanism, possibly serving as a defense against the overwhelming experiences.

Early experiences with caregivers, particularly in the context of play, have a significant impact on the development of a child's sense of self, reality testing, and cognitive flexibility. Erik Erikson (1950/1963) who launched 'identity' as a clinically significant concept in mental health field, stated: ' ... the bizarreness and withdrawal in the behavior of many very sick individuals hide an attempt to recover social mutuality by a testing of the borderlines between senses and physical reality and between words and social meanings'.He continued":Ultimately, the children become neurotic not from frustrations, but from the lack or loss of the societal meaning in these frustrations". Reality perception necessitates taking into account the mutuality of the internal and external worlds. Adversities in childhood disrupt the *psychosocial mutuality*.

The balance between the internal and external worlds is to be optimally established via the caregiver's adequate mirroring. In the 'psychic equivalence' mode, young children may perceive their internal thoughts, fantasies, and desires as equivalent to external reality. They may struggle to differentiate between their subjective experiences and objective reality, leading to magical thinking and a limited understanding of alternative perspectives (Fonagy et al., 2002). The pretend mode, on the other hand, involves imaginative play where children can freely express thoughts and feelings in a fictional context. This mode allows for the exploration of different roles, perspectives, and emotions, promoting cognitive and emotional flexibility. It is considered essential for healthy emotional and psychological development.The opposite of the pretend mode is known as the 'teleological mode' which refers to a more concrete and literal perception of reality, where what is physically apparent is given primary importance. It is characterized by a black-and-white thinking style and a focus on immediate goals and outcomes. In dissociative disorders, internal reality is experienced both in psychic equivalent and pretend modes. This is a further version of the 'dissociation paradox' (Şar et al., 2012).

Involving the pretend mode, playing is used in the emergence of 'transitional objects', such as a favorite toy or blanket, that has the quality for a child of being both real and made-up at the same time. Transitional objects are believed to serve as a bridge between the internal and external worlds, providing comfort, security, and a sense of continuity. They are seen as important tools for soothing and self-soothing, facilitating the transition from dependence on the caregiver to self-regulation. They are all antidotes to early splitting and a rigid thinking style in later. Thus, the basis for splitting and rigid thinking is in fact a diminished ability to play and an incapacity for use of a transitional object.

Mentalization is a construct that provides hints about the developmental and interpersonal origins of perceptions of reality (Fonagy & Allison, 2012). It is defined as the ability to understand the mental state of oneself or others, that underlies overt behavior. The development of mentalization capacity and mirroring experiences with primary caregivers are linked. The so called marked (as opposed to the unmarked) mirroring helps the child to differentiate their (the child's) mirrored emotions from those that are not theirs. Thus, the caregivers should be able to express these (the child's) feelings while indicating that they are not expressing their own. If a parent expresses their own feelings in a way that the child 'reads' as mirroring their own, even though it does not, this provides a basis for the development of dissociation through disruption of psychosocial mutuality (Erikson, 1950/1963).This is the stage of 'mirroring' which allows such interaction about emotions.

Nowadays, concepts such as 'bio-behavioral synchrony' emerged which are components of the interaction between a caretaker and infant characterized by adaptive and reciprocal behaviors that promote a mutually rewarding relationship (Feldman, 2012). The latter is considered as an antecedent for the emergence of self-regulatory function in infants and influences current and future interactions.

Otherwise, the caregiver's expression may seem to mirror the child's own emotion and, consequently *externalize* (as a first example of extratensive processing) the infant's experience and overwhelm the infant due to the mismatch with the origin (Fonagy et al., 2002). As a result, the individual may develop a predisposition to experiencing emotions through others, relying on external cues and feedback to understand and regulate their own emotions. This can lead to difficulties in accurately perceiving and interpreting their own emotions, as well as challenges in effectively regulating them. These early interpersonal experiences and the subsequent emotional dysregulation can shape the individual's perceptions of reality. Their interpretations and reactions to events may be influenced by their emotional state and the external cues they rely on, leading to distortions and misunderstandings of reality. In the context of BPD, this tendency to rely on external cues for emotional regulation can contribute to difficulties in establishing stable and coherent self-identity, as well as challenges in maintaining stable interpersonal relationships. Projective and introjective identifications, where the individual projects their own feelings onto others or internalizes the feelings of others, may be used as defense mechanisms to manage these emotional dysregulations and maintain a sense of stability, albeit at the cost of a fragmented sense of self and distorted perceptions of others.

Subjectivities, in-securities, defenses

Defense mechanisms can be defined as internal processes within an individual that create *barriers between different motivational systems* (Duschinsky & White, 2019). Normally, interaction between different motivational systems is possible. However, when defensive processes come into play, they cause each system to separate and struggle with one another. This can result in one or more systems taking control while others only have a partial influence on behavior. As a consequence, contradictions arise, and behaviors stemming from one system may override those from another. The subject may be unaware or only partially aware of the existence of them. Sigmund Freud (1938/1940 in the 'Outline' summarized in a similar fashion: 'indeed a universal characteristic of the neuroses [is] that there are present in the subject's mental life, as regards some particular behavior, two different attitudes, contrary to each other and independent of each other' (p. 77). Thus, any defense mechanism has an aspect of 'dividedness' (i.e., dissociation) as a basic feature.

Defense mechanisms play a significant role in shaping the awareness and perception of internal and external realities. They also impact to extent to which an individual feels independent in relation to others and the objects in their lives. Battegay (1977) introduced the concept of the three layers of object relationships, each with various degrees of proximity to the subject and influencing how reality is perceived: fusion, active ego performances (defense mechanisms), and the mature (realistic) relationships. Sullivan (1954) coined the term 'parataxic distortion' to describe deviations from reality that arise from projection and are not only defense mechanisms but also a normal aspect of human psychology that can become maladaptive in certain contexts. Parataxic distortion, rooted in early relationships, involves projecting fantasy traits onto others. Attachment theory would have it that the fantasy selves projected onto others in parataxic distortion are informed by our long-term attachment patterns. Not only are these imagined traits the resultant of our earliest bonds and unresolved emotional issues from past relationships, but they are recreated in these fantasy selves for the purpose of recreating that past attachment in the present.

Sullivan (1953) described the 'security operations' formed to avoid anxiety and threats to self-esteem. He developed the 'self system' which emerges in childhood, and reinforced by positive affirmation. This self system is defined as a steering mechanism toward a series of 'I-You' interlocking behaviors that is, what an individual does is meant to elicit a particular reaction. Sullivan called these behaviors 'parataxic integrations', and noted that such action-reaction combinations can become rigid and dominate an adult's thinking pattern, limiting his actions and reactions to relating to the world as he sees it, not as it really is. This is the junction where the human 'psyche' secures its safety by *encrypting to be decrypted* during the I-You situation of psychotherapy.

Communication via layers is critical in addressing defense mechanisms which originate from strivings to maintain security against internal and external threats to the integrated consciousness. Namely, recognizing the 'privacy' of every layer as a separate channel functions like messaging in an encrypted fashion or keeping the safety of a blockchain. Conversation in a 'private room' ('dissociation in the service of the privacy') makes possible to talk about 'therapeutic realities' in a free manner while bypassing 'distortion' by defense mechanisms (i.e., resistances).

'Hidden'

Michael Haneke's 2005 psychological thriller 'Hidden/Cache' serves as an example of the devastating consequences that can arise when previously hidden information or experiences enter one's life in an uncontrollable way. Dissociation involves a sense of hiddenness and secrecy, both from oneself and the external world. This is both due to the struggle of controlling unbearable emotions as well as maintaining of security and safety against an external world which is perceived as threatful. However, when an internal world is closed off and isolated it takes the structure of a ghetto which may lead to the experience of perpetuated abuse inside. The psychological stagnation interferes with hope for psychological change, progress, and maturation unless the circulus vitiosus is broken by an external intervention.Such a 'power-driven' internal world also facilitates abusive relationships in external reality. Before ending up in a depressive condition, this situation may undermine healthy intimacy, cause social withdrawal.

Frontpage and the backstage

Separation-individuation is viewed as the psychological birth of an infant, which occurs over a period of time when the child separates from the mother and begins to individuate (Mahler et al., 1973). For Winnicott (1973), one of the most important and precarious stages of development was in the first three years of life, when an infant grows into a child with an increasingly separate sense of self in relation to a larger world of other people. In health, the child learns to bring his or her spontaneous, real self into play with others. In a 'false self' disorder, however, the child finds this unsafe and hides the 'true self' from other people, and pretend to be as they expect. Playing through a transitional object can be an important early bridge between self and other, which allows a child develop the capacity to be genuine in relationships, and creative.

In 'Sickness unto Death', Kierkegaard (1849/1983) proposes that human spirit (the self) has two aspects: 'self in relation with itself and self in relation with self in relation'. I would propose that actual self is the relation between these two selves. In case of a weakness of this relation, in Carl Gustav Jung's terminology, the departure of the individual's 'persona' (Kalsched, 1996) from one's authentic qualities ends up in a discrepancy between false and true selves (Winnicott, 1973). Sar and Öztürk (2007) underline the clinical and social importance of such departure in their theory of the 'functional dissociation of the self'. A different distinction between aspects of oneself (Van der Hart et al., 2006) is related to evolutionary based psychobiological action systems which serve either for survival of the individual (emotional aspect of personality) or the species and society (apparently normal aspect of personality).

The conceptualization of a set of alternate personality states in dissociative disorders as a 'wall' created and driven by a 'disillusioned angry child' to protect against perceived threats is indeed an intriguing perspective. It highlights the idea that distinct personality states may emerge as a defensive mechanism to shield the individual from overwhelming external or internal threats. Nevertheless, it is essential to differentiate dissociative disorders from a 'false self disorder'. In dissociative disorders, the 'true' self is generally present although it may be obscured or overshadowed by the influence of distinct personality states. The true self may become accessible in certain contexts or during periods of stability when the individual feels safe and secure. However, when there is persistent surface-level narcissism, the true self may be less visible or accessible due to the continuous activation of defense mechanisms. The stretched internal moderator plays a crucial role in managing the expression or hiddenness of the true self and the alternate personality states.

Imposed unity and traumatic narcissism

A defensively created inner world that is no longer sufficient to cope with the discrepancy between the individual's ideal and actual selves (Jacobson, 1972; Şar, 2022b) may be compensated by grandiose narcissism as an additional measure or cover. This compensatory grandiose narcissism involves 'fusing' with 'self-objects' to temporarily bridge the gaps in reality. In fact, Kohut's (1971) three types of self-object relationships (idealization, devaluation, and twin) also align with a dissociated (fragmented) internal world and external reality (Kernberg, 1987).

In a college population study (Şar & Türk-Kurtça, 2021), the Dissociative Experiences Scale (DES) showed positive correlations with both grandiose narcissism and depression scores, despite negative correlations between grandiose narcissism and depression. This apparent contradiction reflects a true definition of dissociation as it suggests that grandiose narcissism and depression can coexist within an individual's dissociated inner world. This is the 'discontinuous narcissist' who is hiddenly dissociated through micro-amnesias and erratic behavior without being aware of them. Outwardly, they may present a unified and composed image, actively engaging in social interactions creating what can be described as a 'mask of unity'. Internally, however, they undergo a range of fluctuating mental states. These include anhedonia, depersonalization-derealization, identity-fragmentation and euphoria, and a sense of omnipotence. Close interpersonal relationships may suffer due to this hidden cycle as partners are forced to share an illusion. Such quasi-connection with the external world cannot be sustained, leading to an inevitable edge of depression.

But this is one possible explanation which needs to be explored empirically. Namely, the statistics may also suggest that different parts of the variance of dissociation may be related to depression and grandiose narcissism in distinct ways, suggesting that they might not always go together. These interpretations should be explored by examining an interactive effect so inquire whether dissociation moderates the relationship of depression and narcissism. For instance, in the same college population study, childhood sexual abuse and physical neglect were also predictors of grandiose narcissism (Şar & Türk-Kurtça, 2021). In fact, traumatic narcissism is an inner withdrawal from a disappointing external world covered by the opposite (i.e., reaction formation). In the above-mentioned college population study, vulnerable narcissism was predicted by preoccupied attachment but not any other type of childhood trauma or dissociation scores. Indeed, disappointment in an allegedly secure relationship was the only other predictor which resulted in depression and defensively recursive grandiose narcissism maintained by dissociation. Thus, the core problem becomes manifest in the vicious cycle between 'traumatic narcissism' and 'dissociative depression'.

Body as container of negative emotions

Renata Gaddini (1977), an Italian psychoanalyst, posited that the failure in the interactional task of the mother takes place during the child's infancy, a time when the child has not yet developed the necessary mental apparatus to take on an object, once associated with the mother, as a symbol for the mother. The process of growing the child moves from sensations to perceptions, feelings, symptoms, and finally, to thoughts. The schemata which develop indicate early symbolization as seen in the transitional object as the first observable step in the development of secondary process (reality-oriented) thinking. In cases in which there has been a poor quality of mother-child interactions, growth and the whole process of individuation are held back, so that the child remains incarcerated in his own physical self. In stressful situations, various psycho-somatic symptoms will form themselves, in the precarious yet pervasive organic apparatus.

Among somatizing patients, the suffering body performed the function of a transitional object (McDougall, 1989) not only for a detached external but also in a divided internal world (Şar et al., 2017). In many of these patients, there seems to be a breakdown in the early introjection of a soothing and caretaking mother image (Krystal, 1978) with which to identify. The positive investment in bodily suffering reminds the infants with incoherent mothering. What should have been supplied from internal sources (that is, some introjected image of the maternal environment that would restore to the infant a feeling of corporeal limits and of the capacity to contain painful emotional states) has to be sought in the suffering body itself. As such, the so-called*earliest childhood trauma* (Şar, 2020) seems to be the common ground of dissociative depression and somatization representing, in fact, an 'anaclitic depression' (Spitz, 1945).

In a study on patients with fibromyalgia or rheumatoid arthritis (Kılıç et al., 2014), both being conditions with strong psychosomatic components, somatic expression of dissociation was associated with a lifetime diagnosis of depressive disorder; i.e., representing a hidden trait. Cognitive-emotional dissociation, however, was associated with the current severity of depressive disorder; i.e., it is a state measure. In an epidemiological study among women, childhood physical abuse, and lifetime diagnosis of major depression and/or dissociative disorder predicted functional neurological (conversion) symptoms (a type of sensori-motor dissociation) (Sar et al., 2009). While depression was linked to a combination of omission and sexual bodily intrusion, physical abuse (non-sexual bodily intrusion) added sensori-motor dissociation to this condition, possibly due to unassimilated bodily perceptions, i.e., somatic memory. Depersonalization and amnesia were the most frequent dissociative symptoms in patients with conversion disorder (Sar et al., 2004).

In summary, childhood abuse (intrusion type of trauma) and cognitive-emotional dissociation appear to act as 'on-makers' in terms of the internal moderator for the switch between experiencing 'inside' and 'outside'. Childhood neglect (omission type of trauma) and somatoform dissociation seem to function as 'off-makers' inhibiting the switch between internal and external. Functional neurological (conversion) symptoms seem to represent both 'on' and 'off' switching as they may have both positive (e.g., dissociative seizures) and negative (e.g., muscle paralysis, anesthesia) qualities. New Zealand-French psychoanalyst Joyce McDougall (1989) proposed that somatizing patients revealed only few 'neurotic' symptoms to such an extent that she referred to them as 'normopaths' as if they were obliged to maintain a camouflage of 'pseudo-normality'. Some of these individuals are rather prone to alexithymia (off mode), including difficulty in identifying or expressing feelings as observed among male patients with alcoholism (Evren et al., 2008) indicating an inner disconnection and emotional dissociation.

Re-petitions: obsessions and possessions

While re-enactment composes an expressed form of repetition ('compulsion'), obsessions are usually hidden and/or hiding. Preliminary observations (Şar, unpublished data) on dissociative experiences in a group of patients with obsessive-compulsive disorder (OCD) suggested the presence of two patterns. The first pattern involves disturbances of sense of self, specifically bodily and cognitive-emotional self-detachment. Bodily self-detachment seems to be related to memory gaps, possibly indicating a hidden trauma history. Cognitive-emotional self-detachment, however, was related to dissociated behavior and generalized amnesia, where dissociated aspects of the self re-emerge ('return of the dissociated'). This pattern may be associated with *expressed and/or internalized anger*, placing it within the spectrum of OSDD (Other Specified Dissociative Disorder) versus BPD/DID.

The second pattern involves disturbances in the sense of agency, particularly experiences of possession and extrasensory perception (the latter being in an inverse relationship with bodily self-detachment). These experiences may be associated with Schneiderian symptoms, characterized by a sense of passive influence or loss of autonomy. Interestingly, this pattern does not appear to be linked to reports of anger. Instead, it involves supranatural experiences and 'magical thinking', suggesting a different underlying process. It is worth noting that the subject may not be fully aware or perceptive of these experiences, suggesting a potential *externalization* followed by *internalization* of these phenomena (Bilu, 1987).

Obsessions which can be seen as one of the resistances of the traumatic self against processing painful material, may hinder self-expression and may lead to a state of mental paralysis or psychological 'arrest'. This state limits further dissociation, including the formation of alternate personality states that could serve as outlets for emotions like anger, such as suicidal or persecutory states. Consequently, this 'locked-in state' of mind impedes both the progression of dissociation and the effectiveness of treatment interventions. This dynamic sets in motion a vicious cycle characterized by an inflation of traumatic obsessions and a sense of detemporalization (Sar & Öztürk, 2006). Not only anger, but fear and shame play significant roles in perpetuating this cycle, as described in Nathanson's (1992) 'compass of shame'. Therapeutic approaches like Eye Movement Desensitization and Reprocessing (EMDR) and psychedelic-assisted psychotherapy have shown promise in interrupting these cycles and promoting healing and recovery (Hofmann et al., 2022).

'Expressed'

For understandable reasons, the popular film industry tends to portray overt and dramatic expressions of dissociation which may not accurately represent the majority of the clinical cases. In reality, many individuals with dissociative experiences hide them for safety and security reasons. Some patients may not even recognize the pathological nature of their experiences and thus do not report them as such. However, there are patients who even give the impression of 'pseudo-false-positive' dissociation due to 'over-expression'; i.e., claiming their disorder (Kluft, 1985). Unfortunately, such 'openness' allows further involvement in potentially abusive relationships and stigmatization, especially when faced with uninformed or ignorant mental health professionals.

'Borderline' phenomena

The relationship between BPD and childhood trauma has been underlined for a long time (Herman et al., 1989). The centrality of borderline phenomena in the context of developmental traumatization and dissociation is of particular interest not only for depression but also for schizophrenic (Sar et al., 2010) and somatic symptom disorders (Kılıç et al., 2014). Once criticized as being 'an adjective in a search for a noun' (Akiskal et al., 1985), total number of the DSM-5 diagnostic criteria for BPD represent the severity of dissociation regardless of the main diagnosis (Şar, 2017a, 2017b). These findings converge around the possibility of a psychological mechanism other than a 'personality' disorder which needs to be identified, defined, and empirically proven yet.Indeed, borderline phenomena seem to describe the *bimodal* quality of several psychological functions (e.g., emotions, interpersonal attachment, cognition, behavior) with either 'on' or 'off' status as represented in 'undermodulation' and 'overmodulation' of emotions in

PTSD (Lanius et al., 2010). This is a condition of general self-regulation: the *internal moderation* (Sar & Öztürk, 2007).

As an internally experienced type of identity disturbance, *mental intrusions from within* predicted both BPD and dissociative disorder (Şar et al., 2017). An alternative to this was the *externally experienced identity disturbances* such as being perceived as a different person, expressing anger, having imaginary friends, and detaching from external reality as a component of derealization. Expectedly, as an undermodulated condition, the latter pattern led to a diagnosis of BPD rather than dissociative disorder. Indeed, evaluations of a young dissociative patient using a projective (Rorschach) test before and after psychotherapeutic treatment yielded that the extratensivity diminished while the concurrent diagnosis of BPD was no longer present (Şar et al., 2002). Apparently, the dyad of internal world (oneself) and external reality (environment) constitutes the ground where the phenomena of DID (introtensitivity) and BPD (extratensivity) prevail.

Schimmenti and Şar (2019) empirically examined the sequence of clusters of dissociative experiences through a network analysis. Namely, an initiating pathway can be identified that goes from confusion about oneself to confusion about the external world. This path way interact with other emerging pathways, such as a path going from an alteration in the perception of self to a detachment from the environment, and another path going from self-detachment to the alterations in the perception of the external world.

(Re-)enactments

In a college population study (Şar, Alioğlu, & Akyüz, 2017; Şar, Alioğlu, Akyüz, Tayakısı, et al., 2017), the BPD-dissociation spectrum was characterized by two poles: 1) an *undulant* course basically with an escape from one's identity (BPD&DID) versus 2) a seemingly *steady* course with intermittent crises and constant distancing from the body (DSM-5 OSDD type 1, i.e., ICD-11 partial DID). The two poles seem to be characterized by different frequencies of on and off switching (higher in BPD/DID pole) of the internal moderator alongside differences in trauma types and coping with them. The somatic component (detaching from the body) is relatively unrelated to the identity component (the undulant pole); e.g., they differ in their relationship to re-enactments as an expressive phenomenon. In fact, alterations related to *body perception* and *identity* both serve as separate transitional objects. While the body is a physical entity existing in the external world, identity is a multifaceted and intangible aspect of a person's being, which primarily resides within the inner world of thoughts, emotions, beliefs, and self-awareness.

In a study on patients with fibromyalgia or rheumatoid arthritis (Kılıç et al., 2014), current severity of depression predicted expressed anger which was associated with loss of control, the number of BPD criteria and dissociative amnesia. This pattern indicates *a crisis state* (nervous breakdown) which seems to be associated with an outburst of the previously overmodulated anger possibly related to 'reminiscences' of trauma.In the same study, loss of control was predicted by all types of abuse, identity fragmentation, and dissociative absorption (narrowing of consciousness). This pattern represents the internal structure of an enactment in terms of co-presence of compartmentalization of identity and altered consciousness as two faces of the same coin. It also points to the relationship of enactment to intrusion type of childhood trauma. Thus, current severity of depression may also represent 'opening' (being more expressive, undermodulated, unstable) of a 'closed' (overmodulated, non-expressive, relatively stable) system. The former constitutes a diagnostic and therapeutic window; i.e., a potentially productive crisis in condition that helpful therapeutic intervention is available.

Psychoticism

Psychotic phenomena may occur both in depressive and dissociative disorders. In depression, delusions and hallucinations, if they happen, are usually mood-congruent while exceptions may exist. Mixed episodes of bipolar disorder are examples of such complex delusional conditions. The relationship of an acute dissociative psychosis to psychotic depression is not known; e.g., the pathogenesis of delusions and hallucinations in psychotic depression. While some authors underline a possible relationship between schizotypal disorders and dissociative psychotic phenomena (Moskowitz & Corstens, 2007), given the benign quality of both domains, a close relationship of dissociation with mood disorders is more likely. On the other hand, psychotic phenomena in dissociative disorder should not be mixed up with dissociative symptoms or disorders seen among individuals with schizophrenia (Sar et al., 2010).

One type of brief psychotic disorder known as 'hysterical psychosis' (Şar, 2022d) originates from a 'revolving door crisis' in chronically dissociated individual (Putnam, 1989) when the alternate personality states enter a loop of rapid switching. The collapse of dissociative barriers also ends up in a similar situation: 'co-consciousness crisis' (Kluft, personal communication, 1995). Amnesias, hallucinations, somatic experiences, and discontinuities in associations may appear like a manic, schizophrenic, or delirious condition. Such brief psychotic attacks may cease in a few hours or a few weeks at the latest and represent a temporary *collapse of the internal moderator*. Nevertheless, there are cases with longer duration that resemble a schizophrenic disorder (Van der Hart et al., 1993). Thus, rather than the duration, mechanism (i.e., dissociation) is important in diagnosis.

There may be personality states which are isomorphic with real people around the patient including friends and family members. In this case, the host personality may mix up the real person with the isomorphic alter. If these personality states are of persecutory nature, the general condition may look like a paranoid psychosis. The solution is for the host to recognize the alter personality state as such and, if possible, fuse them. Another possibility is the existence of an alter personality which has psychotic (paranoid) features and takes full control from time to time or becomes co-conscious. Such alter personalities seem to be related to experiences in relatively early (first few) years of life and severe traumatization (Şar, 2020; Volkan, 1995).

One type of breach between internal world and external reality in dissociative disorders is known as 'internal homicide' (Putnam, 1989). This is an annihilating act driven by a distinct personality state when a patient succeeds in completing such self-destruction by targeting her own body; i.e., in fact a suicidal act. Nevertheless, the ramifications of these internal dynamics and collapses can extend beyond self-directed outcomes, potentially leading to violence against others too (Otnow-Lewis et al., 1997; Sakarya et al., 2012). This is, in fact, an 'external suicide' reminiscent of cases like Munchausen's Syndrome (factitious disorder) by Proxy, among others. The title of a book, penned by a North American forensic psychiatrist (Simon, 2008), 'Bad Men Do What Good Men Dream' powerfully underscores the paramount importance of maintaining the boundary between fantasy and action- a vital function upheld by a well-functioning internal moderator. This juncture necessitates forensic psychiatry to adopt a stance that encompasses not only to ensuring justice but also embracing a proactive role within the societal context including rehabilitation and treatment of offenders where viable, aimed at preventing future incidents. Yet, the application of the 'not guilty by reason of insanity' defense presents a notable challenge in context of dissociative disorders, necessitating careful assessment within the context of the precise circumstances of the act in question. The solution to this question should be sought through transdiagnostic criteria that gauge the extent of the breakdown in moderating functions.

The connection between the perpetuation or replication of stereotypical gender roles and experiences of trauma and dissociation is evident (Howell, 2002).The tragic outcomes that arise from breaching of the boundary between fantasy and action in a scenario where gendered hostility targets a dissociated man's own 'rebellious' *female alternate personality state*, particularly amidst the backdrop of amplified gender role stress fueled by cultural norms, a history of traumatic experiences, and the weight of shame, remain largely unexplored. This complex situation holds the peril of escalating into severe violence as highlighted by a social perspective review on the alarming surge in *femicide* (Koç, 2022). Recent research (Bakır et al., 2023) has unveiled that childhood sexual abuse experienced by men (Gartner, 2001) could predict the development of a *fear of subordination* in adulthood, a central facet of male gender role stress that may contribute to the emergence of aggressive behaviors within intimate relationships, as illustrated by Nathanson's (1992) 'shame compass'. On the other hand, the prevalence of murder as the most common crime type among female prisoners (Öğünç & Şar, 2007) might offer a glimpse into an opposing protective action undertaken by a male 'guardian' personality state of a dissociated woman. This quasi-psychotic breakdown of internal moderation appears to reflect the external world's pervasive power dynamics fostering an expanded sociological self within each individual.

'Purgatory'

The struggle between retaining control over a situation and the possibility of losing that control, or facing setbacks, can be likened to a state of purgatory. This juxtaposition may represent the contrast between resilience and yielding to challenges. However, rather than a clear dichotomy, this is a state of overlap. The internal moderator's on and off modes operate in parallel with various degree of tension: low, normal, or high- each carrying its own outcomes and consequences.

Dissociative mood disorder

Unlike the internal tension characterizing various conditions related to hiddenness or expression, depression often manifests as a state of apparent inaction, where the individuals struggle with reduced motivation, energy, and engagement in life. The internal moderator, responsible for regulating and mobilizing psychological resources, might be in an 'off' state, resulting in a sense of stagnation. Dissociative depression, however, lies in an intermediate stage where the internal moderator still possesses some capacity to toggle between the 'on' and 'off' states. This indicates a degree of flexibility and potential for psychotherapeutic interventions to yield positive outcomes. This juncture should be viewed as a pivotal point by clinicians, serving as the fulcrum for leveraging effective therapeutic endeavors.

Dissociative depression can lead to disturbances in the sense of self and agency, manifested through experiences such as passive influence (Schneiderian) symptoms and even moments of feeling possessed, descriptive features of BPD, and suicidality. They also have more changes in appetite, thoughts of worthlessness and guilt, diminished concentration and indecisiveness (Şar et al., 2013). Experiences of emptiness, boredom, loneliness, and isolation uniquely flavor dissociative depression (Şar et al., 2017). This condition is experienced as an *existential depression* characterized by an ongoing feeling of hopelessness and a struggle to find meaning in life.

Dissociative depression encompasses a *mosaic* of mental functions including emotions and perceptions. These patients experience a range of mood states in a parallel-distinct fashion (Şar et al., 2017). This means that depressive moods are not consistently present but can be triggered by specific contexts or periods during the day. The fluctuation between different mood states can create the appearance of a 'masked depression'. This means that depressive symptoms may not be easily recognizable sometimes. The shifts between mood states may provide temporary relief, masking underlying depressive symptoms and even feelings of suicidality.

Many patients with dissociative depression give the impression of a bipolar disorder as they exhibit periods or moments of heightened mood. However, individuals with clear-cut dissociative disorder of identity can distinguish these periods based on the 'ego-dystonic' quality of their experiences. They may have amnesia even for their own amnesic episodes (Kluft, 1988; Şar et al., 2014a) making it challenging for them to report these lapses in memory. In children and adolescents, emotionally-laden distinct personality states may be more readily apparent. They may display a greater range of identity shifts compared to adults, whose condition is often influenced by adaptive and maladaptive strategies and inner structures developed throughout their lives. In a psychiatric outpatient screening study, 45.5% of the consecutively admitted adolescents with dissociative disorders got the diagnosis of a concurrent major depression (Şar et al., 2014b), and 21.2% bipolar disorder. In a college study (Şar et al., 2017), 37.0% of the young adults reported 'mood changes that one cannot control' to a marked degree. Those who reported subjective and/or objective impairment due to these mood changes constituted 17.2% of the population. Thus, dissociative alterations become manifest not only as identity changes but also in other mental functions (consciousness, sensorimotor functions etc.) including fluctuations of affectivity.

Holding on and falling down

The lack of sense of a healthy self and a persistent confusion caused by mental intrusion and passive influence experiences cause patients lead to internal disruptions. They contribute to feelings of distress and can undermine any hope for a better future. Additionally, the painful experiences from their past continue to exert influence on their present consciousness, further complicating their ability to find stability and a sense of self.Memory difficulties play a significant role in dissociative depression, ranging from everyday forgetfulness to more extensive dissociative amnesia, where significant periods of one's life, including traumatic events, may be inaccessible. These memory disruptions further hinder the development of a coherent and integrated sense of self. It is poignant that individuals who were denied their autonomy as children by their caregivers continue to face barriers in taking control of their own lives in adulthood. They find themselves entrapped within their internal world, unable to break free from the patterns established in their early experiences.

Surviving a period of purgatory may often involves grasping onto various anchors, whether they be a people, ideas, institutions or any internal and external 'object' including substances, food, daydreaming, or even alternate personality states as imaginary companions. Thus, lack of access to alternate personality states or premature 'removal' (including attempts at exorcism) of them may complications potentially even culminating in completed suicide.There are instances where individuals experience chronic suicidal thoughts without reporting other psychiatric symptoms or even overt depressive or dissociative symptoms. This tragic situation can lead to completed suicide while the individual is perceived as 'normal' and may not receive adequate treatment due to the absence of apparent symptoms that fit a specific diagnostic category. In reality, they may be suffering from an 'unperceived' dissociative depression, which hampers their ability to connect with and express themselves and seek the help they need.

Some highly functional individuals with creative capacity might continue to navigate these dynamics throughout their lives, while the 'dark areas of their soul' serve as a driving force for their generativity. This productive lifestyle can serve as a protective factor against descending into prolonged depressive states. Nonetheless, they might possess a subtle awareness of their susceptibility to negative outcomes.

'Healing'

Differentiation of the operations within the tripartite self-system from internal moderation is essential to understanding the mechanism behind dissociative depression. The imbalance of the tripartite self-system due to chronic developmental traumatization indirectly overwhelms the internal moderator. The balance should be re-established by psychotherapeutic interventions via the tripartite self-system that the internal moderator is recovered to secure the return to daily functions.

Paradigm shift

Recognizing dissociative depression and developing of a new conceptualization and common l anguage with the clinician can lead to a *paradigm shift* in the patient. Unlike theories that connect psychopathology to personality and its developmental stages, recognizing the distinct origin and mechanism of the patient's lifelong suffering allows them to differentiate between *the acquired ('musallat'*, the disorder) and the individual's *essence ('fitrat'*, unique personal qualities). This recognition marks the first step of the Dialectical Dynamic Therapy (DDT) (Şar, 2022a, 2023b) which aims to restore balance between a 'detached and expanded' sociological self and a 'restricted and frozen' psychological self. Such repair is possible through a reduction in the mandate of the sociological self and nurturing an 'awakening' of the psychological self.

The therapeutic intervention aims to empower the patient, shifting them from a position of *slave* to a *master* (Şar, 2022a, 2023b). The repair of the *damaged* master identity of the patient (second step of DDT) is a significant step in the therapeutic process, and it occurs through a fusionary-identificatory-narcissistic layer in the therapeutic relationship (Scharff, 1992). The reason of this is the role of introjective identification with the master identity of the therapist in treatment. One dimension of the identificatory processes is the incorporation of the codes obtained from the therapist which is aimed at *fixing the damaged (divided) master identity* of the patient.

The identificatory process develops through questions of the therapist (Sar, 2023a). Dividedness of the master identity of the patient is repaired by the therapist through delivery of their *artificial (copied) self.* This 'transfer' occurs through the therapist's recognition of themselves in the patient, in condition that the patient is aware of this experience.The therapist encourages the patient to challenge their 'master signifiers' (mindset, previously learned knowledge) which helps them to regain a sense of agency and, subsequently, a sense of self. This empowerment increases the patient's desire for recovery, reduces fear and pain, initiates creative learning alongside modeling, and fosters hope, belief, and conviction.

In the therapeutic process, secure and 'encrypted' communication with the therapist through layers ensures safety which is a necessary foundation for activating the patient's psychological self. Conflict resolution attempts can be threatening to the sense of security so the therapist's 'artificial (copied) self' (Şar, 2023b) acts as a transitional object. On the other hand, by identifying with the therapist's artifical self (i.e., introjective identification),patient's psychological self is stimulated and activated. Reciprocally, the therapist ratifies the patient's recognition of themselves in the therapist's pure master identity (Şar, 2023b). This process can be likened to the syringe of a therapist, injecting their artificial self into the patient's psychological self for reconstruction and potential incorporation. Such 'injection' has to occur across the sociological self but must bypass the resistances of the traumatic self. Thus, to initiate a successful clinical improvement, resistances of the traumatic self should be resolved which can be achieved by working through the modalities of the psychological self but rather than the sociological self. Nonetheless, the interaction proceeds as a result of a positive 'domino effect' between these entities.

This is followed by *overcoming the fear of loneliness* (third step) which is a correlate of an emerging healthy self (Şar et al., 2017). In the fourth step, the therapist continues to check the status of the patient to prevent a relapse by providing challenges and ratifications. This is, in fact, an intervention that nurtures the patient's strength in a systematic fashion (i.e., working through). The entire process resembles the developmental phase of separation-individuation (Mahler et al., 1973) with a short period of blues and longing about the personality states.

Layers

Treatment of dissociative depression is akin to the work of an archaeologist or restaurateur where the therapist must carefully and respectfully consider the various layers of the patient's experiences. The therapist's approach involves exploring both the horizontal and vertical layers from surface to depth weaving connections within the inner system beyond just integrating personality states. This requires different approaches to handling the clinical surface, core dissociative dimensions, and *basic dividedness* in the tripartite self-system which is the fertile ground of the clinical phenomena. Clinical surface of dissociative depression may require general psychiatric treatment, including pharmacotherapy, depending on the prevailing conditions. However, the treatment on the surface cannot resolve the chronic depression, necessitating an in-depth evaluation and intervention. Dissociative amnesia, depersonalization, derealization, identity confusion, and identity alteration are core clinical dissociative dimensions (Steinberg & Schnall, 2000). Accessory symptoms such as hallucinations, trance states, behavioral signs of switching between personality states, experiences of possession, and flashbacks may also prevail in the clinical surface.

The Dialectical Dynamic Therapy (DDT) offers various techniques for approaching the tripartite self-system. The main goal is to teach the patient new ways of mental processing that promote longer-lasting and more frequent episodes of integrative mode of consciousness. The ultimate aim is *awaken the psychological self*, with working on personality states and trauma as pathways to achieve this goal. In DDT, communication with the patient should consider separateness of layers which makes such re-learning possible. Addressing through all layers simultaneously without considering their separateness can lead to the persistence of existing patterns, causing resistance and further fragmentation. A mechanistic, quasi-integrative approach should be avoided, as it can hinder progress. The importance of communication by layers is rooted in the need for security and safety. This is an 'encrypted' system which permits communication between only 'trusted' partners who know the 'passwords' to navigate it effectively. It creates a private language that ensures a safe exchange of precious emotional assets. Just as in origami, where each prior step (or 'level' in a computer game) is crucial for the success of subsequent ones. To prevent further fragmentation, the therapist and patient must stay on the same layer when dealing with paradoxes or challenges. Failing to achieve such synchronicity can lead to ineffective or even toxic pseudo-psychotherapy.

Integration

Integration takes place by *letting the individual perceive oneself as oneself in the face of each of the diverse psychological realities, while developing sociopsychological connections between each of these psychological realities and kernels of the self* (Şar, 2017b).Recovery from dissociative disorder relieves dissociative depression. This requires an integrative psychotherapeutic strategy. However, the usual resistance to standard approaches to depression treatment indicates the need for a more specific psychotherapy addressing dissociative psychopathology. The clinical pathways utilized by the patient dictate the course of interventions the clinician has to pursue. As a reason for improvement, at least partly, re-integrated anger can be taken into consideration. Before the treatment, this post-traumatic anger is absorbed in the fragmented or compartmentalized internal world of the patient. The clinical stage is beset by the resistances of the traumatic self: depressive phenomena, traumatic obsessions, and loss of psychosocial mutuality (Öztürk & Şar, 2016). For some of the patients, a chronic PTSD with the classical symptom triad of numbing, intrusions, and hyperarousal may accompany dissociative depression or may become prominent in the middle phases of treatment (concurrent on and off mode); i.e., after abolition of the dissociative coverage.

Conclusions

Dissociative depression is distinct from primary mood disorders in various aspects including its underlying causes, clinical features, comorbidities, course of the condition, and response to treatment. It is characterized by a fragmented affective quality. Individuals with dissociative depression may exhibit expressive patterns, such as borderline phenomena, psychoticism, enactments, or control strategies like somatization, compensatory narcissism, and obsessions. These co-occurring patterns can complicate the clinical presentation and treatment approach.

In a meta analysis, interestingly, while dissociation was often associated with conditions such as BPD and PTSD, it did not consistently rank highest in terms of its association with depression (Lyssenko et al., 2018). It is possible that at least for particular groups of patients, this relationship remains hidden. Indeed, dissociative depression represents a dialectical purgatory, where a disturbance of identity is concealed, while depression often masks behind it. Polarized security concerns, alternating between hiddenness and expression (flight/avoidance versus fight) create tension within the internal moderator. These oscillations between vertical layers (frontpage and backstage) are driven by security concerns related to fears of change and of 'normality' (Steele et al., 2005).The internal moderation capacity of each individual determines whether they lean towards an 'on' or 'off' position. The choice between these two positions is influenced by the type of traumatization experienced, individual coping styles, the therapeutic environment, the clinician's attitude and approach, and the broader cultural context.

Mainstream psychiatry and laymen are relatively well informed about a general concept of depression. However, this has not been sufficient to deliver effective treatment to a considerable proportion of the affected individuals who require more than treatment-as-usual. Psychoanalytic-psychodynamic models and interventions, while valuable, did not sufficiently address related conditions in a specific manner either. Dissociative depression occupies a unique position in this scenario, serving as a bridge between the intensive practice of the psychoanalytical-psychodynamic approaches and the robust clinical power of the medical model in psychiatry. Dialectical Dynamic Therapy (DDT) emerges as a solution to meet this specific need (Şar, 2022a, 2023b). Healing the despair associated with this condition requires considering the internal world in the context of external reality. Recognizing the vertical and horizontal (parallel-distinct) layers of the internal world and external reality facilitates understanding the principles to be pursued; i.e., accepting and being able to follow multiple perspectives within clinical constellations.

In their paper on a search of 'a psyche for psychiatry', Meares (2003) quoted: 'all life reveals itself as a continuous *interchange* between an inner and an outer world (Jaspers, 1913, p. 12)' and added: 'out of this interchange arises the third thing, the experience of *myself*'.In fact, with all these struggles, *the individual strives to save a treasure: the core of the individual existence carrying the potential of a progressive and creative life* (Şar, 2019). This is the fight of realizing one's 'self'-identity to achieve meaning which can only flourish in a responsive social context. Indeed, the words of a patient recovered from dissociative depression reflects the 'rebirth' of a person: '*I am this, this is how I am, this is me'*.

Acknowledgements

The author wish thank to Görkem Ayas, MD for their valuable comments on evolving versions of the manuscript.

Disclosure statement

No potential conflict of interest was reported by the author(s).

References

Akiskal, H. S., Chen, S. E., Davis, G. C., Puzantian, V. R., Kashgarian, M., & Bolinger, J. M. (1985). Borderline: An adjective in search for a noun. *Journal of Clinical Psychiatry*, *46*(2), 41–48.

American Psychiatric Association. (1980). *Diagnostic and statistical manual of mental disorders* (3rd ed.).

American Psychiatric Association. (2013). *Diagnostic and statistical manual of mental disorders* (5th ed.). https://doi.org/10.1176/appi.books.9780890425596

Arieti, S. & Bemporad, J. R. (1980). The psychological organization of depression. *American Journal of Psychiatry*, *137*(11), 1360–1365.

Ataria, Y. (2016). When the body becomes the enemy: Disownership toward the body. *Philosophy, Psychiatry, & Psychology*, *23*(1), 1–15. https://doi.org/10.1353/ppp.2016.0002

Ayas, G., Şar, V., Hun-Şenol, Ş., & Türk-Kurtça, T. (2023). *A novel measure of self-regulation: the Internal Moderation Questionnaire (IMQ)* [Unpublished manuscript].

Bakır, Ç. N., Kılçıksız, C. M., Kaçar, A. Ş., & Şar, V. (2023). The Turkish version of the masculine gender role stress Questionnaire: Dimensions of fears and their correlates in young adults (in review).

Barach, P. M. (1991). Multiple personality disorder as an attachment disorder. *Dissociation*, *4*(3), 117–123.

Battegay, R. (1977). Narzissmus und Objektbeziehungen. In *Über das Selbst zum Object*. Huber.

Beck, A. T., Baruch, E., Balter, J. M., Steer, R. A., & Warman, D. M. (2004). A new instrument for measuring insight: The Beck cognitive insight scale. *Schizophrenia Research*, *68*(2–3), 319–329. https://doi.org/10.1016/S0920-9964(03)00189-0

Berger, J. P. (1972). *Ways of seeing*. British Broadcasting Corp.

Bilu, Y. (1987). Dybbuk possession and mechanisms of internalization and externalization: A case study. In J. Sandler (Ed.), *Projection, identification, projective identification* (pp. 163–178). Routledge Publication. https://doi.org/10.4324/9780429478567-11

Bleuler, E. (1911/1950). *Dementia præcox oder die Gruppe der schizophrenien [dementia præcox or the group of schizophrenias]* (Trans. J. Zinkin). Deuticke and International Universities Press.

Blizard, R. A. (2003). Disorganized attachment, development of dissociative self states, and a relational approach to treatment. *Journal of Trauma and Dissociation*, *4*(3), 27–50. https://doi.org/10.1300/J229v04n03_03

Blizard, R. A. & Bluhm, A. M. (1994). Attachment to the abuser: Integrating object-relations and trauma theories in treatment of abuse survivors. *Psychotherapy: Theory, Research, Practice, Training*, *31*(3), 383–390. https://doi.org/10.1037/0033-3204.31.3.383

Bowlby, J. (1962). Defenses that follow loss: Causation and function. In R. Duschinsky & K. White (Eds.), *Trauma and loss: Key texts from the John Bowlby Archive* (pp. 17–65). Routledge. 2019. https://doi.org/10.4324/9780429329234-2

Bowlby, J. (1980). *Attachment and loss: Vol 3: Loss, sadness, and depression*. Basic Books.

Bowlby, J. (1988). *A secure base: Parent-child attachment and healthy human development*. Tavistock Professional Book.

Bromberg, P. M. (1998). *Standing in the spaces. Essays on clinical process, trauma, and dissociation*. The Analytic Press.

Brown, D. P. & Elliott, D. S. (2016). *Attachment disturbances in adults. Treatment for comprehensive repair*. Norton.

Bühler, K.-E. & Heim, G. D. (2001). General introduction to the psychotherapy of Pierre Janet. *American Journal of Psychotherapy*, *55*(1), 74–91. https://doi.org/10.1176/appi.psychotherapy.2001.55.1.74

Burnham, D. L., Gladstone, A. I., & Gibson, R. W. (1969). *Schizophrenia and the need-fear dilemma*. International Universities Press.

Cade, J. F. J. (1949). Lithium salts in the treatment of psychotic excitement. *Medical Journal of Australia*, *2*(10), 349–352. https://doi.org/10.5694/j.1326-5377.1949.tb36912.x

Chefetz, R. A. (2003). Fishing in dissociative waters: Subjectivity, power, and relatedness in the therapeutic dyad. In *Plenary speech, 20th Annual Conference of the ISSD*.

Dabrowski, K. (1964). *Positive disintegration*. Little Brown.

Deutsch, H. (1934). Über einen Typus der Pseudoaffektivität ("als ob"). *Internationale Zeitschrift für Psychoanalyse*, *20*(3), 323–325.

Diseth, T. H. (2006). Dissociation following traumatic medical treatment procedures in childhood: A longitudinal follow-up. *Development and Psychopathology*, *18*(1), 233–251. https://doi.org/10.1017/S0954579406060135

Duschinsky, R. & White, K. (2019). *Trauma and loss. Key texts from the John Bowlby Archive*. Routledge. https://doi.org/10.4324/9780429329234

Ellickson-Larew, S., Stasik O'Brien, S. M., Stanton, K., & Watson, D. (2020). Dissociation as a multidimensional transdiagnostic symptom. *Psychology of Consciousness: Theory, Research, & Practice*, *7*(2), 126–150. https://doi.org/10.1037/cns0000218

Erikson, E. H. (1950/1963). *Childhood and society*. Norton.

Evren, C., Şar, V., Dalbudak, E., Cetin, R., Durkaya, M., Evren, B., & Çelik, S. (2011). Lifetime posttraumatic stress disorder and quality of life among alcohol dependent men: Impact of childhood emotional abuse and dissociation. *Psychiatry Research*, *186*(1), 85–90. https://doi.org/10.1016/j.psychres.2010.07.004

Evren, C., Şar, V., Evren, B., Semiz, Ü., Dalbudak, E., & Çakmak, D. (2008). Dissociation and alexithymia among men with alcoholism. *Psychiatry and Clinical Neurosciences*, *62*(1), 40–47. https://doi.org/10.1111/j.1440-1819.2007.01775.x

Fairbairn, W. R. D. (1952). *Psychoanalytic studies of the personality*. Routledge & Kegan Paul.

Farina, B., Liotti, M., & Imperatori, C. (2019). The role of attachment trauma and disintegrative pathogenic processes in the traumatic-dissociative dimension. *Frontiers in Psychology*, *10*, 933. https://doi.org/10.3389/fpsyg.2019.00933

Feldman, R. (2012). Bio-behavioral synchrony: A model for integrating biological and microsocial behavioral processes in the study of parenting. *Parenting: Science and Practice*, *12*(2–3), 154–164. https://doi.org/10.1080/15295192.2012.683342

Fonagy, P. & Allison, E. (2012). What is mentalization? The concept and its foundations in developmental research. In N. Midgley & I. Vrouva (Eds.), *Minding the child: Mentalization-based interventions with children, young people, and their families* (pp. 11–34). Routledge Press.

Fonagy, P., Gergely, G., Jurist, E., & Target, M. (2002). *Affect regulation, mentalization, and the development of the self*. Other Press.

Foote, B., Smolin, Y., Neft, D. I., & Lipschitz, D. (2008). Dissociative disorders and suicidality in psychiatric outpatients. *Journal of Nervous and Mental Disease*, *196*(1), 29–36. https://doi.org/10.1097/NMD.0b013e31815fa4e7

Freud, S. (1927). Fetishism. In J. Strachey (Ed.), *The complete psychological works of Sigmund Freud* (Vol. XXI, pp. 147–157). Hogarth and the Institute of Psychoanalysis.

Freud, S. (1938/1940). An outline of psychoanalysis. In J. Strachey (Ed.), *The complete psychological works of Sigmund Freud* (Vol. 23, pp. 139–207). Hogarth and the Institute of Psychoanalysis.

Freyd, J. J. (1994). Betrayal trauma: Traumatic amnesia as an adaptive response to childhood abuse. *Ethics and Behavior*, *4*(4), 307–329. https://doi.org/10.1207/s15327019eb0404_1

Gaddini, R. (1977). The pathology of the self as a basis of psychosomatic disorders. *Psychotherapy and Psychosomatics*, *28*(1/4), 260–271. https://doi.org/10.1159/000287071

Gartner, G. B. (2001). *Betrayed as boys: Psychodynamic treatment of sexually abused men*. Guilford Press.

Guntrip, H. (1969). *Schizoid phenomena, object-relations, and the self*. International Universities Press.

Herman, J. L., Perry, J. C., & Van der Kolk, B. A. (1989). Childhood trauma in borderline personality disorder. *American Journal of Psychiatry*, *146*(4), 490–495.

Hofmann, A., Ostacoli, L., Lehnung, M., Hase, M., & Luber, M. (2022). *Treating depression with EMDR therapy: Techniques and interventions*. Springer Publishing Company. https://doi.org/10.1891/9780826139665

Howell, E. F. (2002). "Good girls," sexy "bad girls," and warriors: The role of trauma and dissociation in the creation and reproduction of gender. *Journal of Trauma and Dissociation*, *3*(4), 2–35. https://doi.org/10.1300/J229v03n04_02

Howell, E. F. (2003). Narcissism, a relational aspect of dissociation. *Journal of Trauma and Dissociation*, *4*(3), 51–71. https://doi.org/10.1300/J229v04n03_04

Jacobson, E. (1972). *Depression*. New York: International Universities Press.

Jaspers, K. (1913). *Allgemeine Psychopathologie* (general psychopathology). Springer Verlag.

Kahneman, D. (2011). *Thinking fast and slow*. Farrar Straus and Giroux.

Kalsched, D. E. (1996). *The inner world of trauma: Archetypal defenses of the personal spirit*. Routledge.

Kandel, E. (2016). *Reductionism in art and brain science: Bridging the two cultures*. Columbia University Press.

Karaaslan, M. F., Orhan, Z., Aloglu, N., Orhan, F. Ö., & Ekerbiçer, H. Ç. (2004). Interference as a depressiogenic factor among housewives. *Proceedings of the 40th Annual Conference of the Psychiatric Association of Turkey*. Psychiatric Association of Turkey.

Karpman, S. B. (1968). Fairy tales and script drama analysis. *Transactional Analysis Bulletin*, *7*(26), 39–43.

Kernberg, O. F. (1967). Borderline personality organization. *Journal of the American Psychoanalytic Association*, *15*(3), 641–685. https://doi.org/10.1177/000306516701500309

Kernberg, O. F. (1987). *Internal world and external reality. Object relations theory applied*. Jason Aronson Inc.

Kierkegaard, S. (1849/1983). *Sickness unto death*. Princeton University Press.

Kılıç, Ö., Şar, V., Taycan, O., Aksoy-Poyraz, C., Erol, T. C., Tecer, Ö., Emül, H. M., & Özmen, M. (2014). Dissociative depression among women with fibromyalgia or rheumatoid arthritis. *Journal of Trauma and Dissociation*, *15*(3), 285–302. https://doi.org/10.1080/15299732.2013.844218

Klein, M. (1987). *The selected Melanie Klein* (J. Mitchell Ed.). Free Press.

Kluft, R. P. (1985). The natural history of multiple personality disorder. In R. Kluft (Ed.), *Childhood antecedents of multiple personality* (pp. 197–238). American Psychiatric Press.

Kluft, R. P. (1988). The dissociative disorders. In J. Talbott, R. Hales, & S. Yudofsky (Eds.), *The American Psychiatric Press textbook of psychiatry* (pp. 557–585). American Psychiatric Press.

Kluft, R. P. (1993). Basic principles in conducting the psychotherapy of multiple personality disorder. In R. P. Kluft & C. G. Fine (Eds.), *Clinical perspectives on multiple personality disorder* (pp 19–26). American Psychiatric Press.

Koç, G. (2022). A study of femicide in Turkey from 2010–2017. *SAGE Open*, *12*(3), 215824402211198. https://doi.org/10.1177/21582440221119831

Kohut, H. (1971). *The analysis of the self: A systematic approach to the psychoanalytic treatment of narcissistic personality disorders*. International Universities Press.

Krystal, H. (1978). Self-representation and the capacity for self-care. In *Annual of psychoanalysis* (Vol. 9, pp. 93–113). International Universities Press.

Kyte, D. H., Hodgdon, H., Suvak, M. K., & DiBiase, R. (2023). Dissociation in a developmental psychopathology framework: Predictors and outcomes among a clinical sample of trauma-impacted adolescents. *Psychological Trauma: Theory, Research, Practice, & Policy*, *15*(Suppl 1), S3–S10. https://doi.org/10.1037/tra0001442

Lanius, R. A., Boyd, J. E., McKinnon, M. C., Nicholson, A. A., Frewen, P., Vermetten, E., Jetly, R., & Spiegel, D. (2018). A review of the neurobiological basis of trauma-related dissociation and its relation to cannabinoid- and opioid-mediated stress response: A transdiagnostic, translational approach. *Current Psychiatry Reports*, *20*(12), 118. https://doi.org/10.1007/s11920-018-0983-y

Lanius, R. A., Vermetten, E., Loewenstein, R. J., Brand, B., Schmahl, C., Bremner, J. D., & Spiegel, D. (2010). Emotion modulation in PTSD: Clinical and neurobiological evidence for a dissociative subtype. *American Journal of Psychiatry*, *167*(6), 640–647. https://doi.org/10.1176/appi.ajp.2009.09081168

Liotti, G. (1992). Disorganized/Disoriented attachment in the etiology of the dissociative disorders. *Dissociation*, *5*(4), 196–204.

Liotti, G. (1999). Understanding the dissociative processes: The contribution of attachment theory. *Psychoanalytic Inquiry*, *19*(5), 757–783. https://doi.org/10.1080/07351699909534275

Liotti, G. (2006). A model of dissociation based on attachment theory and research. *Journal of Trauma and Dissociation*, *7*(4), 55–73. https://doi.org/10.1300/J229v07n04_04

Lynn, S. J., Polizzi, C., Merckelbach, H., Chiu, C. D., Maxwell, R., van Heugten, D., & Lilienfeld, S. O. (2022). Dissociation and dissociative disorders reconsidered: Beyond sociocognitive and trauma models toward a transtheoretical framework. *Annual Review of Clinical Psychology*, *18*(1), 259–289. https://doi.org/10.1146/annurev-clinpsy-081219-102424

Lyons-Ruth, K., Dutra, L., Schuder, M. R., & Bianchi, I. (2006). From infant attachment disorganization to adult dissociation: Relational adaptations or traumatic experiences? *Psychiatric Clinics of North America*, *29*(1), 63–86. https://doi.org/10.1016/j.psc.2005.10.011

Lyssenko, L., Schmahl, C., Bockhacker, L., Vonderlin, R., Bohus, M., & Kleindienst, N. (2018). Dissociation in psychiatric disorders: A meta-analysis of studies using the dissociative experiences scale. *American Journal of Psychiatry*, *175*(1), 37–46. https://doi.org/10.1176/appi.ajp.2017.17010025

Mahler, M. S., Pine, F., & Bergman, A. (1973). *The psychological birth of the human infant*. Basic Books.

Main, M. (1991). Metacognitive knowledge, metacognitive monitoring, and singular (coherent) vs. multiple (incoherent) models of attachment: Findings and directions for future research. In P. Harris, J. Stevenson-Hinde, & C. Parkes (Eds.), *Attachment across the life cycle* (pp. 127–159). Routledge.

Main, M. & Solomon, J. (1986). Discovery of an insecure-disorganized/disoriented attachment pattern. In T. B. Brazelton & M. W. Yogman (Eds.), *Affective development in infancy* (pp. 95–124). Ablex Publishing.

McDougall, J. (1989). *Theatres of the body: A psychoanalytic approach to psychosomatic illness*.

Meares, R. (1999). The contribution of Hughlings Jackson to an understanding of dissociation. *American Journal of Psychiatry*, *156*(12), 1850–1855. https://doi.org/10.1176/ajp.156.12.1850

Meares, R. (2003). Towards a psyche for psychiatry. *Australian and New. Zealand Journal of Psychiatry*, *37*(6), 689–695. https://doi.org/10.1080/j.1440-1614.2003.01256.x

Meares, R. (2012). *A dissociation model of borderline personality disorder*. Norton.

Moskowitz, A. K. & Corstens, D. (2007). Auditory hallucinations: Psychotic symptom or dissociative experience? *Journal of Psychological Trauma*, *6*(2/3), 35–63. https://doi.org/10.1300/J513v06n02_04

Mungan, M. (1982/1990). Punk Lady ve Ümmü-Sübyan. In *Kum Saati*. Remzi Kitabevi.

Nathanson, D. L. (1992). *Shame and pride: Affect, sex, and the birth of the self*. Norton.

Nemeroff, C. B., Heim, C. M., Thase, M. E., Klein, D. N., Rush, A. J., Schatzberg, A. F., Ninan, P.T., McCullough, J.P., Weiss, P.M., Dunner, D.L., & Rothbaum, B.O. (2003). Differential responses to psychotherapy versus pharmacotherapy in patients with chronic forms of major depression and childhood trauma. *Proceedings of the National Academy of Sciences*, *100*, 14293–14296.

Öğünç, N. E. & Şar, V. (2007). Adam öldürme suçu işlemiş kadınların suç motivasyonları ve kişilik özellikleri [Female murderers: motivations for crime and personality features]. *Adli Psikiyatri Dergisi*, *4*(2), 3–11.

Otnow-Lewis, D., Yeager, C. A., Swica, Y., Pincus, J. H., & Lewis, M. (1997). Objective documentation of child abuse and dissociation in 12 murderers with dissociative identity disorder. *The American Journal of Psychiatry*, *154*(12), 1703–1710. https://doi.org/10.1176/ajp.154.12.1703

Öztürk, E. & Şar, V. (2005). 'Apparently normal' family: A contemporary agent of transgenerational trauma and dissociation. *Journal of Trauma Practice*, *4*(3–4), 287–303. https://doi.org/10.1300/J189v04n03_06

Öztürk, E. & Şar, V. (2016). The trauma-self and its resistances in psychotherapy. *Journal of Psychology & Clinical Psychiatry*, *6*(6), 00386. https://doi.org/10.15406/jpcpy.2016.06.00386

Öztürk, M. (1976). The special familial role given to children with symptoms of hysteria. *Çocuk Sagligi ve Hastaliklari Dergisi*, *19*, 93–107.

Öztürk, M. & Öztürk, O. M. (1981). The intra-family role patterns of children with conversion hysterias. *Mediterranean Journal of Social Psychiatry*, *2*, 81–87.

Öztürk, O. M. & Gögüs, A. (1973). Hysterical psychoses presenting with severe regressive symptoms. *Proceedings of the 9th national conference of psychiatry and neurology* (pp. 155–164).

Purtell, J., Robins, E., & Cohen, M. (1951). Observations on clinical aspects of hysteria. *Journal of American Medical Association*, *146*(10), 902–909. https://doi.org/10.1001/jama.1951.03670100022006

Putnam, F. W. (1989). *Diagnosis and treatment of multiple personality disorder*. Guilford Press.

Putnam, F. W. (2016). *The way we are. How states of mind influence our identities, personality and potential for change*. International Psychoanalytic Books.

Renner, W. (2011). *Female Turkish migrants with recurrent depression*. Studia.

Riesman, D. (1950). *The lonely crowd*. Yale University Press.

Ross, C. A. (1997). *Dissociative identity disorder. Diagnosis, clinical features, and treatment of multiple personality*. Wiley Press.

Ross, C. A. (2000). *The trauma model. A solution to the problem of comorbidity in psychiatry*. Manitou Publications.

Sakarya, D., Güneş, C., Öztürk, E., & Şar, V. (2012). "Vampirism" in a case of dissociative identity disorder and PTSD. *Psychotherapy & Psychosomatics*, *81*(5), 322–323. https://doi.org/10.1159/000335930

Sar, I. & Sar, V. (1991). Early birth order in hysteria. *Medical Bulletin of Sisli Etfal Hospital*, *25*, 114–122.

Şar, V. (1989). Depressif kadınlarda çocuklukta anababa yitimi [Parental loss among depressive women]. *Hacettepe Tıp Dergisi*, *22*, 281–287.

Şar, V. (2011). Dissociative depression: A common cause of treatment resistance. In W. Renner (Ed.), *Female Turkish migrants with recurrent depression* (pp. 112–124). Studia.

Şar, V. (2017a). Identity revised: A clinician's perspective on how an identity-based model of mind would look like. In J. Sinnott (Ed.), *Identity flexibility during adulthood: Perspectives on adult development* (pp. 265–288). Springer Publication. https://doi.org/10.1007/978-3-319-55658-1_17

Şar, V. (2017b). Parallel-distinct structures of internal world and external reality: Disavowing and re-claiming the self-identity in the aftermath of trauma-generated dissociation. *Frontiers in Psychology*, *8*, 216. https://doi.org/10.3389/fpsyg.2017.00216

Şar, V. (2019). The Tri-Modal reaction (T-MR) model of complex trauma and dissociation: A proposal. *Quaderni of Psicoterapia Cognitiva*, *44*(44), 50–71. https://doi.org/10.3280/qpc44-2019oa8149

Şar, V. (2020). Childhood trauma and dissociative disorders. In G. Spalletta, D. Janiri, F. Piras, & G. Sani (Eds.), *Childhood trauma in mental disorders: A comprehensive approach* (pp. 333–365). Springer Publication. https://doi.org/10.1007/978-3-030-49414-8_16

Şar, V. (2022a). The dialectical dynamic therapy of trauma. *Journal of Trauma andDissociation*, *23*(4), 339–355. https://doi.org/10.1080/15299732.2022.2079110

Şar, V. (2022b). Dissociation across cultures: A transdiagnostic guide for clinical assessment and management. *Alpha Psychiatry, 23*(3), 95–103. https://doi.org/10.5152/alphapsychiatry.2021.21556

Şar, V. (2022c). Psychiatry shuffles the cards: Toward new subtypes, specifiers, and qualifiers. *Düşünen Adam, 35*, 141–146. https://doi.org/10.14744/DAJPNS.2022.00186

Şar, V. (2022d). Psychotic presentations of dissociative disorders. In M. Dorahy, S. Gold, & J. O'Neil (Eds.), *Dissociation and dissociative disorders: Past, present, future* (pp. 403–413). Routledge Press. https://doi.org/10.4324/9781003057314-31

Şar, V. (2023a). Dialectical Dynamic Therapy (DDT): Allowing progressive change through the subtle repair of master-identity. *European Journal of Trauma & Dissociation, 7*(1), 339–355. https://doi.org/10.1016/j.ejtd.2022.100307

Şar, V. (2023b). Dissociative identity disorder recovery. In H. Tohid & I. H. Rutkofsky (Eds.), *A comprehensive textbook of dissociative identity disorder*. Springer Publication.

Sar, V., Akyüz, G., Dogan, O., & Öztürk, E. (2009). The prevalence of conversion symptoms in women from a general Turkish population. *Psychosomatics, 50*(1), 50–58. https://doi.org/10.1176/appi.psy.50.1.50

Şar, V., Akyüz, G., Kuğu, N., Öztürk, E., & Ertem-Vehid, H. (2006). Axis-I dissociative disorder comorbidity of borderline personality disorder and childhood trauma reports. *Journal of Clinical Psychiatry, 67*(10), 1583–1590. https://doi.org/10.4088/JCP.v67n1014

Sar, V., Akyüz, G., Kundakci, T., Kiziltan, E., & Dogan, O. (2004). Childhood trauma, dissociation and psychiatric comorbidity in patients with conversion disorder. *American Journal of Psychiatry, 161*(12), 2271–2276. https://doi.org/10.1176/ajp.161.12.2271

Şar, V., Akyüz, G., Öztürk, E., & Alioğlu, F. (2013). Dissociative depression among women in the community. *Journal of Trauma and Dissociation, 14*(4), 423–438. https://doi.org/10.1080/15299732.2012.753654

Şar, V., Alioğlu, F., & Akyüz, G. (2017). Depersonalization and derealization in self-report and clinical interview: The spectrum of borderline personality disorder, dissociative disorders, and healthy controls. *Journal of Trauma and Dissociation, 18*(4), 490–506. https://doi.org/10.1080/15299732.2016.1240737

Şar, V., Alioğlu, F., Akyüz, G., & Karabulut, S. (2014a). Dissociative amnesia in dissociative disorders and borderline personality disorder: Self-rating assessment in a college population. *Journal of Trauma and Dissociation, 15*(4), 477–493. https://doi.org/10.1080/15299732.2014.902415

Şar, V., Alioğlu, F., Akyüz, G., Tayakısı, E., Öğülmüş, F. E., & Sönmez, D. (2017). Awareness of identity alteration and diagnostic preference between borderline personality disorder and dissociative disorders. *Journal of Trauma and Dissociation, 18*(5), 693–709. https://doi.org/10.1080/15299732.2016.1267684

Şar, V., Dorahy, M. J., & Krüger, C. (2017). Revisiting the etiological aspects of dissociative identity disorder: A biopsychosocial perspective. *Psychology Research and Behavior Management, 10*, 137–146. https://doi.org/10.2147/PRBM.S113743

Sar, V., Kundakçi, T., Kiziltan, E., Yargiç, L. I., Tutkun, H., Bakim, B., Aydiner, O., Özpulat, T., Keser, V., & Özdemir, Ö. (2003). Axis I dissociative disorder comorbidity of borderline personality disorder among psychiatric outpatients. *Journal of Trauma and Dissociation, 4*(1), 119–136. https://doi.org/10.1300/J229v04n01_08

Şar, V., Necef, I., Mutluer, T., Fatih, P., & Türk-Kurtça, T. (2021). The revised and expanded version of the Turkish childhood trauma Questionnaire (CTQ-33): Overprotection-overcontrol as additional factor. *Journal of Trauma and Dissociation, 22*(1), 35–51. https://doi.org/10.1080/15299732.2020.1760171

Şar, V., Önder, C., Kılınçaslan, A., Zoroğlu, S. S., & Alyanak, B. (2014b). Dissociative identity disorder among adolescents: Prevalence in a university psychiatric outpatient unit. *Journal of Trauma and Dissociation*, *15*(4), 402–419. https://doi.org/10.1080/15299732.2013.864748

Sar, V. & Öztürk, E. (2006). What is trauma and dissociation? *Journal of Trauma Practice*, *4*(1–2), 7–20. https://doi.org/10.1300/J189v04n01_02

Sar, V. & Öztürk, E. (2007). Functional dissociation of the self: A sociocognitive approach to trauma and dissociation. *Journal of Trauma and Dissociation*, *8*(4), 69–89. https://doi.org/10.1300/J229v08n04_05

Şar, V. & Ozturk, E. (2013). Stimulus deprivation and overstimulation as dissociogenic agents in postmodern oppressive societies. *Journal of Trauma and Dissociation*, *14* (2), 198–212. https://doi.org/10.1080/15299732.2013.724346

Şar, V., Öztürk, E., Islam, S., Küçükgöncü, S., Yumbul, Ç., & Ertem-Vehid, H. (2012). Zwischen Selbstreflexion und Selbst-Überzeugtsein: Kognitive Einsicht bei dissoziativen und schizophrenen Störungen und das Dissoziationsparadox. In I. Özkan, U. Sachsse, & A. Streeck-Fischer (Eds.), *Zeit heilt nicht alle Wunden: Kompendium zur Psychotraumatologie* (pp. 161–172). Vandenhoeck Ruprecht. https://doi.org/10.13109/9783666401862.161

Şar, V., Öztürk, E., & Kundakçı, T. (2002). Psychotherapy of an adolescent with dissociative identity disorder: Change in Rorschach patterns. *Journal of Trauma & Dissociation*, *3*(2), 81–95. https://doi.org/10.1300/J229v03n02_05

Sar, V. & Ross, C. A. (2006). Dissociative disorders as a confounding factor in psychiatric research. *Psychiatric Clinics of North America*, *29*(1), 129–144. https://doi.org/10.1016/j.psc.2005.10.008

Sar, V., Taycan, O., Bolat, N., Özmen, M., Duran, A., Öztürk, E., & Ertem-Vehid, H. (2010). Childhood trauma and dissociation in schizophrenia. *Psychopathology*, *43*(1), 33–40. https://doi.org/10.1159/000255961

Şar, V. & Türk-Kurtça, T. (2021). The vicious cycle of traumatic narcissism and dissociative depression among young adults: A trans-diagnostic approach. *Journal of Trauma and Dissociation*, *22*(5), 502–521. https://doi.org/10.1080/15299732.2020.1869644

Şar, V., Ünal, S. N., Kızıltan, E., Kundakçı, T., & Öztürk, E. (2001). HMPAO SPECT study of cerebral perfusion in dissociative identity disorder. *Journal of Trauma and Dissociation*, *2*(2), 5–25. https://doi.org/10.1300/J229v02n02_02

Şar, V., Unal, S. N., & Ozturk, E. (2007). Frontal and occipital perfusion changes in dissociative identity disorder. *Psychiatry Research – Neuroimaging*, *156*(3), 217–223. https://doi.org/10.1016/j.pscychresns.2006.12.017

Scharff, J. S. (1992). *Projective and introjective identification and the use of the therapist's self.* Jason Aronson.

Schimmenti, A. (2022). The relationship between attachment and dissociation: Theory, research, and clinical implications. In M. J. Dorahy, S. N. Gold, & J. A. O'Neil (Eds.), *Dissociation and the dissociative disorders. Past, present, future* (pp. 161–176). Routledge.

Schimmenti, A. & Şar, V. (2019). A correlation network analysis of dissociative experiences. *Journal of Trauma and Dissociation*, *20*(4), 402–419. https://doi.org/10.1080/15299732.2019.1572045

Simon, R. I. (2008). *Bad men do what good men dream. A forensic psychiatrist illuminates darker side of human behavior.* American Psychiatric Publishing.

Soffer-Dudek, N. (2014). Dissociation and dissociative mechanisms in panic disorder, obsessive–compulsive disorder, and depression: A review and heuristic framework. *Psychology of Consciousness: Theory, Research, & Practice*, *1*(3), 243–270. https://doi.org/10.1037/cns0000023

Sommer, J. L., Blaney, C., Mota, N., Bilevicius, E., Beatie, B., Kilborn, K., Chang, U., Sareen, J., & El-Gabalawy, R. (2021). Dissociation as a transdiagnostic indicator of self-injurious behavior and suicide attempts: A focus on posttraumatic stress disorder and borderline personality disorder. *Journal of Traumatic Stress*, *34*(6), 1149–1158. https://doi.org/10.1002/jts.22726

Spiegel, D. (1986). Dissociation, double binds and posttraumatic stress in multiple personality disorder. In B. G. Braun (Ed.), *Treatment of multiple personality disorder* (pp. 61–77). American Psychiatric Press.

Spitz, R. A. (1945). Hospitalism: An inquiry into the genesis of psychiatric conditions in early childhood. *The Psychoanalytic Study of the Child*, *1*(1), 53–74. https://doi.org/10.1080/00797308.1945.11823126

Steele, K., Van der Hart, O., & Nijenhuis, E. R. S. (2005). Phase-oriented treatment of structural dissociation in complex traumatization: Overcoming trauma-related phobias. *Journal of Trauma and Dissociation*, *6*(3), 11–53. https://doi.org/10.1300/J229v06n03_02

Steinberg, M. & Schnall, M. (2000). *The stranger in the mirror*. Cliff Street Books.

Stierlin, H. (1982). *Delegation und Familie*. Suhrkamp Verlag.

Sullivan, H. S. (1953). *The interpersonal theory of psychiatry*. William Alanson White Psychiatric Foundation.

Sullivan, H. S. (1954). *The psychiatric interview*. Norton.

Van der Hart, O. (1983). *Rituals in psychotherapy. Transition and continuity*. Irvington Publishers.

Van der Hart, O. & Horst, R. (1989). The dissociation theory of Pierre Janet. *Journal of Traumatic Stress*, *2*(4), 397–412. https://doi.org/10.1002/jts.2490020405

Van der Hart, O., Nijenhuis, E. R. S., & Steele, K. (2006). *The haunted self: Structural dissociation and the treatment of chronic traumatization*. Norton.

Van der Hart, O., Witztum, E., & Friedman, B. (1993). From hysterical psychosis to reactive dissociative psychosis. *Journal of Traumatic Stress*, *6*(1), 43–64. https://doi.org/10.1002/jts.2490060106

Volkan, V. D. (1995). *The infantil psychotic self and its fates. Understanding and treating schizophrenics and other difficult patients*. New York Jason Aronson.

Watkins, H. H. & Watkins, J. G. (1997). *Ego states: Theory and therapy*. Norton.

Winkelman, M. (2011). A paradigm for understanding altered consciousness: The integrative mode of consciousness. In E. Cardena & M. Winkelman (Eds.), *Altering consciousness: Multidisciplinary perspectives* (Vol. 1, pp. 23–41). Praeger.

Winnicott, D. W. (1973). *The child, the family, and the outside world*. Middlesex, Penguin Publication.

Wright, A. G. C., Ringwald, W. R., Hopwood, C. J., & Pincus, A. L. (2022). It's time to replace the personality disorders with the interpersonal disorders. *The Interpersonal Disorders*, *77*(9), 1085–1099. https://doi.org/10.1037/amp0001087

Yargic, L. I., Tutkun, H., & Sar, V. (1995). Childhood traumas and dissociative experiences in adulthood. In *Proceedings of the 5th ISSD Annual Spring Conference*.

Zhang, J., Wu, Z., Tao, H., Chen, M., Yu, M., Zhou, L., Sun, M., Lv, D., Cui, G., Yi, Q., Tang, H., An, C., Liu, Z., Huang, X., & Long, Y. (2023). Associated socio-demographic and psychological factors of childhood overprotection/overcontrol experiences among Chinese university students: A nationwide survey. Preprint.

Metaphoric, metonymic and psychotic somatoform dissociation

Dana Amir

The present paper seeks to propose, using a combination of psychoanalytic and linguistic thinking, a distinction between three degrees of symbolicity across the somatoform dissociative continuum: the metaphorical, in which there is a symbolic connection between the somatoform phenomenon and the traumatic content, the metonymic, which constitutes a revival of the traumatic experience without the ability to reflect on it, and the psychotic, in which the somatoform phenomenon is experienced as ego-syntonic, thus neither causes distress nor evokes thinking. Three clinical vignettes demonstrate how the higher the degree of symbolization, the more effective the therapeutic process. Finally, a fourth vignette demonstrates how acoustic association in the therapist's countertransference can constitute an antidote to the patient's acoustic dissociation, allowing the reclaiming of the capacity for linking.

One of the questions that bother psychoanalytic clinical and theoretical thinking for decades is the question concerning the recording of traumatic memories. Traumatic experiences often activate a psychic process of self-annihilation. Their acidity creates a type of psychic hole that absorbs the unbearable traumatic substances along with the subject who contains them (Laub, 2005; Modell, 2006; Moore, 1999; Oliner, 1996; Stern, 2012; Van der Kolk et al., 1996), leaving the subject imprisoned in a territory of *negative possession* (Amir, 2012) in which the traumatic contents are neither digested nor worked through. The earlier the traumatic events are, and the more severe their intensity, the more they are prone to create an inner enclave that on the one hand allows no way in – and on the other hand allows no way out (Amir, 2016a, 2016b, 2019a). This enclave is the traumatic lacuna (LaCapra, 1994).

Caruth (1996, pp. 91–92) writes about the traumatic paradox in which the most direct contact with the violent event may occur only through the very inability to know it. Trauma is not only an experience, but also the failure to experience that experience: not merely the threat itself, but the fact that the threat was recognized as such only a moment too late. As it was not experienced in time, the event is condemned not to be fully known (Caruth, 1996, p. 62). As such, it returns to claim its presence, trying to cover the experiential void through various symptoms. This reclaiming can take diverse psychological as well as somatic forms, which simultaneously preserve as well as prevent contact with the traumatic materials. This deeply touches on the subject of dissociation in general, and of somatoform dissociation in particular.

Dissociation & somatoform dissociation

Traditional understanding of dissociation considers it a mechanism that is both defensive and adaptive: a process in which traumatic memories and feelings become disconnected from each other and get displaced in different parts of the personality (Bromberg, 1998; Chefetz, 2015; Kluft, 2000; O'Neil, 2009; Schimmenti & Caretti, 2016), preventing in this way from the traumatic experience, or certain aspects of it, to enter consciousness, thus allowing the individual to avoid processing or integrating information that is intolerable and inescapable. The more extreme the traumatic experience, the more massively the dissociative mechanism will be deployed (Bromberg, 1998; Chefetz, 2015). Van der Hart, Van der Kolk, and Boon (1996) suggest that pathological dissociation can be divided into three forms. In *primary dissociation*, a traumatic experience is processed in parts, rather than as an integrated whole. *Secondary dissociation* involves the individual perceiving an event without experiencing its full emotional impact. *Tertiary dissociation* involves the development of separate identities, each of which contains emotional and cognitive material that is unavailable (or only partially available) to the other identities. This distinction has later been refined (Nijenhuis & Van der Hart, 1999) to focus on the psychological dysfunctions involved in each form: while *primary dissociation* involves traumatic experiences being seen as isolated from the individual rather than as isolated from each other (as suggested by Van der Kolk et al., 1996), in *secondary dissociation* there is a division of the components of an experience (e.g., remembering a trauma without the affective component). Finally, *tertiary dissociation* involves the formation of distinct ego states (Waller et al., 2000).

Somatoform dissociation includes dissociative symptoms that phenomenologically involve the body and are related to the sensory and motor components of experiences, such as hearing, feeling, seeing, speaking, and moving, including conversion symptoms (Ellert & Nijenhuis, 2001; Nijenhuis et al., 1996). Although the tendency is to treat dissociation as a mechanism related to psychological symptoms and factors, patients with dissociative disorders report many somatoform symptoms, and many meet the diagnostic criteria of somatization disorder or conversion disorder (Ellert & Nijenhuis, 2001; Pribor et al., 1993; Ross et al., 1989; Saxe et al., 1994). In addition, patients with somatization disorder often have amnesia (Ellert & Nijenhuis, 2001; Othmer & DeSouza, 1985). Although somatoform disorders are not conceptualized as dissociative disorders in the DSM, the strong correlation between dissociative and somatoform disorders indicates that dissociation and conversion symptoms, particularly somatization symptoms, may be manifestations of a single underlying principle (Ellert & Nijenhuis, 2001). Among various types of traumas, physical and especially sexual abuse, best predicts somatoform dissociation (Coons, 1994; Ellert & Nijenhuis, 2001; Hornstein & Putnam, 1992; Kluft, 1995; Lewis et al., 1997).

Psychoanalytic thinking, beginning with the study of hysteria, strongly coincides with these data. The concept of somatization has its origins in the work of Freud (Breuer & Freud, 1893–1895), who proposed the idea of conversion as a main defense mechanism. The nineteenth century symptoms of hysteria are very characteristic of the twentieth century dissociative disorders. In fact, the items of the Somatoform Dissociation Questionnaire (SDQ-20) comprise many of the symptoms that mark hysteria as described by Janet, whose clinical observations suggested that hysteria involves psychological as well as somatoform functions and reactions (Janet, 1889/1973, 1893, 1901/1977/1907/1965).

Ferenzci (1932) argued that the human individual has two memory systems: while the subjective memory system includes feelings and bodily sensations, the objective memory system includes external events and sensations ascribed to one's surroundings. The earlier an event, the more likely it is to have been encoded in the subjective memory, that is, as a bodily sensation or response. Having been inscribed in the body, certain types of memory can only re-surface in the body. Ferenczi considered the occurrence of bodily symptoms during psychotherapy as evidence of the return of this type of memories – a return made possible because and as part of the process of therapeutic regression. Winnicott (1954), too, regarded bodily experience as the substrate of psychic formation. He described the developing individual as a mode of being within which psyche and soma are inextricable and become distinct only as a function of the observer's viewpoint. In his article 'Ego distortions in terms of true and false self' (1960) he focuses on the stage by which the patient allows contact, however partial, with hitherto inaccessible regions associated with his or her true self. It happens often that the patient falls ill during this process, thereby giving the therapist the opportunity to assume the role previously taken by the false self.

French thinkers linked the psychosomatic drama with difficulty in transforming body into language, or the raw primary data of experience into words and symbols. When the mother-infant relation is dysfunctional, the infant finds it hard to internalise the maternal object enough to dare losing and recreating it as a symbol, thus form a representation of its absence (Green, 1998; Kristeva, 1987). In such cases the infant goes on generating physical symptoms as a way of keeping the mother close as well as expressing his inability to mourn her in the process of internalisation Amir, 2014). MacDougall (McDougall, 1989) argued that where experiences are not successfully repressed, thus gaining no internal representation, they cannot even serve to generate neurotic symptoms. When temporarily, or for a longer stretch of time, the psyche is unable to restore what has been expelled from consciousness in the form of symptoms, the release of dreams or any other type of mental activity, it enters a state of deprivation. It is likely, in such a case, that the psyche will respond by somatisation. Like in early pre-linguistic childhood, the somatically reacting psyche will directly access the 'thing' – not the word that represents it. The bodily reaction is a primitive representation of the experience – but one that cannot turn it into a meaningful experience or enable release. MacDougall mentions in this context a phenomenon she calls 'archaic hysteria'. Unlike its neurotic counterpart, which is a more developed form mainly related to anxiety associated with sexual satisfaction and desires – archaic hysteria concerns the very desire or right to exist. These are not anxieties of the more 'developed' kind, but ones that occur where personal identity or life itself are under a threat of extinction. These states are marked by damage to a body part or bodily function without organic reason. Since the anxieties involved are unavailable to symbolic, reflective, verbal representation – no neurotic symptoms evolve. What remains is the thing itself, without any possibility of distancing.

In 'A question prior to any possible treatment of psychosis' (1958/2007) Lacan writes about the notion of 'forclusion' in the context of psychosis. Repression and forclusion differ in that while the former aims to remove a thought or an image from consciousness, the latter removes it from the unconscious. In other words, while repression strives to fix the materials in the unconscious, forclusion casts them out of it. While repression is part of normal psychic functioning, though under certain conditions it has neurotic outcomes that impair functioning – forclusion consists of a violent rejection of psychic reality and its implications are catastrophic. It leads to psychosis rather than neurosis.

I would like to differentiate now between three states of somatoform dissociation which are located between the pole of repression and the pole of forclusion: The metaphorical, in which there is a symbolic connection between the somatoform phenomenon and the traumatic content, the metonymic, which constitutes a revival of the traumatic experience without the ability to reflect on it, and the psychotic, in which the somatoform phenomenon is experienced as ego-syntonic, thus neither causes distress nor evokes thinking.

Metaphoric, metonymic, and psychotic somatoform dissociation

Metaphor and metonymy are two forms of semantic shift, that is, two modes of transition from one semantic field to another. Metaphor is the use of a word or expression in a borrowed rather than simple sense, or rather the use of the characteristics of one concept to illuminate another. Metaphor is based on analogy, namely on a relationship of similarity between two semantic fields. The sentence 'My love is a rose' does not imply that the rose itself is the beloved one but that something in the beloved one's features resembles those of a rose.

Metonymy, by contrast, is a figurative tool that illustrates something by replacing it with another that is situated close to it in time or space, or that belongs in the same context. The result is not logical in the simple sense, thus can only be understood through the proximity between the two elements. This is how the expression 'the White House' comes to stand for the notion of 'the President's spokesperson'. As opposed to metaphor, in metonymy there is no transfer of characteristics between the two elements (the President's spokesperson is not meant to share features with the White House). The connection between them is associative only in a way that allows us to perceive the one as representative of the other (Amir, 2014; Efrati and Israeli, 2007).

In his article 'Two aspects of language and two types of linguistic disturbances' (Jacobson, 1956/1971), Roman Jakobson presents metaphor and metonymy as opposites rather than parts of the hierarchical order in which they are more commonly seen. He stresses the similarity that metaphor installs between its signifiers versus the contiguity typical of metonymy. Each of these modes of transposition, he argues, relies on different cognitive skills. While metaphor is based on the cognitive ability to convert, metonymy implies the cognitive ability to connect and contextualise. Jakobson divides the aphasic patients with whom his article is concerned into those who suffer from impaired identification of similarities as opposed to patients whose ability to combine and contextualise is affected.

Lacan's distinction between metaphor and metonymy diverges from Jakobson's. Though, following the latter, he associates metaphor with the axis of linguistic selection and metonymy with that of combination, metaphor for him acts to constitute meaning while metonymy resists meaning: the metonymic drive is related to the desire to recover the lost Real. Metaphor, by contrast, is associated with the symptom whose creation is a constructive process in which new meaning is generated.

What is a metaphorical somatoform dissociation versus a metonymical one?

Symbolic somatic phenomena, those which while resisting consciousness nevertheless participate in the symbolic order – can be considered 'metaphorical somatoform dissociation'. The metaphorical somatoform dissociation is an estranged formulation, in a 'foreign language', of something a person either cannot or is not willing to fully recognise. It resembles the conversion phenomena typical of neurotic hysteria. The more primitive somatic phenomena may be seen as 'metonymic somatoform dissociation'. Here there is no rich expression – not even in a different language – of repressed material, but rather a limited shift from the psychic scene to that of the body, or from one physical scene to another physical one (Amir, 2014). It creates a continuity with the traumatic materials, resurrecting them in the vivid present, in a way that is more reminiscent of what MacDougall called 'archaic hysteria' (McDougall, 1989). One can think of the metaphorical somatoform dissociation as a layered structure in which what is located on the surface (the somatic phenomenon itself) is perceived, consciously or unconsciously, as covering another level of consciousness. In contrast, the metonymic somatoform dissociation is a transverse structure. It is not a structure in which one level covers another, but rather a structure in which one phenomenon is connected to another in a more primitive way, where, as mentioned, association replaces analogy.

Finally, there is a third type of somatoform dissociation which I term 'psychotic somatoform dissociation' (Amir, 2014, 2016a, 2016b, 2019a. This phenomenon neither allows for reflection nor does it resurrect the traumatic experience as is. It is a massive attack on thinking and linking. Unlike metaphoric and metonymic expressions which through the distress they cause make a connection, even if a primitive one, with the excluded content – psychotic somatoform dissociation does not only fail to hold meaning (as metaphoric somatoform dissociation does) or preserve continuity (in the way of metonymic somatoform dissociation), but also simply numbs the distress itself, thereby turning any thinking redundant.

And yet, why psychotic?

In both the case of metaphoric somatoform dissociation, where the severed part symbolizes something directly associated with the traumatic memory, and that of metonymic somatoform dissociation, which consists of a vague resurrection of the traumatic experience by producing a kind of contiguity with it, somatoform dissociation is felt to be ego-dystonic (foreign to the self) with the resulting mental distress that accompanies it. These two types of somatoform dissociation, therefore, re-kindle the amputated traumatic contents through the distress they arouse, constituting a kind of invitation, even a demand, for thinking. Psychotic somatoform dissociation, on the other hand, is felt to be ego-syntonic rather than ego-dystonic. What we observe here is neither a symptom demanding meaning (as in the metaphoric somatoform dissociation), nor a contiguity which revives the traumatic real in the here and now and connects to it in this way (as would be the case in metonymic somatoform dissociation), but rather a somatic formation that stays transparent to the subject and hence arouses neither distress nor curiosity. In Bion's terms, this type of somatoform dissociation constitutes the most serious attack on linking (Bion, 1959) not because it blocks the way to the traumatic material but because it does not evoke any mental movement in relation to it, leaving the subject in a state of terminal apathy.

Even though these three types of somatoform dissociation are described here as distinct formations, every single somatoform-dissociative phenomenon might display various combinations of the three types, with each acting as a different dimension of the same phenomenon (see the 4th clinical illustration). While the two first formations are responsive to in-depth interpretations (in the case of metaphoric somatoform dissociation) or experience-near interpretations (in the case of metonymic somatoform dissociation), the psychotic formation remains unresponsive to either form of interpretation. It is this psychotic element which produces a 'negative therapeutic reaction' (Riviere, 1936) in cases of somatoform dissociation, because in relation to it any linking is felt as unbearable threat. And so, chances of a successful psychodynamic psychotherapy depend on the extent to which the metaphoric and metonymic dimensions dominate the somatic dissociative register, indicating that the therapeutic alliance must be made with them.

Clinical Illustrations[1]

Metaphoric somatoform dissociation

A., a man about 30 years old, seeks therapy following a traumatic event in which he forgot his son in the car. The baby lost consciousness and A. was alerted by passers-by who noticed the unconscious child, smashed the window, and activated the car alarm. During the long hours at the intensive care unit, A. began to feel an intense tingling in his right arm. This condition, which remained without any neurological indication, deteriorated, growing so bad that he would suffer severe pains in his arm for days on end (the kind of pain one feels when one's arm goes numb). At other times he lost all feeling in this arm. He sought therapy after medical examinations came up with nothing and the doctors suggested that the origins of his complaint might be emotional, pointing to the fact that the problem had started immediately upon the traumatic event of his forgetting his son in the car. The patient told me, in response to my question, that it was his right arm with which he usually reached back when he was driving and wanted to caress the feet of the baby who was strapped in his baby seat in the back of the car. The tingling in his arm came and went for months. Gradually it stopped, but tended to return when he was somehow in transition. We understood this as related to the fact that in such situations (say moving from car to playschool) he was prone to repeat the traumatic failure of leaving his child behind. In time, as our processing of the traumatic event deepened, the tingling in his arm disappeared. I offer this as an illustration of metaphoric somatoform dissociation because it involves two examples of symbolicity. First, the loss of sensation was in the arm that connected the father with the child, symbolizing the moment in which this connection was 'numbed' enough to enable the father to leave the child behind. Second, the numbness symbolized the state of mental numbness in which the father found himself on the morning of the incident, and which, probably, caused the traumatic forgetting.

Here is an example of a 'metaphorical interpretation', in this context: 'Your numbness is a bodily recording of what happened in your mind, namely the dimming of consciousness, which made it possible to leave your baby in the car. And it is placed in the right hand, the hand you describe as connecting between you two, at the same time as an indication of the traumatic wound and as a warning signal'.

Metonymic somatoform dissociation

B., a woman about 30 years old, was raised by a depressed and dysfunctional mother. Though she did not experience intended abuse, she spent her entire childhood being severely neglected, both physically and emotionally.

According to what a few relatives told her after her mother's death from cancer (when the patient was in her twenties), the mother, who was suffering from extreme post-natal depression, could have for instance changed her diaper, on the one hand, yet forget to feed her on the other; or might put the child to sleep while she was crying with hunger, or alternatively feed her but fail to notice that the baby's entire body was covered in an itchy nappy rash because she was leaving her diapers unchanged. The patient developed a habit of ignoring her hunger and pain. The dissociating function she internalized was activated whenever she experienced either distress or arousal. For instance, she may walk for miles without noticing that her feet are bleeding into her shoes, she forgets to eat for entire days, and one of the things that distresses her the most is her falling asleep during sexual activity.

The reason why this illustrates metonymic somatoform dissociation is because the phenomenon does not symbolize the patient's mother's detachment by means of creating a metaphoric distance, but rather revives it in its raw form, creating in this way an experiential contiguity between daughter and mother through the resurrection of the primary maternal environment. And yet, these dissociations are attended by clear distress that opens a window of opportunity for working through.

Here is an example of a 'metonymic' interpretation following the patient's report of an entire day in which she forgot to eat and drink and ended it in a state of nausea and dehydration (the patient stated that alongside the physical distress there was also a feeling of 'familiarity', even a sense of 'being at home'): 'Being dehydrated, or neglected, is a familiar physical feeling. That's why it's a bit like feeling at home. And maybe this is also your way, when you miss your mother too much, to call her back'.

What is the difference between the 'metaphoric' and the 'metonymic' interpretation?

The former is based on the metaphorical connection between the physical and mental numbness: the hand symbolizes the parental connection between father and son, and the numbness located in this hand is a physical record of the catastrophic rupture of this connection. The interpretation uses, therefore, relatively developed symbolic capacity from the patient's side. The metonymic interpretation, on the other hand, links one thing to another not symbolically but in a way that is experience-near. The dehydration does not symbolize the neglect, or is analogous to the neglect, but is a reproduction of the neglect itself: the experience of the physical distress caused by the dehydration is a kind of memory in action, a revival of the early childhood environment.

In both cases, despite the differences in the level of symbolism, the interpretation was part of prolonged process of working through of a traumatic content that the somatoform symptom allowed access to.

Psychotic somatoform dissociation

C., a woman of about 40, known to the social services for years, is introduced to me by her therapist who comes in for supervision. The problem at hand is C'.s inexplicable somatic phenomenon: a muscular rigidity which breaks up her movement, so that both arms and legs move in a manner reminiscent of what one would call *staccato* in music, as opposed to the *legato* of more naturally flowing motion. The patient herself seems to have no obvious awareness that she is moving in this way, and she does not seem troubled by it. The neurological tests she has done over the years yielded no significant results.

C. was diagnosed with one psychotic-paranoid episode in her early twenties. This diagnosis was based, in part, on her claim that her father was a secret agent who pretended to be a gynecologist (which he really was) to implant 'chips' illicitly collecting information about his patients.

This accusation was related to another complaint C. expressed about having suffered long term sexual abuse from her father. She reported that he would make her recline in his gynecological examination chair every time she was menstruating, penetrating her with his penis, pretending he was carrying out an ultrasound of her ovaries. She told her mother about it on several occasions, but the latter silenced her by explaining that he 'was only checking her to make sure she was developing properly'. The psychotic episode drove the last nail into the coffin of this accusation: now that she was diagnosed with psychosis, any validity her reports might have had becomes compromised in both her mother's and her therapists' views, as well as in her own.

The beginning of her fragmented motor movement can be traced back to her first psychotic breakdown. She was put on medication during a two-month hospitalization and then released. No more episodes of this type occurred, and medication was discontinued. The motor symptom, however, did not vanish. None of the behavioral therapies to which she was referred in the passing years was effective. Presently she is living with her sick mother in what used to be their family home. Her father, apparently taken aback both by the intensity of her psychotic breakdown and her accusations, left home for good while she was hospitalized. She looks after herself physically, and assists her mother with simple chores, but does not maintain relations with anyone other than a few close relatives. Her case was presented to me for supervision, as part of a supervision group for social workers, run by the social services.

I mention it as an illustration of psychotic rather than metaphoric somatoform dissociation (representing, for example, the mental attack on linking through the physical attack on motorial continuity) because of the patient's own attitude to the physical phenomenon, or rather: her non-attitude to it. She treats it as something in need of neither diagnosis nor treatment, something transparent to her, and therefore arousing neither curiosity nor distress. When the examining neurologist asked her whether it did not hinder or trouble her, she answered – 'it troubles my mother'. Upon being asked whether she understood what it was that troubled her mother, she replied she had no idea. Her bizarre motor behavior seems to have erected a barrier between herself and her past trauma, now contained in an untouchable psychosomatic capsule. As long as psychotic somatoform dissociation endures, she is protected, if not entirely from external impingements – than at least from internal seepage in the form of her traumatic memories.

As opposed to the two earlier mentioned types of somatoform dissociation, which produced ambivalent contact (both distancing and beckoning) with the dissociated material, thereby enabling psychic movement in relation to it, psychotic somatoform dissociation not merely thwarts contact with the excluded material, but also neutralizes all motivation to search for meaning.

When it comes to areas of psychotic somatoform dissociation alongside which one can also identify areas of somatoform dissociation that have a metonymic or metaphorical quality – one can work dynamically with the other areas, attempting to increase their surface area in relation to the psychotic surface area. But in cases like the above one, where the dominant area is of psychotic somatoform dissociation, psychodynamic therapeutic work will be much less effective in the absence of any motivation for encounter with depth and meaning.

Vocal Association as Antibody to Vocal Dissociation: Reclaiming of Linking in the Countertransference

D., a woman in her forties, seeks psychoanalysis following continuous traumatization. Between age three and thirteen she was repeatedly raped by her older brother, to whom she felt deeply attached. It happened behind closed doors while her parents were downstairs watching TV.

D. developed a vocal somatoform dissociation, characterized by episodes of either voice-loss or alterations in her voice. She describes episodes during which she is unable to produce any sound, along with episodes in which she wakes at night terrorized at having heard herself speaking in a low male voice (this may suggest dissociative identity disorder, but other than these voice alterations there is no indication of it). One may think of the voiceless episodes as well as the male-voice episodes as two formations where traumatic material is being displaced to the body. Thus, the shifts between her nocturnal male voice and the stretches of daily non-speech were interpreted in analysis as oscillations between metaphoric identification with the (male voice of the) aggressor (Ferenczi, 1932/1988 and the metonymic reenactment of the silencing, which was imposed on her both by external as well as internal origins. While the male voice can be considered a manifestation of metaphoric somatoform dissociation (symbolizing the abuser's voice forcing itself on her voice), the loss of voice has a more composite, metaphoric-metonymic quality: the metaphoric part is associated, as said, with the silencing imposed on her by herself as well as by her family, while the metonymic quality is related to the creation of contiguity with a long-term experience of helplessness; contiguity with the inability to transform what was physically and emotionally intolerable into speech.

The session I will describe now took place some years into analysis. D. was trying to recollect a lullaby of a Scottish origin her brother used to sing to her when she was a little girl.

She remembered loving the tune even though the words made her sad. Then she recited, her voice rather mechanical, the lullaby's lyrics, which one can understand as both seductive and cautioning. It was not surprising she recited these words in a mechanical voice. I understood it as her way of creating metonymic contiguity with the experience of being made into a silent, inanimate object used to gratify her brother's needs. It housed, in the form of a phantom object (Sopher, 2018), her absent, amputated voice – as if marking the site of its burial. Maybe this was what led me to ask her, almost inadvertently, whether she would like to sing the song in her own voice. To my surprise she sat up on the couch, facing the open window, and sang it in a clear voice I had never heard from her before. When she finished singing, she began to weep. Seated behind her, I, too, teared up:

The water is wide, I cannot cross over
Nor do I have light wings to fly
Build me a boat, that can carry two
And both shall row, my love and I

Love is gentle, and love is kind
The sweetest flower when it's first new
But love grows old and waxes cold
And fades away like morning dew

There is a ship that sails the sea
She's loaded deep as deep can be
But not as deep as the love I'm in
I know not how I sink or swim

Botella (2014) writes about what he calls 'acoustic figurability' (pp. 919, 927): a moment when a melody playing in his own head allowed contact with a certain content belonging to his patient, and which completely escaped representation. Listening to my patient at that moment, reciting the song's lyrics in a way that dissociated both lyrics from music and lyrics from vivid experience, I remember holding the music, even singing it, in my head. With a hindsight, I understood that what I stored at that moment was not the melody – but rather the possibility of *a link* between melody and words, as representing the very possibility of linking. As opposed to the patient's dissociative mechanism of silencing, which was rendered both through the formation of no-voice and the voice's transposition to a male register, my singing, and the patient's singing following it, acted as antibody.

Novalis writes beautifully: 'Disease is a musical problem. Cure is a musical solution'.[2] What stood up at that moment against the 'musical problem' of the *acoustic dissociation* was the 'musical solution' of the *acoustic association*. This unique example represents a central guiding principle in the treatment of somatoform dissociation: the therapist must be alert to any cue that allows for the restoration of the patient's capacity for linking, whether located in the patient – or in the therapist's own countertransference.

Caruth, in her book 'unclaimed experience' (1996), suggests that sometimes we speak in a voice that anticipates us. That voice, as D'.s singing illustrates, is a miracle of life preserved inside the inferno: a testimony to the human psyche's capacity not only to bypass that inferno, as in the case of dissociation, but also to pass through it; not only to find a way out, but also to reclaim a way in.

Disclosure statement

No potential conflict of interest was reported by the author(s).

Notes

1. All the details that may reveal the identity of the patients described in this paper have been disguised in a way that does not allow identification.
2. https://quotefancy.com/quote/1346880/Novalis-Every-disease-is-a-musical-problem-Its-cure-a-musical-solution-The-more-rapid-and.

ORCID

Dana Amir http://orcid.org/0000-0002-1574-5844

References

Amir, D. (2012). The inner witness. *The International Journal of Psycho-Analysis*, *93*(4), 879–896. https://doi.org/10.1111/j.1745-8315.2012.00618.x

Amir, D. (2014). Nausea as the refusal of a mother-tongue: The psychosomatic metaphoric, metonymic and psychotic expression. In *Cleft tongue: The language of psychic Structures* (pp. 111–132). Karnac Books. https://doi.org/10.4324/9780429472916-6

Amir, D. (2016a). The metaphoric, the metonymic and the psychotic aspects of obsessive-sympomatology. *International Journal of Psychoanalysis*, *97*(2), 259–280. https://doi.org/10.1111/1745-8315.12442

Amir, D. (2016b). When language meets the traumatic lacuna: The metaphoric, the metonymic and the psychotic modes of testimony. *Psychoanalytic Inquiry*, *36*(8), 620–632. https://doi.org/10.1080/07351690.2016.1226045

Amir, D. (2019a). *Bearing witness to the Witness: A psychoanalytic perspective on four modes of traumatic testimony*. Routledge. https://doi.org/10.4324/9781315146508

Bion, W. (1959). Attacks on linking. *International Journal of Psycho-Analysis*, *40*, 308–315.

Botella, C. (2014). On Remembering: The notion of memory without recollection. *The International Journal of Psycho-Analysis*, 95(5), 911–936. https://doi.org/10.1111/1745-8315.12220

Breuer, J. & Freud, S. (1893–1895). Studies on hysteria. In J. Strachey (Ed.), *Standard edition of the complete psychological works of Sigmund freud* (Vol. 2, pp. xxix–305–). Hogarth.

Bromberg, P. M. (1998). *Standing in the spaces: Essays on clinical process, trauma, and dissociation*. The Analytic Press.

Caruth, C. (1996). *Unclaimed experience: Trauma narrative and history*. Johns Hopkins University Press.

Chefetz, R. A. (2015). *Intensive psychotherapy for persistent dissociative processes: The fear of feeling real*. Norton.

Coons, P. M. (1994). Confirmation of childhood abuse in child and adolescent cases of multiple personality disorder and dissociative disorder not otherwise specified. *The Journal of Nervous and Mental Disease*, *182*(8), 461–464. https://doi.org/10.1097/00005053-199408000-00007

Efrati, D. & Israeli, Y. (2007). *The philosophy and psychoanalysis of Jacques Lacan*. Ministry of Defense Publishing House.

Ellert, R. S. & Nijenhuis, E. R. S. (2001). Somatoform dissociation. *Journal of Trauma & Dissociation*, *1*(4), 7–32. https://doi.org/10.1300/J229v01n04_02

Ferenczi, S. (1932). In J. Dupont, M. Balint, & N. Z. Jackson (Eds.), *The clinical diary*. Cambridge, MA. Harvard University Press.

Ferenczi, S. (1932/1988). *The clinical diary*, and Judith Dupont, Ed.). Harvard University press.

Green, A. (1998). The primordial mind and the work of the negative. *International Journal of Psycho-Analysis*, *79*, 649–665.

Hornstein, N. L. & Putnam, F. W. (1992). Clinical Phenomenology of child and adolescent dissociative disorders. *Journal of the American Academy of Child and Adolescent Psychiatry*, *31*(6), 1077–1085. https://doi.org/10.1097/00004583-199211000-00013

Jacobson, R. (1956/1971). Two aspects of language and two types of aphasic disturbances. In Jacobson, R. (Ed.), *Selected writings—Word and language* (Vol. 2, pp. 239–259). Mouton.

Janet, P. (1889/1973). *L'Automatisme Psychologique*. Félix Alcan. Reprint: Société Pierre Janet.

Janet, P. (1893). *L'etat Mental des Hystériques: Les Stigmates Mentaux* [the mental state of hystericals: The mental stigmata]. Rueff & Cie.

Janet, P. (1901/1977). *The mental state of hystericals*. Putnam & Sons: Reprint: University Publications of America. https://doi.org/10.1037/10597-000

Janet, P. (1907/1965). *Major symptoms of hysteria*. Macmillan. Reprint: Hafner. https://doi.org/10.1037/10008-000

Kluft, R. P. (1995). The confirmation and disconfirmation of memories of abuse in DID patients: A naturalistic clinical study. *Dissociation*, *8*(4), 251–258.

Kluft, R. P. (2000). The psychoanalytic psychotherapy of dissociative identity disorder in the context of trauma therapy. *Psychoanalytic Inquiry*, *20*(2), 259–286. https://doi.org/10.1080/07351692009348887

Kristeva, J. (1987). *Black sun: Depression and Melancholia* (Leon S. Roudiez, Trans). Columbia University Press.

Lacan, J. (1958/2007). *Écrits* (B. Fink, Trans.). W. W. Norton.

LaCapra, D. (1994). *Representing the holocaust: History, theory, trauma*. New York, NY: Cornell University.

Laub, D. (2005). Traumatic shutdown of narrative and symbolization. *Contemporary Psychoanalysis*, *41*(2), 307–326. https://doi.org/10.1080/00107530.2005.10745863

Lewis, D. O., Yeager, C. A., Swica, Y., Pincus, J. H., & Lewis, M. (1997). Objective documentation of child abuse and dissociation in 12 murderers with dissociative identity disorder. *American Journal of Psychiatry, 154*(12), 1703–1710. https://doi.org/10.1176/ajp.154.12.1703

McDougall, J. (1989). *Theatres of the body.* Free Association Books.

Modell, A. (2006). *Imagination and the meaningful brain.* MIT Press.

Moore, R. (1999). *The creation of reality in psychoanalysis.* The Analytic Press.

Nijenhuis, E. R. S., Spinhoven, P., Van Dyck, R., Van der Hart, O., & Vanderlinden, J. (1996). The development and psychometric characteristics of the Somatoform Dissociation Questionnaire (SDQ-20). *The Journal of Nervous and Mental Disease, 184*(11), 688–694. https://doi.org/10.1097/00005053-199611000-00006

Nijenhuis, E. R. S. & Van der Hart, O. (1999). Forgetting and reexperiencing trauma: From anesthesia to pain. In J. Goodwin & R. Attias (Eds.), *Splintered reflections: Images of the body in trauma*, (pp. 39–65). Basic Books/Hachette Book Group.

O'Neil, J. A. (2009). Dissociative multiplicity and psychoanalysis. In P. F. Dell & J. A. O'Neil (Eds.), *Dissociation and the dissociative disorders—DSM-V and beyond* (pp. 287–325). Routledge.

Oliner, M. (1996). External reality: The elusive dimensions of psychoanalysis. *Psychoanalytic Quarterly, 65*(2), 267–300. https://doi.org/10.1080/21674086.1996.11927491

Othmer, E. & DeSouza, C. (1985). A screening test for somatization disorder (hysteria). *American Journal of Psychiatry, 142*(10), 1146–1149. https://doi.org/10.1176/ajp.142.10.1146

Pribor, E. F., Yutzy, S. H., Dean, J. T., & Wetzel, R. D. (1993). Briquet's syndrome, dissociation and abuse. *American Journal of Psychiatry, 150*(10), 1507–1511. https://doi.org/10.1176/ajp.150.10.1507

Riviere, J. (1936). A Contribution to the Analysis of the negative therapeutic reaction. *The International Journal of Psychoanalysis, 17*, 304–320.

Ross, C. A., Heber, S., Norton, G. R., & Anderson, G. (1989). Somatic symptoms in multiple personality disorder. *Psychosomatics, 30*(2), 154–160. https://doi.org/10.1016/S0033-3182(89)72296-9

Saxe, G. N., Chinman, G., Berkowitz, M. D., Hall, K., Lieberg, G., Schwartz, J., & Van der Kolk, B. A. (1994). Somatization in patients with dissociative disorders. *American Journal of Psychiatry, 151*(9), 1329–1334. https://doi.org/10.1176/ajp.151.9.1329

Schimmenti, A. & Caretti, V. (2016). Linking the overwhelming with the unbearable: Developmental trauma, dissociation, and the disconnected self. *Psychoanalytic Psychology, 33*(1), 106–128. https://doi.org/10.1037/a0038019

Sopher, R. (2018). An allegiance to absence: Fidelity to the internal void. *The Psychoanalytic Quarterly, 87*(4), 729–751. https://doi.org/10.1080/00332828.2018.1518084

Stern, D. B. (2012). Witnessing across time: Accessing the present from The past and the past from the present. *The Psychoanalytic Quarterly, 81*(1), 53–81. https://doi.org/10.1002/j.2167-4086.2012.tb00485.x

van der Hart, O., van der Kolk, B. A., & Boon, S. (1998). Treatment of dissociative disorders. In J. D. Bremner & C. R. Marmar (Eds.), *Trauma, memory, and dissociation* (pp. 253–283). American Psychiatric Association.

Van der Kolk, B., McFarlane, A., & Weisaeth, L. (1996). *Traumatic stress: The effects of overwhelming experience on mind, body, and society.* The Guilford Press.

Waller, Waller, G., Hamilton, K., Elliott, P., Lewendon, J., Stopa, L., Waters, A., Kennedy, F., Lee, G., Pearson, D., Kennerley, H., Hargreaves, I., Bashford, V., & Chalkley, J. (2000). Somatoform dissociation, psychological dissociation, and specific forms of trauma. *Journal of Trauma & Dissociation, 1*(4), 81–98. https://doi.org/10.1300/J229v01n04_05

Winnicott, D. W. (1954). Mind and its relation to the psyche-soma. *Brit. J. Med. Psychol, 27*, 201–209.

Self-medication, traumatic reenactments, and dissociation: a psychoanalytic perspective on the relationship between childhood trauma and substance abuse

Antonino Costanzo, Gianluca Santoro and Adriano Schimmenti

This article explores the relationship between developmental trauma, dissociation, and substance abuse within the framework of the self-medication hypothesis. By means of presenting a clinical vignette, the article illustrates how substance abuse can serve as a maladaptive coping strategy for managing overwhelming emotions that stem from traumatic experiences in attachment relationships during childhood. Individuals who have undergone developmental trauma may dissociate negative attachment memories and their related emotions, which consequently leads to compartmentalization of their internal states and hinders their self-regulation abilities. In such scenario, substances can act as external regulators of distressing emotions, distancing these individuals from their traumatic memories and facilitating the adoption of an omnipotent and self-reliant attitude. Hence, it is of utmost importance for clinicians to accurately identify and address the self-medication needs of these individuals. This is fundamental in facilitating these clients' capacity to acknowledge, explore, and integrate their distressing memories as intrinsic elements of their identity, thereby fostering the development of a unified and cohesive self-concept.

The focus of this article is on case formulation and treatment principles for individuals who underwent traumatic experiences in their childhood and presently manifest issues related to substance abuse. It utilizes the self-medication hypothesis (Khantzian, 1985) as the framework for analysis.

From a nosographic perspective, substance use disorder is defined as a problematic pattern of substance use that leads to significant impairment or distress. This impairment can manifest in various aspects of an individual's life, including relationships, work or academic performance, and overall well-being (American Psychiatric Association [APA], 2022). Extensive research has been conducted on substance use disorder and other addictive behaviors within the realm of psychodynamic theories, with various authors focusing on elucidating crucial aspects of treatment (Baurer, 2021; Khantzian, 2021; Potik, 2020).

Efforts have also been made to integrate psychoanalytic models of addiction with neurobiological findings (Alvarez-Monjaras et al., 2019; Scarna, 2020), develop psychoanalytic-informed assessment tools (Caretti et al., 2018), and provide evidence to support Khantzian's self-medication hypothesis (Alfonso, 2021).

The self-medication hypothesis acknowledges that substance abuse can present itself in various ways among individuals, as a result of their psychological condition and the contextual factors surrounding their use of substances. Nevertheless, it also proposes that individuals have a propensity to favor specific substances for abuse, influenced by their distinct vulnerabilities. Stated differently, the individuals' motivation to address these vulnerabilities may compel them to actively search for particular substances that may alleviate their distress (Khantzian, 1997). Accordingly, Khantzian (1999) suggests that self-regulation plays a crucial role in substance abuse. Specifically, the following difficulties are transversal conditions to the multifaceted aspects of substance abuse: (a) difficulty recognizing and regulating feelings; (b) difficulty establishing and maintaining a coherent sense of self and adequate self-esteem; (c) difficulty establishing and maintaining adequate and comforting relationships; (d) difficulty establishing and maintaining adequate behavioral regulation, especially self-care (Khantzian, 2012). As Khantzian (2003) further explained, 'from a psychodynamic perspective, resorting to addictive drugs, more than anything, represents attempts at self-correction that ultimately fall short (...) Drug-dependent individuals, in their drug use, are continuously trying to regulate their emotions, their sense of self, their relationship with others, and their behaviors' (p. 9).

This is particularly true for individuals who were exposed to traumatic experiences and severe parental failures during their childhood and who developed an addictive disorder (Lotzin et al., 2019; Zhang et al., 2020). Developmental trauma encompasses childhood experiences involving loss, neglect, and abuse within attachment relationships, which have not been adequately addressed and processed on both cognitive and emotional levels (Schimmenti & Caretti, 2016). The relevant literature indicates that these experiences have a negative impact on adult psychological functioning (Bifulco & Schimmenti, 2019; Midolo et al., 2020) and contribute to the development of dissociative symptoms (Dalenberg et al., 2012; Schimmenti, 2018; Vonderlin et al., 2018). Furthermore, developmental trauma increases the likelihood of both acute and chronic dissociative responses to distressing situations (Bryant, 2007; Carlson et al., 2012; Dalenberg et al., 2012).

Dissociation involves a disruption or discontinuity in the normal integration of mental functions, including consciousness, memory, identity, emotion, perception, body representation, motor control, and behavior (APA, 2022). Within the psychoanalytic tradition, dissociation is conceptualized as a defense mechanism that establishes a separation between different elements constituting one's self-perception and/or perception of the external world. This mechanism is already present during the early stages of human development, and it serves as a way for individuals to protect themselves from conflicting stimuli and temporarily avoid emotional distress (Bromberg, 1998). However, if dissociation becomes a person's primary response to stress, it can become pathological and can lead to severe symptoms.

Several studies confirmed the positive associations between developmental trauma, dissociation, and substance abuse (Baudin et al., 2022; Schäfer et al., 2007, 2010; Schimmenti et al., 2022; Somer, 2003; Somer et al., 2019). This is because the vulnerabilities associated with developmental trauma: (a) compromise the ability to recognize and regulate emotions (Dvir et al., 2014; Dye, 2018; Pollak et al., 2009), (b) compromise the cohesion of the self (Frewen & Lanius, 2015; International Society for the Study of Trauma and Dissociation [ISSTD], 2011; Krystal, 1995); (c) foster maladaptive personality functioning (Granieri et al., 2018), also generating mentalization failures (Santoro et al., 2021) and insecurity in intimate relationships (Midolo et al., 2020). Consequently, individuals who were exposed to developmental trauma often face significant difficulties in effectively regulating their emotions and engaging in mentalizing activities (Schimmenti & Caretti, 2016). As a result, they may resort to using psychotropic substances as a means to cope with internal conflicts and painful feelings.

This aligns with existing literature (Najavits & Walsh, 2012; Somer, 2022; Somer et al., 2010, 2019) suggesting that traumatized individuals may actively seek for a 'chemical' form of dissociation induced by substances. In this context, substances lead to altered states of consciousness, temporarily enhancing the physical and mental well-being of these individuals. Consequently, chemical dissociation serves as a method of self-regulation and can be considered a form of self-medication for coping with emotion dysregulation. Accordingly, Khantzian (1997) had already observed that a heavy use of alcohol and other drugs by individuals with posttraumatic stress disorder (PTSD) might serve to self-medicate the affective flooding or numbing involved in this condition. This can be experienced, even more vividly, by individuals who were exposed to complex and cumulative trauma within their childhood attachment relationships.

The case of Charles

The case of Charles will help illustrating the articulate relationship between developmental trauma, dissociation, and substance abuse from a self-medication perspective. The name of patient is changed and details of the case are omitted or disguised to protect confidentiality.

The case implies that substance abuse might, somewhat paradoxically, provide a short-term improvement in an individual's well-being by excluding traumatic memories with their painful emotions from the awareness. Consequently, as a counterphobic reaction to the dissociated traumatized mental states, there could be a mental and behavioral shift toward a sense of omnipotence. This shift can sometimes be marked by increased aggressiveness and the emergence of feelings of hatred.

Hence, substance abuse carries the capacity to uphold an unhelpful perception of self-efficacy and inner equilibrium by blocking conscious access to traumatic memories. However, the dissociation of developmental trauma can contribute to its reenactment, whether symbolically or in actual form. This, in turn, reinforces the dependence on substances for self-medicating emotional wounds. In the absence of appropriate treatment, dissociating developmental trauma ultimately perpetuates the destructive cycle of addiction.

Leap forward: a glimpse of interaction

It was a sunny Monday morning when Charles, a patient who had been regularly attending therapy for the past seven months, unexpectedly sent a text message to his therapist. Charles and his therapist seldom communicated outside of their weekly consultations. Nonetheless, that Monday he sent a message expressing his confusion and impossibility to wait until Thursday, when the next session was scheduled. The therapist found this surprising, since Charles usually displayed an unwavering reticence and persistent aversion to exposing his vulnerability or seeking assistance.

Driven by Charles's unexpected request, the therapist made the decision to call him and was taken aback by the change in his demeanor. Instead of the confident and pragmatic 27-year-old man the therapist was accustomed to, Charles now displayed a strong sense of underlying apprehension. He spoke with a tangled flow of words, repeatedly asking, 'Do you understand me, doctor?' in an attempt to alleviate his distress and seek comfort. Additionally, the therapist observed a noticeable shift in Charles's voice, as it became higher in pitch, resembling that of a pubescent youngster on the verge of adolescence.

In an unprecedented display of vulnerability, Charles was weeping and clearly overwhelmed with emotions. He revealed that the night before, he had received a new contract that would require him to relocate, both professionally and residentially. This news apparently triggered intense emotions that he could not handle. In an attempt to cope, Charles admitted to drinking wine on an empty stomach before going to bed. The next morning, he woke up to his father's distressed voice reverberating through the mobile phone and accusing him of taking drugs. It was at this point that Charles suddenly realized he had been engaged in a conversation with his father for at least five minutes, the contents of which had escaped his consciousness entirely.

While Charles was talking, the therapist continued to notice the unusual shift in his voice: he seemed like a completely different, younger person. After the therapist helped Charles regain some control of himself – speaking to him as if Charles was a scared child who needed reassurance – they agreed to anticipate the Thursday session to that Monday afternoon.

During the therapy session, it seemed that Charles had come to his sense. He went into detailed explanations of the events that led him to urgently seek his therapist's help that very morning. He had carefully examined the archived call logs and text messages on his phone and was shocked to discover a continuous pattern of constant calls to his fiancée and close friends, starting as early as 4:30 am. He had called them each about ten times, but he could not remember any of it. What further perplexed him was discovering explicit pleas for assistance within the chat logs, without any accompanying explanation or justification for his state of distress. Charles had later reached out two of these friends, and they reported that during the calls he had been acting strangely, speaking in a childish manner.

Charles also mentioned that his desk housed a mere trio of cigarettes before he succumbed to slumber. However, when he woke up, he was astounded to discover an inexplicable transformation had taken place – two complete packages of cigarettes now resided upon the very same desk. This occurrence forged in him the conviction that he had indeed acquired two packages of cigarettes amidst the bewilderments of his 'mental blackout'. He stressed that he had not experienced anything like this before. However, he recalled a memory of being found locked in the refrigerator by his parents when he was five years old. Although there was no other evidence of sleepwalking during his childhood, he attributed this experience to somnambulism.

Anamnestic information

In order to establish context, pertinent information regarding Charles is presented. Charles was a 27-year-old male employed in the field of human resources. He was the sole offspring of his parents, who underwent a divorce when Charles was twelve years old. Charles provided a depiction of his American mother as a weak woman plagued by problems with alcohol addiction and a proclivity for selecting aggressive partners. He depicted his father as a successful individual who, during Charles's formative years, displayed considerable commitment to his professional obligations at the detriment of fostering familial connections. Post his parents' divorce, Charles resided with his mother until reaching the age of nineteen. Approximately at the age of twelve, Charles commenced consuming cannabis and alcohol. By the time he turned sixteen, he progressed to using cocaine and sporadically experimenting with synthetic substances. As he entered adulthood, Charles, despite displaying a clear dedication to his pursuits and fulfilling his obligations commendably, frequently found himself engaging in violent and delinquent behaviors that also attracted the attention of law enforcement. Intriguingly, these behaviors seemed incongruous with his aesthetically pleasing appearance and his adeptness at displaying formal etiquette in social interactions. Charles was involved in a romantic relationship with a woman who was two years younger than him.

First session

Charles began psychotherapy seven months prior to the amnesic episode mentioned earlier, subsequent to a bout of aggression that resulted in him being reported to the authorities. During this incident, he was engaged in excessive alcohol consumption and embroiled in a heated confrontation with his fiancée. Subsequently, she sought assistance from her previous partner, but upon his arrival, Charles physically assaulted him and caused damage to his vehicle.

During the first therapy session, Charles expressed his belief that a significant portion of his anger episodes stemmed from challenges in effectively managing his emotional states, particularly as a consequence of his relationship with his fiancée. However, Charles also confessed that he had previously exhibited violent tendencies, though confined to male individuals, including the most recent confrontation that impelled him to seek psychological treatment. Furthermore, he acknowledged that his violent tendencies were linked to his alcohol abuse. During the consultation, Charles also conveyed his commitment to ending both substance abuse and violent behavior. However, he indicated his intention to reduce alcohol consumption rather than quitting it entirely. Subsequently, a therapeutic agreement was established to ensure that Charles would not attend therapy sessions while under the influence of drugs or alcohol. Furthermore, it was mutually agreed that if Charles failed to decrease his substance abuse within a year, he would be referred to the National Health Service for addiction therapy. In the event that Charles refused to participate in the recommended treatment, the therapist would evaluate whether to continue or terminate their therapy sessions.

Assessment and treatment goals

To effectively prepare for therapy, a preliminary assessment was conducted, wherein psychodiagnostic instruments were employed to explore Charles's personality functioning, traumatic experiences, attachment style, and dissociative symptoms.

The Shedler-Westen Assessment Procedure-200 (SWAP-200; Shedler & Westen, 1998) was used as a clinician-report instrument to assess Charles's personality functioning. A personality profile characterized by explosive and dramatic behavior, strong expressed emotionality, egocentrism, and low empathy was observed. Specifically, based on the Personality Disorder Types (PD-T) of the SWAP-200, which references the diagnostic criteria outlined in the DSM-5-TR (APA, 2022), Charles fulfilled the criteria for both antisocial personality disorder and borderline personality disorder; clinically significant scores were also observed for the paranoid, narcissistic, and histrionic scales. Also, when analyzing the Q-factors of the SWAP-200 (these are factor scores on personality disorders that are empirically derived from actual and well-documented cases), it emerged that Charles had an antisocial personality, combined with clinically relevant paranoid, histrionic, dysphoric, dependent-masochistic, and hostile traits.

The Traumatic Experiences Checklist (TEC; Nijenhuis et al., 2002) was used to assess Charles's lifetime exposure to traumatic events, including childhood experiences of neglect and abuse. Charles reported several traumatic experiences endured in his formative years, and among them: (1) family problems (e.g., his mother had depression and alcohol problems), (2) divorce of his parents (e.g., he suffered for his relocation from his father's residence to reside with his mother), (3) threat to his life (e.g., he was physically threatened by one of his mother's partners); (4) witnessing others undergo trauma (e.g., one evening he discovered his mother in an unconscious state lying on the floor, having sustained a head injury); (5) emotional neglect (e.g., he received insufficient affection from his father); (6) emotional abuse (e.g., he was belittled and humiliated by more than one of his mother's partners, also overhearing his mother engaging in sexual activities with strangers).

The Relationship Questionnaire (RQ; Bartholomew & Horowitz, 1991) was used to assess Charles's attachment style in close relationships. The RQ further elucidated Charles's inclination towards perceiving both self and others in a negative light. His fearful attachment style brought him to yearn for intimate connections with others, yet his capacity to fulfill this longing was hindered by intense fear pertaining to the prospects of rejection and abandonment.

The Dissociative Experiences Scale-II (DES-II; Carlson & Putnam, 1993) was used to assess Charles's dissociative symptoms. Charles reported severe experiences of depersonalization, identity alteration, and amnesia. Charles observed that these experiences were particularly prominent during periods of increased distress or a decline in mood. However, his alcohol and substance abuse hindered a more comprehensive assessment of his dissociative symptoms – he was frequently under the influence of alcohol or drugs, which alter the consciousness and its functions.

Following the assessment conducted through clinical interviews and the use of psychodiagnostic tools, a complex profile has been revealed. This profile indicated the presence of unprocessed traumatic experiences and rigid dissociative processes, which had resulted in the compartmentalization and autonomy of different aspects of self. Additionally, there was evidence of reenactments of traumatic dynamics in his life.

In light of the initial assessment, the therapist presented Charles with a set of treatment goals to achieve. A main goal for treatment was to reduce his substance and alcohol consumption, by fostering a more profound understanding of his internal states and processes that drove his addictive substance use. To achieve this, the therapist explained that Charles would need to: (a) develop emotion regulation skills and a greater capacity to tolerate negative emotional experiences (Siegel, 1999), also maintaining physical and psychological safety during both therapy sessions and his daily life (ISSTD, 2011); (b) enhance his ability to interpret and reflect upon his own and others' mental states (Bateman

& Fonagy, 2006), also to improve the quality of his close relationships; (c) acquire a balanced sense of self-esteem and self-efficacy that would enable him to navigate life's challenges without relying on substances or aggressive behaviors (Yeomans et al., 2015).

Inside the addictive mind

During subsequent sessions, Charles expounded on his addiction to substances – a reward, he maintained, for his unwavering focus and diligent task completion at work. In fact, he had cleaved his identity into compartmentalized and extremely polarized parts: the working Charles versus the Charles who used substances, the emotional Charles versus the cynical Charles, the dependent Charles versus the self-sufficient Charles, and so on.

As therapy progressed, Charles's inclination for compartmentalization became increasingly apparent. He contended that substances were necessary to unwind and sharpen his thoughts after a hard day's work, but this only bolstered the polarities within his identity, with his opposite parts operating almost autonomously. He seemed to conceive of these polarities as separate and distinct parts of self, each acting independently of the other. Charles's self-experiences proved challenging to integrate. Two dynamic processes appeared to support the consolidation of polarized identity states, specifically, the processes of shifting and the narcissistic investment in one of the compartmentalized poles. Identity shifting enabled Charles to internally transition from a vulnerable and conflicted self to an idealized and grandiose self – a phenomenon akin to the vertical splitting process previously documented in the literature (Goldberg, 1995, 1999; Kohut, 1971). Vertical splitting is a dissociative-like defense mechanism that occurs when the individuals separate the contents of their inner experience into two distinct parts: one characterized by grandiosity or idealization, and the other marked by devaluation or depreciation. The grandiose part represents a narcissistic defense that allows the individual to preserve a sense of worth and importance, while the devalued part helps contain negative and self-deprecating emotions. However, vertical splitting usually results in a lack of integration between these two polarities, leading to overwhelming internal conflict and psychological distress.

In fact, it seemed that Charles actively employed substances as a means to facilitate the transition between these opposite parts, paradoxically for the purpose of avoiding their integration (Bromberg, 1998). Especially when he was distressed, the shifts occurred towards mental states that were omnipotent and gave him a sense of mastery. Accordingly, this process of shifting can be clarified by applying the theory of chemical dissociation (Somer et al., 2010, 2019). In this context, it is plausible to suggest that the altered state of consciousness resulting from his use of alcohol and substances allowed him to experience the desired sense of grandiosity. Upon further examination, it became clear that his transition towards a self-reliant and overly confident state was primarily influenced by his intense feelings of shame regarding the vulnerable and depressive parts of his personality. These parts were closely linked to his traumatic experiences during childhood.

Kluft (1984) explained that from a young age, individuals might excessively invest in certain parts of themselves for the purpose of physical and mental survival in response to traumatic situations. Nevertheless, this tendency can lead to dissociation of mental states and can contribute to severe symptoms. Thus, in order to comprehend the fundamental mechanisms that propelled Charles's addiction, violence, and dissociation, it becomes imperative to explore the ways in which he internally processed his developmental trauma.

During his childhood and teenage years, Charles experienced the unfortunate challenges of his mother's depression and alcoholism, resulting in a lack of reliable support and care from her. He perceived his mother as a victim of her own struggles and constantly in need of assistance. On the other hand, Charles's father was a successful businessman but often absent, fulfilling only Charles's material needs. As time passed, their relationship evolved, and although Charles began to appreciate his bond with his father more, it remained mixed with conflicting feelings: while his father could be a source of understanding and support on certain occasions, he often could not comprehend Charles's personal struggles. Furthermore, Charles discovered that during his father's own youth, his father engaged in even more excessive drug and alcohol consumption than Charles's mother and Charles himself. Gradually, Charles developed an unconscious sense of competition with his father regarding their respective work, which became more evident over the years. However, Charles also admired his father, who represented a role model for him, and even associated his father's professional success and authority with boundless power. This admiration took the form of a partial Oedipal identification with his father's power, which established a dissociated and omnipotent self-image in Charles. Such omnipotent self-image served as a protective mechanism to avoid succumbing to the challenges of everyday life and to prevent experiencing feelings of powerlessness with significant individuals in his life.

Charles's upbringing was further defined by his parents' divorce when he was twelve, thrusting him into the care of his mother. At the time, Charles's mother had an affinity for unsavory characters and a proclivity for associating with criminals due to her addictions. From his small room, Charles often heard his mother engaging in sexual activities with strangers, and he also witnessed horrific acts of violence committed against her on more than one occasion. These experiences had a profound and long-lasting impact on him. When he was sixteen, Charles returned from a night with his friends to find his mother in a perilous condition, lying unconscious on the entrance landing with a serious head injury. Filled with panic and desperation, he called his father, who was vacationing with a new partner in another part of the country. In that situation, Charles received no assistance whatsoever – in fact, his father was unresponsive and suggested that Charles contact an uncle instead. In a moment of complete abandonment, Charles took control of the situation and rushed his mother to the hospital to receive the treatment she so desperately needed.

Therefore, Charles had undergone a number of traumatic experiences in his formative years, from living with parents with psychiatric condition to emotional neglect, from witnessing violence to growing up in an incestuous climate (Racamiere, 1995). Notably, as an adolescent Charles had witnessed terrible violence against his mother, and felt helpless as she descended into self-destruction, with little support or protection. Such experiences left their mark, and Charles started to live in a constant state of alertness. Furthermore, Charles's adult relationships with women seemed to replicate the strains and conflicts inside his family relationships. While women caused him to be in a continuous state of hypervigilance, they also gave him the opportunity to perform the role of the omnipotent father. Charles indeed acted as a surrogate father for most of them, as he practically helped the women in his life and provided for their financial and material needs; yet, similar to his father, he remained almost unable to establish and maintain an intimate connection with them.

Therefore, it seems probable that Charles had developed traumatic identifications (Schimmenti, 2017) in his family relationships, which stimulated unconscious inclinations towards both dissociation and violence. Specifically, Charles demonstrated damaged emotional connections with female figures, which resulted in compulsive caregiving and constant concern for them, the echoes of a primitive internalization of the connection with a weak and frail mother. Concurrently, Charles's caregiving of frail women allowed him to feel accomplished and essential, ultimately leading to identification with the all-powerful and distant father.

Furthermore, Charles experienced internal conflicts and intense anger towards men, perceiving them as threatening and destructive. In response, he exhibited violent behavior toward them, as a form of narcissistic rage (Kohut, 1971). This not only demonstrates the Oedipal conflict Charles had with his father and at the same time his tendency to adopt similar dismissive traits, but also implies his effort to portray himself as strong enough to shield his mother from the significant harm caused by her sexual partners. Accordingly, the fact that Charles primarily directed his violent behaviors towards males can be meaningfully understood when analyzed through the lens of the identification with the aggressor (Ferenczi, 1932/1988). This defense mechanism sheds light on the reason why Charles displayed acts of violence towards men who were connected to the women in his life: by acting out his aggression, Charles could reject the perception of being a victim and instead adopt the role of the perpetrator in relation to those individuals who symbolically represented his mother's past aggressors. Actually, the identification with the aggressor facilitates the shifting from feelings of shame and powerlessness to a sense of strength, fearlessness, and dominance. Its underlying principle is, 'in order to no longer fear you, I become like you'.

However, as a result of traumatic experiences, Charles had developed different parts of himself that were not integrated, together with intensely aversive and antagonistic motivations (Lichtenberg et al., 1992, 1996, 2011). It is possible that this rift represented the heart of his violent tendencies.

Notably, Charles displayed a range of destructive and self-harming behaviors, especially when consuming alcohol and engaging in arguments with his partners. It is worth reiterating that he directed his anger both towards other men and towards himself, but he never resorted to physical violence against his partners, who symbolized his vulnerable mother. Charles had self-inflicted cuts on his arms, broke his knuckles by hitting walls, and on one occasion, even jumped out of a second-story window while intoxicated and without taking any safety precautions. As suggested by the assessment of his adult attachment style through the Relationship Questionnaire, which indicated a fearful attachment, it is conceivable that Charles utilized these behaviors as an unconscious, maladaptive strategy to alleviate his unrecognized separation anxiety and to cope with his difficulties in maintaining intimate relationships with his partners. By engaging in self-destructive actions, he might have indirectly conveyed a need for emotional support from them, triggering their innate caregiving system (Lichtenberg et al., 1992, 1996, 2011). However, the concurrent activation of attachment and aversive motivational systems – almost always in relation to substance or alcohol use – thwarted Charles's attempts to develop more effective emotion regulation and relational strategies. Instead, he found himself caught in a vicious cycle of chaotic behavior, brought on by the contradictory and irreconcilable nature of his traumatized parts, each with its own activated motivational system.

Self-medication

The case of Charles serves as an illustration of how traumatic experiences and dissociative processes are intertwined with challenges in regulating emotions, maintaining a cohesive sense of self, developing secure interpersonal relationships, and controlling behaviors (Khantzian, 1997). Charles relied on substances as an external, objectified means to regulate his emotions, as he struggled to directly express his own vulnerability and fragility.

In fact, Charles tended to adopt a grandiose, all-powerful, dominant, and aggressive persona in his life, which further perpetuated the dissociation of his parts and hindered his ability to perceive himself as a complete individual. This compartmentalization was evident in Charles's compulsive alcohol use, which both reenacted and denied his relational trauma (Mezzalira et al., 2023). Specifically, alcohol addiction of his mother served as the driving force behind the need to safeguard her during Charles's formative years, which fostered his grandiose parts. Furthermore, given that Charles's father also engaged in alcohol abuse, alcohol became a means for Charles to establish a sense of competition with, and at the same time, separation from, his omnipotent and distant paternal figure, thus allowing Charles to partially resolve his Oedipal conflict. Additionally, alcohol served as a coping mechanism for Charles, granting him a temporary sense of mastery and agency as he navigated through challenging circumstances.

Therefore, Charles's addictive behaviors could be interpreted as a manifestation of self-medication (Khantzian, 1985, 1997). Alcohol and substances were employed as a means to manage the diminishing dissociative boundaries and the ensuing potential for conscious recognition of segregated aspects of the self, along with all the associated distressing memories and emotions. In this context, the use of substances aimed to reestablish the imbalance between the compartmentalized parts, constituting an attempt to entrench the dominance of the all-powerful part.

However, when faced with particular triggers, compartmentalization can break or weaken, potentially resulting in an overwhelming flooding of traumatic contents within the self. Indeed, keeping compartmentalization necessitates a substantial amount of emotional energy and is often unsustainable over long periods. Simultaneously, it is crucial to note that the process of integrating the distinct aspects of one's identity and harmonizing the burden of traumatic memories into a coherent self is frequently an arduous and tense expedition (Bromberg, 1998). This journey necessitates the dismantling of defensive barriers, but for the addicted individuals these barriers represent a bulwark against mental disorganization (Schimmenti, 2021): this is among the factors explaining why it is intrinsically difficult to treat individuals who have suffered from developmental trauma and exhibit substance abuse.

Navigating the countertransference

Also because of their unrecognized parts that are traumatized, clients exposed to developmental trauma who suffer from substance use disorder may evoke intense countertransference responses. Indeed, Charles had developed a habitual pattern of turning to alcohol as a coping mechanism in response to feelings of sadness, powerlessness, or distress. During an online therapy session, Charles shared his plans to relocate to a new city and how his father had reluctantly offered him financial assistance. Charles felt troubled because he believed his father was devaluing his professional choice to relocate. This made Charles feel insignificant. Suddenly, he got up and moved towards his kitchen while declaring, 'Doctor, I'm going to get a bottle of wine and drink it all'. The therapist inquired why Charles felt the need to consume alcohol at that moment, and Charles responded by stating that drinking allowed him to release his anger with full intensity.

While exploring his internal response to Charles's abrupt decision to drink, the therapist understood that Charles might require emotional recognition and appreciation for the inner turmoil he was experiencing. In the end, Charles was seeking a difficult integration between his attachment needs and his needs for autonomy in the relationship with his father. This formulation was shaped by the therapist's countertransference reaction. The therapist, in fact, experienced a sense of being overlooked and disarmed by Charles's statement. Initially, the therapist's reaction was to intervene with a raised voice, reprimanding Charles as if he were a challenging child rather than an adult man. By regulating his countertransference response, the therapist empathetically tried to convey a sense of emotional boundaries combined with recognition to the patient. He discouraged Charles from drinking, suggesting that his desire to drink likely stemmed from difficulty managing his conflicting emotions towards his father, as well as his therapist, in that particular moment. Furthermore, the therapist conveyed to Charles that his urge to drink might be linked to previous experiences where alcohol allowed him to attain a mental state where he no longer felt ashamed of seeing himself as powerless or helpless. The therapist proposed that Charles occasionally experiencing a sense of powerlessness was a positive sign of advancement in his self-regulation capacities, as it indicated a higher level of emotional processing and potential for personal growth, which can facilitate the healing process. Additionally, the therapist recognized and praised Charles for his efforts to improve his overall mental functioning and well-being.

Significantly, the therapist's adequate responsiveness (Lindon, 1994; Stolorow, 1988) through the management of his countertransference reaction played a role in fostering mutual regulation (Beebe & Lachmann, 1998) within the analytic dyad. Charles began reflecting on his internal processes. He acknowledged that his expressions of anger were sometimes motivated by a desire for emotional closeness and recognition from his father. At the same time, he also realized that his compulsive need for his father's validation obstructed his ability to assess the consequences of his actions and identify his own personal needs. Notably, these types of regulatory interactions were pivotal in facilitating Charles' internalization of more advanced and effective emotion regulation strategies throughout the course of his treatment.

Therefore, this clinical excerpt reveals that Charles's inclination towards shifting into his grandiose and aggressive persona, which he unconsciously perceived as a source of power, served to deny his feelings of powerlessness. With the help of the therapist, Charles improved his capacity to regulate and mentalize his own emotions, thereby transforming the overwhelming feelings that derived from developmental trauma – and that were previously unmanageable due to the alcohol-induced dissociation – into new information for better processing and integrating his internal and interpersonal experiences.

Promoting therapeutic change

If clients are not sufficiently prepared to address their developmental trauma, the clinician's efforts to assist them in resolving internal conflicts and integrating different parts of themselves might lead to a deterioration of their condition and the emergence of feelings of psychic fragmentations. Despite generating multiple and incompatible self-states, compartmentalization may be paradoxically comforting for traumatized individuals, as it provides a semblance of self-continuity, albeit fictional, and protects the most vulnerable parts of the self by excluding them from awareness. Accordingly, in the context of therapeutic interventions, it is crucial for clinicians to recognize how substance use might serve as a form of self-medication for these clients and how chemical dissociation has the function of protecting them from disorganization. Only with this awareness, can clinicians proceed at an appropriate pace based on the clients' needs in the intricate process of trauma processing.

Additionally, it is evident that in cases of developmental trauma, the use of substances can also serve as a counterphobic response (Glover, 1932a, 1932b) with a regulatory function. In such situations, a shift occurs, leading to the denial of trauma and the reinforcement of counterphobic and omnipotent states, as observed in Charles's case. This often results in the clients' inability to learn from relational experiences, perpetuating unconscious feelings of shame, guilt, abandonment, and loneliness (Schimmenti, 2021). Hence, substance addictions may serve as compensatory but ineffective attempts at self-regulation and self-medication.

For Charles, substance abuse indeed resulted from a need of self-medication, as substances allowed him to temporarily escape from his vulnerable, depressed, and traumatized internal parts. However, this came at the cost of further insulating these parts and making them independent entities – exemplified by the instance when a 'preadolescent Charles' seeking for help called his friends at 4:30 in the morning. Therefore, although substances may appear as a viable self-medication option for individuals like Charles, they ultimately do not contribute to genuine healing and integration of different parts of the self.

Within the therapeutic process, it was imperative to address Charles's substance use for self-medication, and promote the integration of his dissociated parts in a manner that ensured safety. A critical aspect involved examining the underlying causes contributing to the dissociation of his parts, which had made him susceptible to recurring trauma and engagement in violent behaviors throughout his life. This entailed the crucial task of addressing developmental trauma, a process that necessitates therapists to approach it with utmost sensitivity in order to prevent overwhelming dysregulation and potential disorganization (Schimmenti, 2022)

When considering the disintegrative relational experiences that have contributed to the development of different parts in clients like Charles, it is imperative for the clinician to generate moments of transformative and self-delineating experiences (Atwood & Stolorow, 1984; Stolorow et al., 1987). These experiences, enabled by constructive intersubjective interactions, emancipate these clients from viewing themselves exclusively as individuals who have undergone trauma and struggle with substance abuse, thereby reinstating their self-esteem, mastery, and sense of agency. This empathetic approach aids in reducing the risk of retraumatization during therapy, as self-delineating experiences align with the concept of corrective emotional experiences (Alexander, 1950; Alexander & French, 1946). Within the therapeutic context, these experiences assume a pivotal role in validating and restoring dignity and coherence to the addicted clients' internal world, as they actively navigate and ultimately process their developmental trauma.

By implementing targeted interventions tailored to his specific psychological difficulties, Charles witnessed a notable enhancement in his overall well-being. After undergoing therapy for a year and a half, Charles successfully reduced his alcohol consumption and completely refrained from using illicit substances.

Discussion

The case of Charles demonstrates how addictive behaviors often stem from developmental trauma and dissociation (Schimmenti et al., 2022). Throughout his childhood and teenage years, Charles experienced several traumatic events, such as observing his mother's self-destructive behaviors and witnessing aggression towards her. Additionally, he had to confront parental conflicts and endure the separation from his father. Charles was actually exposed to severe developmental trauma, that is, to a 'traumatic configuration of the relational field between the child and his or her caregivers, characterized by a lack of emotional reciprocity and a disavowal of the child's affective needs' (Schimmenti & Caretti, 2016, p. 109). In developmental trauma, the child is subjected to the desires, conflicts, fears, and unprocessed emotions of the parents (Borgogno, 2007).

Several authors, including Bromberg (1998) and Stolorow and Atwood (1992), have emphasized that these relational failures in attachment relationships can hinder the development of a coherent and unified sense of self in the child. Instead, they can lead to self-fragmentation (Kohut, 1971, 1977) and the introduction of alien transplants (that is, foreign elements deriving from the caregivers' projections; see Ferenczi, 1932/1988) into the child's mind. In other words, the self becomes compartmentalized into different parts, some of which maintain a primitive identification with specific aspects of the caregivers (e.g., the frightened part and the frightening part; see Schimmenti, 2017).

Kilborne (2002) proposed that children may even dismantle their own self-structure to protect their internal representation of parents who have caused psychological harm. Charles's case provides an alternative perspective: it is plausible that some individuals who have experienced developmental trauma defensively use compartmentalization to push away from the awareness the overwhelming experiences of parental intrusion, rejection and neglect. However, this compartmentalization impedes the formation of a cohesive self and hinders the development of adequate mentalizing processes.

Also, in individuals who suffered developmental trauma, substance use might be employed as a means to facilitate and strengthen the dissociation between parts. Indeed, by engaging in altered states of consciousness induced by substances (Somer et al., 2010, 2019), individuals can evade the emotional depths where the unbearable emotions (Schimmenti & Caretti, 2016) that have led to the compartmentalization still possess their annihilating and harmful power. It is noteworthy that these individuals may perceive self-preservation through the continuation of dissociation, which is supported by substance abuse.

Dissociation represents indeed a normal process of the mind that enables adaptation to reality by allowing the emergence of specific configurations of self, other, and self-other representations (Schimmenti, 2022). However, an excessive and repetitive activation of the dissociative processes following traumatic experiences may hinder the integration of different self-states, leading to their compartmentalization instead (Bromberg, 1998). In a psychodynamic perspective, dissociation is also conceptualized as a defense mechanism that renders traumatic experiences inaccessible to consciousness (Beresford, 2012; Vaillant, 1992; Vaillant & Drake, 1985). The presence of persistent dissociative processes manifests through symptoms such as dissociative amnesia, depersonalization, derealization, identity confusion, and identity alteration (Steinberg, 2023). Referring to the case of Charles, major dissociative processes might be identified in his episodes of amnesia and identity alteration, for example, when a frightened, child-like state that he could not recognize as a part of his own identity emerged after the communication of work relocation. Specifically, the part identified with his omnipotent father was unable to recognize the vulnerable part identified with his frail and depressed mother.

Indeed, an excessive use of dissociation may impair the integration of bodily and mental states, hindering the development of capacities for self-regulation and interpersonal regulation of emotions, as well as limiting the individual's reflective functioning (Schimmenti & Caretti, 2016). In accordance with the self-medication hypothesis (Khantzian, 1997, 2003), substance abuse can be precisely interpreted as a maladaptive strategy for emotion regulation. Within this framework, substances act as external regulators for emotions that remain unprocessed and unbearable, intertwined with traumatic memories (Schimmenti et al., 2022).

It is also the case that in certain instances, pathological dissociation emerges as a direct outcome of thoughts and emotions that are genuinely too overwhelming for the child to manage. This is because they could be so distressing that they might even lead to psychic disintegration. The disrupting emotions resulting from severe abuse, neglect, and rejection in attachment relationships can generate conflicting and highly competitive mental states that, if not excluded from awareness, have the potential to jeopardize the child's entire sense of self (Schimmenti, 2022). In the case of Charles, the omnipotent part was established as a result of the identification with an image of a grandiose father, which came about due to the existence of an opposing polarity stemming from experiences of maternal weakness and paternal rejection, leading to the internalization of a devalued and fragile part. It is important to note that the division between these two parts is not contingent upon the dichotomy of a positive and negative internal object (Klein, 1935); instead, it pertains to the manner in which relationally traumatic experiences in childhood are structured within different systems of meaning, involving their own distinct processes of identification.

Considering this psychological context, the role of substance abuse becomes more comprehensible. The self-medication hypothesis posits that the physiological effects of substances significantly influence their usage (Khantzian, 1997). Thus, individuals may use certain substances in order to attain a psychobiological state that enables them to cope with their specific vulnerabilities. Accordingly, Charles consumed alcohol and other substances to experience feelings of competence and grandiosity in both professional endeavors and close relationships, as opposed to feelings of fragility and powerlessness. His substance abuse facilitated the shifting from a vulnerable part to a grandiose part, occasionally leading him to engage in aggressive behavior.

Also, Wurmser (2003) postulated that severe attachment failures can give rise to an archaic, authoritarian superego which fosters feelings of shame and guilt. This archaic superego emerges as a means of coping with the overwhelming emotions stemming from traumatic interactions with caregivers, and it serves a regulatory purpose: self-regulation is manifested through engaging in self-punitive and sadomasochistic behaviors. When Charles was under the influence of substances and confronted with the potential separation from his partners, his anger surfaced and he resorted to self-harm and destructive actions. These incidents could potentially indicate the presence of this archaic and punitive superego, which was connected to the early internalization of a grandiose and harsh paternal image. Through its disinhibition effects, alcohol consumption facilitated Charles's shifting toward the polarity of grandiosity and invulnerability, that is, alcohol gave him the possibility to inhabit the same psychic place of the authoritarian and omnipotent superego. Consequently, this shift may be interpreted as a ruthless posttraumatic dynamic, as it represents a primitive attempt to insulate, exclude, or even eliminate the most vulnerable, ashamed, and fragile parts of the self.

Hence, treating individuals with substance addiction who have been relationally traumatized in their childhood presents a significant challenge. In order to effectively treat these individuals, therapeutic interventions must aim not only to foster integration in their object representations, but also to enhance their capacity to tolerate the internal inconsistencies and potential destructiveness associated with the identification with these internal objects. It is essential for these individuals to develop the necessary abilities to manage and process the emotional distress that emanates from their partial identification with aggressive, distant, unaffectionate, and abusive objects. This is crucial in order to diminish the disruptive influence that these internal objects have on their lives. With the acquisition of emotion regulation and mentalization skills, addicted individuals with a history of developmental trauma may overcome their traumatic identifications (Schimmenti, 2017) and restore a sense of wholeness, authenticity, and integrity (Bromberg, 2013).

Conclusions

The case of Charles served as an illustration of the self-medication hypothesis (Khantzian, 1985) and its applicability in understanding substance abuse in individuals with a history of developmental trauma. Within this framework, substance abuse can be regarded as a method for strengthening the dissociation between different parts of the self and reinforcing the defensive exclusion of the unbearable emotions associated with developmental trauma from awareness.

Clinical and empirical research should delve deeper into the importance of dissociative mechanisms in the realms of both behavioral and substance addictions. Notably, the notions of 'psychic pits' linked to developmental trauma (Schimmenti & Caretti, 2010, 2017) and the quest for 'chemical dissociation' in traumatized individuals (Somer, 2003) provide valuable insights into how dissociative processes contribute to the continuation of addictive behaviors. These concepts offer insights into the efforts made by some individuals struggling with addiction to disavow their relational trauma, their reliance on addictive behaviors as a form of emotion regulation, and the transient feelings of well-being stemming from altering their consciousness through these behaviors. All of these dynamics can be seen as attempts at self-medication, driven by the vulnerable states induced by developmental trauma.

The case of Charles also exemplifies the seemingly contradictory nature of substance abuse in people who were exposed to developmental trauma. On one hand, engaging in substance abuse can enable the transition from a vulnerable and helpless state to an omnipotent state, serving as a counter-phobic strategy for coping with feelings of shame, inadequacy, and powerlessness without experiencing disorganization or fragmentation. On the other hand, substance abuse can also be seen as a reenactment of the original process of compartmentalization that resulted from the impossibility for the child to tolerate the traumatic experiences and integrate them into a cohesive system of meaning.

Clinical interventions with traumatized individuals suffering from addiction should prioritize improving their ability to endure distressing emotions and feelings without resorting to substances or engaging in other addictive behaviors (Yeomans et al., 2015). For this reason, it is critical to perform a thorough assessment as an indispensable prerequisite of substance use treatment. It is strongly recommended to employ empirically validated instruments along with compassionate interviews during the assessment phase. It is essential to evaluate various facets of the addicted clients' history and mental functioning, thus encompassing not only substance use patterns but also elements like traumatic experiences, personality traits, attachment styles, quality of relationship, self-regulation capacities, mentalizing abilities, and dissociative processes. All of these factors may play a substantial role in shaping therapeutic plans and providing personalized treatments.

Especially, a comprehensive exploration of the clients' dissociative processes can help the clinician to develop tailored and more effective interventions aimed at addressing the clients' vulnerabilities. Also, providing these clients with insights on their use of dissociation can encourage them to adopt a curious attitude towards their psychic processes, promoting their self-reflectivity and increasing their feeling of security in the therapeutic relationship (Chefetz, 2015).

Once a sense of relational security is established and a solid therapeutic alliance is formed, the clinician can assist these clients in increasing their tolerance for dysregulated emotions that lead to impulsive behaviors and substance abuse (Siegel, 1999). Accordingly, it is recommended that the clinician adopts a compassionate, supportive, respectful, and empathetic approach (Baurer, 2021; Khantzian, 2021) when interacting with addicted clients. This approach also entails the ability to understand and connect with the dissociated states of these clients, alongside the clients themselves (Bromberg, 1998).

In conclusion, Khantzian's self-medication hypothesis could inform clinical interventions targeting substance abuse in individuals who have endured developmental trauma and exhibit persistent dissociative processes. Through an in-depth comprehension of the vulnerabilities that underlie their pursuit of external regulators for emotions, such as drugs and alcohol, personalized interventions can be tailored to improve self-regulation skills and promote a unified and cohesive self-concept. Furthermore, by accurately identifying and addressing the self-medication tendencies of these clients, the clinician can facilitate the recognition and harmonious integration of the dissociated parts of their identity. This process fosters a sense of coherence and enhances their ability to live in a more authentic and spontaneous manner.

Disclosure statement

No potential conflict of interest was reported by the author(s).

Funding

The author(s) reported that there is no funding associated with the work featured in this article

ORCID

Gianluca Santoro http://orcid.org/0000-0002-9762-1510

Adriano Schimmenti http://orcid.org/0000-0001-5181-2648

References

Alexander, F. (1950). Analysis of the therapeutic factor in psychoanalytic treatment. *Psychoanalytic Quarterly*, *19*(4), 482–500. https://doi.org/10.1080/21674086.1950.11925819

Alexander, F., & French, T. M. (1946). *Psychoanalysis and psychotherapy: Principles and application*. Ronald Press.

Alfonso, C. A. (2021). An overview of the psychodynamics of addiction. *Psychodynamic Psychiatry*, *49*(3), 363–369. https://doi.org/10.1521/pdps.2021.49.3.363

Alvarez-Monjaras, M., Mayes, L. C., Potenza, M. N., & Rutherford, H. J. V. (2019). A developmental model of addictions: Integrating neurobiological and psychodynamic theories through the lens of attachment. *Attachment & Human Development, 21*(6), 616–637. https://doi.org/10.1080/14616734.2018.1498113

American Psychiatric Association. (2022). *Diagnostic and statistical manual of mental disorders* (5th rev. ed.). https://doi.org/10.1176/appi.books.9780890425787

Atwood, G., & Stolorow, R. (1984). *Structures of subjectivity: Explorations in psychoanalytic phenomenology.* The Analytic Press.

Bartholomew, K., & Horowitz, L. M. (1991). Attachment styles among young adults: A test of a four-category model. *Journal of Personality and Social Psychology, 61*(2), 226–244. https://doi.org/10.1037/0022-3514.61.2.226

Bateman, A., & Fonagy, P. (2006). *Mentalization-based treatment for borderline personality disorder: A practical guide.* Oxford University Press.

Baudin, G., Barrault, S., El Ayoubi, H., Kazour, F., Ballon, N., Maugé, D., Hingray, C., Brunault, P., & El-Hage, W. (2022). Childhood trauma and dissociation correlates in alcohol use disorder: A cross-sectional study in a sample of 587 French subjects hospitalized in a rehabilitation center. *Brain Sciences, 12*(11), 1483. https://doi.org/10.3390/brainsci12111483

Baurer, F. M. (2021). Psychodynamic treatment with the addicted person. *Psychodynamic Psychiatry, 49*(3), 404–424. https://doi.org/10.1521/pdps.2021.49.3.404

Beebe, B., & Lachmann, F. M. (1998). Co-constructing inner and relational processes: Self- and mutual regulation in infant research and adult treatment. *Psychoanalytic Psychology, 15*(4), 480–516. https://doi.org/10.1037/0736-9735.15.4.480

Beresford, T. P. (2012). *Psychological adaptive mechanisms: Ego defense recognition in practice and research.* Oxford University Press.

Bifulco, A., & Schimmenti, A. (2019). Assessing child abuse: "we need to talk!" *Child Abuse & Neglect, 98*, 104236. https://doi.org/10.1016/j.chiabu.2019.104236

Borgogno, F. (2007). Ferenczi's clinical and theoretical conception of trauma: A brief introductory map. *The American Journal of Psychoanalysis, 67*(2), 141–149. https://doi.org/10.1057/palgrave.ajp.3350022

Bromberg, P. M. (1998). *Standing in the spaces: Essays on clinical process, trauma, and dissociation.* Analytic Press.

Bromberg, P. M. (2013). Prefazione [Foreword]. In V. Caretti, G. Craparo, & A. Schimmenti (Eds.), *Memorie traumatiche e mentalizzazione, teoria, ricerca e clinica* (pp. 7–12). Astrolabio Ubaldini.

Bryant, R. A. (2007). Does dissociation further our understanding of PTSD? *Journal of Anxiety Disorders, 21*(2), 183–191. https://doi.org/10.1016/j.janxdis.2006.09.012

Caretti, V., Gori, A., Craparo, G., Giannini, M., Iraci-Sareri, G., & Schimmenti, A. (2018). A new measure for assessing substance-related and addictive disorders: The addictive behavior questionnaire (ABQ). *Journal of Clinical Medicine, 7*(8), 194. https://doi.org/10.3390/jcm7080194

Carlson, E. B., Dalenberg, C., & McDade Montez, E. (2012). Dissociation in posttraumatic stress disorder part 1: Definitions and review of research. *Psychological Trauma: Theory, Research, Practice, & Policy, 4*(5), 479–489. https://doi.org/10.1037/a0027748

Carlson, E. B., & Putnam, F. W. (1993). An update on the Dissociative Experiences Scale. *Dissociation: Progress in the Dissociative Disorders, 6*(1), 16–27.

Chefetz, R. A. (2015). *Intensive psychotherapy for persistent dissociative processes: The fear of feeling real.* WW Norton & Company.

Dalenberg, C. J., Brand, B. L., Gleaves, D. H., Dorahy, M. J., Loewenstein, R. J., Cardeña, E., Frewen, P. A., Carlson, E. B., & Spiegel, D. (2012). Evaluation of the evidence for the trauma and fantasy models of dissociation. *Psychological Bulletin, 138*(3), 550–588. https://doi.org/10.1037/a0027447

Dvir, Y., Ford, J. D., Hill, M., & Frazier, J. A. (2014). Childhood maltreatment, emotional dysregulation, and psychiatric comorbidities. *Harvard Review of Psychiatry*, *22*(3), 149–161. https://doi.org/10.1097/HRP.0000000000000014

Dye, H. (2018). The impact and long-term effects of childhood trauma. *Journal of Human Behavior in the Social Environment*, *28*(3), 381–392. https://doi.org/10.1080/10911359.2018.1435328

Ferenczi, S. (1932/1988). *The clinical diary.*

Frewen, P., & Lanius, R. (2015). *Healing the traumatized self: Consciousness, neuroscience, treatment.* WW Norton & Company.

Glover, E. (1932a). On the aetiology of drug-addiction. *International Journal of Psychoanalysis*, *13*, 298–328.

Glover, E. (1932b). The relation of perversion-formation to the development of reality-sense. In E. Glover (Ed.) (1956), *On the early development of mind* (pp. 216–234). Imago Publishing Co.

Goldberg, A. (1995). *The problem of perversion: The view from self psychology.* Yale University Press.

Goldberg, A. (1999). *Being of two minds: The vertical split in psychoanalysis and psychotherapy.* Analytic Press.

Granieri, A., Guglielmucci, F., Costanzo, A., Caretti, V., & Schimmenti, A. (2018). Trauma-related dissociation is linked with maladaptive personality functioning. *Frontiers in Psychiatry*, *9*, 206. https://doi.org/10.3389/fpsyt.2018.00206

International Society for the Study of Trauma and Dissociation. (2011). Guidelines for treating dissociative identity disorder in adults (Third revision). *Journal of Trauma & Dissociation*, *12*(2), 115–187. https://doi.org/10.1080/15299732.2011.537247

Khantzian, E. J. (1985). The self-medication hypothesis of addictive disorders: Focus on heroin and cocaine dependence. *The American Journal of Psychiatry*, *142*(11), 1259–1264. https://doi.org/10.1176/ajp.142.11.1259

Khantzian, E. J. (1997). The self-medication hypothesis of substance use disorders: A reconsideration and recent applications. *Harvard Review of Psychiatry*, *4*(5), 231–244. https://doi.org/10.3109/10673229709030550

Khantzian, E. J. (1999). *Treating addiction as a human process*. Jason Aronson.

Khantzian, E. J. (2003). Understanding addictive vulnerability: An evolving psychodynamic perspective. *Neuropsychoanalysis*, *5*(1), 5–21. https://doi.org/10.1080/15294145.2003.10773403

Khantzian, E. J. (2012). Reflections on treating addictive disorders: A psychodynamic perspective. *The American Journal on Addictions*, *21*(3), 274–279. https://doi.org/10.1111/j.1521-0391.2012.00234.x

Khantzian, E. J. (2021). Psychodynamic psychotherapy for the treatment of substance use disorders. In N. el-Guebaly, G. Carrà, M. Galanter, & A. M. Baldacchino (Eds.), *Textbook of addiction treatment* (pp. 383–389). Springer. https://doi.org/10.1007/978-3-030-36391-8_26

Kilborne, B. (2002). *Disappearing persons: Shame and appearance*. State of University New York Press.

Klein, M. (1935). A contribution to the psychogenesis of manic-depressive states. *International Journal of Psychoanalysis*, *16*, 145–174.

Kluft, R. P. (1984). Aspects of the treatment of multiple personality disorder. *Psychiatric Annals*, *14*(1), 51–55. https://doi.org/10.3928/0048-5713-19840101-09

Kohut, H. (1971). *The analysis of the self: A systematic approach to the psychoanalytic treatment of narcissistic personality disorders*. University of Chicago Press.

Kohut, H. (1977). *The restoration of the self.* University of Chicago Press.

Krystal, H. (1995). Disorders of emotional development in addictive behavior. In S. Dowling (Ed.), *The psychology and treatment of addictive behaviors* (pp. 65–100). International University Press.

Lichtenberg, J. D., Lachmann, F. M., & Fosshage, J. L. (1992). *Self and motivational systems: Towards a theory of psychoanalytic technique*. Analytic.

Lichtenberg, J. D., Lachmann, F. M., & Fosshage, J. L. (1996). *The clinical exchange: Techniques derived from self and motivational systems*. Analytic.

Lichtenberg, J. D., Lachmann, F. M., & Fosshage, J. L. (2011). *Psychoanalysis and motivational systems: A new look*. Routledge.

Lindon, J. A. (1994). Gratification and provision in psychoanalysis should we get rid of "the rule of abstinence"? *Psychoanalytic Dialogues*, *4*(4), 549–582. https://doi.org/10.1080/10481889409539038

Lotzin, A., Grundmann, J., Hiller, P., Pawils, S., & Schäfer, I. (2019). Profiles of childhood trauma in women with substance use disorders and comorbid posttraumatic stress disorders. *Frontiers in Psychiatry*, *10*, 674. https://doi.org/10.3389/fpsyt.2019.00674

Mezzalira, S., Santoro, G., Bochicchio, V., & Schimmenti, A. (2023). Trauma and the disruption of temporal experience: A psychoanalytical and phenomenological perspective. *The American Journal of Psychoanalysis*, *83*(1), 36–55. https://doi.org/10.1057/s11231-023-09395-w

Midolo, L. R., Santoro, G., Ferrante, E., Pellegriti, P., Russo, S., Costanzo, A., & Schimmenti, A. (2020). Childhood trauma, attachment and psychopathology: A correlation network approach. *Mediterranean Journal of Clinical Psychology*, *8*(2). https://doi.org/10.6092/2282-1619/mjcp-2418

Najavits, L. M. & Walsh, M. (2012). Dissociation, PTSD, and substance abuse: An empirical study. *Journal of Trauma & Dissociation*, *13*(1), 115–126. https://doi.org/10.1080/15299732.2011.608781

Nijenhuis, E. R., Van der Hart, O., & Kruger, K. (2002). The psychometric characteristics of the traumatic experiences checklist (TEC): First findings among psychiatric outpatients. *Clinical Psychology & Psychotherapy*, *9*(3), 200–210. https://doi.org/10.1002/cpp.332

Pollak, S. D., Messner, M., Kistler, D. J., & Cohn, J. F. (2009). Development of perceptual expertise in emotion recognition. *Cognition*, *110*(2), 242–247. https://doi.org/10.1016/j.cognition.2008.10.010

Potik, D. (2020). *Psychodynamic approaches for treatment of drug abuse and addiction: Theory and treatment*. Routledge.

Racamiere, P.-C. (1995). *L'inceste et l'incestuel*. Les Éditions du Collège.

Santoro, G., Midolo, L. R., Costanzo, A., & Schimmenti, A. (2021). The vulnerability of insecure minds: The mediating role of mentalization in the relationship between attachment styles and psychopathology. *Bulletin of the Menninger Clinic*, *85*(4), 358–384. https://doi.org/10.1521/bumc.2021.85.4.358

Scarna, H. (2020). Genesis of the heroin-induced addictive process: Articulation between psychodynamic and neurobiological theories. *Frontiers in Psychiatry*, *11*, 524764. https://doi.org/10.3389/fpsyt.2020.524764

Schäfer, I., Langeland, W., Hissbach, J., Luedecke, C., Ohlmeier, M. D., Chodzinski, C., Kemper, U., Keiper, P., Wedekind, D., Havemann-Reinecke, U., Teunissen, S., Weirich, S., Driessen, M., & TRAUMAB-Study Group. (2010). Childhood trauma and dissociation in patients with alcohol dependence, drug dependence, or both–A multi-center study. *Drug & Alcohol Dependence*, *109*(1–3), 84–89. https://doi.org/10.1016/j.drugalcdep.2009.12.012

Schäfer, I., Reininghaus, U., Langeland, W., Voss, A., Zieger, N., Haasen, C., & Karow, A. (2007). Dissociative symptoms in alcohol-dependent patients: Associations with childhood trauma and substance abuse characteristics. *Comprehensive Psychiatry*, *48*(6), 539–545. https://doi.org/10.1016/j.comppsych.2007.05.013

Schimmenti, A. (2017). Traumatic identification. *Attachment: New Directions in Relational Psychoanalysis and Psychotherapy*, *11*(2), 154–171. https://doi.org/10.33212/att.v11n2.2017.154

Schimmenti, A. (2018). The trauma factor: Examining the relationships among different types of trauma, dissociation, and psychopathology. *Journal of Trauma & Dissociation*, *19*(5), 552–571. https://doi.org/10.1080/15299732.2017.1402400

Schimmenti, A. (2021). The aggressor within: Attachment trauma, segregated systems, and the double face of shame. In O. B. Epstain (Ed.), *Shame matters: Attachment and relational perspectives for psychotherapists* (pp. 114–132). Routledge. https://doi.org/10.4324/9781003175612

Schimmenti, A. (2022). The relationship between attachment and dissociation: Theory, research, and clinical implications. In M. J. Dorahy, S. N. Gold, & J. A. O'Neil (Eds.), *Dissociation and the dissociative disorders: Past, present, future* (2nd ed., pp. 161–176). Routledge.

Schimmenti, A., Billieux, J., Santoro, G., Casale, S., & Starcevic, V. (2022). A trauma model of substance use: Elaboration and preliminary validation. *Addictive Behaviors*, *134*, 107431. https://doi.org/10.1016/j.addbeh.2022.107431

Schimmenti, A., & Caretti, V. (2010). Psychic retreats or psychic pits? Unbearable states of mind and technological addiction. *Psychoanalytic Psychology*, *27*(2), 115–132. https://doi.org/10.1037/a0019414

Schimmenti, A., & Caretti, V. (2016). Linking the overwhelming with the unbearable: Developmental trauma, dissociation, and the disconnected self. *Psychoanalytic Psychology*, *33*(1), 106–128. https://doi.org/10.1037/a0038019

Schimmenti, A., & Caretti, V. (2017). Video-terminal dissociative trance: Toward a psychodynamic understanding of problematic internet use. *Clinical Neuropsychiatry*, *14*(1), 64–72.

Shedler, J. & Westen, D. (1998). Refining the measurement of Axis II: A Q-sort procedure for assessing personality pathology. *Assessment*, *5*(4), 333–353. https://doi.org/10.1177/107319119800500403

Siegel, D. J. (1999). *The developing mind: Toward a neurobiology of interpersonal experience*. Guilford Press.

Somer, E. (2003). Prediction of abstinence from heroin addiction by childhood trauma, dissociation, and extent of psychosocial treatment. *Addiction Research & Theory*, *11* (5), 339–348. https://doi.org/10.1080/1606635031000141102

Somer, E. (2022). Opioid misuse and dissociation: Two powerful modes of distress regulation. In M. J. Dorahy, S. N. Gold, & J. A. O'Neil (Eds.), *Dissociation and the dissociative disorders: Past, present, future* (2nd ed., pp. 564–572). Routledge.

Somer, E., Abu-Raya, H. M., & Nsairy Samaan, Z. (2019). Maladaptive daydreaming among recovering substance use disorder patients: Prevalence and mediation of the relationship between childhood trauma and dissociation. *International Journal of Mental Health and Addictions*, *17*(2), 206–216. https://doi.org/10.1007/s11469-018-0011-9

Somer, E., Altus, L., & Ginzburg, K. (2010). Dissociative psychopathology among opioid use disorder patients: Exploring the "chemical dissociation" hypothesis. *Comprehensive Psychiatry*, *51*(4), 419–425. https://doi.org/10.1016/j.comppsych.2009.09.007

Steinberg, M. (2023). *The SCID-D interview: Dissociation assessment in therapy, forensics, and research*. American Psychiatric Association Publishing.

Stolorow, R. D. (1988). Transference and the therapeutic process. *Psychoanalytic Review*, *75*(2), 245–254.

Stolorow, R. D., & Atwood, G. E. (1992). *Contexts of being. The intersubjective foundations of psychological life*. The Analytic Press.

Stolorow, R. D., Brandchaft, B., & Atwood, G. E. (1987). *Psychoanalytic treatment: An intersubjective approach*. Analytic Press, Inc.

Vaillant, G. E. (1992). *Ego mechanisms of defense: A guide for clinicians and researchers*. Harvard University Press.

Vaillant, G. E., & Drake, R. E. (1985). Maturity of ego defenses in relation to DSM-III Axis II personality disorder. *Archives of General Psychiatry*, *42*(6), 597–601. https://doi.org/10.1001/archpsyc.1985.01790290079009

Vonderlin, R., Kleindienst, N., Alpers, G. W., Bohus, M., Lyssenko, L., & Schmahl, C. (2018). Dissociation in victims of childhood abuse or neglect: A meta-analytic review. *Psychological Medicine*, *48*(15), 2467–2476. https://doi.org/10.1017/S0033291718000740

Wurmser, L. (2003). The annihilating power of absoluteness: Superego analysis in the severe neuroses, especially in character perversion. *Psychoanalytic Psychology*, *20* (2), 214–235. https://doi.org/10.1037/0736-9735.20.2.214

Yeomans, F. E., Clarkin, J. F., & Kernberg, O. F. (2015). *Transference-focused psychotherapy for borderline personality disorder: A clinical guide*. American Psychiatric Publishing, Inc.

Zhang, S., Lin, X., Liu, J., Pan, Y., Zeng, X., Chen, F., & Wu, J. (2020). Prevalence of childhood trauma measured by the short form of the childhood trauma questionnaire in people with substance use disorder: A meta-analysis. *Psychiatry Research*, *294*, 113524. https://doi.org/10.1016/j.psychres.2020.113524

OPEN ACCESS

Addressing dissociation symptoms with trauma-focused mentalization-based treatment

E. Rüfenacht, L. Shaverin, J. Stubley, M. L. Smits, A. Bateman, P. Fonagy and P. Luyten

A significant number of individuals receiving mental health care exhibit a history of traumatic experiences. Accompanying dissociative symptoms often amplify the complexity of their required treatment. This article introduces a novel understanding and treatment approach for post-traumatic stress symptoms, inclusive of dissociation, derived from attachment and mentalization theories. Initially, we outline the different expressions of dissociation and the prevailing knowledge concerning their associations with diverse clinical manifestations and their role in trauma. We subsequently reinterpret these clinical symptoms through an attachment and mentalization lens, then proceed to elaborate on the new trauma-focused mentalization-based treatment and its therapeutic objectives. The article culminates with a case study that exemplifies the application of this approach in a clinical setting.

Dissociative experiences, as natural reactions to stress, are not only found in the general population but are also prevalent across various mental health disorders (American Psychiatric Association, 2013; Carlson, 1998; Dalenberg & Paulson, 2009; Spiegel et al., 2011). There's considerable research evidence linking these experiences to a history of adverse childhood experiences. In a clinical setting, dissociation can add another layer of complexity to patient treatment, potentially impacting outcomes. Thus, it is imperative for clinicians to learn to navigate dissociative experiences, integrating them into treatment goals for trauma patients to enhance their care.

This article presents an exploration of dissociation, its manifestations, its connection with several mental health disorders, its origin, and its role. We will also delve into recent advances in the understanding of trauma through the lens of attachment and mentalizing theory. Subsequently, we introduce a novel therapeutic method, trauma-focused mentalization-based treatment (MBT-TF), and delineate its therapeutic goals which encompass addressing epistemic mistrust, dissociation, shame, and alien-self experiences, and promoting embodied mentalizing. The article concludes with a real-world case study that demonstrates this approach.

Dissociation

Definition and clinical manifestations

Dissociation, as defined by the American Psychiatric Association, is a discontinuity or lack of integration in subjective experiences like emotions, memory, somatic sensations, consciousness, and identity (American Psychiatric Association, 2013). Dissociative experiences span a wide spectrum, from normative behaviors like daydreaming to intense symptoms like depersonalization, derealization, and in its most acute form, dissociative identity disorder (DID). Depersonalization involves a sense of unreality about oneself or one's body, experiencing an 'autopilot' mode, out-of-body experiences, disconnectedness from thoughts or emotions, or lack of usual bodily sensations. On the other hand, derealization involves feeling as though the external world is unreal or as if looking through a fog (Allen, 2013b). These symptoms, which typically co-occur, are identified as psychological forms of dissociation, contrasted with somatic forms like alterations in pain perception or loss of voluntary motor control (Krause-Utz et al., 2021; Spiegel et al., 2011).

Dissociative experiences occurring during traumatic events are called peritraumatic dissociation. Another way to categorize these experiences is into detachment and compartmentalization. Detachment refers to disconnection from oneself or the external world and includes absorption, depersonalization, or derealization. Compartmentalization involves instances where parts of a person's experience or personality become inaccessible to others, as seen in dissociative amnesia or dissociative identity disorder (Allen, 2013a). Further, dissociation can be classified into negative dissociative symptoms, denoting a loss of memory or self-information or a loss of bodily control, and positive dissociative symptoms characterized by intrusive symptoms like flashbacks (Spiegel et al., 2011). Both negative and positive dissociative symptoms disrupt an individual's functioning, personal narrative, and self-perception (Spiegel et al., 2011).

There exists considerable debate over the precise classification of dissociative experiences and the demarcation point at which such experiences become pathologized (Carlson, 1998; Dalenberg & Paulson, 2009; Spiegel et al., 2011). It's critical to recognize that several dissociative manifestations are observable within the general population and can function as adaptive coping mechanisms in certain contexts, notably in response to stress. This dynamic further complicates the task of discerning 'normal' from pathological dissociation.

Etiology and function

While the origins of dissociation and its models remain subject to debate, particularly since such symptoms can emerge in the absence of adverse life events, substantial evidence underscores the link between traumatic experiences and dissociation (Dalenberg et al., 2012; Krause-Utz et al., 2021; Loewenstein, 2018; Lyssenko et al., 2018). A meta-analysis encompassing 65 studies revealed that early onset, prolonged abuse duration, and parental maltreatment significantly contribute to heightened dissociation levels (Vonderlin et al., 2018). The trauma etiological model proposes that dissociative symptoms function as protective shields against overwhelming and emotionally distressing experiences (Loewenstein, 2018). From an evolutionary and biological viewpoint, they may represent survival strategies when fight or flight responses are impracticable or ineffective.

Dissociation is typically part of the involuntary stress response spectrum, beginning with a freeze state (characterized by immobility but heightened danger awareness) or a fight/flight reaction, ultimately transitioning into tonic immobility, a state of surrender and shutdown (Fanselow & Lester, 1988; Schauer & Elbert, 2010). These conceptual frameworks are often used to understand dissociation symptoms in individuals exposed to developmental trauma (Allen, 2013b). From an attachment and mentalizing perspective, dissociation could serve an unconscious defensive role by inhibiting children from mentalizing the mental states of abusive caregivers, especially when escape is impossible, and survival is contingent on caregiver attachment (Allen, 2013b; Fonagy & Target, 1997). Although dissociation aids survival by disconnecting from bodily experiences and mental states, it also obstructs self-development, identity formation, and affect regulation. The result is a fragmented self-experience that leads to self-alienation and estrangement from others, leaving individuals more susceptible to stress and predisposed to automatic dissociative coping mechanisms in response to life's later challenges (Classen et al., 1993).

Dissociation in clinical populations

Dissociative symptoms are often experienced by individuals with mental health conditions, and several manifestations of dissociation are listed among the diagnostic criteria in the DSM-5 (American Psychiatric Association, 2013) for various disorders including post-traumatic stress disorder (PTSD) and borderline personality disorder (BPD) (Krause-Utz et al., 2021; Lyssenko et al., 2018). Alongside this, childhood abuse is also known to be a risk factor for many mental health disorders later in life, including schizophrenia, bipolar disorder, complex post-traumatic stress disorder (complex PTSD), and BPD (Maercker et al., 2022; Struck et al., 2020; Zanarini & Frankenburg, 1997), as well as numerous physical health conditions (Felitti et al., 1998). Complex PTSD includes the three symptom clusters found in PTSD (avoidance of traumatic reminders, re-experiencing of the traumatic events and hypervigilance), but additionally encompasses three symptom clusters linked to pervasive disturbances in self-organization: emotion regulation difficulties, negative self-concept and relational difficulties. The disorder appears in the aftermath of chronic and repetitive traumatic experiences of horrific or threatening nature, from which escape is either difficult or impossible (Cloitre, 2020; Maercker et al., 2022; World Health Organization, 2019/2021).

BPD, complex PTSD, and PTSD are associated with a high psychosocial burden (Maercker et al., 2022), are highly comorbid to the extent that they greatly overlap, and are negatively associated with treatment response (Barnicot & Crawford, 2018; Ford & Courtois, 2021; Pagura et al., 2010; Scheiderer et al., 2015). Currently, the prevalence of dissociative symptoms in individuals with BPD is estimated at around 80% (Krause-Utz et al., 2021) and these symptoms seem to be particularly present in patients with complex PTSD compared with PTSD (Hyland et al., 2020; Longo et al., 2019; Møller et al., 2021). In adults with BPD, severity of sexual abuse and co-occurring PTSD were significantly linked to dissociative symptom (Zanarini et al., 2023). Studies also suggest considerable heterogenicity in the level of dissociation symptoms experienced by BPD patients, ranging from absorption to amnesia and depersonalization (Zanarini et al., 2000). While the severity of dissociation appears to decrease over time in BPD patients, these symptoms may persist and remain problematic, particularly in patients with complex trauma (Zanarini et al., 2008). Additionally, dissociative symptoms may account for impeded psychological functioning and symptom severity, and they are associated with increased levels of suicidality in clinical populations compared with patients without dissociative symptoms (Haaland & Landrø, 2009; Lyssenko et al., 2018; Webermann et al., 2016). Interestingly, a recently published prospective follow-up study (Shah et al., 2020) showed that a reduction of dissociative symptoms over time was associated with recovery in BPD, suggesting its potential role in the course of BPD.

Given the considerable influence of dissociation on treatment outcomes and the effectiveness of clinical interventions, assessing dissociative symptoms and developing specific interventions to address dissociative states is essential in order to improve care for patients who have experienced childhood maltreatment and who present with complex PTSD and/or BPD.

The mentalizing approach to trauma and dissociation

Theoretical background

Significant strides have recently been made towards adapting existing interventions for BPD to treat complex trauma, a necessary advancement considering the dearth of treatment guidelines for complex PTSD (Maercker et al., 2022). This section delves into recent developments in the mentalizing approach to psychopathology for trauma treatment, with a specific focus on dissociative phenomena. The discussed approach has been expressly developed for patients with histories of traumatic childhood attachment experiences, which can present as complex PTSD with or without BPD traits or diagnosis. While this paper delves into dissociative symptoms within CPTSD, it does not extend to more severe clinical presentations like DID. Detailed exploration of DID would demand a broader theoretical framework, though certain clinical phenomena in both CPTSD and DID share similarities.

Mentalizing, or reflective functioning, signifies the ability to interpret oneself and others in the context of mental states. Extensive evidence validates the deleterious effects of adverse and traumatic experiences on mentalizing capacities (Luyten et al., 2020). From a developmental perspective, childhood maltreatment is known to create the potential for attachment insecurity, which can profoundly compromise the development of mentalizing. The processes of attachment and mentalizing are intricately interconnected and mutually reliant throughout their developmental journey. The capacity to mentalize initially emerges within early attachment relationships, cultivated by caregivers who perceptively mirror the child's experiences, thus encouraging the development of a stable self-sense (crucial for self-organization) and affect regulation (Fonagy & Luyten, 2016; Fonagy et al., 2002).

Widespread neglect by caregivers can impair mentalizing by not adequately mirroring mental states, while abuse can cause repeated instances of highly distorted and/or intrusive mirroring. Under these conditions, insecure attachment patterns can form, manifesting as either avoidant (deactivated attachment needs) or anxious (hyperactivated attachment needs) tendencies in self and relational contexts (Allen, 2013a; Fonagy & Luyten, 2016). When a child is raised in a hostile environment by an abusive or neglectful caregiver, and without appropriate mirroring, an approach – avoidance conflict can surface early, with the simultaneous activation of attachment and threat systems, creating self and other confusion. These characteristics are typical of disorganized attachment patterns, commonly observed in individuals with BPD and complex PTSD (Luyten et al., 2020).

As a consequence, patients may exhibit a continuous hyperactivation or deactivation of their attachment system, contributing to their relational vulnerability, along with the internalization of various 'alien-self' experiences from abusive caregivers. This condition impedes the development of authentic self-experiences, typically facilitated through consistent and coherent mirroring by caregivers. The mind may become trapped in a pervasive state of avoidance of mental states over time, leading to diminished ability to mentalize self and others, fragmentation of identity, and lack of narrative coherence. Attempts to manage post-traumatic stress symptoms (including hyperarousal, avoidance, and re-experiencing) and the negative effects on self-organization (affect dysregulation, negative self-concept, relationship disturbances) may further limit the individual's internal world and lead to social withdrawal.

Traumatic experiences may also breed a deep sense of mistrust in others, including hypervigilance toward externally imparted knowledge, or epistemic mistrust, and shame. Both these factors contribute to increased isolation and mental closure to social learning throughout life (Luyten et al., 2020; Sharp et al., 2012). Epistemic mistrust hinders the ability to benefit from and integrate knowledge from social contexts, leading to prevalent epistemic hypervigilance, which perpetuates a mental 'freeze' state, hindering recovery from past traumas and isolating the individual from potential support and help available through relationships (Luyten et al., 2020; Sharp et al., 2012). Consequently, individuals exposed to extensive relational trauma may face heightened vulnerability in life's adversities and greater challenges in navigating relational complexities (Sharp et al., 2012).

Trauma, mentalizing and trauma reminders

Central to the mentalizing approach to trauma is the understanding that the trauma doesn't lie in the event itself, but in the associated experience wherein the individual feels isolated in insurmountable emotional pain (Allen, 2013a). Adverse experiences typically entail a failure in mentalizing. However, when a secure environment offers a safe space for reflection, the traumatic experience can be processed with another mind through marked mirroring, enabling the recontextualization of the experience (Luyten et al., 2020). Understanding the experience with the help of a validating and empathetic other aids in restoring agency and selfhood, as well as trust and a sense of belonging. This process also offers an opportunity to integrate and construct new knowledge about oneself, others, and the world.

The challenge with developmental trauma is the absence of a supportive other, combined with profound mistrust and shame, leaving the individual isolated and bearing the traumatic experiences in an unmentalized form. These can be recurrently triggered later in life by reminders of the original event. Without a reflective process following the event to integrate the experience into the individual's narrative and distinguish the past from the present, such reminders continue to elicit intense distress due to the emotional experience associated with the memory and its sense of immediacy, as if continually reliving the event. The mental experiences tied to the memory, triggered by reminders of the event, can become unbearable for the individual, leading to the need to avoid them through cognitive or emotional psychological processes, or even physical action.

Moreover, reminders of trauma may often initiate the emergence of prementalizing modes of self and other experiences. There are three forms of prementalizing modes in mentalization-based treatment: psychic equivalence (mental states are viewed as defining physical reality), pretend mode (captures a disconnect between mental states and the external reality, and importantly, without any undertones of intentionality), and teleological functioning (characterized by actions taking precedence over reflective thought) (Bateman & Fonagy, 2016). For instance, individuals with post-traumatic stress symptoms experience a high degree of psychic equivalence: thoughts of the traumatic event, or reminders of it, trigger mental states linked to the event that feel as real as if the event is happening again. In other words, these individuals feel as if they are reliving the event and are trapped in the past (Luyten et al., 2020). This phenomenon is exemplified in dissociative symptoms such as flashbacks of the traumatic event. A varying degree of disconnection between objective reality and subjective experience can occur, leading to disorientation and confusion. In these circumstances, patients may become ensnared in intense feelings of defeat and powerlessness, feeling as though there is no escape from their emotional pain and no hope of recovery.

The chronic condition of hypervigilance, a manifestation of hyperarousal, and the activation of the fight/flight system can also be seen through the lens of psychic equivalence. Patients endure a continuous sense of threat, both physically and mentally. A persistent, distorted perception of danger and lack of safety is maintained and experienced as if it were an actual reality.

Psychic equivalence can also surface in the form of maladaptive and ego-destructive feelings of shame, frequently elicited when an individual encounters trauma reminders or social situations viewed through the trauma lens as a repetition of past experiences. Alien-self experiences, defined as internalized derogatory attributions from past abusers (e.g., 'You are worthless', 'You deserve it'), or beliefs ascribed to the abusive figure (e.g., 'I must be awful for them to treat me this way'), become activated, leading to deep-seated feelings of shame, self-defectiveness, vulnerability, and helplessness. These feelings can provoke a sense of overwhelming humiliation and a need for social withdrawal. Moreover, this repetitive pattern can help sustain shame over time, leaving patients feeling ill-equipped to handle everyday adversities, as many situations can swiftly and unpredictably trigger this state (due to the lower activation threshold of the attachment system and simultaneous fight/flight response), resulting in overwhelm. Moreover, in the absence of a social buffer and with diminished mentalizing abilities, feelings of shame are experienced with even greater intensity. Consequently, hypervigilance toward potential threats to the self is sustained, and both physical and mental avoidance become pervasive survival mechanisms, as well as dissociation, ranging from emotional numbing to full-blown symptoms of depersonalization and derealization. Therefore, chronic and alienating shame can contribute to and perpetuate the tendency to dissociate due to its potent self-dissolving effect (Bateman et al., 2023; Luyten et al., 2020). The emotional threat prompted by alien-self experiences might result in a disconnection from one's internal emotions and a detachment from external surroundings. This disengagement can manifest in various degrees, from emotional numbing to more severe states of depersonalization and derealization. However, readers should remember that this description doesn't encapsulate the intricate nature of identity shifts inherent to DID.

Depersonalization and derealization, or emotional numbing, can also be triggered when arousal levels rise, as traumatic reminders can provoke intense physical responses or activate overwhelming mental states and emotional distress through the fight/flight response. The disconnection between external reality, bodily experience, and mental state can be viewed as an extreme form of 'pretend mode' that serves a protective function. The term 'pretend' does not imply intentionality, and can be understood in this case as a form of psychological escape from painful and intense mental states.

Escaping painful experiences and regaining a semblance of control can also be achieved through action in the teleological mode. As distressing mental states remain unmentalized, self-destructive behaviors are utilized for relief, sometimes as a result of alien-self experiences or in the context of traumatic events being reenacted in an attempt to change the outcome. However, in some situations, individuals might view self-harming actions as a necessary means to regain a sense of control and reconnect with their body. Indeed, dissociative symptoms can lead to extreme anxiety and feelings of losing control over bodily functions, thereby adding a layer of self-distrust. Patients can struggle to identify their triggers and, due to a lack of understanding of these experiences, may feel vulnerable, with no solution other than to act in order to regain control over their bodies.

These manifestations define the three prementalizing modes (psychic equivalence, pretend mode, and teleological functioning) that signal a breakdown in mentalizing and potentially a shift into dissociative states after exposure to trauma triggers. Thus, identifying these different modes, potential shifts into dissociative states, and their triggers is of paramount importance in Mentalization-Based Treatment for Trauma (MBT-TF).

The MBT approach to trauma and dissociation: treatment strategy and interventions

Treatment structure and setting

Trauma-focused mentalization-based treatment (MBT-TF) is a specialized, group-based intervention designed to treat trauma and dissociation in patients with a history of complex trauma. This research emphasizes PTSD treatment, especially targeting dissociative symptoms within the realm of complex trauma. While adaptations are underway to address DID more comprehensively, such discussions remain outside the scope of this paper. This approach can be used as a standalone treatment or in conjunction with other therapeutic interventions. MBT-TF is an adaptation of the standard mentalization-based treatment (MBT), specifically developed to address posttraumatic stress symptoms and to improve mentalizing in relation to traumatic events that the patient identifies as consistently distressing. The underlying hypothesis is that fostering a reflective process around these events may lead to generalized improvements in the patient's overall mentalizing capacity. MBT-TF may offer an additional framework for clinicians using MBT and therapists interested in the model to treat patients with complex trauma.

The treatment consists of a group intervention structured into three phases that reflect established practices in the field of trauma therapy (Herman, 1998): (i) stabilization and psychoeducation on trauma and mentalizing; (ii) processing traumatic memories; and (iii) mourning, acceptance of loss, and moving on. The program can be implemented over a period of 6 months as an adjunct to standard MBT, or over 9 to 12 months as a standalone intervention. It places particular emphasis on working through traumatic memories in the group sessions (Bateman et al., 2022, 2023).

In MBT-TF, similar to standard MBT, patients are encouraged to collaboratively work with the therapist to develop a formulation that assesses their mentalizing difficulties in four domains: (i) mentalizing of the traumatic event-(s), (ii) mental avoidance/isolation, (iii) vigilance, and (iv) mentalizing of the self and experienced shame. In addition, prototypical trauma memories are elicited, and the patient is asked to identify which aspects of these memories they feel comfortable discussing in the group setting. These specific aspects are then targeted in the group therapy sessions, supplemented by individual sessions as necessary. A particular emphasis is put on supporting the development of reflective function through each stage of the treatment, individually and in the group.

The initial phase of MBT-TF emphasizes psychoeducation, mental function stabilization, and risk management. This includes learning to manage dissociative symptoms and cultivating a safe mental space during times of high anxiety, building a therapeutic alliance, and agreeing on a therapeutic focus. The second phase prioritizes working with traumatic memories and facilitating mentalizing of these traumatic experiences. This helps in developing a more coherent self-narrative around these events and integrating them into the individual's life narrative. The final phase focuses on reflecting on the insights gained from the second phase, mourning and accepting loss, and looking towards the future, including life post-therapy, and moving forward.

In both group and individual sessions of trauma-focused mentalization-based treatment (MBT-TF), the aim is to foster epistemic trust by cultivating a shared group experience, progressively encouraging curiosity about self and others, and effectively addressing conflicts that arise within the group. The group component of this intervention is designed to counteract the sense of isolation that patients often experience due to feelings of shame and a state of hypervigilance.

The group setting provides a unique opportunity for patients to engage in new social interactions, which can be particularly beneficial for those grappling with the effects of complex trauma. Observing other group members who are dealing with similar challenges can make it easier for patients to open up about their own traumatic experiences. Furthermore, it allows them to gain a deeper understanding of how these traumatic events have affected them not only on a personal level, but also in their relationships with others. The group also offers a space where trauma symptoms may be reflected on with others that share comparable difficulties, allowing for direct exchanges of experiences between patients that may also be received with greater epistemic trust.

In essence, the group therapy component of MBT-TF helps create a safe space where individuals can share their experiences and learn from others in similar situations. This collaborative environment can help reduce feelings of isolation, validate individual experiences, and promote the development of new coping strategies and insights.

Specific focus on dissociation

Addressing dissociation is a crucial component of the MBT-TF process, and several strategies are put in place to facilitate this.

Identifying Dissociative Symptoms and Integrating Them into the Treatment Goals: During the initial stages of MBT-TF, a comprehensive assessment of the patient's symptoms, including any dissociative symptoms, is conducted. Recognizing the specific manifestations of dissociation in each patient's life allows for the tailoring of the treatment plan to the individual's needs. Once these symptoms are identified, they are integrated into the treatment goals. Additionally, psychoeducation is provided to help patients understand dissociation's function and manifestation, with the goal of increasing their ability to recognize and manage their symptoms.

Building Epistemic Trust: Developing trust between the therapist and the patient is fundamental to the success of the therapy. This trust enables the patient to believe in the relevance and helpfulness of the therapist's insights and suggestions, allowing them to be open to changing their thinking and behavior patterns. Epistemic trust can be cultivated through consistent, reliable, and empathetic interactions over time.

Embodied Mentalizing: As a part of MBT-TF, patients are encouraged to become more aware of their physical sensations and experiences, particularly those associated with dissociative states. This process of embodied mentalizing helps patients to understand how their bodily experiences relate to their emotions and thoughts, providing another layer of insight into their mental states.

Addressing Shame and Alien-Self Experiences: Feelings of shame and alien-self experiences, which involve feeling detached or estranged from oneself, are common among individuals who have experienced trauma. These feelings can be detrimental to mentalizing, leading to avoidance and withdrawal. In MBT-TF, therapists work with patients to explore these feelings, understand their origins, and develop strategies for managing them.

By systematically addressing these elements, MBT-TF supports patients in managing dissociation, improving their mentalizing capabilities, and ultimately enhancing their emotional and social well-being.

Identifying dissociative symptoms and integrating them into the treatment goals

The therapeutic journey in Trauma-focused Mentalization-based Treatment (MBT-TF) commences with a comprehensive evaluation undertaken by the individual therapist. This primary appraisal seeks to understand the impact of dissociative occurrences on the patient's psychosocial functioning and daily life, their presentation in various settings, and their manifestations within therapeutic encounters. The therapist may discern, in collaboration with the patient, potential deficits in the recognition of triggers and the transitions into dissociative episodes, thus establishing the need for guided facilitation to enhance the patient's comprehension and introspection into their unique experiential world.

In order to construct a more profound understanding within the patient of their own dissociative processes, an educational approach, psychoeducation, is employed from the treatment's inception. Psychoeducation serves as a critical tool to elucidate the functional aspects of dissociation and its manifold representations. The aim is to foster a heightened embodied awareness within the patients, augmenting their ability to perceive and attend to their own experiences. This knowledge facilitates the normalization of symptoms, offers explanations for their existence, and aids in shifting the focus from potential shame associated with such symptoms towards empowerment through enhanced understanding.

The psychoeducational component may particularly benefit from articulating the detrimental effects of trauma on the capacity for mentalization and attachment, along with the impact on self-regulatory mechanisms. It can be valuable to convey to patients the restricted emotional responses resulting from trauma, often limited to states of anxiety, rage, fear, or numbness, coupled with a decreased threshold for activation of the fight/flight response and the onset of dissociation. An essential aspect of the process then becomes the identification of personal triggers and early indicators (prodromal symptoms) of dissociative episodes, both mental and bodily, as well as the cultivation of skills to discern the patient's arousal level to prevent full-blown dissociative states.

Additionally, it is vital for the patient to consent to jointly tackle dissociative symptoms within the context of individual and group sessions, acknowledging the necessity of mitigating these symptoms. This collaborative process necessitates the patient's receptivity to feedback from clinicians and group members when dissociative states appear imminent during therapy sessions, and the effort to anchor themselves and reengage with their bodily sensations. Such demands may provoke ambivalence in the patient for various reasons, including the patient's entrenched patterns of mental state avoidance, fear of relinquishing the perceived protective function of this avoidance against distressing experiences, and heightened exposure to discomfiting emotions. These conditions may be perceived as threatening, potentially inducing feelings of vulnerability. Furthermore, the patient may struggle with the perception of a lack of control over these symptoms, doubting their ability to address them effectively, leading to heightened anxiety about experiencing these symptoms in a social setting.

Acknowledging these difficulties is crucial while also taking into consideration the limitations imposed by the patient's current functional state, and juxtaposing these with their aspirations and desire for future change. The discomfort encountered while traversing novel experiences can be validated, while concurrently contemplating the critical importance of acquiring the skill to manage dissociative states for the overall treatment process, as these states may hinder effective mentalization and obstruct the integration of new social learning. This process might offer an opportunity for the patient to reclaim a sense of agency and work toward desired future changes.

Building epistemic trust

Another A crucial phase of the therapeutic process is the gradual cultivation of a sense of security within the therapeutic framework, as well as towards the therapists and group members. To facilitate this, it is important for the therapists (group facilitators and individual therapist) to adopt a stance of mentalization, working in collaboration with the patient from a humble, not-knowing position that focuses on exploring mental states and working explicitly through situations that foster the development of epistemic trust (Bateman & Fonagy, 2013). This approach involves transparency, clarification of misunderstandings and intentions, admission of errors, and a readiness to mend the therapeutic relationship following any ruptures. It is crucial to maintain a process of reflection on what transpires during the sessions, and to draw connections to relational challenges arising from the patient's traumatic past.

In addition, the therapist supports the patient's sense of agency and control, a vital recovery step following traumatic events that may have left the patient feeling helpless and powerless. The therapist aids the patient in gradually constructing a shared understanding of their difficulties while modeling curiosity about the patient's experiences. The patient's expertise about their own experiences is recognized, and the therapist shows a thoughtful and genuine interest in understanding the patient's functioning and challenges. The therapy also involves helping the patient express boundaries regarding what they can manage and tolerate during sessions, which aids in preventing feelings of being overwhelmed and supports the development of agency. The clinical challenge lies in balancing the treatment focus and working through the patient's avoidance tactics.

Patients may at times display explicit (e.g., refusing to explore further or answer questions) or implicit (e.g., avoiding specific questions, changing the subject) resistance to sharing their experiences with the therapist and group members. Acknowledging and working through the discomfort and hypervigilance that may arise from exploring mental states in self and others is critical. Building epistemic trust is a gradual process; learning to accept and trust information from therapists or other group members can be challenging for patients who have previously experienced harm from others. This, therefore, may become an important treatment goal. Learning to navigate relationships in new ways to benefit from them and reduce isolation can be identified as a crucial recovery step, as well as engaging in a process of reflection on the balance between adaptive trust and mistrust.

In cases where traumatic experiences are reactivated, leading to a strong psychic equivalence mode in the patient, it's crucial to aid the patient in engaging in reflective processes to begin differentiating past traumatic experiences from the present, thereby reducing confusion and emotional arousal. For instance, the patient might perceive receiving attention as particularly painful or even threatening, indicative of an approach-avoidance conflict resulting from the simultaneous activation of attachment and the fight/flight response. This can be particularly pronounced in patients who have suffered emotional manipulation and abuse. A titrated approach can be beneficial, focusing on slowing down, sharing different perspectives, and reflecting on the patient's activations, conflicting affects, and associated discomfort and confusion. A connection can gradually be made between the impact of past events and the patient's current coping mechanisms for distress and relational difficulties, which may often involve an immediate attempt to manage problems independently. The discomfort associated with negotiating new experiences and the accompanying uncertainty may need acknowledgment.

Embodied mentalizing

Integrating bodily experiences is a fundamental aspect of trauma work, as described in this field (Cloitre et al., 2011; van der Kolk, 2006). Frequently, trauma victims start viewing their bodies as dangerous territories due to their symptoms and a perceived lack of control (Herman, 1998). Hence, fostering embodied mentalizing, which is the ability to introspectively consider one's bodily experiences and sensations and their connection to intentional mental states in oneself and others (Luyten et al., 2012), is a pivotal aspect of trauma recovery and managing dissociative symptoms.

Identifying dissociation necessitates heightened self-awareness and attention to both mental and physical states, which the patient may have consistently avoided due to their threatening nature. The clinician will need to collaboratively monitor the patient's response to increased attention to their mental and physical states, noting changes in arousal and the activation of protective mechanisms designed to avoid distress or maintain relational or emotional distance. These challenges can be progressively worked through with the patient to build a shared understanding of the ongoing experiences. The therapist, in turn, mirrors back to the patient their understanding of the patient's experiences and explores potential methods to manage the distress and possible dissociative symptoms. A personalized toolkit and approach may be necessary for each patient due to the diversity of clinical presentations.

Special attention is given to learning how to identify and trust interoceptive and proprioceptive signals, which might signify changes in arousal and mental states. The goal is to aid the patient in initiating a reflective process and forge connections between their bodily and mental states to foster an understanding of their subjective experience. Sensorimotor processes can also be employed for this purpose (Ogden & Fisher, 2015; Ogden & Minton, 2000). Patients are progressively guided towards finding a balance between top-down (using the mind to recognize and soothe the body) and bottom-up (using the body to identify and soothe the mind) processes to regulate their arousal level. Excessive top-down regulation can lead to over-management and disconnection into a pretend mode, while too much bottom-up processing can cause bodily experiences to become reality without reflective processing, leading to psychic equivalence (Bateman & Fonagy, 2021).

In individual sessions, the therapist is urged to periodically check in with the patient, guided by the patient's external bodily cues, and to take a moment to assist the patient in recognizing their internal experiences. The therapist may share their observations with the patient, noting nonverbal physical signs such as agitation, avoidance of eye contact, fixed gaze, change of tone, silence, or signs of withdrawal and disengagement from the external environment. All these may be indicative of a pretend mode and potential disconnection from the body and emotional experience, thereby averting further disconnection.

This method enables both the patient and therapist to closely track and observe changes in internal states and the emergence or presence of dissociation, which may disrupt mentalizing. Subsequently, the patient is guided to evaluate their level of arousal and engage with their body to calm or ground themselves. Maintaining an external focus on this soothing activity can help lower arousal by redirecting attention from the internal state to a joint distraction effort. The therapist can join the activity with the patient (e.g., using a stress ball, grounding and breathing exercises), mirroring the patient's experiences. The therapist and patient monitor the effect of this intervention, and the patient is encouraged to observe any impact it has on their internal state or any other mental states brought about by the process. Once arousal has decreased to a level where some reflective functioning is restored, the clinician and patient can jointly explore triggers, reflect on the function of the body, and share the experience of working through this together. This helps to build a shared understanding and mentalize the experience. Repetition of this exercise over time can bolster the patient's self-confidence and their ability to manage these symptoms, both independently and with the help of others.

In group therapy, activities might include group-wide breathing or grounding exercises. Check-ins could incorporate an embodied mentalizing approach that encourages patients to identify bodily sensations and make connections to their current mental states. Individual interventions may be necessary during group sessions if a patient dissociates. These interventions would begin by clearly identifying the dissociative state, then assessing the patient's individual needs to soothe or ground them, clarifying what the group can contribute, allowing the patient to self-regulate, and agreeing to check back with them later. The group can support this process, offering a space to reflect on the dissociative experience and mentalize it later. In both group and individual sessions, attention is given to the body, recognizing it as a resource to aid the mentalizing process.

Addressing shame and alien-self experiences

In treatment, significant focus is directed towards feelings of shame and the emergence of alien-self experiences. Developmental trauma often impacts patients, leaving them with a deep-rooted mistrust of their own experiences in relation to past events. This bolsters their belief that they are incapable of making decisions to ensure their own safety and that they are inherently flawed as individuals. Moreover, their chronic disconnection from and avoidance of mental states and bodily sensations can lead them to be perplexed about their own experiences and lack self-knowledge. Revealing these difficulties has the potential to intensify feelings of shame and trigger alien-self experiences.

The aim during MBT-TF (Mentalization-Based Treatment for Trauma) is to provide a space that is attuned to allow and support the development of curiosity and the generation of compassion towards oneself and others. Sessions strive to cultivate new authentic self-experiences, which are highlighted and reflected back by the therapist and the rest of the group members. This process involves providing empathetic validation in response to the intense psychic equivalence of the patient's alien-self experiences, while also demonstrating curiosity and maintaining differences between minds. The goal is to integrate new perceptions. This process may provide patients with opportunities to gain new insights that challenge their internalized beliefs about themselves and help distinguish past internalized beliefs from their current self-experience.

Case illustration

Case history: Rose

This case illustration amalgamates the experiences of several patients with dissociative symptoms who received Mentalization-Based Treatment with a trauma focus. We'll call the composite patient Rose. In her thirties, Rose lived alone and had minimal contact with her two younger siblings since leaving home at 18. Rose's avoidance of her family was later linked to her effort to avoid reminders of her past. She completed school but dropped out of university due to struggles with her studies and mental health. Rose had been working in retail sales for several years. She was referred for treatment by her general practitioner due to persistent symptoms connected to her traumatic childhood.

Throughout her assessment and treatment sessions, Rose described a history of childhood trauma that included physical abuse and witnessing domestic violence. Rose's father had left the family before her birth, and her mother and stepfather were unpredictable. Rose felt continuously on edge, never knowing whether her actions might incite hostility or anger. This state of hypervigilance persisted into adulthood, causing difficulties with sleep as she felt perpetually unsafe. Rose also endured emotional abuse and neglect. Her parents showed little interest in her emotional well-being and were intrusive and controlling. Growing up, Rose lacked supportive adult figures and was constantly trying to manage her issues alone. This reinforced her belief that no one could be trusted.

School was also challenging for Rose. She was often bullied by her peers and felt different, noticing that her clothes were unkempt compared to her classmates. Witnessing the family lives of her peers only amplified her feelings of shame about her own circumstances. This early shame influenced Rose to shy away from forming close relationships, fearing further rejection. Rose carried the belief that if others knew about her past, they would reject her, confirming the feelings of unworthiness and 'badness' she held about herself. To escape her life and distress, Rose often disconnected from both the outside world and her internal experiences.

Identifying dissociative symptoms and integrating them in the treatment

During the assessment phase, Rose expressed feeling isolated despite having friends and colleagues. She struggled to understand her own emotions, which were either extremely intense without clear triggers, or completely absent, causing her to feel detached. Others would often notice when she seemed off or distant, making her self-conscious. Because of previous emotional outburst in the past, she learned to avoid her internal experience, as it felt easier to avoid her feelings and too dangerous to experience and share them. Rose spoke of the effort she put into appearing tough and self-reliant, and how important it was for her to hide any vulnerability from others. She easily dissociated in work situations or during conflicts, as she would later describe, going numb, feeling as if she was not really there and experiencing loss of time. Rose's protective disconnection from her feelings and maintenance of appearances, along with her depersonalization symptoms, all suggested multiple levels of pretend mode.

Rose also shared that she often felt hypervigilant at home, regularly checking her apartment for security purposes if she heard any suspicious noises. She constantly felt in danger, leading to sleep difficulties. These states of hyperarousal can be viewed as psychic equivalence (a feeling of danger interpreted as actual danger) and teleological mode (only physical actions like checking locks could provide a sense of safety). She cycled between states of hyperarousal, intense anxiety, anger, or helplessness, and states of numbness, with little room for more nuanced or positive emotions. When distressed, Rose reported excessive drinking and use of sleep medication to numb herself – another example of teleological mode. She described intense feelings of self-hatred, which she was certain were shared by others. This belief reinforced her social withdrawal and avoidance of intimate relationships, and could be triggered by situations where she felt out of place or self-conscious. These states represented alien-self experiences, often linked to shame experienced in psychic equivalence.

In her individual treatment sessions, Rose initially came and presented well and very articulate in the description of her difficulties, with some disconnection from her emotional experiences. In her narratives, there was little regard of her internal experience and how these affected her. Her therapist noticed signs of hyperarousal, as Rose tended to look repeatedly at the time, talked fast and seemed physically agitated, shaking her legs, looking around the room, with crossed arms. After a few sessions, she appeared at times more silent and withdrawn. Her therapist explored these moments asking Rose what she noticed was going on on the inside, while explaining what she was seeing from the outside. She marked her curiosity towards Rose's experience and stated her uncertainty of what was taking place for her. Rose often answered that she did not know, that she felt numb. As they slowly began to focus on her feelings of numbness over several sessions, more information came out on its frequency and how it led Rose to feel lost and uncertain of what was going on for her. Her therapist gave her information about dissociation and its functions, which helped Rose build an initial understanding of her reactions when she seemed to close down. This opened up more conversations on the topic. Later in treatment, it was also possible to link how she feared coming to the therapy and her high levels of arousal during the sessions. She talked about how anxiety provoking it was to talk to someone, especially to have to think about her feelings and then to 'go numb'. She experienced a sense of threat and would feel angry after the sessions, feeling as if she lost control, would be judged for not knowing and for her silences. This would lead her to regret her efforts she put into trying to trust and a feeling of helplessness would then ensue, as she felt stuck in her current situation and acknowledged that she needed support. Rose talked about her fear of coming in with these mixed feelings and at risk if she were to express her anger towards her therapist. Through the exploration of these hyperarousal, angry and dissociative states, Rose was able to talk about her difficulties to slow down and bring awareness to her bodily sensations that were indicating that her anxiety was rising, leaving her struggling with what she was feeling and then going numb during the session. Collaboratively they aimed to work on increasing her awareness of these symptoms, noticing the rise in her heartbeat, her breathing and the pace of her speech. They focused on attending to her bodily sensations, identifying her anxiety level, linking it to a sense of threat and to her emerging understanding of the ambivalence she felt of opening up on her feelings and connecting to her inner experiences. This process took repetitions of loops of explicit observation, rewinding to the events before she would go numb during the sessions, and reflecting to build an understanding of them when she felt grounded again. This could take whole sessions, at times she would leave with some level of persisting dissociation symptoms, that she felt was manageable for her. This supported Roses' capacity to trust her ability to manage through her emotional experience and come back from the numbing. As this process was worked through during the session, trauma triggers outside of the sessions became apparent as well. Rose worked on noticing when she felt disconnected or numb, and recognizing triggers for these states. She noticed that reading news about childhood abuse or experiencing anger – such as aggressive tones – could trigger a fight/flight state (her body going tense, her heart rate increasing and feeling in danger, wanting to escape), depersonalization (feeling as if she was unreal), and derealization (others becoming increasingly distant and as if they were actors). Before these episodes, she experienced symptoms like feeling light-headed, tingling, a racing heart, faster breathing, and an increasing urge to escape, all coupled with a rising sense of danger. These symptoms could present with different durations and intensity, depending on the trigger she encountered and her state of being.

Rose and her therapist noted that her difficulty identifying her feelings and connecting them with her bodily sensations led to confusion about her needs and a fragmented self-experience. The vulnerability she felt in relation to these states resulted in her preferring to keep up her mask, appearing pleasant to others as a means of maintaining a semblance of safety and distancing herself from intense emotions related to past memories. This strategy felt safer but isolated her in the pain she felt and maintained her perpetual feelings of difference and displacement.

Formulating a shared understanding of Rose's experiences in relation to her past was crucial for Rose and her therapist to make sense of her struggles and consider treatment options. This also initiated Rose's reflection on her relational patterns and their impact on her present interactions with others and herself. Among her treatment goals, Rose hoped to develop compassion for herself, establish connections in the group, be more open about her feelings, and gain more control over her dissociative symptoms.

Building epistemic trust

Throughout the course of her treatment, Rose gradually began to experience a newfound sense of safety with her therapist and fellow group members. This progress unfolded gradually over the first 4 months (phase 1 of treatment) and further deepened during phase 2. A full year of individual therapy before the group sessions began also significantly facilitated this process. A crucial initial step was recognizing and articulating the feelings of unsafety she sometimes experienced during therapy sessions, as mentioned above. Being given the opportunity to express her feelings with her therapist, associated with a sense of safety and not resulting in catastrophic consequences opened up new perspectives for Rose. Experiencing closeness and more transparency concerning what she was feeling supported the emergence of a sense of agency in relation to herself and to others. She was learning to trust her emotional experience and the process of sharing it, in that it brought conversations that increased her awareness of herself and allowed her to connect with others. This changed from her belief that others mainly judged or misunderstood her. This acknowledgement allowed her to begin challenging her presumptions about what others might be thinking or intending towards her.

This development was further supported and generalized to the group experience. When misunderstandings in the group sparked anger in Rose, these instances provided opportunities for her to move beyond the façade she preferred to maintain and expose her genuine inner emotions, despite her fear. This step brought with it the new realization that expressing her true feelings did not inevitably lead to immediate danger or negative repercussions.

This therapeutic journey was supported by a consistent curiosity about Rose's mental states and a quest to understand the situations that triggered her hypervigilance and anger. As these differences were explored and clarified, Rose often experienced feelings of guilt and shame, which sometimes led to avoidance of therapy sessions. However, the therapists (including co-facilitators and individual therapist) remained present, demonstrating humility, genuine interest, and respect for her agency. They also frequently reassured her that she was kept in their minds, which encouraged her to return to therapy.

Being explicit about relational difficulties and expressing willingness to work through them was crucial. Reminding patients of the possible coexistence of contradictory emotional states and offering a safe space to navigate through them allowed a process of building trust in themselves and with others. Concurrently, reminding all group members of their belonging within the group seemed to foster trust and provide opportunities for repairing and transforming their various relationships. These collective efforts helped Rose confront her past traumas and foster healthier relationships with herself and others.

Working with the body

Fostering a stronger trust in Rose's own self-experience was greatly assisted by the process of embodied mentalizing, which encouraged her to attune to her physical sensations with curiosity and kindness. Some bottom-up processes were used when her anxiety rose. When during a conversation she would go silent, appeared to shut down and presented a fixed gaze, her therapist would take out a small stress ball. They had agreed together that her therapist could offer her a distraction from the discussion, as she would focus on throwing the ball gently back and forth. This strategy helped stop her arousal level from increasing. Thus, silences often prompted the question whether to take out the ball, which would then go back and forth between Rose and her therapist. As she became more active and was able to speak again, after having a few informal exchanges at times out of topic, the therapist would gently assess with her current state of arousal. After confirmation she was ready to explore further, they would go back and try to think about what had happened earlier and reflect together and build a shared understanding on what had taken place. Another strategy was to use putties and she would concentrate on giving them different shapes. Other techniques included breathing exercises, inhaling the scent of perfume on her scarf, or grounding herself by pushing her feet firmly into the ground. Progressively, Rose found ways to use her body to help manage her level of arousal. She would work towards identifying when her arousal went up (heart rate, breathing rate, muscular tension) or decreased (going numb, feeling zoned out) and mobilize her resources. These grounding strategies helped her build confidence in her abilities to manage her body as her understanding of herself grew and navigate through her internal experiences with or without external support.

As she allowed herself to engage more deeply with her feelings, this at times triggered episodes of dissociation, as her arousal heightened and anxiety surged. However, with time, Rose became increasingly adept at identifying the onset of dissociation, which allowed her to use strategies to manage the symptom and bring herself back. Rose explicitly talked about the loop becoming less time-consuming and feeling less anxiety.

Rose also learned to inform her therapist and the group when a dissociative episode was occurring during a session. The other group members supported her by helping her notice and engage with what they observed in her and by sharing their own experiences and methods for managing dissociation. Adapted short mindfulness exercises prompting patients to notice signals from their bodies further supported her capacity to notice her bodily sensations and monitor her level of arousal in a top-down process. This complemented the individual and group work focusing on helping patients to check within themselves and try to make links between their bodies signals and their mental states, and reflect on how this informed them and helped them build an understanding of themselves in relation to their environment and current experience.

As time passed, Rose began to express feeling less vulnerable as she achieved improved awareness and control over her internal experiences. This growth facilitated her ability to identify her bodily sensations and correlate them with her emotional states. The group and individual therapy sessions assisted Rose in reflecting on herself, thinking about and making sense of her bodily experiences, and understanding her mental states in relation to specific events and relational contexts. This process led to a deeper comprehension of her own identity and emotions, and better equipped her to navigate her interpersonal relationships and manage her symptoms of dissociation.

Addressing shame

Finally, the group setting provided valuable opportunities for Rose to cultivate new relational experiences that helped alleviate her chronic feelings of shame.

The shame fluctuated through the psychoeducation phase. As acquiring knowledge seemed to helped her build more understanding about her difficulties, the acknowledgement of the impact the traumatic experiences brought up painful realizations of her current functioning. Part of the shame reduced over time as she learned to gain more agency in relation to the management of her dissociative symptoms. Navigating through those dissociative states in a safe environment supported her in gaining more control and confidence that she could regain control over herself on her own or with the support of others when needed.

Sharing a traumatic memory within the group allowed her to receive feedback from others and learn about their own experiences. Both individual and group sessions provided a safe space for these explorations, and the feedback she received from others gave her insight into how she was perceived and the impact she had on those around her.

This interactive process enabled Rose to challenge some of the long-held beliefs and assumptions she had about herself and others – beliefs and assumptions that had been impeding the formation of meaningful relationships. This process appeared to offer some valuable insight, as Rose reported an increase in her understanding of how her past experiences had affected her, and how they were impacting her present relationships. Importantly, she noticed that as she developed empathy towards others in the group, it facilitated the cultivation of self-compassion – a critical component in her healing process and ongoing recovery.

Discussion and conclusions

This paper provided an overview of the latest developments in Mentalization-Based Therapy (MBT) and introduced MBT with a trauma focus (MBT-TF), an innovative mentalizing approach to addressing trauma and dissociation in patients with a history of complex trauma. This treatment was implemented for the first time as an independent group intervention for less than a year within a clinical service providing specialized psychotherapeutic treatments for adults who have experienced trauma. Patients underwent individual psychotherapy before joining the group, following either a trauma-adapted psychodynamic model or a trauma-adapted MBT approach. Individual sessions continued alongside group sessions to reinforce the therapeutic work carried out in groups. Notably, the program had no dropouts.

Patient feedback indicated that although the group experience was challenging, it was generally deemed acceptable and useful in facilitating a meaningful understanding of trauma symptoms and offering an experience of relationship building with others. Additionally, patients reported some reduction in feelings of shame and isolation, as well as an increased ability to connect with feelings and emotions, accept changes, and reduce experiences of numbness.

MBT has already proven its efficacy as a treatment for patients with severe Borderline Personality Disorder (BPD), and its adaptation to an expanding range of disorders suggests its potential as a promising new approach for patients suffering from posttraumatic stress symptoms, including dissociative symptoms. A particular emphasis on dissociation and embodied mentalizing seems necessary to manage the clinical complexities that arise from traumatic experiences. Nonetheless, more research is required concerning the treatment process and outcomes.

Disclosure statement

No potential conflict of interest was reported by the author(s).

Funding

Eva Rüfenacht was supported by an Early Postdoc Mobility Grant [P2GEP3_195239] from the Swiss National Science Foundation.

ORCID

P. Luyten http://orcid.org/0000-0002-1161-2817

References

Allen, J. G. (2013a). *Mentalizing in the development and treatment of attachment trauma.* Karnac Books.

Allen, J. G. (2013b). *Restoring mentalizing in attachment relationships: Treating trauma with plain old therapy.* American Psychiatric Publishing, Inc.

American Psychiatric Association. (2013). *Diagnostic and statistical manual of mental disorders* (5th ed.). https://doi.org/10.1176/appi.books.9780890425596

Barnicot, K., & Crawford, M. (2018). Posttraumatic stress disorder in patients with borderline personality disorder: Treatment outcomes and mediators. *Journal of Traumatic Stress*, *31*(6), 899–908. https://doi.org/10.1002/jts.22340

Bateman, A., & Fonagy, P. (2013). Mentalization-based treatment. *Psychoanalytic Inquiry*, *33*(6), 595–613. https://doi.org/10.1080/07351690.2013.835170

Bateman, A., & Fonagy, P. (2016). *Mentalization based treatment for personality disorders: A practical guide.* Oxford University Press. https://books.google.ch/books?id=WeJOCwAAQBAJ

Bateman, A., & Fonagy, P. (2021). *Trauma-focused mentalization-based treatment (MBT-TF) Core Manual In.*

Bateman, A., Fonagy, P., Campbell, C., Luyten, P., & Debbané, M. (2023). A history of mentalizing and mentalization-based treatment. In *Cambridge guide to mentalization-based treatment (MBT)* (Cambridge Guides to the Psychological Therapies, pp. 1–3). Cambridge: Cambridge University Press. https://doi.org/10.1017/9781108896054.002

Bateman, A., Rüfenacht, E., Perroud, N., Debbané, M., Nolte, T., Stubley, J., Shaverin, L., & Fonagy, P. (2022). Childhood maltreatment, dissociation, and borderline personality disorder: The role of mentalizing in the development of complex post-traumatic stress disorder. *Psychology and Psychotherapy: Theory, Research and Practice (PAPTRAP)*. (manuscript submitted 2022–2023).

Carlson, E. A. (1998). A prospective longitudinal study of attachment disorganization/disorientation. *Child Development*, *69*(4), 1107–1128. https://doi.org/10.1111/j.1467-8624.1998.tb06163.x

Classen, C., Koopman, C., & Spiegel, D. (1993). Trauma and dissociation. *Bulletin of the Menninger Clinic*, *57*(2), 178–194.

Cloitre, M. (2020). ICD-11 complex post-traumatic stress disorder: Simplifying diagnosis in trauma populations. *British Journal of Psychiatry*, *216*(3), 129–131. https://doi.org/10.1192/bjp.2020.43

Cloitre, M., Courtois, C. A., Charuvastra, A., Carapezza, R., Stolbach, B. C., & Green, B. L. (2011). Treatment of complex PTSD: Results of the ISTSS expert clinician survey on best practices. *Journal of Traumatic Stress*, *24*(6), 615–627. https://doi.org/10.1002/jts.20697

Dalenberg, C. J., Brand, B. L., Gleaves, D. H., Dorahy, M. J., Loewenstein, R. J., Cardeña, E., Frewen, P. A., Carlson, E. B., & Spiegel, D. (2012). Evaluation of the evidence for the trauma and fantasy models of dissociation. *Psychological Bulletin*, *138*(3), 550–588. https://doi.org/10.1037/a0027447

Dalenberg, C. J., & Paulson, K. (2009). The case for the study of "normal" dissociation processes. In P. F. Dell & J. A. O'Neil (Eds.), *Dissociation and the dissociative disorders: DSM-V and beyond* (pp. 145–154). Routledge/Taylor & Francis Group.

Fanselow, M. S., & Lester, L. S. (1988). A functional behavioristic approach to aversively motivated behavior: Predatory imminence as adeterminant of the topography of defensive behavior. In *Evolution and learning* (pp. 185–212). Lawrence Erlbaum Associates, Inc.

Felitti, V. J., Anda, R. F., Nordenberg, D., Williamson, D. F., Spitz, A. M., Edwards, V., Koss, M. P., & Marks, J. S. (1998). Relationship of childhood abuse and household dysfunction to many of the leading causes of death in adults. The adverse childhood experiences (ACE) study. *American Journal of Preventive Medicine*, *14*(4), 245–258. https://doi.org/10.1016/s0749-3797(98)00017-8

Fonagy, P., Gergely, G., Target, M., & Jurist, E. L. (2002). *Affect regulation, mentalization, and the development of the self.* Other Press. https://books.google.ch/books?id=EDHi3N-ebykC

Fonagy, P., & Luyten, P. (2016). A multilevel perspective on the development of borderline personality disorder. In D. Cicchetti (Ed.). *Developmental psychopathology* (pp. 1–67). https://doi.org/10.1002/9781119125556.devpsy317

Fonagy, P., & Target, M. (1997). Attachment and reflective function: Their role in self-organization. *Development and Psychopathology*, *9*(4), 679–700. https://doi.org/10.1017/S0954579497001399

Ford, J. D., & Courtois, C. A. (2021). Complex PTSD and borderline personality disorder. *Borderline Personality Disorder and Emotion Dysregulation*, *8*(1), 16. https://doi.org/10.1186/s40479-021-00155-9

Haaland, V., & Landrø, N. I. (2009). Pathological dissociation and neuropsychological functioning in borderline personality disorder. *Acta Psychiatrica Scandinavica*, *119* (5), 383–392. https://doi.org/10.1111/j.1600-0447.2008.01323.x

Herman, J. L. (1998). Recovery from psychological trauma. *Psychiatry and Clinical Neurosciences*, *52*(S1), S98–S103. https://doi.org/10.1046/j.1440-1819.1998.0520s5S145.x

Hyland, P., Shevlin, M., Fyvie, C., Cloitre, M., & Karatzias, T. (2020). The relationship between ICD-11 PTSD, complex PTSD and dissociative experiences. *Journal of Trauma & Dissociation*, *21*(1), 62–72. https://doi.org/10.1080/15299732.2019.1675113

Krause-Utz, A., Frost, R., Chatzaki, E., Winter, D., Schmahl, C., & Elzinga, B. M. (2021). Dissociation in borderline personality disorder: Recent experimental, neurobiological studies, and implications for future research and treatment. *Current Psychiatry Reports*, *23*(6), 37. https://doi.org/10.1007/s11920-021-01246-8

Loewenstein, R. J. (2018). Dissociation debates: Everything you know is wrong. *Dialogues in Clinical Neuroscience*, *20*(3), 229–242. https://doi.org/10.31887/DCNS.2018.20.3/rloewenstein

Longo, L., Cecora, V., Rossi, R., Niolu, C., Siracusano, A., & DiLorenzo, G. (2019). Dissociative symptoms in complex post-traumatic stress disorder and in post-traumatic stress disorder. *Journal of Psychopathology*, *25*, 212–219.

Luyten, P., Campbell, C., & Fonagy, P. (2020). Borderline personality disorder, complex trauma, and problems with self and identity: A social-communicative approach. *Journal of Personality*, *88*(1), 88–105. https://doi.org/10.1111/jopy.12483

Luyten, P., van Houdenhove, B., Lemma, A., Target, M., & Fonagy, P. (2012). A mentalization-based approach to the understanding and treatment of functional somatic disorders. *Psychoanalytic Psychotherapy*, *26*(2), 121–140. https://doi.org/10.1080/02668734.2012.678061

Lyssenko, L., Schmahl, C., Bockhacker, L., Vonderlin, R., Bohus, M., & Kleindienst, M. (2018). Dissociation in Psychiatric disorders: A meta-analysis of studies using the dissociative experiences scale. *The American Journal of Psychiatry*, *175*(1), 37–46. https://doi.org/10.1176/appi.ajp.2017.17010025

Maercker, A., Cloitre, M., Bachem, R., Schlumpf, Y. R., Khoury, B., Hitchcock, C., & Bohus, M. (2022). Complex post-traumatic stress disorder. *The Lancet*, *400*(10345), 60–72. https://doi.org/10.1016/s0140-6736(22)00821-2

Møller, L., Bach, B., Augsburger, M., Elklit, A., Søgaard, U., & Simonsen, E. (2021). Structure of ICD-11 complex PTSD and relationship with psychoform and somatoform dissociation. *European Journal of Trauma & Dissociation*, *5*(3), 100233. https://doi.org/10.1016/j.ejtd.2021.100233

Ogden, P., & Fisher, J. (2015). *Sensorimotor Psychotherapy: Interventions for trauma and attachment (Norton series on interpersonal neurobiology)*. W. W. Norton. https://books.google.ch/books?id=8hN0AwAAQBAJ

Ogden, P., & Minton, K. (2000). Sensorimotor Psychotherapy: One method for processing traumatic memory. *Traumatology*, *6*(3), 149–173. https://doi.org/10.1177/153476560000600302

Pagura, J., Stein, M. B., Bolton, J. M., Cox, B. J., Grant, B., & Sareen, J. (2010). Comorbidity of borderline personality disorder and posttraumatic stress disorder in the U.S. population. *Journal of Psychiatric Research*, *44*(16), 1190–1198. https://doi.org/10.1016/j.jpsychires.2010.04.016

Schauer, M., & Elbert, T. (2010). Dissociation following traumatic stress etiology and treatment. *Zeitschrift für Psychologie / Journal of Psychology*, *218*(2), 109–127. https://doi.org/10.1027/0044-3409/a000018

Scheiderer, E. M., Wood, P. K., & Trull, T. J. (2015). The comorbidity of borderline personality disorder and posttraumatic stress disorder: Revisiting the prevalence and associations in a general population sample. *Borderline Personal Disord Emot Dysregul*, *2*(1), 11. https://doi.org/10.1186/s40479-015-0032-y

Shah, R., Temes, C. M., Frankenburg, F. R., Fitzmaurice, G. M., & Zanarini, M. C. (2020). Levels of depersonalization and derealization reported by recovered and non-recovered borderline patients over 20 years of prospective follow-up. *Journal of Trauma & Dissociation*, *21*(3), 337–348. https://doi.org/10.1080/15299732.2020.1719259

Sharp, C., Fonagy, P., & Allen, J. G. (2012). Posttraumatic stress disorder: A social-cognitive perspective. *Clinical Psychology: Science & Practice*, *19*(3), 229–240. https://doi.org/10.1111/cpsp.12002

Spiegel, D., Loewenstein, R. J., Lewis-Fernández, R., Sar, V., Simeon, D., Vermetten, E., Cardeña, E., & Dell, P. F. (2011). Dissociative disorders in DSM-5. *Depression and Anxiety, 28*(12), E17–E45. https://doi.org/10.1002/da.20923

Struck, N., Krug, A., Yuksel, D., Stein, F., Schmitt, S., Meller, T., Brosch, K., Dannlowski, U., Nenadić, I., Kircher, T., & Brakemeier, E. L. (2020). Childhood maltreatment and adult mental disorders – The prevalence of different types of maltreatment and associations with age of onset and severity of symptoms. *Psychiatry Research, 293*, 113398. https://doi.org/10.1016/j.psychres.2020.113398

van der Kolk, B. A. (2006). Clinical implications of neuroscience research in PTSD. *Annals of the New York Academy of Sciences, 1071*(1), 277–293. https://doi.org/10.1196/annals.1364.022

Vonderlin, R., Kleindienst, N., Alpers, G. W., Bohus, M., Lyssenko, L., & Schmahl, C. (2018). Dissociation in victims of childhood abuse or neglect: A meta-analytic review. *Psychological Medicine, 48*(15), 2467–2476. https://doi.org/10.1017/s0033291718000740

Webermann, A. R., Myrick, A. C., Taylor, C. L., Chasson, G. S., & Brand, B. L. (2016). Dissociative, depressive, and PTSD symptom severity as correlates of nonsuicidal self-injury and suicidality in dissociative disorder patients. *Journal of Trauma & Dissociation, 17*(1), 67–80. https://doi.org/10.1080/15299732.2015.1067941

World Health Organization. (2019/2021). *International classification of diseases, eleventh revision (ICD-11).*

Zanarini, M. C., & Frankenburg, F. R. (1997). Pathways to the development of borderline personality disorder. *Journal of Personality Disorders, 11*(1), 93–104. https://doi.org/10.1521/pedi.1997.11.1.93

Zanarini, M. C., Frankenburg, F. R., Jager-Hyman, S., Reich, D. B., & Fitzmaurice, G. (2008). The course of dissociation for patients with borderline personality disorder and axis II comparison subjects: A 10-year follow-up study. *Acta Psychiatrica Scandinavica, 118*(4), 291–296. https://doi.org/10.1111/j.1600-0447.2008.01247.x

Zanarini, M. C., Martinho, E., Temes, C. M., Glass, I. V., Aguirre, B. A., Goodman, M., & Fitzmaurice, G. M. (2023). Dissociative experiences of adolescents with borderline personality disorder: Description and prediction. *Borderline Personality Disorder and Emotion Dysregulation, 10*(1), 9. https://doi.org/10.1186/s40479-023-00217-0

Zanarini, M. C., Ruser, T., Frankenburg, F. R., & Hennen, J. (2000). The dissociative experiences of borderline patients. *Comprehensive Psychiatry, 41*(3), 223–227. https://doi.org/10.1016/s0010-440x(00)90051-8

OPEN ACCESS

Dissociation in suicidal depression: a Reformulated Object-Relations Theory (RORT) perspective

Golan Shahar, Morgan Robison and Thomas E. Joiner

The Interpersonal-Psychological Theory of Suicidal Behavior (IPTS) posits that suicide stems from *a motivation* to die by suicide, emanating from perceived-burdensomeness and failed belongingness, and *a capacity* to kill oneself. We propose a bridge between IPTS and dissociation theory/research via a recent reformulation of Melanie Klein's notion of the depressive position, as comprised of three elements: Demeaning affect, compensatory affect-regulatory maneuvers, and mental representation of self-as-deficient and others as judgmental/punitive and at times seductive. This position is formed in childhood, proceeds to adulthood, and is projected into the future with the hope of finding respite from criticism. This hope is then thwarted by the sufferer's interpersonal action leading to interpersonal strife. We posit that, in the *Basic Level*, a trauma-based, dissociative structure is formed, whereby the reformulated depressive position disengages from benign and benevolent mental processes, in turn creating interpersonal havoc. In the *Advanced Level*, dissociative mechanisms are utilized to assist the now depressed-suicidal position to succeed in its mission: Killing the self. A chilling case illustration of this pattern is presented and discussed. Clinically, we recommend a routine measurement of both dissociation and suicide risk, and appraisal of the psychodynamic connecting dissociation and suicidality.

The purpose of this article is to propose a conceptualization that ties together three bodies of literature: The Interpersonal-Psychological Theory of Suicide (IPTS [Joiner, 2005; Van Orden et al., 2010]), dissociation theory and research, and psychoanalytic object-relations theory, with a particular focus on social-cognitive reformulations of this theory. Guiding this integrative framework is a case illustration of an adult psychotherapy patient attempting a serious, near-lethal suicide attempt. The patient, treated by the first author (GS), is described below, followed by the proposed theoretical viewpoint.

1. 'Nirity': a case illustration[1,2]

'I would like to hug Nirity of twenty-one years ago and ten years ago'. This is how Nirit's suicide letter starts. It continues as follows: *'Unfortunately, Niriti is 49 years old (in two days, if I live that long) and she is exactly at the same place she was then, with the very same regrets, insights, anguish, and self-reproach, What a waste of life. Perhaps, if I wasn't a physician. Perhaps if my mother would really love me. Or if I had not married an emotionally crippled thief'*.

The letter then continues extensively. Twenty-one pages of sorrow, reproach for self-and-others, poignant reflections of life, expression of love for her children, guidelines to close friends as to what to do with her property, and how to take care of her children after she kills herself. All of this is juxtaposed against unbelievably witty utterances completely in synchrony with the pertinent political period (e.g., to her younger son: 'Always vote Meretz [a left-wing party, GS] and never to Bibi! [Binyamin Netanyahu, the right-wing prime minister of Israel]'). The same wit, sense-of-humor, and sparkling intelligence that has made her an adored star among her peer physicians, a role model for her residents, and a much-feared threat among her supervisors.

Nirit did not kill herself, albeit not for lack of trying. During the weekend where she spent time alone in her house, intermittently writing her suicide letter, watching TV, and texting with family members, she also tried several times to hang herself. When this did not work, she tried swallowing a wide array of pills. For an experienced physician to not complete the task of ending a human life is noteworthy. But something within her – or someone – stubbornly kept her alive, and we will get to know that someone later in this article. Eventually, Nirit texted a family member that she is about to die by suicide. The text was immediately circulated around to other family members, who rushed to her house and stormed in, finding her half-conscious and taking her to a general hospital on the other side of the country, to protect her confidentiality. There, after a very brief hospitalization and medical stabilization, Nirit was discharged to the care of her family members. Two weeks later, she was at my (GS) office, examining me suspiciously while at the same time making me laugh using her stand-up-comedian-like quips.

We therapists all have a certain patient – if we are lucky more than one but never numerous – the encounter with whom is going to transform our lives forever. I am one of those fortunate therapists, and Nirit is one of those 'transformational objects' (Bollas, 1979), changing the way I think and feel about my creed and life. The change continues. Nirit has been in therapy with me for the past 4 years now, and counting. During which time, a lot has happened, enabling me to learn a great deal about the potentially tragic fate of physicians, both worldwide and especially in Israel, particularly the most conscientious and successful ones (Shahar, 2021a). But Nirit also introduced me to something very unique about suicide attempts, and arguably suicide death: The potential, always formidable, presence of *dissociation* in the unfolding of this horrendous undertaking. This is what we – the three authors of this article – are attempting to unpack.

Nirit was a little child when her parents immigrated from the former Soviet Union to Israel. She was the eldest of two brothers and one sister. As immigrants, the parents were economically disadvantaged, managing to make do but always with huge efforts, and always in the face of the kind of discrimination directed against 'Russians'. The family was close-knit, and Nirit was viewed, from early childhood, as a rising star, both intellectually and physically. Her appearance was adorable, her tenacity fierce, and her intellectual powers highly apparent. She excelled in everything she did, in and out of school. While exhibiting a passion for literature and creative writing, Nirit ultimately focused on biology and the life sciences, with the aim of becoming a physician.

Despite these favorable descriptions made by Nirit of her childhood, she also alluded – hesitantly at first but gradually more forcefully – to very tumultuous relationships between her and her parents. The latter's parental style was authoritarian, clashing with Nirit's independence and reactance. This has led to countless quarrels, during which Nirit described instances that could only be defined as consistent with emotional and physical maltreatment. As is frequently the case, these altercations co-existed with the admiration and care Nirit continued to receive from her parents, leaving her (also quite customarily) confused, often feeling aggrieved and downright betrayed. Her recollections of these childhood incidents suggest that it was then that the seeds of depression and post-traumatic stress symptoms were planted.

As a teenager and then a young woman, Nirit was considered very attractive, and she was intensely sought out by young men. Nevertheless, she was quite selective in her romantic choices. After completing an illustrious mandatory army service, Nirit immediately applied to medical school and was accepted, thus embarking on the intensely long and hard journey of becoming an Israeli physician. Overall, things went very well for her. She excelled in medical school and was accepted into a very competitive residency, fell in love with a man her age and got married, had two adorable children, and – further down the road – applied and was admitted to a top-notch clinical and research fellowship in Europe. It was during the fellowship that her marital relationships went sour. She got divorced, completed the fellowship (again, with distinction), and went back to work at her 'Alma Mater' hospital in Israel. In this hospital, which she considered as 'her home and second family', she quickly rose within the ranks to become the head of an innovative medical unit treating high-risk patients.

It was then, at the peak of her career, that her mental health began to deteriorate. The clear triggers were work-related: Agreements made with the hospital for personnel and resources were not fulfilled, propelling Nirit to feel betrayed by her 'second family', as she had been by the original one. Worse for Nirit was her increasingly growing conviction that the medical services that she and her team are providing are actually substandard, and that she is in fact responsible for several patients' fatalities. Repeated attempts made by her to force the hospital leadership to fulfill the agreements have failed, in turn increasing her distress and alienation. She experienced nightmares and a severe loss of appetite, and was completely burned out.

2. The interpersonal-psychological theory of suicide

Suicide is, and has been, a severe global public health concern (World Health Organization, 2021). Over 700,000 people each year die by suicide (World Health Organization, 2021). Although all aspects of suicidality (suicidal thoughts, suicidal behaviors, death by suicide) are relatively rare, they are, in principle, preventable. As such, there is urgency in understanding factors that may explain suicide; dissociation may be one such factor, facilitating process, or condition that enables lethal suicide attempts (Centers for Disease Control and Prevention, 2022; Orbach, 1994).

Theories in the late 70s interlaced psychopathology and social processes (e.g., Abramson et al., 1978; Brown et al., 2012) presenting a heavily interpersonal lens into understanding why people suffer and why they die by suicide. The Interpersonal-Psychological Theory of Suicide (IPTS) further refined this view by presenting the first ideation-to-action theory, interacting with four essential constructs: thwarted belongingness, perceived burdensomeness; a sense of hopelessness towards changes regarding the two prior factors; and capacity for suicide (Joiner, 2005; Van Orden et al., 2010).

The first three constructs address suicidal desire (i.e., suicidal ideation). Thwarted belongingness encompasses the internal perception of societal detachment and its correlates (e.g., isolation; loneliness). Perceived burdensomeness includes the belief that others would benefit from one's death. Hopelessness about the first two facets of IPTS creates a sense of despondency (cf. helplessness) and a worldview that one's life is a series of fatalistic failures (cf. negative expectancy (Abramson et al., 1989; Beck, 1967)). Finally, an important contribution of IPTS was the distinction between those who contemplate suicide compared to those who enact it; the theory suggests there are biological (i.e., genetic) and experiential (i.e., habituation) differences (Joiner, 2005). Accordingly, when a desire to die is combined with capacity (i.e., fearlessness towards death and dying; considerable tolerance for physical pain; and an applied and accessible knowledge surrounding the prepared method [e.g., firearm familiarity; Joiner, 2005; Klonsky & May, 2015], the theory predicts a lethal or near-lethal suicide attempt (see Van Orden et al., 2010 for a full review)).

2.1. IPTS in Nirit's case

Thwarted belongingness and perceived burdensomeness were very prominent in Nirit's suicide attempt. With those friends and family members she actually met, Nirit refrained from revealing her turmoil. As a consequence, she was incredibly lonely when she reached that weekend. Perceived burdensomeness was apparent in her conviction that she was providing substandard medical services, in turn convincing her that her patients were better off if she were dead. The logic proceeded as follow: If she is dead, her hospital will have to shut down the unit. When this happens, her patients will be referred to a hospital elsewhere in Israel, where physicians and patients enjoy safer working conditions not supplied by her own hospital. In hindsight, Nirit felt that she was better off either leaving the hospital and moving to another, or renouncing her medical career altogether. However, Nirit maintained that these two alternatives were highly unfeasible at the time because 'you don't leave a family' and 'I couldn't fathom myself not being a doctor'.

3. Dissociative processes in suicidality

Dissociation includes a constellation of clinical presentations, evoking some empirical and clinical controversy (e.g., Dalenberg et al., 2012; Lynn et al., 2014). Historical definitions of dissociation range, such as defining it as a lack of integration of two or more mental processes or defining it as a separation between the mind and the body (Calati et al., 2017; Cardeña, 1994; Orbach, 1994). The DSM-5 defines dissociation as a combination of the above: 'disruption of and/or discontinuity in the normal integration of consciousness, memory, identity, emotion, perception, body representation, motor control, and behavior' (American Psychiatric Association, 2022). Clinically, it presents as a spectrum of severity including symptoms of depersonalization (i.e., self-detachment and/or significant alterations to the sense of self and/or identity), derealization (i.e., loss of perception of one's surroundings as real), and amnesia (i.e., inability to recall memory; Mitra & Jain, 2023; Rabasco & Andover, 2020; Rossi et al., 2019).

Current research has divided dissociative symptoms into two predominant domains: *compartmentalization and detachment* (Holmes et al., 2005; Rabasco & Andover, 2020; Rossi et al., 2019). Compartmentalization (i.e., dissociative amnesia and conversion disorders) is characterized by an inability to maintain cognitive agency and voluntary motor control (Holmes et al., 2005; Rabasco & Andover, 2020; Rossi et al., 2019). Detachment (i.e., depersonalization and derealization) is characterized by a transmutation of the consciousness, or an 'alienation' of the self, others, or the world. Self-detachment can manifest as a blunting of emotion (e.g., flat affect), alteration of bodily sensations (e.g., numbing or out-of-body experiences), or the loss of tangibility of one's environment (e.g., dreamlike states; Holmes et al., 2005; Rabasco & Andover, 2020; Rossi et al., 2019). Detachment has been reported across a variety of mental states (e.g., under the influence of illicit substances, during states of fatigue and sleepiness, and during the occurrence of trauma) and holds clinical relevance as a diagnostic subtype of post-traumatic stress disorder (American Psychiatric Association, 2022).

There is further evidence suggesting dissociative detachment may be transdiagnostic, relevant in a host of other types of psychopathology (e.g., substance abuse, borderline personality disorder, eating disorders, and depression (Lyssenko et al., 2018; Scalabrini et al., 2017; Soffer-Dudek, 2014)). Each of the aforementioned disorders shares a heightened risk for another, particularly grave outcome: suicide (Andover et al., 2005; Centers for Disease Control and Prevention, 2022; Shahnaz & Klonsky, 2021; Smith et al., 2018). Thus, dissociative detachment may, additionally, be particularly informative when understanding suicide risk.

Orbach (1994) hypothesized that suicide attempts, especially distinctly violent ones, may be marked by dissociation presenting as an insensitivity to physical pain and bodily indifference (Orbach, 1994). When differentiating between the two modes of dissociation (i.e., compartmentalization and detachment), detachment through depersonalization and derealization most aligns with Orbach's theory and may be the more likely to impart suicide risk (Caulfield et al., 2022; Holmes et al., 2005). Joiner's (2005) interpersonal theory of suicide (IPTS) – which, though it did not emphasize dissociation, nonetheless owes an intellectual debt to Orbach (1994)—proposed one aspect of capacity, i.e., a heightened ability to inflict lethal injury, helps explain critical differentiations between those who contemplate and those who enact lethal suicide attempts (Joiner, 2005; Van Orden et al., 2010). An integration of Orbach's (1994) theory and IPTS would suggest that dissociation may increase the threshold for pain, decrease bodily sacredness, and increase a fearlessness towards death. Additionally, Joiner and colleagues suggest that diminished eye blink rate – an indication of fearlessness – may serve as a non-specific biobehavioral marker of imminent suicidality (Duffy et al., 2022; Joiner et al., 2016; Rubin et al., 2017). This marker may be one observable manifestation of dissociation.

Indeed, some research supports such claims: higher self-reported dissociative experiences associate with painful and lethal methods of suicide attempts (e.g., stabbing, falling, and hanging compared to drug overdose; Fakhry, 2015). Furthermore, in a meta-analysis conducted by Calati et al. (2017), dissociative symptoms or disorders remained a transdiagnostic risk factor for lifetime history of suicide attempts in psychiatric patients (Calati et al., 2017). Five of the studies in that meta-analysis specifically compared symptoms of dissociation, independent of a disorder, using the Dissociative Experiences Scale (Bernstein & Putnam, 1986), and found high scores differentiated between suicide-attempting and non-suicide-attempting psychiatric patients (Hedges' $g = 0.52$, 95% CI = 0.32–0.72; Calati et al., 2017).

When experimentally assessing relationships between dissociation, pain tolerance, suicidal ideation, and suicide attempts, respectively, dissociation and suicidal ideation, but not pain tolerance, were significantly cross-sectionally associated with an increased number of past suicide attempts (Rabasco & Andover, 2020). The three-way interaction of dissociation, physiological pain tolerance, and suicidal ideation was significantly related to an increased number of past suicide attempts such that those high in suicidal ideation and dissociation, but low pain tolerance, had more attempts (Rabasco & Andover, 2020). Pachkowski et al. (2021) examined two samples and found that dissociation cross-sectionally differentiated individuals with a history of suicide attempts from those with ideation alone ($d = 0.28$; $d = 0.46$; $ps = 0.01$) in both samples, and pain tolerance did not explain the association (see Study 2; importantly, associations diminished when including clinical covariates) (Pachkowski et al., 2021). Conversely, among clinical samples of patients with borderline personality disorder, researchers have found a relationship between dissociation and pain tolerance (Bekrater-Bodmann et al., 2015; Ludäscher et al., 2007). Finally, Levinger et al. (2015) found that adolescent inpatients with suicide attempts reported higher levels of mental pain, in combination with a lower tolerance for the accompanying symptoms, in conjunction with a greater sense of physical dissociation, compared to non-suicidal adolescent inpatients and nonclinical participants (Levinger et al., 2015). Taken together, these findings may suggest that mental pain and physical dissociation (e.g., out-of-body experiences) relate to suicide risk, while mental dissociation (e.g., self-detachment) may affect the relationship between physical pain tolerance and suicide risk. Further research is needed to examine the role of dissociation in the interplay between it, pain tolerance, and suicide attempts.

Caulfield et al. (2022) also found significant cross-sectional associations between lifetime dissociation and past year suicidal ideation, and past suicide attempts (Caulfield et al., 2022). Furthermore, symptoms of dissociation, particularly derealization and depersonalization, increased a participant's likelihood of selecting suicide in a virtual reality paradigm (though statistical significance dissipated when controlling for other correlated factors; Caulfield et al., 2022). Thus, there appears to be some connection between dissociation, suicide attempts, and capacity. Nevertheless, research has yet to investigate if dissociation impacts one's psychological and physical proximity to pain and methods, other facets of capacity that may impact the lethality of a suicide attempt (Rogers et al., 2019).

Dissociation was the strongest correlate of suicide attempts among Israeli high schoolers, more so than experiences of trauma including emotional abuse, physical abuse, sexual abuse, and neglect (Zoroglu et al., 2003). Findings here have been clinically replicated, as those with dissociative subtypes of posttraumatic stress disorder (PTSD-D) have reported significantly more current suicidal thoughts and suicide attempts; moreover, symptoms of depression in the past month and lifetime suicide attempts significantly predicted PTSD-D (Mergler et al., 2017). Longitudinally, severe dissociation was predictive of future suicide attempts among those with borderline personality disorder (BPD; $n = 290$) 16 years later, albeit the increase in risk was marginal (Wedig et al., 2012). Therefore, dissociation appears to be relevant in suicide risk across a variety of clinical diagnoses (e.g., PTSD-D and BPD, though see conflicting evidence: Lieberman et al., 2023).

3.1. Dissociation and suicidal ideation

More recent efforts, though preliminary, have begun to assess and parse through the role that dissociation plays in suicidal ideation (see Caulfield et al., 2022; Mergler et al., 2017; Pachkowski et al., 2021; Rabasco & Andover, 2020). As noted above, this work is predominately cross-sectional (see Caulfield et al., 2022; Mergler et al., 2017; Pachkowski et al., 2021; Rabasco & Andover, 2020); nevertheless, dissociation differentiated between those with prior suicide attempts and those with lifetime suicidal ideation (Pachkowski et al., 2021). Therefore, though research on causation is warranted, there may exist an important distinction between dissociation's relationship to suicidal ideation vs. to suicide attempts.

Thoughts and behaviors surrounding suicide can cause significant distress and impairment in their own right and warrant clinical attention and intervention (Jobes & Joiner, 2019). To our knowledge, there is a dearth of research to date studying the theoretical relationships (i.e., see the IPTS above) between dissociation and the interpersonal facets of suicidal ideation. One study, among a clinical sample of bulimia nervosa participants, found that dissociation did not share zero-order correlations with suicidal ideation, but did with self-hatred (i.e., a proxy of perceived burdensomeness), a proxy of thwarted belongingness, and capability (Lieberman et al., 2023). Therefore, additional research is warranted to determine if depersonalization and derealization relate to thwarted belongingness and perceived burdensomeness. Theoretically, depersonalization results in blunted emotions, and can display externally as a flat affect, which may impede an individual's ability to socially connect to others (Holmes et al., 2005). Additionally, depersonalization may result in feeling disconnected from one's community, described as if one was separated by a glass wall (Holmes et al., 2005). Derealization, on the other hand, can alter one's perception into a dreamlike state, with full awareness of this environmental alteration, furthering experiences of social disconnection (Holmes et al., 2005). This dreamlike state may further disrupt perceptions of time and impact ability to complete tasks, relevant to perceived burdensomeness. This imprisonment of the mind may drive a desire to die as an unfortunate method to awaken from the dream state that is dissociation. Those who experience dissociative states, in both episodic and continued intervals, may find it particularly challenging to recollect uninterrupted periods of time (e.g., memories) without states of distress. This may create tension within the self between a desire towards life and a calling to death as a means to escape. This simultaneous process of planning life while planning death has been noted in past accounts of lethal suicide attempts (Jamison, 1995;

Joiner, 2005); thus, further understanding dissociation's role in suicidal ideation may be a critical direction forward in understanding the suicidal mind.

Given that dissociation is defined by disruptions in memory, bodily connection, and integration of consciousness, it follows that dissociative symptoms should result in cognitive dysfunction. Indeed, a review of the literature suggests that dissociation and cognitive dysfunction may share psychological mechanisms and their neurobiological bases, resulting in dissociation impacting cognitive performance relating to attention, executive functioning, memory, and social cognition (McKinnon et al., 2016). Therefore, there may be neurobiological similarities between dissociation and suicide (Comparelli et al., 2022; Fernández-Sevillano et al., 2021). However, it is cautioned against generalizing neurobiological findings in suicide risk across all clinical diagnoses, as stronger associations between executive dysfunction and suicidality have been found in depressive disorders more so than in bipolar or psychotic disorder samples (Bredemeier & Miller, 2015). Nevertheless, these preliminary cognitive associations appear to mirror theoretical and empirical support towards associations between detachment dissociation and suicide (rather than compartmentalization [e.g., memory] and suicide, though see [McKinnon et al., 2016]).

3.2. Clinical implications

Taken together, dissociative tendencies, particularly detachment, may aid in the facilitation of suicide. Work to date has linked dissociation to suicide attempts; clients are safest when embracing their bodily awareness and experiencing life with lethal means secured far away (Rogers et al., 2019). Dissociation interferes with many components of this safety (e.g., bodily and life awareness, sacredness of self) and while simultaneously impacting capability (e.g., fearlessness about death and pain), this hinges the safety of a higher suicide risk client upon securing lethal methods. Moreover, dissociation has been associated with poorer therapeutic outcomes, nonadherence, and dropout rates in a variety of clinical diagnoses (Bae et al., 2015; Kleindienst et al., 2011; Rufer et al., 2005). On the other hand, a review assessing treatment outcomes for dissociative disorders has shown neighboring reductions in suicidal ideation and attempts (Brand et al., 2009; Brand & Stadnik, 2013).

As dissociation has been associated with more violent suicide attempts (Fakhry, 2015; Orbach, 1994), and global suicide deaths oftentimes involve methods that are more violent (e.g., self-poisoning through pesticides, ligature, and firearms [World Health Organization, 2021]), accurate assessment of dissociation symptoms may help inform treatment protocols. The Brief Dissociative Experiences Scale (DES-B) is an 8-item measure which assesses an individual's frequency of dissociation within the past week, where higher sum scores indicate a greater severity of dissociative experiences (C. Dalenberg & Carlson, 2010). This scale has shown strong 10-week test–retest reliability and good validity (Kira et al., 2022). Incorporating routine measurement of dissociation, in conjunction with gold standard measurements of suicide risk (see Batterham et al., 2015; Gutierrez et al., 2019), may help clinicians assess for heightened suicide attempt risk.

3.3. Dissociative experiences in Nirit's suicide attempt

Nirit remembers talking to herself loudly during the entire weekend proceeding her suicide attempt. She remembers a very stormy dialogue between two self-aspects. The first she called *The Terminator*, which pushed her repeatedly to kill herself, ridiculing her in the face of her 'failures' to do so. The second was 'Niriti', a cute little girl 'who did not want to die'. As therapy progressed, and with the occurrence of two additional dissociative episodes getting Nirit closer to suicide attempts, it became clear that each self-aspect had a different role in Nirit's inner world. The Terminator was in charge of summoning the courage to cross daunting challenges, including the maltreatment she had suffered during her childhood (i.e., courage which could have manifested as a reduction in blink rate, a sign of imminent suicide risk (Duffy et al., 2022; Rubin et al., 2017)). Niriti, on the other hand, was in charge of relationships: With romantic partners, her children, and – of course – with me in therapy: An affectionate, caring but concurrently highly sensitive and vulnerable – protagonist that represents what Blatt (Blatt, 2004; Blatt, 2008) would label as anaclitic-dependent needs: The need to be nurtured, protected, and supported, so that she could stay alive. Upon discovering and delineating the two self-aspects, Nirit was particularly alarmed – not by their presence – but by the fact that they are so disconnected in their daily experience. Which brings us to Melanie Klein's notion of positions, and particularly the depressive-suicidal one.

4. The Reformulated Object Relations Theory (RORT) and the reformulated suicidal-depressive position

A central tenet of this article is that the underlying dissociative processes are relatively stable, i.e., structural, representations of self-and-others, characterized by a particular affective tone and specific ways to regulate such affect (i.e., defense mechanisms and coping strategies). The combination of mental representations, affect, and affect-regulation conforms to Melanie Klein's (1935) notion of positions (Thieberger, 1991). Over approximately two and a half decades of theoretical work Shahar and colleagues have attempted to reformulate psychoanalytic object-relations theory in general and Klein's notion of positions in particular (Klein, 1928, 1935, 1940, 1945; Klein et al., 1993) with the aim of freeing these important intellectual and professional bodies of literature from what is often deemed an idiosyncratic, stifling jargon (e.g., 'bad breast') that is highly unappealing to thinkers both within and outside psychoanalysis (Shahar, 2004, 2006a, 2006b, 2010, 2011, 2015a, 2016, 2021a, 2021b, 2023; Shahar, Cross, et al., 2004; Shahar et al., 2003; Shahar & Davidson, 2009; Shahar & Schiller, 2016). Another important aim of this theoretical work is to inform object-relations theory and the notion of Kleinian positions with extant, up-to-date findings from psychological and neuropsychological work focusing on emotions and the self. As repeatedly acknowledged, this theoretical work stands on the shoulders of earlier pioneers integrating psychoanalysis and empirical research (Blatt, 2004; Blatt, 1974; Fonagy, 1995; Kemberg et al., 2008; Westen, 1991, 1998). The products of this extensive theoretical work are the Reformulated Object-relations Theory (RORT) and the reformulated depressive (−suicidal) position. Both will be summarized succinctly below.

4.1. RORT and a new definition of positions

Shahar and Schiller (2016) posit that the central content of the psychodynamic unconscious conforms to what Klein labeled as position: An amalgamation of – in her terms – object-relations, anxiety, and defense mechanisms. Readers of this journal hardly need to be taught about the two positions featuring in Klein's theory, namely, the schizoid-paranoid position and the depressive position. The former, more 'primitive' (developmentally younger) position consists of a polarized experience of the world as split between 'good' and 'bad' segments, including self and others ('objects'). The corresponding anxiety is that of annihilation of the good by the bad, and the principal defense mechanisms geared to regulate this very dramatic anxiety operate on the basis of a split, sharp divide, between good and bad. As long as good is kept away from bad, the former is relatively secure, although it is constantly threatened. With the accumulation of positive (pleasurable and nurturing) experiences, the more developmentally advanced, depressive position germinates. In this position, self and others are multifaceted, namely, they include both 'good' and 'bad' aspects. This paves the way to an entire plateau of hitherto unexperienced emotions such as sadness, guilt, regret, and ambivalence, and to a type of anxiety very different from the schizoid-paranoid one: An anxiety about one's own ability to destroy the 'good' within the object via my own 'bad' (aggressive) aspects. Defense mechanisms utilized in this position are much more moderate, conforming to the descriptions of Sigmund and Anna Freud of 'neurotic defenses'. Instead of erasing vast segments of experiences, such defenses obscure circumscribed experimental aspects, namely, impulses, thoughts, and emotions (Greenberg & Mitchell, 1983; Ogden, 1992). As elaborated on by Klein and her followers, positions are different than stages in that they co-exist within the same person at the same period of time, in turn accounting for rapid oscillation between primitive and advanced levels of personality organization and behavioral maturity.

Shahar and colleagues applauded numerous aspects of Klein's notion of positions, including (1) its depiction of psychological development as characterized by increasing cognitive-affective complexity (see Blatt, 1995), (2) avoiding common fallacies committed by stage theories (e.g., such as Piaget's and Freud's) via emphasizing the co-existence positions, and (3) describing personality as a dynamic structure in which various components work in tandem. This latter strength is paramount, because it allies Klein's notion of positions with similar theories, both within and outside psychoanalysis, that view personality as a dynamic (dis)equilibrium of numerous forces (Beck, 1996; Block, 2002; Horowitz, 1998; Kelly, 1955; Kernberg, 1984; Mischel & Shoda, 1995). On the other hand, Shahar and colleagues note two major flaws of Melanie Klein's theory: (1) the above-noted use of the idiosyncratic jargon and (2) Its seclusion of key findings from psychological and neuroscientific research. Both flaws are addressed by reformulating the notion of positions, and hence object-relations theory itself, using social-cognitive nomenclature, which is clear, empirically testable, and encourages integration between psychoanalysis and empirical science (Blatt et al., 1997; Bornstein, 2001; Westen, 1991, 1998).

Specifically, the following are several empirically supported principles that Shahar and colleagues incorporated into their reformulated version of object-relations theory (RORT) and, by extension, Kleinian positions:

- Instead of a sole emphasis on anxiety as the affective 'prime mover' of personality, RORT emphasizes the importance of a nuanced perspective on emotions. Particularly, RORT acknowledges that numerous negative emotions may fuel the dynamic interplay between personality components, and that negative and positive affect – which are largely orthogonal – are likely to each independently impact personality.
- Instead of embracing the idea of a thick 'repressive line' clearly separating unconscious and (sub)conscious material, RORT adopts research findings that attest to the continuous nature of consciousness: Material can go in and out of awareness depending on individuals' goals and developmental tasks (for empirical support, see Erdelyi, 2006; Green et al., 2009; Sedikides & Green, 2009; Shahar, 2006a); for a similar theoretical view within psychoanalysis, see (Eagle, 2011; Stolorow et al., 1987). Perhaps, the biggest advantage of this modification is that it allows treating both defense mechanisms (hitherto considered 'unconscious') and coping strategy (previously considered 'conscious') as equal manifestation of 'affect regulatory maneuvers' (Shahar, 2021b, 2023).
- Instead of focusing on past and present as the focal tenses impacting personality, RORT elevates the role of the future in the psyche. Specifically, drawing from both early (Sullivan, 1953) and recent (Summers, 2003) developments in psychoanalytic theory, as well as from voluminous research on the effect of future representations on *human* cognition, affect, and behavior (Amati & Shallice, 2007; Austin & Vancouver, 1996; Gilbert & Wilson, 2007; McDaniel & Einstein, 2007; Seligman et al., 2013), Shahar and colleagues highlighted the centrality of

the future as 'an object of desire': People project themselves into the future in order to become what they think they might be and ought to be (Shahar, 2011).

- Instead of the Kleinian tendency to focus mostly on intrapsychic processes (e.g., fantasy), Shahar and colleagues extract the only interpersonal aspect of Klein's theory – projective identification. As is probably obvious to readers of this journal, projective-identification is a split-based, interpersonal defense mechanism whereby individuals force significant others in their lives to behave in a way that is consistent with segments of their personality which they (the initiators) unconsciously disown: I am full of hatred, thus I will force you – e.g., through a wide array of provocations – to behave in a hateful manner toward me. The Kleinian notion of projective identification is not only consistent with numerous other ideas within psychoanalysis (e.g., Joseph Sandler's role responsiveness (Sandler, 1976), Karen Horney's externalization and the vicious cycle (Horney, 1936)), but also with ideas propagated in cognitive, behavioral, and family-systems schools of psychopathology, according to which individuals, propelled by their personal characteristics, create the very social environment that lead to their distress (e.g., Coyne, 1976a, 1976b; Depue & Monroe, 1986; Hammen, 1991; Joiner, 1994, 2000; Shahar, 2006b).

Weaving it all together, we arrive at the following, reformulated definition of Melanie Klein's position:

'A position is an amalgamation of affect, its regulation, and schemas and scripts of self-in-relationships, with all augmenting each other and forming a distinct and coherent experience of the world. Positions are formed throughout childhood and adolescence and are maintained via interpersonal action. They are projected into the future, representing individuals' hope and fears, and as such are guiding cognition, motivation, emotion, and behavior. Although all positions strive to be confirmed in the interpersonal arena, some positions, occupying a large space in the psyche, are likely to create a maladaptive social environment that culminates in psychopathology'.

(Shahar, 2023).

Building on Shahar (2023), several aspects of this definition need further emphasis:

(1) Affect, its regulation, and schemas and scripts are co-causative.
(2) Positions enable a clear worldview: 'This is what the world looks like, and I should act accordingly'.
(3) All positions translate into action: people constantly shape social reality in accordance with their worldview. Wachtel titles this vector 'cyclical psychodynamics' (see, in particular, [Wachtel, 1994]).

(4) All positions are projected into the future. Future representations are thus the pillar of the psyche.
(5) Whereas Klein focused on two 'super-' positions, we posit that, in fact, there are likely to be many positions in the psyche. This is in line with other personality theories highlighting the role – and multiplicity – of various components of intertwined affect and cognition, such as Beck's (1996) modes (see also in Schema Therapy, Lazarus & Rafaeli, 2023), and sets, (Lynn et al., 2014, 2019) and this point is paramount for the understanding of dissociation. In addition to Melanie Klein's positions, i.e., the schizoid-paranoid and depressive, one may imagine obsessive, somatic, grandiose-manic, playful, humorous, affiliative, and so on. We postulate that each of these positions includes all the elements described above. An important issue concerning personality organization and psychopathology is the extent to which the various positions occupying the psyche of each are interconnected. Arguably, the more positions a person has, and the stronger these positions are interconnected, the greater is a person's sense of coherence, comprehensiveness, and completeness. Correspondingly, a high number of interconnected positions enable a person a greater repertoire of responses under threat.
(6) In psychopathology, a small number 'eclipse the others', in that they occupy a disproportionally large segment of the psyche. When this happens, a concerted effort is made by the individuals to confirm these positions in the interpersonal arena, and this – in turn – is likely to lead to calamitous outcomes.

Each of these points will now be utilized to reformulate Klein's depressive position.

4.2. The reformulated depressive position

Shahar's reformulation of the depressive position (2016, 2018, 2021b, 2023) rests firmly on decades of empirical research into the role of personality in unipolar depression. Such research was largely inspired by the theories and studies of Blatt (1974, 1998, 2004) and Beck (1996). One of the clear patterns emanating from this research is the centrality of self-criticism as a dimension of vulnerability to all types of unipolar depression, as well as to other, related psychopathologies (Shahar, 2015b; Werner et al., 2019). Self-criticism activates a host of emotions, including sadness, fear, anger, shame, and contempt (Whelton & Greenberg, 2005). Self-critics may regulate this pain through maladaptive defense mechanisms such as acting out, undoing, projection, devaluation, denial, isolation, and splitting, and turning against oneself and others (Besser & Priel, 2011), as well as more conscious, maladaptive coping strategies such as venting distress to others without attempting to solve the putative problem (Dunkley et al., 2003), and highly maladaptive motivational regulative endeavors, namely, attempting to suppress authentic interest in activities (Shahar et al., 2003). Some of these defense mechanisms – projection, turning against others, splitting – actually shed light on a very close link – also likely to be reciprocal – between self-criticism and representations of other people. Specifically, self-criticism is shown to be strongly associated with the perception of others as harsh, punitive, and judgmental (Mongrain, 1998). Finally, painful affect may feed-back, increasing the intensity of self-criticism (Shahar, Blatt, et al., 2004; Shahar & Henrich, 2019).

Synthesizing such research and substituting it in the above, reformulated structure of Klein's position, Shahar proposed that a reformulated depressive position includes (a) criticism-based affect; (b) regulatory processes that reinforce this affect; (c) schemas and scripts associated with self-criticism; (d) a time axis that considers past and present influences as well as projections of the self in the future; and (e) interpersonal actions, primarily externalizing self-criticism, which creates a vicious cycle (Shahar, 2018, 2021b). Allow us to explicate below.

4.2.1. Affect

The most dominant affect in the reformulated depressive position is neither sadness nor fear, but rather a demeaning, *criticism-based affect*. It consists of emotions such as anger, shame, guilt, contempt, disgust, disappointment, hatred, and envy. The overall affective tone is that of putting down (either self or other) and focusing on deficiencies. Nevertheless, alongside this type of affect, we propose that there also exists a positive one: hope. This hope emanates almost inevitably from the theme of criticism: 'I am flawed, but I know why. If I correct my flaws, I will be ok'. As we explicate below, this form of hope turns out to be problematic.

4.2.2. Affect regulation

Demeaning, criticism-based affect is defended against using three clusters of affect-regulatory maneuvers: counteracting deficiency, downregulating authenticity, and maintaining hope through 'prospection', or compulsive purposefulness. *Counteracting deficiency* is experiencing oneself consciously, as well as behaving, as if one is actually flawless, in a manner consistent with the Kleinian notion of *manic defenses* (see also Barrett, 2006; Ogden, 1992; Winnicott, 1958). *Downregulating authenticity* pertains to one's tendency to do what is right, instead of what one wishes to do. It is tantamount to an assault on spontaneity, the latter deemed by self-critics as a constant threat because it is so unpredictable. Preparedness, rather than spontaneity, is perceived as an ultimate life demand. Finally, *Compulsive purposefulness* is an affect-regulatory mechanism espoused in the service of hope: 'In order to eradicate my flaws, I must constantly self-improve!'.

4.2.3. Schemas and scripts

Schemas/scripts of the self are characterized by self-criticism and schemas/ scripts of others as punitive and judgmental (Mongrain, 1998). Note, however, that self and others are schematized and scripted in the psyche as acting upon each other (Shahar, 2004), what I have labeled previously as 'agents in relationships' (AIR; Shahar, 2010). The other conveys judgment and disappointment, and the self as actively attempting to shield against these punitive judgments and disappointment in two ways: appeasing the other and protesting against the other. Appeasement is done by way of what Klein calls 'reparation' (see [Thieberger, 1991]): a fantasy of re-constituting the other as good is accompanied by solicitous behavior. The self is trying 'to be good' so that the other deems the self as non-deficient. Protests come to the fore either when the self does not succeed in appeasing the other, or by way of a 'preemptive strike': for example, 'Are you mad at me?' The tone of this question is angry rather than inquisitive. It is 'how dare you be mad at me when I am so good!'

In addition, there is a subtle experience of the other as seductive, in an evaluative – rather than erotic – sense: 'If you only accomplish this or that, or be this or that, then I will cease judging you and will lovingly accept what you are'. Such a seduction is, of course, reciprocally related to the hope that we described earlier, which – also subtly – dwells within the person's affective spectrum. This is highly consistent with the notion of the 'exciting object' coined by Ronald Fairbairn (1944). The exciting object promises a bright future in which the self is accepted, thus summoning love (see, for instance, Celani, 1999) and is – we submit – useful to the understanding of the reformulated depressive position.

4.2.4. Time axis

The reformulated depressive position considers the relevance of the past, the present, and the future. The past produces a storage of autobiographical memories from which the person draws the experience of being wronged (maltreated) by the other, but also the possibility of being at least partly responsible to the wrongdoing because the person somehow offended the other (Ferenczi, 1988). Hence, 'You have hurt me. Had I hurt you before?'

In the present, there are active exchanges – both internally and externally, between self and others that revolve around hurt, grievance, and wrongdoing: Someone is always hurting someone else. These schemas and scripts surface, but are also amalgamated, by the aforementioned regulatory maneuvers shifting blame from self to other and vice versa. Thus, 'You are hurting me. Do I deserve it?'

Following Sullivan (1953) and Summers (2003), however, we are highlighting the role of the future. This is where both dread and hope lie. The self yearns for an experience of the accepting other, but dreads a scenario whereby, despite all efforts, the other will remain judgmental and punitive. The tragedy is that the self – via interpersonal action – actually solidifies this punitive judgement by evoking rejections, confrontations, and interpersonal loss.

4.2.5. Interpersonal action

Voluminous research demonstrates compellingly that self-critics create a maladaptive social environment comprising interpersonal life stress (rejections, confrontations, breakups) and a dearth of positive experiences and social support (for a review, see Shahar, 2015b). Filling this pattern with psychodynamic depth, Shahar argued that, propelled by the reformulated depressive position, individuals project into their future both their hope for an accepting other and their expectations for a judgmental and punitive one. Their actions, however, automated throughout the years, are more consistent with the latter than the former. In a manner consistent with Klein's 'projective identification' and Sandler's (1976) 'role responsiveness', but also with Coyne's (1976a, 1976b) and Joiner's (Joiner, 1994, 2000) research on excessive reassurance-seeking, these individuals' actions exert pressure on others to react negatively rather than with compassion, ultimately yielding the above-noted interpersonal stress and dearth of positive events and social support.

It should be noted here that the above reformulation of the depressive position not only enhances and upgrades Klein's description but actually alters this description in fundamental ways. In fact, as Shahar has noted recently (2021b, 2023), Klein was not at her best in describing unipolar depression as a clinical entity. She was much more astute in describing the more psychotic psychopathologies, to which 'her' paranoid-schizoid position conformed. In describing depression, she either quickly 'regresses' into describing paranoia and/or mania (Klein, 1935, p.158) or provide an ultra-benign, if not downright favorable, account. This favorable account emphasizes the capacity for integration of good and bad objects and the ability of reparation of the relationships – actual and internalized – with the good object (Thieberger, 1991). Integration and reparation both protect the 'self' (a term Klein did not use but that was introduced subsequently in object-relations theory) not only as a fundamentally worthy being but also as a historical-narrative being that rests on a relatively cohesive life story. This is probably why Ogden (1992) proposed re-titling 'the depressive position' as 'the historical position' (Ogden, 1992). In a subsequent publication, we hope to elaborate more on the difference between a pathological, genuinely depressive, position, and a favorable, benevolent, 'historical position' that tallies with some of Klein's accounts.

4.4. How does the reformulated depressive position spiral into suicidality?

An enormous mental pain is experienced by depressed individuals when they project their hoped-for self-with-other representations onto the future only to be met with interpersonal stress and a dearth of social support and positive events. The failure to 'generate' an accepting other erodes hope and introduces frustration and resultant agitation, and these affects further alienate others, thereby trapping the person in interpersonal turmoil. Others thus are either abandoning, leading to *thwarted belongingness*, or fiercely accusing, and as such begetting *perceived burdensomeness*: 'My mere existence is an offense'. The person is left alone at the mercy of their inner world, which at this point is completely merciless. Because depression 'locks the person' into their inner world (depressive rumination), the encounter with this world becomes harsher and harsher. Depressed-suicidal patients in one of our practices (GS) regularly describe their suicidal ruminations as stormy. Often, the person has already burnt all interpersonal bridges and/or realizes that they are likely to invoke hurt in any interpersonal maneuver. The only way to stop the pain is to cease being aware, and the only way to secure this is to die (Baumeister, 1990). This state of affairs pertains to what Joiner and colleagues title acute suicidal risk (Rogers et al., 2019). Now the sufferer has a new goal, a new sense-of-meaning, a new way to salvage their self-image: They can capably enact death. This is incumbent on two conditions. The first is stealth: If people close to the sufferer knew that they were going to kill themselves, they would interrupt. This is why acute suicide risk may go under clinicians' radar. The second is fear of death, which requires practice leading to what Joiner and colleagues term *capacity*. After sufficient practice has occurred, the sufferer is ready to stare death down (Van Orden et al., 2010).

4.5. What is the role of dissociation in the above-described descent into suicidality?

We posit that, for the reformulated depressive position to spiral into suicidality, it should not only 'eclipse' other available positions but must downright annihilate these positions. Put differently, dissociative mechanisms enable depressed individuals, when they sink into an acute suicide crisis (Rogers et al., 2019), to smoothly sail into the tragic faith *without interference.*

What would such an interference look like? Suicide research is replete with empirical evidence of the ambivalence sufferers are harboring between life and death, often till the very last minute (Joiner, 2005; Orbach, 1994; Steel, 2006). Police negotiation teams are aware of this ambivalence, and when they attempt to dissuade sufferers from jumping off roofs or bridges, they are aiming at this very ambivalence, or, more accurately, at the inner voices within the sufferer who do not wish to die by suicide (Briggs & Mellinger, 2015). In the terms advanced here, during acute suicide crisis, there is a mighty struggle between, on the one hand, the reformulated-depressive-position-turned-suicidal, and any other position that is 'benign', namely, incompatible with killing oneself. Benign positions are those which include soothing affect (e.g., serenity, curiosity), mature defenses and coping style (humor, sublimation), and representations of self-and-others which include even a modicum of compassion. For the reformulated-depressive-position-turned-suicidal to materialize itself, such benign positions must be moved out of the way.

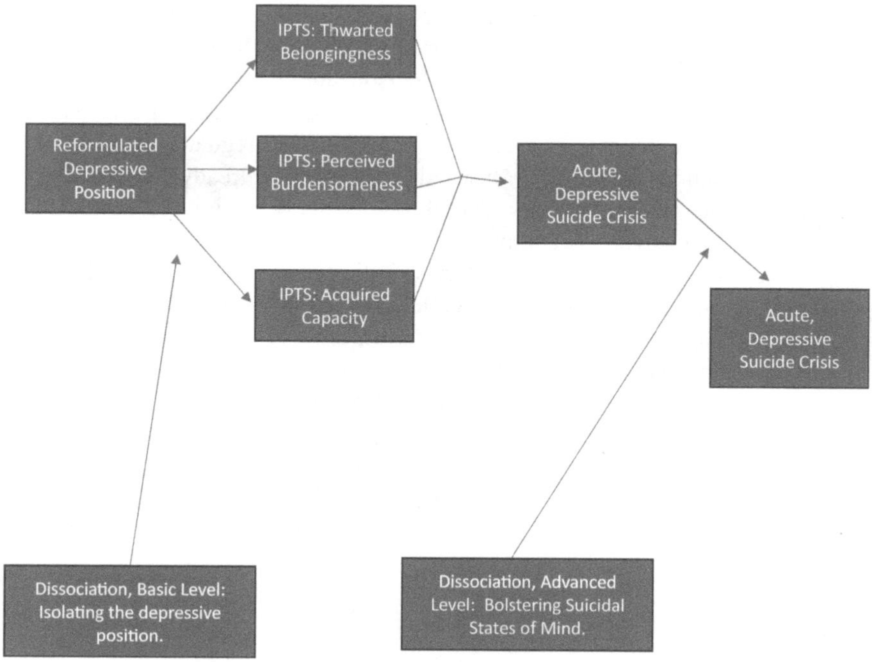

Figure 1. Proposed role of dissociation in the progression of the depressive position into suicidality.

The way these benign positions are neutralized is depicted in Figure 1. There are two levels in which dissociative mechanisms 'keep at bay' benign positions. On a more basic level, throughout development individuals learn to distrust benign positions: They experience them as signaling weakness and as potentially leading to mental injury. Consequently, such positions are either downplayed or downright ostracized (Strenger, 1998), whereas positions that promise, seductively and elusively, 'to toughen up' are elevated and are acted upon. Ultimately, an isolated depressive position is likely to propel the above-described IPTS-related factor leading to an acute suicidal crisis, in turn descending into suicidal behavior. On the more advanced level, within the acute suicide crisis itself, dissociative mechanisms operate online to banish thoughts, affect, and inner dialogues emanating from the benign positions, leaving the sufferers on their own with the reformulated-depressive-position-turned-suicidal, namely, with the perpetrator. Thus, this advanced level bolsters suicidal states of mind.

Which leads us back to Nirit's case, and to some speculations as to how she got to where she seriously tried to kill herself, and why she ultimately did not die.

5. Back to Nirit's case: how dissociation led to suicide and how suicide was derailed

5.1. Basic-level Dissociation

Surviving a tumultuous childhood, Nirit learned to disengage from 'Niriti', a soft, mellow, arguably anaclitic-dependent position whereby the other is supportive and nurturing, the self is trusting and unguarded, affect is largely pleasant, fueled by affect-regulatory mechanisms aimed at increasing closeness, intimacy, and positive affect more generally (Fredrickson, 1998). Instead, ascended to dominance in her inner world was a position elevating performance, sharpness, reactance, and wit. Nirit learned that this position is her road to safety. To the extent that she is governed by it, others will adore and respect her: First her parents, then men in her life, commanders in the army, and ultimately the medical establishment. This dissociated personality structure, where two central positions – a soft, care-based one and a tough, go-getter one – are actively separated – worked well for Nirit for most of her life. Nirit has built what appeared to be a satisfying life on all fronts. Things got more complicated during her fellowship abroad, when her marriage went sour and she got divorced. Returning to Israel and investing all her energy in work, she again ascended to professional heights, only to discover that she is again betrayed, this time by 'her second family' – the very medical establishment that embraced her – by denying her the resources and means necessary for her to meet her professional and ethical standards. She was fiendishly trapped. On the one hand, not being the kind of physician she had to be, Nirit felt that she is a burden to her patients. In IPTS terms, perceived burdensomeness has set in. On the other hand, she kept her plight to herself, actively alienating herself from friends and colleagues, in turn propelling – in IPTS terms – thwarted belongingness. Both factors have increased the desire to kill by suicide, bringing her to the weekend where she actually tried to kill herself.

5.2. Advanced-Level Dissociation

The above description of the weekend during which Nirit has made numerous attempts to kill herself (by hanging, swallowing pills) is marred by dissociative elements. Intense depersonalization and de-realization were evident by a dream-like altered consciousness throughout the weekend, a spontaneous, uncontrollable inner-dialogue accompanied by sporadic, seemingly uncontrollable and at times incoherent journaling (including writing the suicide note). There were also out-of-body experiences, motor behaviors that were not fully voluntary (searching for a rope to hang herself) and an intense and massive dissociative amnesia, manifested by inability to recall a lot of what has happened during this weekend. Such dissociative amnesia also transpired in other instances occurring during therapy where Nirit was highly agitated, including one instance in which she was over the phone with GS for almost an hour, threatening to swallow sedatives and eventually dissuaded from doing so, but recalling nothing from this incident. Thus, active and intense cognitive processes conforming to both compartmentalization and detachment were highly operative during this prolonged suicide attempt.

The common denominator of both levels of dissociation, basic and advanced, is – we believe – childhood trauma. After decades of debate within the trauma and dissociation field, a consensus is gradually forming regarding the ability of massive trauma, particularly in childhood, to propel both a dissociative personality structure and dissociative, hypnotic-like mental processes. Interestingly, even scholars suspicious of the most severe and eccentric manifestations of dissociative disorders, such as Dissociative Identity Disorder (DID), acknowledge the role of trauma in leading to a fragmented self-organization (van Heugten van der Kloet and Lynn, 2020). Similarly, even scholars who emphasize the possibility of dissimulation of dissociation agree that such a dissimulation is difficult to identify (Lynn et al., 2019). In Nirit's case, there was no indication for DID, neither there was any indication of dissimulation. In fact, over time dissociative states became her greatest fear, the outcome she attempted to avoid most.

It was this very fear of dissociation that, we believe, ultimately saved her life. It is our contention that the dissociative personality structure (*Basic Level*) and dissociative processes (*Advanced Level*), aimed at keeping The Terminator and 'Niriti' at bay were simply not strong enough. 'Niriti', the anaclitic-relational position seeking nurturance, comfort, and support, withstood the vicious dissociative attacks, managed to voice herself in via WhatsApp texts to family members, in turn summoning her own evacuation. Fortunately, 'Niriti' saved Nirit.

Why was 'Niriti' able to survive these attacks? This, we believe, has to do with the presence of love and care in Nirit's childhood, co-existing alongside the maltreatment and turmoil. It was this love, we believe, that instilled enough positive inner presences ('good objects') that enabled Nirit to not only refrain from killing herself but also to embark upon a very profound therapeutic process that allowed her to begin working through both levels of dissociation. This working through is indeed a work in progress, as is our current understanding of the psychodynamics of depression, dissociation, and suicide – a frustration we seemed bound to bear for the foreseeable future. So, we will have to stop here and bear the frustration.

Notes

1. In Hebrew, when the letter 'y' is added to a first name (e.g., 'Golany'), it conveys affection and care by the speaker toward the person addressed. A possible British/American equivalent would be 'Nirit-dear'.
2. The case description is distorted demographically but faithful clinically. The patient has read and approved this description, and consented to its publication.

Disclosure statement

No potential conflict of interest was reported by the author(s).

References

Abramson, L. Y., Metalsky, G. I., & Alloy, L. B. (1989). Hopelessness depression: A theory-based subtype of depression. *Psychological Review, 96*(2), 358–372. https://doi.org/10.1037/0033-295X.96.2.358

Abramson, L. Y., Seligman, M. E., & Teasdale, J. D. (1978). Learned helplessness in humans: Critique and reformulation. *Journal of Abnormal Psychology, 87*(1), 49–74. https://doi.org/10.1037/0021-843X.87.1.49

Amati, D. & Shallice, T. (2007). On the emergence of modern humans. *Cognition, 103* (3), 358–385. https://doi.org/10.1016/J.COGNITION.2006.04.002

American Psychiatric Association. (2022). *Diagnostic and statistical manual of mental disorders* (5th ed., text rev.). American Psychiatric Association Publishing. https://doi.org/10.1176/appi.books.9780890425787

Andover, M. S., Pepper, C. M., Ryabchenko, K. A., Orrico, E. G., & Gibb, B. E. (2005). Self-mutilation and symptoms of depression, anxiety, and borderline personality disorder. *Suicide and Life-Threatening Behavior, 35*(5), 581–591. https://doi.org/10.1521/suli.2005.35.5.581

Austin, J. T. & Vancouver, J. B. (1996). Goal constructs in psychology: Structure, process, and content. *Psychological Bulletin, 120*(3), 338–375. https://doi.org/10.1037/0033-2909.120.3.338

Bae, H., Kim, D., & Park, Y. C. (2015). Dissociation predicts treatment response in eye-movement desensitization and reprocessing for posttraumatic stress disorder. *Journal of Trauma & Dissociation, 17*(1), 112–130. https://doi.org/10.1080/15299732.2015.1037039

Barrett, L. F. (2006). Are emotions natural kinds? *Perspectives on Psychological Science, 1*(1), 28–58. https://doi.org/10.1111/j.1745-6916.2006.00003.x

Batterham, P. J., Ftanou, M., Pirkis, J., Brewer, J. L., Mackinnon, A. J., Beautrais, A., Kate Fairweather-Schmidt, A., & Christensen, H. (2015). A systematic review and evaluation of measures for suicidal ideation and behaviors in population-based research. *Psychological Assessment, 27*(2), 501–512. https://doi.org/10.1037/PAS0000053

Baumeister, R. F. (1990). Suicide as escape from self. *Psychological Review, 97*(1), 90–113. https://doi.org/10.1037/0033-295X.97.1.90

Beck, A. (1967). *Depression*. Harper and Row. https://psycnet.apa.org/record/1967-35022-000

Beck, A. T. (1996). Beyond belief: A theory of modes, personality, and psychopathology. In P. M. Salkovskis (Ed.), *Frontiers of Cognitive Therapy* (pp. 1–25). The Guilford Press.

Bekrater-Bodmann, R., Chung, B. Y., Richter, I., Wicking, M., Foell, J., Mancke, F., Schmahl, C., & Flor, H. (2015). Deficits in pain perception in borderline personality disorder: Results from the thermal grill illusion. *Pain, 156*(10), 2084–2092. https://doi.org/10.1097/J.PAIN.0000000000000275

Bernstein, E. M. & Putnam, F. W. (1986). Development, reliability, and validity of a dissociation scale. *The Journal of Nervous and Mental Disease, 174*(12), 727–735. https://doi.org/10.1097/00005053-198612000-00004

Besser, A. & Priel, B. (2011). Dependency, self-criticism and negative affective responses following imaginary rejection and failure threats: Meaning-making processes as moderators or mediators. *Psychiatry: Interpersonal & Biological Processes, 74*(1), 31–40. https://doi.org/10.1521/psyc.2011.74.1.31

Blatt, S. (2004). *Experiences of depression: Theoretical, clinical, and research perspectives*. American Psychological Association (APA).

Blatt, S. J. (1974). Levels of object representation in anaclitic and introjective depression. *The Psychoanalytic Study of the Child*, *29*(1), 107–157. https://doi.org/10.1080/00797308.1974.11822616/ASSET//CMS/ASSET/8E9EE78B-6367-423E-8382-A7B38B975FBD/00797308.1974.11822616.FP.PNG

Blatt, S. J. (1995). Representational structures in psychopathology. In D. Cicchetti & S. L. Toth (Eds.), *Rochester symposium on developmental psychopathology: Vol. 6. Emotion, cognition, and representation* (pp. 1–33). University of Rochester Press.

Blatt, S. J. (1998). Contributions of Psychoanalysis to the understanding and treatment of depression. *Journal of the American Psychoanalytic Association*, *46*(3), 723–752. https://doi.org/10.1177/00030651980460030301

Blatt, S. J. (2008). Polarities of experience: Relatedness and self-definition in personality development, psychopathology, and the therapeutic process. *American Psychological Association*. https://doi.org/10.1037/11749-000

Blatt, S. J., Auerbach, J. S., & Levy, K. N. (1997). Mental representations in personality development, psychopathology, and the therapeutic process. *Review of General Psychology*, *1*(4), 351–374. https://doi.org/10.1037/1089-2680.1.4.351

Block, J. (2002). *Personality as an affect-processing system: Toward an integrative theory*. Lawrence Erlbaum Associates Publishers.

Bollas, C. (1979). The transformational object. *The International Journal of Psycho-Analysis*, *60*(1), 97–107. http://www.ncbi.nlm.nih.gov/pubmed/457346

Bornstein, R. F. (2001). The impending death of psychoanalysis. *Psychoanalytic Psychology*, *18*(1), 3–20. https://doi.org/10.1037/0736-9735.18.1.2

Brand, B. L., Classen, C. C., McNary, S. W., & Zaveri, P. (2009). A review of dissociative disorders treatment studies. *The Journal of Nervous and Mental Disease*, *197*(9), 646–654. https://doi.org/10.1097/NMD.0B013E3181B3AFAA

Brand, B. L. & Stadnik, R. (2013). What contributes to predicting change in the treatment of dissociation: Initial levels of dissociation, PTSD, or overall distress? *Journal of Trauma & Dissociation: The Official Journal of the International Society for the Study of Dissociation (ISSD)*, *14*(3), 328–341. https://doi.org/10.1080/15299732.2012.736929

Bredemeier, K. & Miller, I. W. (2015). Executive function and suicidality: A systematic qualitative review. *Clinical Psychology Review*, *40*, 170. https://doi.org/10.1016/J.CPR.2015.06.005

Briggs, K. & Mellinger, S. (2015). *Guardian of the Golden Gate : Protecting the line between hope and despair*. Ascend Books.

Brown, G. W., George, W., & Harris, T. O. (2012). *Social origins of depression : A study of psychiatric disorder in women*. Routledge. https://www.routledge.com/Social-Origins-of-Depression-A-study-of-psychiatric-disorder-in-women/Brown-Harris/p/book/9780415510929

Calati, R., Bensassi, I., & Courtet, P. (2017). The link between dissociation and both suicide attempts and non-suicidal self-injury: Meta-analyses. *Psychiatry Research*, *251*, 103–114. https://doi.org/10.1016/J.PSYCHRES.2017.01.035

Cardeña, E. (1994). The domain of dissociation. In S. J. Lynn & J. W. Rhue (Eds.), *Dissociation: Clinical and Theoretical Perspectives* (pp. 15–31). The Guilford Press.

Caulfield, N. M., Karnick, A. T., & Capron, D. W. (2022). Exploring dissociation as a facilitator of suicide risk: A translational investigation using virtual reality. *Journal of Affective Disorders*, *297*, 517–524. https://doi.org/10.1016/J.JAD.2021.10.097

Celani, D. P. (1999). Applying Fairbairn's object relations theory to the dynamics of the battered woman. *American Journal of Psychotherapy*, *53*(1), 60–73. https://doi.org/10.1176/APPI.PSYCHOTHERAPY.1999.53.1.60

Centers for Disease Control and Prevention. (2022). *Risk and protective factors suicide*. https://www.cdc.gov/suicide/factors/index.html

Comparelli, A., Corigliano, V., Montalbani, B., Nardella, A., De Carolis, A., Stampatore, L., Bargagna, P., Forcina, F., Lamis, D., & Pompili, M. (2022). Building a neurocognitive profile of suicidal risk in severe mental disorders. *BMC Psychiatry*, *22*(1), 1–8. https://doi.org/10.1186/s12888-022-04240-3

Coyne, J. C. (1976a). Depression and the response of others. *Journal of Abnormal Psychology*, *85*(2), 186–193. https://doi.org/10.1037/0021-843X.85.2.186

Coyne, J. C. (1976b). Toward an interactional description of depression. *Psychiatry*, *39* (1), 28–40. https://doi.org/10.1080/00332747.1976.11023874

Dalenberg, C. J., Brand, B. L., Gleaves, D. H., Dorahy, M. J., Loewenstein, R. J., Cardeña, E., Frewen, P. A., Carlson, E. B., & Spiegel, D. (2012). Evaluation of the evidence for the trauma and fantasy models of dissociation. *Psychological Bulletin*, *138*(3), 550–588. https://doi.org/10.1037/a0027447

Dalenberg, C. & Carlson, E. (2010). New versions of the dissociative experiences scale: The DES-R (revised) and the DES-B (brief). *Annual Meeting of the International Society for Traumatic Stress Studies*. Montreal, Quebec.

Depue, R. A. & Monroe, S. M. (1986). Conceptualization and measurement of human disorder in life stress research: The problem of chronic disturbance. *Psychological Bulletin*, *99*(1), 36–51. https://doi.org/10.1037/0033-2909.99.1.36

Duffy, M. E., Buchman-Schmitt, J. M., McNulty, J. K., & Joiner, T. E. (2022). *Eyes fixed on heaven's gate: An empirical examination of blink rate and suicide*. https://doi.org/10.1080/13811118.2022.2083536

Dunkley, D. M., Zuroff, D. C., & Blankstein, K. R. (2003). Self-critical perfectionism and daily affect: Dispositional and situational influences on stress and coping. *Journal of Personality and Social Psychology*, *84*(1), 234–252. https://doi.org/10.1037/0022-3514.84.1.234

Eagle, M. N. (2011). Psychoanalysis and the enlightenment vision: An overview. *Journal of the American Psychoanalytic Association*, *59*(6), 1099–1118. https://doi.org/10.1177/0003065111428611

Erdelyi, M. H. (2006). The unified theory of repression. *Behavioral and Brain Sciences*, *29*(5), 499–511. https://doi.org/10.1017/S0140525X06009113

Fairbairn, W. R. D. (1944). Endopsychic structure considered in terms of object-relationships. *International Journal of Psychoanalysis*, *25*, 70–93.

Fakhry, H. (2015). Dissociative phenomena in attempted suicide. *Egyptian Journal of Psychiatry*, *36*(1), 45. https://doi.org/10.4103/1110-1105.153779

Ferenczi, S. (1988). Confusion of tongues between adults and the child. *Contemporary Psychoanalysis*, *24*(2), 196–206. https://doi.org/10.1080/00107530.1988.10746234

Fernández-Sevillano, J., Alberich, S., Zorrilla, I., González-Ortega, I., López, M. P., Pérez, V., Vieta, E., González-Pinto, A., & Saíz, P. (2021). Cognition in recent suicide attempts: Altered executive function. *Frontiers in Psychiatry*, *12*, 12. https://doi.org/10.3389/FPSYT.2021.701140

Fonagy, P. (1995). *Psychoanalytic and empirical approaches to developmental psychopathology: An object-relations perspective* (T. Shapiro & R. N. Emde, eds.; pp. 245–260). International Universities Press, Inc.

Fredrickson, B. L. (1998). What good are positive emotions? *Review of General Psychology*, *2*(3), 300–319. https://doi.org/10.1037/1089-2680.2.3.300

Gilbert, D. T. & Wilson, T. D. (2007). Prospection: Experiencing the future. *Science*, *317* (5843), 1351–1354. https://doi.org/10.1126/science.1144161

Greenberg, J. R. & Mitchell, S. A. (1983). *Object relations in psychoanalytic theory*. Harvard University Press.

Green, J. D., Sedikides, C., Pinter, B., & Van Tongeren, D. R. (2009). Two sides to self-protection: Self-improvement strivings and feedback from close relationships

eliminate mnemic neglect. *Self and Identity*, *8*(2–3), 233–250. https://doi.org/10.1080/15298860802505145
Gutierrez, P. M., Joiner, T., Hanson, J., Stanley, I. H., Silva, C., & Rogers, M. L. (2019). Psychometric properties of four commonly used suicide risk assessment measures: Applicability to military treatment settings. *Military Behavioral Health*, *7*(2), 177–184. https://doi.org/10.1080/21635781.2018.1562390
Hammen, C. (1991). Generation of stress in the course of unipolar depression. *Journal of Abnormal Psychology*, *100*(4), 555–561. https://doi.org/10.1037/0021-843X.100.4.555
Holmes, E. A., Brown, R. J., Mansell, W., Fearon, R. P., Hunter, E. C. M., Frasquilho, F., & Oakley, D. A. (2005). Are there two qualitatively distinct forms of dissociation? A review and some clinical implications. *Clinical Psychology Review*, *25*(1), 1–23. https://doi.org/10.1016/J.CPR.2004.08.006
Horney, K. (1936). Culture and neurosis. *American Sociological Review*, *1*(2), 221. https://doi.org/10.2307/2084481
Horowitz, M. J. (1998). Cognitive psychodynamics: From conflict to character. *The American Journal of Psychiatry*, *155*(Issue 2). https://doi.org/10.1176/AJP.156.2.331
Jamison, K. R. (1996). An unquiet mind: A memoir of moods and madness. *VIntage*.
Jobes, D. A. & Joiner, T. E. (2019). Reflections on suicidal ideation. *The Crisis*, *40*(4), 227–230. https://doi.org/10.1027/0227-5910/a000615
Joiner, T. E. (1994). Contagious depression: Existence, specificity to depressed symptoms, and the role of reassurance seeking. *Journal of Personality and Social Psychology*, *67*(2), 287–296. https://doi.org/10.1037/0022-3514.67.2.287
Joiner, T. E. (2000). Depression's vicious scree: Self-propagating and erosive processes in depression chronicity. *Clinical Psychology: Science & Practice*, *7*(2), 203–218. https://doi.org/10.1093/CLIPSY.7.2.203
Joiner, T. E. (2005). *Why people die by suicide*. Harvard University Press.
Joiner, T. E., Hom, M. A., Rogers, M. L., Chu, C., Stanley, I. H., Wynn, G. H., & Gutierrez, P. M. (2016). Staring down death: Is abnormally slow blink rate a clinically useful indicator of acute suicide risk? *Crisis: The Journal of Crisis Intervention and Suicide Prevention*, *37*(3), 212–217. https://doi.org/10.1027/0227-5910/a000367
Kelly, G. A. (1955). *The psychology of personal constructs: Vol. 1. A theory of personality. Vol. 2. Clinical diagnosis and psychotherapy*. Norton.
Kemberg, O. F., Yeomans, F. E., Clarkin, J. F., & Levy, K. N. (2008). Transference focused psychotherapy: Overview and update. *The International Journal of Psycho-Analysis*, *89*(3), 601–620. https://doi.org/10.1111/J.1745-8315.2008.00046.X
Kernberg, O. F. (1984). *Severe personality disorders: Psychotherapeutic strategies*. Yale University Press, Ed.
Kira, I. A., Shuwiekh, H., & Laddis, A. (2022). The linear and non-linear association between trauma, dissociation, complex PTSD, and executive function deficits: A longitudinal structural equation modeling study. *Journal of Loss & Trauma*, *28*(3), 217–234. https://doi.org/10.1080/15325024.2022.2101734
Klein, M. (1928). Early stages of the Oedipus conflict. *International Journal of Psychoanalysis*, *9*, 167–180.
Klein, M. (1935). A contribution to the psychogenesis of manic-depressive states. *International Journal of Psychoanalysis*, *15*, 145–174.
Klein, M. (1940). Mourning and its relation to manic-depressive states. *International Journal of Psychoanalysis*, *21*, 125–153.
Klein, M. (1945). The Oedipus complex in the light of early anxieties. *International Journal of Psychoanalysis*, *26*, 11–33.
Kleindienst, N., Limberger, M. F., Ebner-Priemer, U. W., Keibel-Mauchnik, J., Dyer, A., Berger, M., Schmahl, C., & Bohus, M. (2011). Dissociation predicts poor response to

dialectial behavioral therapy in female patients with borderline personality disorder. *Journal of Personality Disorders*, *25*(4), 432–447. https://doi.org/10.1521/pedi.2011.25.4.432

Klein, M., Kupfer, D. J., & Shea, M. T. (1993). *Personality and depression: A current view.* Guilford press.

Lazarus, G. & Rafaeli, E. (2023). Modes: Cohesive personality states and their interrelationships as organizing concepts in psychopathology. *Journal of Psychopathology and Clinical Science*, *132*(3), 238–248. https://doi.org/10.1037/abn0000699

Levinger, S., Somer, E., & Holden, R. R. (2015). The importance of mental pain and physical dissociation in youth suicidality. *Journal of Trauma and Dissociation*, *16*(3), 322–339. https://doi.org/10.1080/15299732.2014.989644

Lieberman, A., Robison, M., Wonderlich, S. A., Crosby, R. D., Mitchell, J. E., Crow, S. J., Peterson, C. B., Le Grange, D., Bardone-Cone, A. M., Kolden, G., & Joiner, T. E. (2023). Self-hate, dissociation, and suicidal behavior in bulimia nervosa. *Journal of Affective Disorders*, *335*, 44–48. https://doi.org/10.1016/J.JAD.2023.05.015

Ludäscher, P., Bohus, M., Lieb, K., Philipsen, A., Jochims, A., & Schmahl, C. (2007). Elevated pain thresholds correlate with dissociation and aversive arousal in patients with borderline personality disorder. *Psychiatry Research*, *149*(1–3), 291–296. https://doi.org/10.1016/J.PSYCHRES.2005.04.009

Lynn, S. J., Lilienfeld, S. O., Merckelbach, H., Giesbrecht, T., McNally, R. J., Loftus, E. F., Bruck, M., Garry, M., & Malaktaris, A. (2014). The trauma model of dissociation: Inconvenient truths and stubborn fictions. Comment on Dalenberg et al. (2012). *Psychological Bulletin*, *140*(3), 896–910. https://doi.org/10.1037/a0035570

Lynn, S. J., Maxwell, R., Merckelbach, H., Lilienfeld, S. O., Kloet, D. V. H. D., & Miskovic, V. (2019). Dissociation and its disorders: Competing models, future directions, and a way forward. *Clinical Psychology Review*, *73*, 101755. https://doi.org/10.1016/j.cpr.2019.101755

Lyssenko, L., Schmahl, C., Bockhacker, L., Vonderlin, R., Bohus, M., & Kleindienst, N. (2018). Dissociation in psychiatric disorders: A meta-analysis of studies using the dissociative experiences scale. *The American Journal of Psychiatry*, *175*(1), 37–46. https://doi.org/10.1176/APPI.AJP.2017.17010025

McDaniel, M. A. & Einstein, G. O. (2007). Prospective memory: An overview and synthesis of an emerging field. *Prospective Memory: An Overview and Synthesis of an Emerging Field*, 1–264. https://doi.org/10.4135/9781452225913

McKinnon, M. C., Boyd, J. E., Frewen, P. A., Lanius, U. F., Jetly, R., Richardson, J. D., & Lanius, R. A. (2016). A review of the relation between dissociation, memory, executive functioning and social cognition in military members and civilians with neuropsychiatric conditions. *Neuropsychologia*, *90*, 210–234. https://doi.org/10.1016/J.NEUROPSYCHOLOGIA.2016.07.017

Mergler, M., Driessen, M., Lüdecke, C., Ohlmeier, M., Chodzinski, C., Weirich, S., Schläfke, D., Wedekind, D., Havemann-Reinecke, U., Renner, W., & Schäfer, I. (2017). Relationships between a dissociative subtype of PTSD and clinical characteristics in patients with substance use disorders. *Journal of Psychoactive Drugs*, *49*(3), 225–232. https://doi.org/10.1080/02791072.2017.1296209

Mischel, W. & Shoda, Y. (1995). A cognitive-affective system theory of personality: Reconceptualizing situations, dispositions, dynamics, and invariance in personality structure. *Psychological Review*, *102*(2), 246–268. https://doi.org/10.1037/0033-295X.102.2.246

Mitra, P. & Jain, A. (2023). Dissociative identity disorder. *Current Psychosis and Therapeutics Reports*, *4*(3), 112–116. https://doi.org/10.1007/BF02629332

Mongrain, M. (1998). Parental representations and support-seeking behaviors related to dependency and self-criticism. *Journal of Personality*, *66*(2), 151–173. https://doi.org/10.1111/1467-6494.00007

Ogden, T. H. (1992). The matrix of the mind: Object relations and the psychoanalytic dialogue. *The Matrix of the Mind: Object Relations and the Psychoanalytic Dialogue*, 1–270. https://doi.org/10.4324/9780429482403/MATRIX-MIND-THOMAS-OGDEN

Orbach, I. (1994). Dissociation, physical pain, and suicide: A hypothesis. *Suicide and Life-Threatening Behavior, 24*(1), 68–79. https://doi.org/10.1111/J.1943-278X.1994.TB00664.X

Pachkowski, M. C., Rogers, M. L., Saffer, B. Y., Caulfield, N. M., & Klonsky, E. D. (2021). Clarifying the relationship of dissociative experiences to suicide ideation and attempts: A multimethod examination in two samples. *Behavior Therapy, 52*(5), 1067–1079. https://doi.org/10.1016/J.BETH.2021.03.006

Rabasco, A. & Andover, M. S. (2020). The interaction of dissociation, pain tolerance, and suicidal ideation in predicting suicide attempts. *Psychiatry Research, 284*, 112661. https://doi.org/10.1016/J.PSYCHRES.2019.112661

Rogers, M. L., Hom, M. A., Stanley, I. H., & Joiner, T. E. (2019). Brief measures of physical and psychological distance to suicide methods as correlates and predictors of suicide risk: A multi-study prospective investigation. *Behaviour Research and Therapy, 120*, 103330. https://doi.org/10.1016/J.BRAT.2018.11.001

Rossi, R., Longo, L., Fiore, D., Carcione, A., Niolu, C., Siracusano, A., Di, L. G., & Di, L. G. (2019). Dissociation in stress-related disorders and self-harm: A review of the literature and a systematic review of mediation models. *Journal of Psychopathology, 25*, 162–171.

Rubin, M., Hien, D., Das, D., & Melara, R. (2017). Inhibitory control under threat: The role of spontaneous eye blinks in post-traumatic stress disorder. *Brain Sciences, 7* (12), 16. https://doi.org/10.3390/brainsci7020016

Rufer, M., Held, D., Cremer, J., Fricke, S., Moritz, S., Peter, H., & Hand, I. (2005). Dissociation as a predictor of cognitive behavior therapy outcome in patients with obsessive-compulsive disorder. *Psychotherapy and Psychosomatics, 75*(1), 40–46. https://doi.org/10.1159/000089225

Sandler, J. (1976). Countertransference and role responsiveness. *International Review of Psycho-Analysis, 3*(1), 43–47.

Scalabrini, A., Cavicchioli, M., Fossati, A., & Maffei, C. (2017). The extent of dissociation in borderline personality disorder: A meta-analytic review. *Journal of Trauma & Dissociation: The Official Journal of the International Society for the Study of Dissociation (ISSD), 18*(4), 522–543. https://doi.org/10.1080/15299732.2016.1240738

Sedikides, C. & Green, J. D. (2009). Memory as a self-protective mechanism. *Social and Personality Psychology Compass, 3*(6), 1055–1068. https://doi.org/10.1111/j.1751-9004.2009.00220.x

Seligman, M. E. P., Railton, P., Baumeister, R. F., & Sripada, C. (2013). Navigating into the future or driven by the past. *Perspectives on Psychological Science, 8*(2), 119–141. https://doi.org/10.1177/1745691612474317

Shahar, G. (2004). Transference-countertransference: Where the (political) action is. *Journal of Psychotherapy Integration, 14*(4), 371–396. https://doi.org/10.1037/1053-0479.14.4.371

Shahar, G. (2006a). Clinical action: Introduction to the special section on the action perspective in clinical psychology. *Journal of Clinical Psychology, 62*(9), 1053–1064. https://doi.org/10.1002/JCLP.20290

Shahar, G. (2006b). Repression, suppression, and oppression (in depression). *Behavioral and Brain Sciences, 29*(5), 533–534. https://doi.org/10.1017/S0140525X06459112

Shahar, G. (2010). Poetics, pragmatics, schematics, and the psychoanalysis-research dialogue (rift). *Psychoanalytic Psychotherapy, 24*(4), 315–328. https://doi.org/10.1080/02668734.2010.513544

Shahar, G. (2011). Projectuality versus eventuality: Sullivan, the (ambivalent) intentionalist. *Journal of Psychotherapy Integration*, *21*(2), 211–220. https://doi.org/10.1037/A0022909

Shahar, G. (2015a). Object Relations Theory. In R. Cautin & S. Lillinfeld (Eds.), *The Encyclopedia of Clinical Psychology*. New York: Wiley. https://doi.org/10.1002/9781118625392.wbecp189

Shahar, G. (2015b). *Erosion: The psychopathology of self-criticism*. New York: Oxford University Press. https://doi.org/10.1093/MED:PSYCH/9780199929368.001.0001

Shahar, G. (2016). Criticism in the self, brain, relationships, and social structure: Implications for psychodynamic psychiatry. *Psychodynamic Psychiatry*, *44*(3), 395–421. https://doi.org/10.1521/pdps.2016.44.3.395

Shahar, G. (2018). The (suicidal-) depressive position: A scientifically informed reformulation. *Psychodynamic Psychiatry*, *46*(2), 265–293. https://doi.org/10.1521/pdps.2018.46.2.265

Shahar, G. (2021a). Integrative psychotherapy with physicians in the trenches: Convergence of cognitive, existential, and psychodynamic processes. *Journal of Humanistic Psychology*, 002216782110655. https://doi.org/10.1177/00221678211065580

Shahar, G. (2021b). Reformulated object relations theory: A bridge between clinical psychoanalysis, psychotherapy integration, and the understanding and treatment of suicidal depression. *Frontiers in Psychology*, *12*, 12. https://doi.org/10.3389/fpsyg.2021.721746

Shahar, G. (2023). *Complex depression: The role of personality dynamics and social ecology*. American Psychological Association Press.

Shahar, G., Blatt, S. J., Zuroff, D. C., Kuperminc, G. P., & Leadbeater, B. J. (2004). Reciprocal relations between depressive symptoms and self-criticism (but not dependency) among early adolescent girls (but not boys). *Cognitive Therapy and Research*, *28*(1), 85–103. https://doi.org/10.1023/B:COTR.0000016932.82038.d0

Shahar, G., Cross, L. W., & Henrich, C. C. (2004). Representations in action. *The Psychoanalytic Study of the Child*, *59*(1), 261–293. https://doi.org/10.1080/00797308.2004.11800741

Shahar, G. & Davidson, L. (2009). Participation-engagement: A philosophically based heuristic for prioritizing clinical interventions in the treatment of comorbid, complex, and chronic psychiatric conditions. *Psychiatry: Interpersonal & Biological Processes*, *72*(2), 154–176. https://doi.org/10.1521/psyc.2009.72.2.154

Shahar, G. & Henrich, C. C. (2019). Role of adolescent exposure to rockets in the links between personality vulnerability and psychopathology. *Development and Psychopathology*, *31*(4), 1367–1380. https://doi.org/10.1017/S0954579418000792

Shahar, G., Henrich, C. C., Blatt, S. J., Ryan, R., & Little, T. D. (2003). Interpersonal relatedness, self-definition, and their motivational orientation during adolescence: A theorical and empirical integration. *Developmental Psychology*, *39*(3), 470–483. https://doi.org/10.1037/0012-1649.39.3.470

Shahar, G. & Schiller, M. (2016). Treating the depressive self: A psychodynamic-integrative approach. In M. N. K. Kyrios, S. Bhar, G. Doron, M. Mikulincer, & R. Roulding (Eds.), *The self in understanding and treating psychological disorders* (pp. 29–39). Cambridge University Press.

Shahnaz, A. & Klonsky, E. D. (2021). Clarifying the association of eating disorder features to suicide ideation and attempts. *Journal of Clinical Psychology*, *77*(12), 2965–2977. https://doi.org/10.1002/jclp.23266

Smith, A. R., Zuromski, K. L., & Dodd, D. R. (2018). Eating disorders and suicidality: What we know, what we don't know, and suggestions for future research. *Current Opinion in Psychology*, *22*, 63–67. https://doi.org/10.1016/j.copsyc.2017.08.023

Soffer-Dudek, N. (2014). Dissociation and dissociative mechanisms in panic disorder, obsessive–compulsive disorder, and depression: A review and heuristic framework. *Psychology of Consciousness: Theory, Research, & Practice*, *1*(3), 243–270. https://doi.org/10.1037/cns0000023

Steel, E. (2006). *The Bridge*. https://watchdocumentaries.com/the-bridge/

Stolorow, R. D., Brandshaft, B., & Atwood, G. E. (1987). *Psychoanalytic treatment: An intersubjective approach*. Analytic.

Strenger, C. (1998). East of Eden: Clinical and theoretical aspects of the sense of excommunication. *Journal of Humanistic Psychology*, *38*(4), 41–64. https://doi.org/10.1177/00221678980384004

Sullivan, H. S. (1953). *The interpersonal theory of psychiatry*. Norton.

Summers, F. (2003). The future as instrinsic to the psyche and Psychoanalytic Therapy. *Contemporary Psychoanalysis*, *39*(1), 135–153. https://doi.org/10.1080/00107530.2003.10747206

Thieberger, J. (1991). The concept of reparation in Melanie Klein's writing. *Melanie Klein & Object Relations*, *9*(1), 32–46.

van Heugten van der Kloet, D. & Lynn, S. J. (2020). Dreams and dissociation—Commonalities as a basis for future research and clinical innovations. *Frontiers in Psychology*, *11*. https://doi.org/10.3389/fpsyg.2020.00745

van Orden, K. A., Witte, T. K., Cukrowicz, K. C., Braithwaite, S. R., Selby, E. A., & Joiner, T. E. (2010). The interpersonal theory of suicide. *Psychological Review*, *117* (2), 575–600. https://doi.org/10.1037/a0018697

Wachtel, P. L. (1994). *Cyclical psychodynamics and the contextual self : The inner world, the intimate world, and the world of culture and society*. https://www.routledge.com/Cyclical-Psychodynamics-and-the-Contextual-Self-The-Inner-World-the-Intimate/Wachtel/p/book/9780415713955

Wedig, M. M., Silverman, M. H., Frankenburg, F. R., Reich, D. B., Fitzmaurice, G., & Zanarini, M. C. (2012). Predictors of suicide attempts in patients with borderline personality disorder over 16 years of prospective follow-up. *Psychological Medicine*, *42*(11), 2395–2404. https://doi.org/10.1017/S0033291712000517

Werner, A. M., Tibubos, A. N., Rohrmann, S., & Reiss, N. (2019). The clinical trait self-criticism and its relation to psychopathology: A systematic review – update. *Journal of Affective Disorders*, *246*, 530–547. https://doi.org/10.1016/j.jad.2018.12.069

Westen, D. (1991). Social cognition and object relations. *Psychological Bulletin*, *109*(3), 429–455. https://doi.org/10.1037/0033-2909.109.3.429

Westen, D. (1998). The scientific legacy of Sigmund Freud: Toward a psychodynamically informed psychological science. *Psychological Bulletin*, *124*(3), 333–371. https://doi.org/10.1037/0033-2909.124.3.333

Whelton, W. J. & Greenberg, L. S. (2005). Emotion in self-criticism. *Personality and Individual Differences*, *38*(7), 1583–1595. https://doi.org/10.1016/J.PAID.2004.09.024

Winnicott, D. W. (1958). The capacity to be alone. *International Journal of Psychoanalysis*, *39*(5), 416–420.

World health organization. (2021). *Suicide*. https://www.who.int/news-room/fact-sheets/detail/suicide

Zoroglu, S. S., Tuzun, U., Sar, V., Tutkun, H., Savaş, H. A., Ozturk, M., Alyanak, B., & Kora, M. E. (2003). Suicide attempt and self-mutilation among Turkish high school students in relation with abuse, neglect and dissociation. *Psychiatry and Clinical Neurosciences*, *57*(1), 119–126. https://doi.org/10.1046/J.1440-1819.2003.01088.X

Epilogue: the formidable human need to "not know"

Dana Amir, Richard Chefetz, Antonino Costanzo, Paul Cundy, Thomas E. Joiner, Morgan Robison Vedat Şar, Gianluca Santoro, Adriano Schimmenti, Golan Shahar, Nirit Soffer-Dudek and Eli Somer

It is widely recognized that mainstream psychoanalysis has maintained a distance from dissociation studies, even though its founders were initially drawn to psychotherapy by their dissociative patients. Object relations theorists may be an exception, as they emphasized the need to address the clinical fragmentation of consciousness observed in their clients albeit through a metapsychological framework. However, the gaps between metapsychology, clinical practice, and empirical research must be bridged to develop an approach that genuinely benefits those who are suffering. This book offers critical insights into understanding dissociative phenomena from multiple psychodynamic perspectives. It explores the topic through several novel perspectives including: absorption as the ultimate form of state dissociation, difficulties in mentalization as the primary correlate of early trauma, intra- and inter-personal psychological dynamics as the key transpersonal algorithm, and melancholia and suicide as the central elements of trait dissociation. Appropriate attention is given to the fact that the subjective experience of detachment from oneself or the environment may co-occur with other clinical manifestations, such as failures in mentalizing, maladaptive daydreaming, suicidal attempts, substance abuse, and depression. Through the various contributions Dissociation is revealed as a rich, nuanced language, not as a kind of dead-end but, on the contrary, as a kind of opening for thought and therapeutic action.

What unites these chapters is the use of the psychoanalytic lens through which the authors view their subjects and the notion of the psychoanalytic unconscious. Whereas in practically all other therapeutic modalities (i.e., cognitive-behavioral, interpersonal, humanistic-existential, family-systems) there is an awareness, and acceptance, of the fact that humans act due to unconscious motivations, it is the unique postulate of psychoanalysis that humans do so with intention, by way of goal-directed action. In accordance with the notion of *defense mechanisms,* the various strands of psychoanalysis hold that people espouse a wide range of cognitive, experiential, and interpersonal maneuvers that enable them *not to know.* Importantly, this "not knowing" never comes for free: It comes with what S. Freud termed the "psychopathology of everyday life" or, quite often, with actual psychopathology, psychiatric disorders, and even death (e.g., by suicide). From this perspective, dissociation represents an extreme example of the human need to "not know". What is it in human nature that propels, and enables, such a massive reluctance to be aware? From both an evolutionary and existential perspective, the answer might be that people operate based on what *they believe* to be "a need to know" basis. People are busy trying to survive the world into which they have been thrown and they encounter various threats in their environment. In prehistoric times this could be a predator, whereas in modern times it is more likely to be a human traumatizer. There is no time to stop and ponder. In order to survive one dissociates and acts. Unlike other, more neurotic (repressive) or even psychotic (projective) defense mechanisms, which elude the subject of specific segments of inner and outer reality, dissociation eliminates awareness of knowledge (typically micro-amnesias, less frequently massive aggregations of knowledge), particularly about self and others, internalized and/or real. And, as cogently demonstrated by the various contributions, the cost to mental health is indeed formidable: Depression, anxiety, post-traumatic stress symptoms, addiction, disrupted identity (dissociative identity disorder, DID), and even suicide.

Dissociation carries implications in the generation of mental illness and significantly interacts with other psychopathologies, creating unique subtypes and challenging comorbid presentations (Loewenstein & Brand, 2023; Costanzo et al., 2023; Sar, 2023; Shahar et al., 2023). An untrained or inexperienced clinician can easily miss dissociative pathology, which is often subtle, contradictory, or confusing (Loewenstein & Brand, 2023) and may manifest at different levels of the mind-body (Amir, 2023). This concern is exacerbated by well-documented data on the prevalence of sexual, physical, and emotional abuse of women and children (Felitti et al., 1998; WHO, 2021). The profound and devastating effects of these assaults on physical sovereignty and mental dignity often underlie much of the psychopathology seen globally, and they also influence genetically based illnesses (Teicher & Samson, 2013). Domestic violence and organized criminal abuse of children in the global pornography industry, estimated to generate over $40 billion annually in the U.S.A. alone, are widespread (Estes & Weiner, 2001) and exacerbate these concerns. This book serves as a call to action for psychotherapists worldwide to recognize, assess, and treat dissociative experiences, which are integral to PTSD, CPTSD, and dissociative disorders (Cloitre et al., 2013) and often shape the presentations of comorbid anxiety and depressive disorders, eating disorders, and Emotionally Unstable Personality Disorder. Although clinical interventions for dissociative disorders and related phenomena may draw on various therapeutic approaches, it is crucial to adopt a sensitive and empathetic approach that addresses not only dissociative symptoms but also the dysregulated feelings rooted in childhood trauma. We must improve how we educate members of our professions about dissociative processes and experiences (Brand et al., 2019; Kumar et al., 2022).

References

Amir, D. (2023). Metaphoric, metonymic and psychotic somatoform dissociation. *Psychoanalytic Psychotherapy, 37*(4), 429–442. https://doi.org/10.1080/02668734.2023.2251552

Brand, B. L., Schielke, H. J., Putnam, K. T., Putnam, F. W., Loewenstein, R. J., Myrick, A., … & Lanius, R. A. (2019). An online educational program for individuals with dissociative disorders and their clinicians: 1-year and 2-year follow-up. *Journal of Traumatic Stress*, *32*(1), 156–166.

Cloitre, M., Garvert, D. W., Brewin, C. R., Bryant, R. A., & Maercker, A. (2013). Evidence for proposed ICD-11 PTSD and complex PTSD: a latent profile analysis. *European Journal of Psychotraumatology*, *4*, 10.3402/ejpt.v4i0.20706. https://doi.org/10.3402/ejpt.v4i0.20706

Costanzo, A., Santoro, G., & Schimmenti, A. (2023). Self-medication, traumatic reenactments, and dissociation: A psychoanalytic perspective on the relationship between childhood trauma and substance abuse. *Psychoanalytic Psychotherapy, 37*(4), 443–466. https://doi.org/10.1080/02668734.2023.2272761

Estes, R. J., & Weiner, N. A. (2001). The commercial sexual exploitation of children in the US, Canada and Mexico. University of Pennsylvania, School of Social Work, Center for the Study of Youth Policy. In Cooper et al., (Eds): *Medical, legal, social aspects, of child sexual exploitation*. STM Learning, pp. 297–335.

Felitti, V. J., Anda, R. F., Nordenberg, D., Williamson, D. F., Spitz, A. M., Edwards, V., Koss, M. P., & Marks, J. S. (1998). Relationship of childhood abuse and household dysfunction to many of the leading causes of death in adults. The Adverse Childhood Experiences (ACE) Study. *American Journal of Preventive Medicine*, *14*(4), 245–258. https://doi.org/10.1016/s0749-3797(98)00017-8

Kumar, S. A., Brand, B. L., & Courtois, C. A. (2022). The need for trauma training: Clinicians' reactions to training on complex trauma. *Psychological Trauma: Theory, Research, Practice, and Policy*, *14*(8), 1387.

Loewenstein, R. J., & Brand, B. (2023). Dissociative identity disorder: A disorder of diagnostic and therapeutic paradoxes. *Psychoanalytic Psychotherapy, 37*(4), 339–380. https://doi.org/10.1080/02668734.2023.2272771

Sar, V. (2023). Dissociative depression. *Psychoanalytic Psychotherapy, 37*(4), 381–428. https://doi.org/10.1080/02668734.2023.2254824

Shahar, G., Robison, M., & Joiner, T. E. (2023). Dissociation in suicidal depression: A Reformulated Object-Relations Theory (RORT) perspective. *Psychoanalytic Psychotherapy*, 37(4), 492–520. https://doi.org/10.1080/02668734.2023.2271969

Teicher, M. H., & Samson, J. A. (2013). Childhood maltreatment and psychopathology: A case for ecophenotypic variants as clinically and neurobiologically distinct subtypes. *The American Journal of Psychiatry*, *170*(10), 1114–1133. https://doi.org/10.1176/appi.ajp.2013.12070957

World Health Organization. (2021). *Violence against women prevalence estimates, 2018: Global, regional and national prevalence estimates for intimate partner violence against women and global and regional prevalence estimates for non-partner sexual violence against women.* World Health Organization.

Index

Note: *Italic* page numbers refer to figures and page numbers followed by "n" denote endnotes.

Kolibri 360 GmbH
Ferdinand-Jühlke-Straße 7
99095 Erfurt, Deutschland
produktsicherheit@kolibri360.de